Caen:

Alexander McKee, OBE

CAEN
Anvil of Victory

SOUVENIR PRESS

First published 1964 by
Souvenir Press Ltd.,
43 Great Russell Street, London WCIB 3PA

Reissued with additional material 1984
Reissued in paperback 2000

ISBN 0 285 63559 X

Printed in Great Britain by
The Guernsey Press Co. Ltd., Guernsey, Channel Islands

CONTENTS

5

CONTENTS

ILLUSTRATIONS

Field Marshal Erwin Rommel inspects 21 Panzer Division a week before D-Day. *Photo Lt. Höller.*

Oberfeldwebel Hans Erich Braun in 'walking out' dress.

Radio operator Heinz Trautmann on duty in Tiger 134.

Leutnant Hans Höller on D-Day, during the battle of Benouville

A 75 mm SP gun of 21 Panzer Division dug-in at Cairon, just before D-Day. *Photo: Lt. Höller.*

Lt. Höller with one of his 75 mm anti-tank guns disguised as a bush.

Churchill tank at Maltot, in the shadow of Hill 112, awaits a possible counter-attack. *Photo: Imperial War Museum.*

British infantry on the start-line, waiting to attack. *Photo: Imperial War Museum.*

Heinz Trautmann's Tiger 134 after a hard-fought action in Normandy. *Photo: Heinz Trautmann's Collection.*

A tank of 7 Armoured Division ' brewing up ' after being knocked out by a Tiger of S.S. Heavy Tank Battalion 502. *Photo: Heinz Trautmann's Collection.*

Grenadier of 10 S.S. Panzer Division digging in under a knocked-out Sherman, to get overhead cover. *Photo: Heinz Trautmann's Collection.*

Teenagers of 12 S.S. Panzer Grenadier Division ' Hitler Jugend ' on the march, heavily laden. *Photo: Heinz Trautmann's Collection.*

Le Bon Sauveur Convent, Caen, before and after the bombing. *Photos: Sister Malone's Collection.*

Le Bon Sauveur nuns fleeing from the convent at Pont l'Abbe. *Photo: Sister Malone's Collection.*

ILLUSTRATIONS

Sherman tanks in battle order firing on the enemy near Cheux during the Odon offensive. *Photo: Imperial War Museum.*

Shermans of 13/18 Hussars in 'harbour'.

The strong-point village of Sannerville before 'Goodwood'. *Photo: Imperial War Museum.*

Aiming Point picture of Sannerville taken from F/Lt. Linacre's Lancaster, 18 July. *Photo Imperial War Museum.*

Sannerville after the bombing. *Photo: Imperial War Museum.*

Young German sniper, captured during the Odon battle, is urged on in no uncertain manner. *Photo: Imperial War Museum.*

British soldier takes cover by a knocked-out German tank and a dead sniper. *Photo: Imperial War Museum.*

One of Wittmann's Tigers knocked out in Villers-Bocage during the June battle. *Photo: Imperial War Museum.*

An Allied soldier gazes dumbly at the ruins of Caen. *Photo: Imperial War Museum.*

Serjeant Sears of 23 Hussars accepts his due. *Photo: Imperial War Museum.*

Canadian Scottish soldier supervises a POW burial party. *Photo: Author's Collection.*

CHAPTER ONE

THE LONG WAIT

1940 - 1944

The thin grey line on the horizon was France. As it came closer it grew trees, houses, church spires, sand dunes; and billowing clouds of smoke, alive with spurting debris. Not all saw it. Corporal Raymond Arthur Hill, having eaten for breakfast one tin of self-heating soup, was boxed down inside his Sherman tank beside the gun, and could see nothing. " I just heard shellfire, rockets, and so on, and presumed we'd arrived." Most of the men had had no breakfast, nor did they want it. They wanted only to get ashore. Most of yesterday's half-digested meals were spewed, still reeking, on the steel-plated decks of the landing craft, and sloshed to and fro in the ' heads ' with each sickening lurch and heave of the ugly, clumsy vessels, as they punched through half-gale seas towards the shore. " It wasn't too bad for us sailors," said Ronald McKinlay of the R.N. Commandos, " but I think one of the main reasons why Normandy was a great success was that the soldiers would much rather have fought thousands of Germans than go back into those boats and be sea-sick again." Serjeant Leo Gariepy, of the Canadian 6th Armoured Regiment, ' skipper ' of a 30-ton tank temporarily turned into a boat by means of a canvas hull supported by frail struts, found himself wallowing in a near-sinking condition; and, to make matters worse, he was not allowed to invade France until 0730 hours, in ninety minutes' time, if his ' D.D.' tank stayed afloat that long. " I cautioned my crew of the situation, but three of them were so sea-sick they did not care any more."

By that time, the airborne troops would have been fighting in France for seven hours already. The first seaborne troops ashore to support them would land behind armour plate—in ' D.D.' tanks to quell the beach defences and Engineer tanks (AVREs) to blast open beach exits for the infantry and ordinary tanks to pass through. Perched on one of the AVREs, incon-

gruously, was an officer in R.A.F. uniform, Squadron Leader
A. E. L. Hill, commanding a unit responsible for flying the
protective barrage balloons from part of the invasion armada.
He was going in with the first wave, having arranged to meet his
men on the beach shortly afterwards. They said he wouldn't.
" You'll have been shot by then, sir." What most impressed him
now was not so much the fury of the covering bombardment as
the number of wild ducks flying about, presumably stirred up
by it. A thousand heavy bombers had already struck; now the
defences were being swamped at short-range by massed rocket
salvos from special landing craft, the whistle-swoosh of their
missiles thickened up by the express-train roar of heavy shells
from the warships. "Awe-inspiring," said Petty Officer Johnson,
an expert in these matters; and when he noted that a few
German guns were replying, his reaction was—" Cheek!"

Johnson and McKinlay were friends and both had the same
job: to go in with the ' D.D.' tanks and immediately erect signs
to mark the beach exits and to bring in the follow-up landing
craft to the right places; for a seaborne invasion requires more
precise planning and organisation than any other military operation. McKinlay's ' D.D.' was about to launch into the rough
sea, when the landing craft shuddered under the impact of an
explosion at the bows, which jammed the ramp. Out of control,
the vessel began to drift helpless with the tide along the Normandy coast, bullets whining and cracking overhead, mortar
bombs throwing up fountains of water alongside. " We were
pretty annoyed: we had been practising for so long, and this
was our day; and now it looked as if we were not going to make
it." For Johnson, matters were not going right, either. There
should have been a long stretch of sand in front of them, so
that they would ground in the shallows short of the mined beach
obstacles which stood near the high water mark. But the strong
wind, on this particular beach, at Courseulles, was literally
driving the flooding tide before it up the sand; the sea was
rising faster and higher than had been predicted, foaming
already among the angle-iron obstacles; and the tank landing
craft directly ahead was driving inexorably at the explosive-
ridden barrier. " She just about hit everything," said Johnson.
But she had punched a hole in the defences all the same, and

the LCT Johnson was in manoeuvred alongside the wreck, using it as a quay. Johnson scrambled across her and got ashore on the far side. He had taken part in three small commando raids on the French coast, escaped from a sunken landing craft during the Dieppe raid, carried out two similar landings in North Africa, and had even served aboard a suicide Fire-ship intended to stop the German invasion of 1940. But Dieppe was his most vivid memory—the sight of the helpless Churchill tanks, piled up on the beach by the exits, unable to get off it and into the town—the classical bad moment of any seaborne assault. The time for the counter-attack.

Now, as he looked round on this beach, Johnson discovered that he was alone; the inexperienced lads he was leading thought the German fire to be much heavier than it really was—and were still sheltering inside the landing craft. And this, too, the lack of practical experience among the assault troops and their commanders, was to be typical, not merely of D-Day, but of the campaign which followed. However, he got them out at last, including the two who were supposed to be his personal body-guards, and, together with a midshipman, started looking for the Beachmaster who was to direct the placing of the signposts. Then, enemy fire becoming really effective, they went to ground momentarily before Johnson, jumping to his feet, shouted to the bodyguards to get up again. As they obeyed, a blow as swift and savage as the kick of a mule bowled Johnson clean over, leaving him totally breathless, squirming in the sand like a hooked fish. Shell or mortar bomb, whatever it was, it had accounted for one of the bodyguards, too, a lad who had killed one man only in his Commando career—a fellow soldier by accident on the pistol range.

Almost instantly, Johnson was grabbed by an Army officer's batman, dragged to a shallow depression, rolled onto his back, and forcibly held down, to keep him out of the line of fire. " He tried to keep me down, and I tried to get up, because it was so hard to breathe; there was pain in my arm, which started to stiffen up in very quick time, and I was spitting blood on the sand. Some extra fear had crept in, because I did not know what had happened to me." Johnson had always managed to conceal fear and been contemptuous of who those could not. He had wondered whether he would ever be hit—and where. He had heard wounded men scream, and had sworn to himself, " I'm not going to yak, if I'm hit, I'm not going to look a loon." Now, spitting gouts of blood, he was badly shocked, shaking with nervous reaction, and ready for argument with Midshipman Richard Cole who was cutting away the bloodied uniform at the arm, while Johnson steadily cursed him. " You bloody fool, there's nothing there—it's my back! "

" Nothing wrong with your back! " snapped the midshipman.

" Spitting blood threw me right out of gear, so I was happy to go along with the midshipman to a small group of medics and wounded who by then had formed up in the lee of a couple of tanks," recollected Johnson. " Two tanks had blown themselves up on the only exit from the beach, and so a mass of newly-landed tanks was piling up there; queuing to get off the beach. Just like Dieppe all over again, I thought." Having landed at dawn, by teatime Johnson was on his way back to England. He did not know whether the tanks had got off the beach or not, or whether the inevitable German counter-attack had caught the invaders still milling around on the sand. At the hospital, no notice was taken of his back; in fact, they were about to discharge him when a check X-ray showed that the two small punctures in his shoulder were entry wounds and that the splinters were still in his lung. However, the damage had healed itself and Johnson hitched a lift back to his unit in Normandy, without bothering about documentation. " It was easy, everyone was going that way." Things got boring, when the armies broke out from the beachhead, so he and McKinlay decided to join the frogmen for a bit of excitement. McKinlay is still a diver, but Johnson last saw action in 1952, in the cruiser *Ceylon*, off Korea. And the last picture he had of Normandy on D-Day had proved to be typical, not exceptional. A mass of men, vehicles and equipment piling up on the beaches, the strip of sand steadily narrowing as the tide came in; the beach exits blocked or inadequate: the leading troops pushing on, but the follow-up formations delayed; the slowing down process inexorably trans-mitted to the giant organisational machine behind them, in England, inevitably affecting the tempo of the whole campaign. Above all, the university town of Caen and the dominating heights around it should have fallen quickly and easily to the British on D-Day. But because they advanced only six miles instead of ten that day, it was not to fall for another six weeks —and only after it had become a cemetery for its inhabitants and the soldiers of three armies.

* * *

German thinking on the subject was affected, not only by the lessons of the Dieppe Raid of 1942, but of those which resulted from their own experiences while preparing for Operation ' Sealion,' the proposed invasion of England, in 1940. During that year a large-scale exercise was held, in which part of the German invasion fleet left Boulogne and attempted to land troops on another part of the French coast. " Even the private soldier could see that it was not on," commented one German naval observer, who had seen the shambles on the beach, the infantry struggling through the water towards the dunes, the guns, ammunition and transport still hopelessly stuck in the barges, reaching the shore only in driblets after a long struggle, much of it never arriving at all. He had been told that a cross-Channel invasion was only an assault river crossing on a large scale; and clearly it was not. The fatal factor was the lack of specialised landing craft. In 1940, only the Japanese had them. In no sense were Rhine barges a substitute, even when their bows were removed and hinged ramps fitted instead. Most of a barge hull is below the waterline, whereas a landing craft is built to the opposite specification, so that it can ride right up onto a beach before the ramp is lowered. At best, the barges would ground hundreds of yards out to sea; and at worst, half a mile or more. Time and place of arrival were problematical, because the barges were almost unmanageable in open sea, and many had no engines and would therefore have to be towed in pairs by tugs, veering continually on the ends of their tow ropes. And since the deep-draught tugs could not approach the shore, the barges would have to be pushed into the shallows by motor boats; but in any wind at all the motor boats were moved by the barges, and not the other way round. Even the embarkation times were laid down by the Channel tide and not by the staff, for the vessels had to be loaded from quaysides, and with a rise and fall of between 15 and 20 feet, neither the tanks nor the trucks could negotiate the gangplanks except at around high water. Nor could the horses. With no experience of loading tables, the staff had decided that the 38,000 men of von Manstein's corps, for instance, plus their vehicles, should embark in 330 barges—but they found that 38,000 into 330 wouldn't go, so decided to cut out the petrol-driven vehicles and substitute pack-horses, which could be re-fuelled on the English countryside.

As originally planned, Army Group A was to land between Ramsgate and Portsmouth, a front of nearly 120 miles, and form a beachhead 20 miles deep. Army Group B, which four years later was to be on the receiving end in Normandy, was to land west of Portsmouth. The naval and merchant shipping resources to do this simply did not exist, but the German Army could never really bring themselves to believe it. Although the maritime strength of the Allies in 1944 was immensely greater than that of the Germans in 1940, the Allied plan, as finalised by General Montgomery, was to land on a front of about 40 miles and form an initial beachhead ten miles deep, complete control of the air and sea space being assured. Nevertheless, the impractical German Operation 'Sealion' of 1940, long since moulting in a pigeon-hole, was to have its effect on the Allied Operation 'Overlord' of 1944.

Three legacies of that abortive invasion lasted into 1944, to mislead the Germans fatally. Firstly, their own landings had been timed for near high water on a falling tide, to reduce the open space between the assault infantry and the defenders and also to enable the landing barges to 'dry out', the only effective way most of them could be unloaded. Assuming that the Allies would do the same, the Germans therefore sited their defence obstacles accordingly, high up the beach. But the Allies planned to land near low water on a rising tide, both to allow time for the demolition of the German beach obstacles and also to enable their landing craft to back off and return for the next load within minutes of disembarkation, instead of lying helplessly aground for hours under the muzzles of the enemy guns. Secondly, the Germans continued to underestimate the amount of shipping required, failing to realise the need for a stream of transport ships moving to-and-fro across the Channel continuously, like some vast conveyor belt, bringing in reinforcements and supplies for the crucial battle of the build-up; and therefore they believed it logistically possible for the Allies to mount more than one cross-Channel invasion. Thirdly, because of the deficiencies of their own landing craft, the Germans had planned to make most use of the shortest sea crossing, that between Kent and Pas de Calais. Therefore they assumed that the Allies must do the same, and that any landing elsewhere would most probably be a large-scale diversion. The Allies went to extraordinary lengths to encourage the idea that this was where, in fact, they would land. Consequently, the Germans built their strongest defences here and manned them with the nineteen divisions of their 15th Army. And so, while the battle in Normandy raged to its climax around Caen, this German army remained in its fixed positions, staring out to sea for an invasion force which never came and, indeed, did not exist.

For the British, the legacy of 1940 was emotional. Then, the Germans had seemed to have an overwhelming superiority in men, machines, and sheer professional preparedness. ' Now it's our turn ', was the feeling of 1944; and, indeed, the Germans in their turn bitterly called the Battle of Normandy the war of ' men against material '. Petty Officer Johnson, the R.N. Commando, whose experience spanned the four years between, could vividly remember leaving the battlecruiser *Hood* on 25 August, 1940, and joining the naval oil-tanker *War Nawab*, which, with some half-a-dozen other oilers, had been fitted up with gun cotton charges designed to fire the crude oil in her tanks; she was now a gigantic, floating incendiary bomb. Under cover of smoke, they were to enter the German invasion ports, point the ship at the largest concentration of landing craft, set the fuses, and " gracefully retire with the getaway boats." This suicidal fire mission, dependent for any chance of success on the wind and the smokescreen, was contemplated at all only because the situation was desperate—the fate of the British Empire hung on 600 fighter aircraft and three dozen destroyers. In 1944, the positions were reversed, but not exactly. The German air and sea forces were very nearly impotent in face of the overwhelming strength of the Allies; but whereas the British Army of 1940 could have put up little effective resistance, being, after Dunkirk, by far the weakest of the three Services, in 1944 the German Army holding 'Fortress Europe' was far from negligible. Nevertheless, it would have to do the brunt of the work—the fate of the 'New Order' depended largely upon some ten Panzer divisions, which the British and Canadians were to try to pin down at Caen, in order to allow their American allies to make the decisive breakthrough at the other end of the beachhead.

The beachhead battle, on the Allied side, was to be controlled by General Sir B. L. Montgomery, victor of Alamein and a master of the 'set piece' battle. Another reason for the choice of a British commander was that there would be three British and Canadian beaches as against only two American beaches; the British naval force would be stronger than the American and the bulk of the merchant shipping would be British. Under Montgomery would be three Army Commanders —General Omar Bradley (American First Army), General Sir Miles Dempsey (British Second Army), and General H. D. G. Crerar (First Canadian Army). Operations on D-Day would be carried out by negligible forces on both sides; the decisive factor would be the speed and efficiency with which both the Allies and the Germans could funnel the bulk of their armies to the battlefield during June, July and August. Later, when the strength of the American forces had been built up to equal those of the British and Canadians, Montgomery and Bradley would become equal, as Army Group Commanders, under the Supreme Commander, General Eisenhower. But during the period of the build-up in the beachhead, with which we are concerned, the Allied forces had a single commander—Montgomery.

The German command set-up was illogical from the purely military viewpoint, because it was political, being designed to give Hitler not merely the supreme command but the power of interference at all levels, and also to prevent, in the prevailing dangerous atmosphere, any possible combination of generals against the Führer. Command was divided four ways. Field Marshal von Rundstedt was Commander-in-Chief West—he believed that the main Allied effort would be against Pas de Calais. Field Marshal Rommel was commander of Army Group B, covering the potential invasion coast from Holland to Brittany —he believed that Normandy was a dangerous weak spot; and from what he already knew of Allied air power, judged that Germany would lose a battle of the build-up. He therefore recommended that the armoured reserves be held near the coast, ready for immediate counter-attack, to break the invasion actually on the beaches, on D-Day. General Geyr von Schweppenburg commanded Panzer Group West, a planning staff and tank training organisation which had been set up on the opposite assumption—that it would be best to hold back the bulk of the armour in order to fight a great tank battle well inland, out of reach of the Allies' naval guns. Such encounters had often proved decisive on the Russian front, in one case netting 750.000 prisoners; it was hoped that tank attack by night, also proved successful in the East, would help to counter the disadvantages of mounting massed armoured operations under skies dominated by an enemy air force. These conflicting views had not been resolved by June, 1944, least of all by Hitler, who intended to solve all problems, as they occurred in the West, from his headquarters far away in the East: the static divisions holding the coastal defences could fire at any invader, but no one could move the strategic armoured reserve without the Führer's express permission. And, when D-Day came, the Führer was asleep and no one dared wake him.

*   *   *

Unfortunately for those who will over-stress the ' ideological ' nature of the conflict, the war rulers on all sides had found it necessary to impose conscription even before making war. Most of the fighting men arrived at the battlefield as a direct consequence of a call-up notice delivered by the postman, backed by King's Regulations or an Order of the Führer. Some would have joined in any case, once war was declared, for reasons of patriotism or adventure, but these tended to siphon off into the elite units, such as the British paratroops and commandos or the German Waffen S.S. The Canadian Army was distinctly exceptional, being composed entirely of such volunteers, men who had made up their own minds that there was a cause worth fighting for, and were prepared to take the possible consequences of death or wounds. But, unlike 1914, most unit commanders were faced with a mass of basically unwilling, very varied individuals, who hated the army, felt like herded cattle, bitterly resented it, and intended, not to win a decoration for gallantry, but to survive the war, if they could. The recruit training procedures of the British and German armies, basically similar and dating approximately from the time of Frederick the Great, did nothing to improve their temper; however, the German Army had one great advantage over the British, for the German recruits knew they would soon be in action. What they were doing was real, and had a purpose. But the British Army was stale, and bored, and bitter. Four years of endless route marches up and down England, raggedly singing:

> *We had to join,*
> *We had to join,*
> *We had to join*
> *Old Churchill's army . . .*

Down the roads they went, the packs of the knowing ones stuffed with cardboard and old socks, the recruits carrying full load, fearful of a snap inspection; shoulders aching under the burden of obsolete and often useless weapons, belts cutting them in two, feet burning in the big army boots, chafed by the tough, unyielding leather.

> *Ten bob a week,*
> *Flip-all to eat,*
> *Great big blisters*
> *On yer bleedin' feet . . .*

And the singing rising to a howl on the pay-off line:

> *Churchill—yer bastard!*

And the younger officers looking relieved, for sometimes it was their names, instead of that of the great war leader, which occurred at this point.

> *We had to join,*
> *We had to join,*
> *We had to join*
> *Old Churchill's army . . .*

Sweat running down their chests inside the rough, collarless khaki shirts, the clips of the battledress collars chafing their

necks, they hooked their thumbs under the shoulder-straps, to
ease the strain, and shifted Bren guns, mortars, anti-tank rifles
to a different angle, so that the weight fell on a different muscle,
marching from Otley to Ilkley, from New Alresford to Basing-
stoke, while the German Army drove to the Caucasus, or inflicted
yet another defeat on yet another incompetent English general.
Blinded with sweat, unthinking, uncaring, they marched on,
bawling the song of the wasted years:

> *Sittin' on the grass,*
> *Polishin' yer brass,*
> *Great big spiders*
> *Crawlin' up yer arse . . .*

With no faith in their leaders, or in themselves, their voices
rose to a howl of derision:

> *Churchill—yore barmy!*

And the officers looked relieved. Thump—thump—thump—
went the heavy studded boots on the road, the files bobbing
down the endless road to nowhere. Back in the camp there was
an enormous scavenger of a rat, big and bold and cunning, an
altogether exceptional, bullet-proof rat; and they called him
'Rommel', because he was big and bold and cunning, and
because it would annoy the officers, an act of calculated insub-
ordination not contemplated in K.R.s, a unanimous vote of 'no
confidence' in the British Army. But also, it was a call for a
Cromwell, not some ridiculous figure in Bermuda shorts with
bony knees. They wanted a leader who could look the part, as
well as act it; and what they got was a very fine actor, who had
perceived what was wrong, and was also a perfectly adequate
general, wearing the necessary halo of victory. Towards the end
of 1943, General Montgomery arrived in England to take command of the 'Overlord' forces and almost simultaneously his
old opponent, Field Marshal Rommel, was sent to France to take
up the exactly opposite appointment—to stop him. Neither
commander was particularly pleased at what he found: the
morale of the men was not good and the operational plans were
unsatisfactory.

In France, security was a particularly weak spot, because of the 'couldn't care less' attitude of the troops, and also of some of the commanders. Allied propaganda at the time presented a picture of France occupied by fanatical Nazis, opposed by a flamboyantly brave Resistance. The truth was otherwise. The truth was an old greengrocer's van which appeared every day on the coastal road in a vital Normandy sector of the West Wall. "Even though Field Marshal Rommel had given orders—immediately after he had taken over the command—that the entire area of the coastal fortifications should be cleared of civilians, this Frenchman, and no doubt many others too, in different ways, had managed to hang on to the last moment before the invasion, quietly and thoroughly noting every change and reporting it," said Hubert Meyer, in 1944 the senior staff officer of 12 S.S. Panzer Grenadier Division in Normandy. "We found out later, after he had been arrested, that he had spied for years in the River Orne area, and later, too, we saw the results. Our security and counter-espionage measures were insufficient. Admittedly, the conditions were unfavourable—we were occupying enemy territory, the troops had gone slack through years of living in France—but more should have been done. A notable exception was Panzer Group West, but in general the troops were not familiar with nor even interested in the problems of security. Here, the enemy was far ahead of us."

"Actually you could divide the men into two groups," said Karl Max Wietzorek, then a 'browned-off' nineteen year old soldier of 5 Fallschirmjäger Division. "The first lot had been stationed in France for years and did not believe in an invasion, only in the Thousand-Year Reich and their beloved Führer, Adolf Hitler. The second group consisted of all the men who had come from the Russian front; mostly sick soldiers, in shoddy, patched uniforms, not interested in any more fighting." Wietzorek was one of the latter group. While he had been in hospital recovering from wounds, his unit had been annihilated at Zhitomir on the Kiev road, and in February, 1944, he was sent to the Channel coast near St. Malo. "I was a parachute corporal then, wearer of the black wound badge, wearer of the Iron Cross, second class, wearer of the parachute badge; in other words, a 'fully-licensed' parachute soldier, completely entitled to my ration of six cigarettes a week, plus some inferior food, just like all my comrades. While the officers 'lived like God' in France, as the saying went, we felt in our bones, instinctively, that something terrible was to come. And on 6 June, what confusion in our barracks! For we had only dummy cartridges in our pockets and the key of the arms-store was with a corporal who was miles away, playing billiards. . . ."

" Our crews were between 18 and 24, and inexperienced," said Werner Kortenhaus, a tank wireless operator of 21 Panzer Division, the key formation defending Caen, near enough to the beaches to intervene decisively on D-Day. " My own 4th Company was the only one up to its full strength of 17 Mark IVs; but we had had little time for practice with them and had done only one or two range-shoots. We were expecting invasion, of course, but had no idea where it would come, when, or in what strength. In fact, we knew nothing except our daily duties. These became more and more exhausting. First, single-sentries. Then double-sentries were added. Then the double-sentries were forbidden to talk to each other while on duty. This continuous tightening up convinced us that something was afoot. We cut down trees to give a field of fire, then had to drive the trunks into the ground as an anti-glider precaution, the so-called ' Rommel Asparagus '. This job was not much appreciated, as we doubted its effectiveness. Finally, we had to leave our billets and sleep in tents beside our tanks, and then we knew that invasion was imminent. We did realise that the battle would be decisive, but as we thought the war lost anyway, there seemed to be no worthwhile goal."

" The waiting became intolerable for the British public, but the soldier knew better than to worry; it would come eventually, whether he willed it or not," commented Serjeant H. Green of 10th Battalion the Highland Light Infantry in a narrative written soon afterwards. "And so the weeks slid by, into the heat of May, the infantryman training in full marching order, sweating, cursing, plodding along with a savage hatred for his superiors for making him do such stupid things. The fiercest wish in every mind was the desire not to be among the first 50,000 to land. One could either face the inevitable or, alternatively, have a last try to swing the lead and get a ' re-grade '; but the M.O.s were well versed in the art of dealing with ' dodgers '.

Meanwhile, the Generals tried their utmost to instil confidence in their armies. Never were such compliments paid to soldiers as yet untried by battle. The superiority of the Allied Armies was so great, that anyone believing this would be apt to pity the Germans facing them across the Channel. But do you think the ordinary soldier believed such statements? Not likely. To him, the German was as formidable as the ' bogey man ' is to a small child. Wasn't the German Army the best the world had ever seen? Hadn't it beaten us thoroughly in Norway, France, Greece, Crete, and Libya? True, Monty had driven them back into the sea in Tunisia, but look what was happening in Italy! Oh, no, the German was far from beaten. Didn't the pamphlets admit he was a magnificent fighter? And how well we knew our German Army pamphlets! Besides, every soldier thought of his own unit as a ' heap ', a useless collection of men. ' The Germans will die, laughing, when they see this shower ', he used to say. Where was the confidence that an army going into battle must have, if it is to succeed? If there was any, it was well and truly hidden: because the Germans did die—and from every complaint except laughing."

It was too late now to touch the deep-seated and substantial reasons for the lack of confidence in Second Army. Over-trained at unit level, almost untrained at formation level; infantry knowing nothing about tanks, and tank crews knowing nothing about infantry; hardly anyone with any experience at all of modern war; and no doctrine at all, apart from sub-unit ' battle drill '. A few divisions brought home from the Mediterranean theatre made very little difference, except that it was un-nerving to sit in a barrack room festooned with pictures of tough Germans sloganed, " He is a master of his Weapons—You must be a Past-Master of Yours ". or " He is Ready to Die for his Führer —Can You Ensure that He Does?" while an 8th Army veteran with one glass eye told how the German tank guns so far out-ranged the British that " Jerry sees you coming, sits down, has his tea, and afterwards pops you off at his leisure." It was little consolation to learn that the Afrika Korps had treated British prisoners decently, particularly the wounded. All that could be done in the time available was to withdraw from infantry batta-lions the totally unsuitable anti-tank weapons, positively guaranteed *not* to pierce the armour of any known type of German tank (but effective against British Bren carriers), and replace them with genuine 6 pounder anti-tank guns and the new ' bazooka '-type weapon, the PIAT.

The only approach remaining was psychological, and this was pushed to the limit with a care and attention not hitherto devoted to military affairs. One of General Montgomery's many visits to units was analysed, in slightly barbed fashion, by the historian of the 2nd Household Cavalry Regiment. " Outwardly simple in character," he wrote, " the parade was really the result of the most detailed instructions which had come direct to 8 Corps HQ from the General's personal staff. Everything, including the ' spontaneous surge forward ', was laid on by the hand of a master of publicity." The General fiddled with an apparently malfunctioning microphone, thus focusing attention on himself; said he wanted to get to know them, and that they might like to take a look at him; and summing up the war to date, " recalled how he had ' been knocked into the sea in 1940 ' and that he did not like it at all, and that at present he was looking for a good sea into which to throw the Germans. This crack went with a swing, and he and the men were on good terms thereafter." He had never started a battle until he had first won the air fight. This was now going on, and when it was won, he would invade. " Not before." The last words positively rang out. " We felt," wrote the historian, " that here was a captain who would not even let us out of the pavilion until he had morally won the match. It was ruthlessly twentieth century. The Press and public lapped it up."

The Prime Minister also appeared, an even greater actor, equally intent on instilling confidence. At his visit to the 43rd (Wessex) Infantry Division he was preceded, as is customary, by lesser members of the cast—Field Marshal Smuts, the Prime Ministers of Canada and Southern Rhodesia. "At last, wearing a curious brown, square bowler hat, of a type apparently worn about 1898 by foremen carpenters, and with the usual cigar, the greatest man of his age, leaving a haze of cigar smoke behind him in the corridor, stepped out onto the platform and immediately called for the station-master," wrote the division's historian. " This official was unearthed with some difficulty and thanked for the privilege of using his station." Radiating " the spirit of offensive battle and conviction of overwhelming success," Mr. Churchill saw a demonstration of flame-throwers which " filled him with youthful delight." Field Marshal Smuts had only one line to speak, a stage whisper to a gunner: " It's coming very soon now, boys."

" England and the Allied world needed a hero," commented Serjeant Leo Gariepy, of 6th Canadian Armoured Regiment, " but we had none except for aces such as ' Screwball' Burling, ' Sailor' Malan, ' Cobber' Kane. But an air force hero is not like a flamboyant General of the Armies. The Germans on the other hand had a myriad heroes, and also the Russians; we of the Commonwealth had none, and they were sorely needed. Monty looked more like a college professor, or some ascetic, and he made a very poor impression when he said at our reviewing, ' Let them approach and see me'. The Canucks did not go for that. And when he began his traditional hand-picking of some 8 or 10 cigarettes to scatter in a throng of thousands of Canadians who had more cigarettes than they could smoke, the men were insulted. For us, Monty was a zero." The only unqualified, one hundred per cent success with the Canadian volunteer soldiers was a shy and self-effacing man. " He practically looked at each tank man individually. His visit made a very good impression on all troops. The Canadian soldiers were deeply proud of their King, and after that visit, we all felt that we were going to see to it personally that he remained the reigning monarch of England."

While the German tank crews of 21 Panzer Division were getting what battle practice they could, in between tree-felling and sentry-go, the men of Gariepy's unit were training secretly in the Solent with their ' D.D.' tanks. The only new thing about the German Mark IV was the gun—the excellent ' long ' 75 mm. But the ' Duplex Drive ', or ' swimming ' tanks, were so secret that sea training had to take place at night, sometimes in the middle of the shipping lanes, where awkward encounters took place. " Ship's officers could not believe their eyes, when they switched on a spotlight and saw this strange collection of canvas boats roaming aimlessly, and received a greeting of real Canadian curses." The ' D.D.' mechanism enabled an ordinary tank's engines to be coupled at will to twin propellers; a heavy canvas screen then converted the tank into a boat with a freeboard of only two feet. When at sea, the tank commander was the only man with his head above water-level, consequently they were all put through a short 'submarine escape' course at Portsmouth. The Canadians lost tanks, but no men. The British, however, because they insisted that the crews should wear full equipment and look properly Regimental, as at Bunker Hill, lost not merely a tank, but the entire crew as well. The men were never found, but the regulation was changed thereafter.

Gariepy, a French-Canadian married to a Toronto girl, had volunteered for this hazardous job because he was a regular soldier, his army number being preceded by ' P ' (for ' Permanent Force '). " It did not matter to what unit you were attached, that magical ' P ' was infallible. ' Just the man we've been waiting for,' they beamed. Immediately, a long list of soldiers described as ' rebellious ', ' hard heads ', ' permanent defaulters ', etc., was read out; because we were regarded as strict, parade square Serjeant-Majors, it became our duty to ' straighten them out '. But being assigned to the ' awkward squad ' was more terrible to the peacetime soldier than being given a sentence in the ' glass-house '. Consequently, volunteering became a ritual; any-thing would have been acceptable as long as it meant action."

The entire formation—2nd Canadian Armoured Brigade— had reached a high state of training. In gunnery, they no longer aimed at a tank, but a particular weak point of it, an individual bogey or sprocket; in tactics, they trained constantly with 7th Canadian Infantry Brigade, even to letting the infantry drive the tanks, so that 2 CAB and 7 CIB were in effect a fully-integrated flexible formation similar to what the Germans called a Battle Group, much less ponderous than a division. Gariepy's unit, 6th Armoured Regiment (1st Hussars), who were to man the D.D.s and supply the D-Day spearhead, had first to master their strange craft in difficult waters and then, finally, practice launch-ing from the tank landing craft. " These LCTs were so unpre-dictable that each launching was an adventure. With a flat bottom, engine and bridge aft, and a top speed of 10 knots, in a ' beam ' sea they would swing like a pendulum. As the Sherman D.D.s had a speed of only 6 knots, they had to reduce speed until the LCT had hardly any steerage. Then, because of its slab sides which caught the wind, it had first to position itself in the wind, then lower a large ramp which acted like a tremendous scoop or brake in the water, and practically go into reverse so as to allow the tank to make its steep plunge into the sea. And the tank would sink into the sea with the impact until the water was less than six inches from the top of the canvas. No two less sea-worthy vessels ever took part in any naval engagement of the past, or ever will again in the future."

As the troops began to move to their concentration areas, there to discover for the first time how vast was the enterprise on which they were engaged, a mysterious and extraordinary propaganda gambit was played. There existed already a confidential project to reduce the population of Germany after the war by dismantling her industry and crippling her agriculture; it was to become known as the 'Morganthau Plan', after the adviser of President Roosevelt who initiated it; and was codified in an operation order known as 'Eclipse', not actually issued to British Army units until January 1945, under the signature of Montgomery's chief of staff. News of the existence of such a plan was likely to make even the most 'bolshy' or 'couldn't care less' German soldier fight to the bitter end on the beaches, but nevertheless, the news was leaked to the press just before the invasion, the time of maximum impact and of crucial decision, and was instantly picked up by Goebbels. In its issue of 28 May, timed almost to perfection had the editor known it, the newspaper of the German Armies on the Channel coast, *Wacht am Kanal,* re-printed from the London *Daily Express* an article by William Barkley now headlined " Totale Zerstoerung Deutschlands "—" Total Destruction for Germany "—which was a fair summary of the policy outlined. " This plan would teach us again to eat our bread with tears ", ran the commentary. "A Germany without industry, and with an exhausted soil, would inevitably decline to the level of India . . . where millions die every year. This will wake up all those sleepy-headed softies who are crazy enough to believe that a compromise can be reached."[1]

---

[1] The present author picked up this copy of *Wacht am Kanal* from a German billet during the Normandy campaign, and still has it in his collection of interesting enemy and allied documents.

In the perspective of twenty years after, it can be seen that a policy of 'Unconditional Surrender', of prolonging the war until all Germany and half Europe had been ruined, suited Stalin's interests, and perhaps America's interests also, for certainly Roosevelt was prime mover in all these ventures apparently designed to stiffen the German will to fight. But there may have been a deeper reason, for, simultaneously, Goebbels was producing propaganda leaflets which could only convince the Allied soldiers who were supposed to read them that their originators were utterly and unspeakably evil, and that what they stood for must be destroyed.[2] It may be that mutual hatred at the top had grown to frightening proportions, producing an indifference to the fate of the millions who must die because of it; or, as some have speculated, that evil begets evil, like a contagious poison, infecting all who come into contact with it.

The day after publication, 29 May, Field Marshal Rommel was in the Caen area inspecting units of 21 Panzer Division with

The front page of
Wacht am Kanal,
containing the
reprint of the
Daily Express article.

[2] An example soon to come was the " BERLIN and now LONDON " leaflet which accompanied the V1 offensive in June. Simultaneous examples from the Italian campaign are discussed by Denis Johnston in *Nine Rivers from Jordan*, pp. 168-170.

their commander, Generalmajor Edgar Feuchtinger. Among the locations was the anti-tank gun 'hedgehog' at Cairon, halfway to the coast, admirably positioned, as it turned out, to block the advance of 3 Canadian Infantry Division and its supporting armour in eight days' time. But the transport was a hotch-potch of mostly French vehicles, the 75 mm SP (self-propelled) guns being mounted on the chassis of a Renault half-track; the defensive minefields were fenced off with barbed wire, and labelled; and French civilians were still moving around freely, able to inspect all the German preparations. "We found out, when the invasion started, that the enemy knew more about our defences than we did ourselves," commented Leutnant Hans Höller, who commanded a Section of three guns at Cairon. "I took some photographs of Rommel inspecting our division, and the general report was that he was not satisfied with the fortifications in the coastal area. Certainly, the pictures show him looking as black as thunder; but like many German generals at that time, he was balanced on the razor's edge of revolt, forced to think two ways—how to hold off the Allied invasion and, simultaneously, how to overthrow the Führer and the Party. This was not merely suspected by the Führer but known by that time even to the Allied generals waiting across the Channel.[3] The last-minute leakage of the 'Morgenthau Plan', following on the demand for 'Unconditional Surrender', made the latter task, which might have ended the war in 1944, far more dangerous and difficult; indeed, for Rommel, as for many others, it was to prove fatal.

But already the assault forces had been penned into camps fenced with barbed wire. There remained only the loading of vehicles and men into the ships, according to meticulous plans and tables prepared, on inadequate and inaccurate data by the War Office, and peremptorily brushed aside at the last, as the B.A.O.R. historian of 7th Armoured Division recorded, "by knowledgeable men in bowler hats who leant over the side of the ship, shouting: 'Bring on that one there; flick what the bloody officers say, I bin loading ships for forty years and know what they'll 'old'."

[3] See in particular General Omar Bradley's *A Soldier's Story*, pp. 188/9. The Allied military planners had prepared for this contingency as far back as 1943, under the code name 'Rankin C'.

CHAPTER TWO

THAT REMINDS ONE
OF VERDUN!

The Armada Sails—Alerte in France—the Airborne Landings
night of 5/6 June

The German supreme headquarters in the West was at St. Germain, just outside Paris; the Allied invasion headquarters was in an old red-brick fort high on Portsdown Hill behind Portsmouth, built by Lord Palmerston against the menace of French invasion during the Second Empire. It overlooked the great anchorage of Spithead and the Solent, and a great deal of history as well. Here, in the April and May of 1346, almost exactly 600 years before, King Edward III had massed his army and fleet for the invasion of Normandy. He also misled his enemies by pretending to threaten somewhere else—in his case Gascony. And his D-Day was also delayed, but not by a mere 24 hours; he did not get his men ashore until 12 July. The area was exactly covered by the D-Day map which still hangs on the wall of Southwick House, for he landed in the American sector, in the Cotentin, near Cherbourg, the route of his breakout covering the major battles of the 1944 Normandy campaign—Carentan, St. Lo, and Fontenay. And so to a desperate battle for Caen, whereas Bayeux surrendered easily, and on to the crossing of the Seine and the rout of the French King's main army on the battlefield of Crecy, on 26 August. Places and dates were uncannily similar, because geography and the seasons govern all military operations. On the 1944 map, said one witness, "Caen jumped to the eye", and the great massif of Mont Pincon loomed menacingly in the background.

On the morning of 5 June, 1944, the original date for D-Day, the vast armada began to take up its assembly positions in the Solent. " They'll never let us go out in this," thought Squadron Leader A. E. L. Hill, who knew the area well and could guess what it was going to be like once they got into the Channel, outside the shelter of the Isle of Wight. Corporal Raymond Arthur Hill, of 13/18 Hussars, could see the steel deck of his landing craft bending up and down under the combined stress of six Sherman tanks and the heavy seas. It was blowing Force 5 from the south-west—a 'beam' sea for the unwieldy slab-sided landing craft. Nevertheless, recollected Serjeant Leo Gariepy of 6th Armoured Regiment. "At 7 p.m. the word came: 'Go'. We were preceded only by a slow-moving minesweeper which was to clear a channel for us through the German minefields. Watching the sweeper's manoeuvres, one would think they were on a Sunday jaunt, so indifferent they appeared about their grim task. Far off on the port side could be seen a destroyer, leading the advance force. Everywhere excitement ran very high, aboard that LCT that was to carry us to the feared Germans. We were trained to a fine edge, not apparently scared, but very wary of the task ahead. The sealed maps were ordered to be opened and we finally saw that part of the Normandy coast which we were to call Green Mike and Red Mike from now on." This was the stretch Vaux/Graye/Courseulles—the centre of the British assault. " Later, it got very rough, white caps rising everywhere on the water. The great air armada could be heard flying overhead, but we could not see them. Everyone was praying for the coast of France, so that we could get off this LCT, but the interminable snail pace continued, with the plodding minesweeper ahead barely discernible in the darkness, the ghostly shapes of other ships aft, and so the grim procession continued throughout the night." From many other ports between London and Falmouth, similar armadas were converging on an area south of the Isle of Wight, later to be known as 'Piccadilly Circus', and heading south down the 'Spout' towards the minefields.

At 9 p.m. a small group of French people met in Caen, as pre-arranged, for a discussion as to what they could do to help, in case the area became a battle zone. The wailing of the air raid sirens and the sound of waves of planes passing overhead did not disturb them; it was nothing unusual. Among them was Madame L. Corbasson, mother of three children, whose husband was in an extermination camp. From their house was an underground passage leading to the chateau of William the Conqueror, whose tomb was nearby in the great Abbey of St.

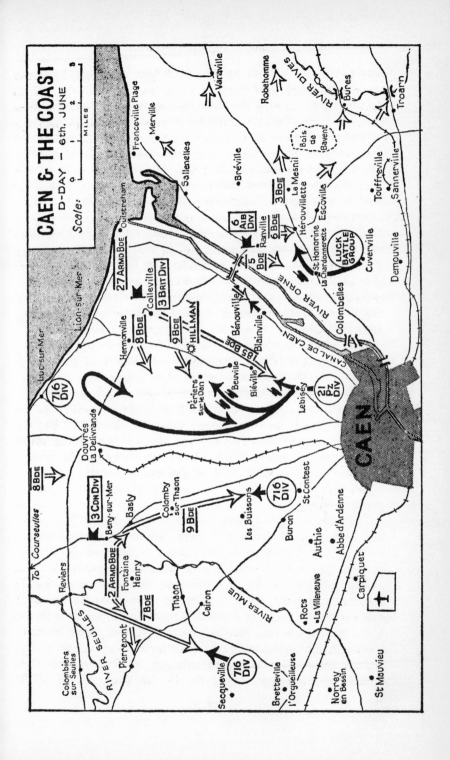

CAEN & THE COAST

D-DAY – 6th. JUNE

Scale: 0 MILES 2 3

Etienne, and she planned to use this passage as a shelter in the event of anything happening.

At 9.15 p.m., those Frenchmen who were really in the know heard a B.B.C. message, " Blessent mon coeur d'une langueur monotone "—the second half of a verse by Verlaine; and they knew what it meant—" Call out the Resistance: invasion within 48 hours." The Germans heard it, too. And they also knew what it meant. Generalleutnant Bodo Zimmermann was sitting in the officers' mess at Field Marshal von Rundstedt's headquarters in St. Germain, when the chief intelligence officer entered excitedly with the news. A general alert was sent out, but Rommel was en route from Germany, and could not be reached, and many of the senior commanders were en route from Rennes, where they had been attending a war game. And for many hours, there were no further reports, so that it seemed like a false alarm.

Madame Corbusson went home and started to pack. Without waking the boys, she quickly got together everything that mattered—documents, jewels, clothes. Peering down into the street through the blinds, she could see plainly that there was 'flap' on: German soldiers were about, armed, and wearing steel helmets, and at one point it seemed that they had captured a Resistance man. " Two of them came along 'fanning' a very young man. He looked very upset; certainly, he was not to go home again, poor young fellow." She had arranged for herself and the three children to share the underground passage shelter with a friend, but a neighbour begged for shelter also, and as she had 18 children and grandchildren, the total number rose immediately to 24.

At Epanay, south of Caen, where Werner Kortenhaus was stationed with 4 Company of Panzer Regiment 22, 21 Panzer Division, a special patrol was sent out to check the whole neighbourhood; but by midnight, everyone was awake anyway, because of the exceptionally heavy air activity. At 0100 hours, the official alarm came through and they prepared their tanks for action; but no further orders arrived and they made no move for another five hours. At Cairon, between Caen and the coast, where Leutnant Höller was stationed with the anti-tank guns of 8 Company, Panzer Grenadier Regiment 192, 21 Panzer Division, the alert was received at about 0200. By that time, said Höller,

" the earth was shaking with the tremors of the bomb carpet and the sky above Caen was glowing red. The French people in my billet had been extremely kind, and with the ground trembling under us, they pressed food and drink on me and said goodbye. We soon loaded up the vehicles and took the road for Bénouville. I cannot remember who gave this order, as in the beginning all the leaders were very uncertain; but probably it was Oberstleutnant Rauch, the Regimental commander, whose whim was always to react immediately to any change in the situation." Bénouville covered the two vital bridges over the twin water barriers of the Orne and the Caen Canal; and was the objective of 5 Parachute Brigade, 6 Airborne Division.

By odd coincidence, the eastern (British) and the western (American) flanks of the invasion were marked by two large convents of the same foundation, Le Bon Sauveur, both some ten miles from the sea. The mother convent at Caen was so enormous that it was known as ' the town within a town '. At this moment, it held 2,000 people, including mental patients, deaf-mute children and ordinary schoolchildren; two days later, an influx of refugees had raised the number to over 10,000. As the sky blazed with the glow of fires, soon shrouded in the drifting dust of the bomb explosions, the air sullen with the throbbing of aircraft engines, split by the high-pitched bark of the flak, the old men began to mutter ominously, " That reminds one of Verdun!" Leaflets came drifting down, warning the people of Caen that the railway station, the power station, and certain other buildings were to be bombed. But what the nuns, and still less the mentally defective, the totally mad, the deaf and the dumb, the sick and the homeless who sheltered there in hope of God's protection did not realise, was how sharply Caen " jumped to the eye " on that great wall map in Fort Southwick across the Channel.

The other great hospital run by the nuns of the Good Saviour foundation was at Pont l'Abbe on the Cherbourg peninsula. The Germans had already, in May, evacuated their own patients, and then sited an artillery battery nearby. The Superiors had, without result, applied to the French authorities for a complete evacuation of the convent buildings. These included ordinary medical hospitals, special-employment schools for deaf-mutes, and mental homes, housing in all about 1,000 patients of both sexes. "We passed two nights of terror", wrote a nun in her diary. "Intense bombardments. Last night, 5th June, the sky from Cherbourg to Harfleur was a sheet of flame, so that we thought the invasion must be taking place there."[1] The nuns could not know that, not Cherbourg, but the beach directly opposite them, some ten miles distant, had been scheduled for the landing of 30,000 American troops next morning; and that on the great war map in Fort Southwick it now bore the code name Utah. Halfway between that beach and the convent, with its mental patients, was the small town of St. Mere-Eglise. Could the nuns have stolen a look at the diagram showing the fly-in routes of the 82nd and 101st American Airborne Divisions, they would have seen that their dropping zones were on either side of St. Mere-Eglise, five miles away, and that the great fleets of transport aircraft must pass almost directly over the convent. In fact, the night of 5/6 June was chaotic. Bombs fell around them, destroying the laundry, forge and stables, while above them, lost, frightened, under fire, most of them for the first time, the American transport pilots scattered their unfortunate comrades like casual confetti all over the Cherbourg peninsula. The insanity of war was about to overwhelm the insane.

*   *   *

Shortly after midnight, six gliders came whistling down towards the two vital bridges in the British sector. The leading glider, commanded by Major R. J. Howard, bumped to earth 47 yards from the canal bridge by Bénouville; of the six, only one went astray, and both bridges were rushed and taken. Shortly afterwards, the parachutists of 5 Brigade began to drop to reinforce them; they were in position soon after 0300 hours, by which time Leutnant Höller's unit was already moving out of Cairon for the counter-attack. 5 Brigade had the static role: hold the bridges. The chaotic, disruption task was allotted to Brigadier S. James L. Hill's 3 Parachute Brigade; they were to operate eastward, beyond the Orne bridges, cause maximum confusion

[1] The diaries kept by the nuns of both Bon Sauveur convents were collected and translated into English, early in 1945, by Sister Eilis Malone of the Good Saviour Convent at Holyhead, Anglesey, who had trained for several years at the Caen foundation.

and then retire to form a bridgehead. The most important destruction targets were the coastal battery at Merville, positioned so as to rake the beaches on which 3 (British) Infantry Division was to land some seven hours later, and the bridges over the River Dives at Troarn and Bures, across which German armoured reserves would come for the counter-attack. The battery, heavily fortified, was to be taken by Lieutenant-Colonel Otway's 9 Para Battalion, assisted by three gliders which were to land right on top of it, as in the classic German assault on Fort Eben Emael in 1940. The Dives bridges were to be blown by the Brigade Engineers, covered by part of Lieutenant-Colonel Pearson's 8 Para Battalion. The remainder of this battalion, plus the Canadian Para Battalion, were to form a firm base to which the destruction parties could withdraw after their missions had been carried out. They would then be the left flank of the entire Allied assault, holding a small triangular bridgehead over the Orne; a cramped and difficult position, inviting counter-attack.

Although the airborne troops arrived first, they had started last. The evening sky was pink and stormy as their aircraft rose up above their airfields; half-an-hour after midnight, they were going out across the Channel, the aircraft rocking and bumping and the white horses on the waves down below clearly visible. Brigadier Hill spared a thought for the landing craft and the 'swimming tanks', and for his relative, Squadron Leader Hill, somewhere down there in an LCT. "As Brigade Commander," he said, " one's task was temporarily done; there was a sense of almost peace. Fourteen months of intense training was now a page out of the past, and one's plans were inexorably in motion. I knew they would go wrong; I had told all my chaps to expect that, and to go anyway to the rendezvous. I also realised that we were embarking on a momentous event, and that the number of men in the Brigade who had any previous experience of fighting could have been counted on the fingers of one hand. That gave me no cause for worry. Each Battalion had a personality of its own, moulded by the stock from which it was raised and the characteristics of the leaders within it. With one Canadian and two British battalions, the Brigade combined the vitality, élan and dash of the New World with the discipline, doggedness and staying power of the old."

35

The entry of the Brigadier into the D-Day battle was not dignified: nor did it go according to plan. His first operational task, to drop onto the beach defences a couple of bricks and a football daubed in luminous paint to resemble the Führer's face, proved more difficult than anticipated owing to the lurching of the aircraft in face of the flak barrage; and because of the half-gale conditions, it was hard for the navigator, let alone anyone else, to tell the difference between the very similar mouths of the Orne and the Dives, only some five miles apart. He saw a blazing seaside town, which was Cabourg, then suddenly there was a shout of: "*Green on—go!*" A blast of cold air, a violent jerk, then a moment of peace and quiet, drifting down. "The moon was then hidden, but the illumination was sufficient to show that something was very wrong. I was approaching a vast sheet of water. There was just time to loosen the harness for a water landing, then bang into four feet of it I went. We had been dropped into the valley of the Dives, flooded by the Germans as a defensive measure, and well to the north of our objective." One by one, they floundered towards drier land, the Brigadier weighed down by the reserve tea bags (for a quick 'brew up') which had been sewn onto his trouser tops by his batman. "So, for the first few minutes of the invasion," he said, rather bitterly, "I was wading around in the river, making cold tea. I heard shots almost at once—but it was only two members of my bodyguard mistaking each other for Germans." It took them three hours, by which time the Brigadier had gathered together 38 soldiers, two sailors, and a parachute dog, to reach the rendezvous. Their only consolation was, that by landing in the River Dives, they had begun their invasion where William the Conqueror had started his; and that he, too, had lost touch with his units, due to bad weather, and for a time appeared to be invading England on his own.

The drop of Lieutenant-Colonel Otway's 9 Para Battalion was even more scattered but the adjutant, Captain H. H. T. Hudson, had a surprise of a different kind. "The first thing that impressed me when I jumped, was that I found myself looking down on the dropping zone and could clearly see the battalion rendezvous. This had never previously been my good fortune on a night drop. Nor had I ever previously landed in a

tree; fortunately it was not very high, but I got out of it just
as fast as I could. I should, if the drop had gone according to
plan, have been one of the last to arrive at the R.V. In fact,
when I got there, there was nobody at all. I remember the feeling
that it was all mad and that some nightmare change must have
been made in the location of the R.V. and that I had not been
told. I wandered about and found Wigg, the C.O.'s batman: we
exchanged greetings and the password, in that order, and set
about trying to entice the battalion to the R.V. by blowing on
our bird whistles; my bird noise was a screech owl and quite
effective. When the C.O., Terence Otway, arrived we mustered
about 120 men, rather a poor performance; and among the 600
odd men who had been dropped in the wrong place there were
some vital chaps who carried important equipment for the
assault on the battery. However, we set off hopefully and I took
my Battalion H.Q. staff in with the second wave of the assault.
In the minefield, halfway to the wire, I felt a tremendous smack.
I thought it was a stone flung up from a mortar explosion and
was surprised to find that I could not stand up. Vaguely, I saw
the chaps streaming through the apparently solid wall of tracer
along the wire. I thought I ought to do something to help before
I died, so I got out my revolver and wavering it at the nearest
emplacement, I managed after a physical effort to pull the trigger.
In fiction, of course, the bullet would have gone through the
heart of the German battery commander: in real life, it went
straight through my right foot."

When he fired that shot, Hudson had eighteen pieces of
shrapnel in him; it was years before he recovered from his terrible
wounds. And at the moment when he fell, it seemed that the
assault must fail. A complete Battalion of 750 men had been
allotted the task of capturing the Merville Battery, because it
was a fortress. The four 75 mm guns (reported as 150 mm pieces)
were mounted in concrete emplacements 6½ feet thick, the
entrances being barred by steel doors. The perimeter defences
consisted of an anti-tank ditch, a minefield 100 yards deep, and
a barbed wire fence 15 feet wide, covered by machine-gun posts,
trenches and 2 cm flak, and manned by a garrison believed to
be 200 strong (but actually numbering 130). Most of the
engineer equipment to breach these defences was with the

missing 600 men of the battalion, as was the equipment to illuminate the battery for the glider landings; and consequently none landed on the battery and one only nearby. The assault would have to be carried out by about 120 men, entirely from outside the perimeter, and with small arms only. And furthermore, the task had to be completed within 60 minutes; for if the success signal was not fired by 0530 on 6 June, naval guns would open a bombardment on the target. And at 0500 the success signal was lit by the survivors. In the ruins of the battery, some 75 parachutists and about 20 Germans were still on their feet. An epic had ended, and one of the two major tasks allotted to the Brigade had been completed.

The other was the blowing of the vital bridges over the Dives, of which that at Troarn was the most important. Like all the airborne operations on D-Day, this had been meticulously planned and rehearsed. Just before midnight on 5 June, 30 of the Brigade Engineers were to drop near Touffreville, move one mile to the Troarn bridge, prepare it for demolition in 60 minutes, and blow at 1.30 on the morning of 6 June, covered meanwhile by reconnaissance patrols. In practice, 10 men moved 7 miles and blew the bridge in 7 minutes, at 5.20, completely on their own and unprotected. "This ratio of manpower, time and achievement was roughly but successfully typical of most airborne tasks undertaken on D-Day." said David A. Breese, then a lieutenant of Major Roseveare's Parachute Squadron, R.E. "As commander of troops in my aircraft, I was No. 1 to drop. After landing and preparing my equipment and weapons, an eternity of some ten minutes must have lapsed before there was sound or sight of friendly or enemy troops; then one of my Stick, Sapper 'Sam' Peachey arrived, and together we sought and loaded the stores onto the special airborne folding trolley, which was as the packhorse or jeep is to conventional heavier-equipped units. Other figures appeared, asking for the D.Z. R.V. and identifying themselves as members of units of 5th Brigade. The sound of hunting horn rallying aids, foreign to 3rd Brigade, confirmed my assessment that we had been dropped on the wrong D.Z. Success of our mission was vitally dependent on surprise and speed onto the objectives, before the enemy could properly organise.

Instead of a mile, we had now to move on foot seven miles, and success was therefore seriously jeopardised."

The balance between success and failure was tipped 2½ miles short of Troarn when Major A. J. C. Roseveare held an 'O' (Orders) Group and devised a new plan, based on a commandeered R.A.M.C. jeep and trailer. The medical stores were thrown out, and the engineers stores put on, then the Major took the wheel and ordered Lieutenant Breeze to get his section aboard. Heavily laden with explosives and ten armed men, jeep and trailer reached the outskirts of Troarn where they ran into an unmanned barbed wire barricade. Reversing out only wrapped the wire more firmly round the front axle, and there was a painful wait, during which a German soldier walked across the road in front of them, before it was cut. While Major Roseveare drove on, to check direction at the road junction ahead, a German cyclist rode towards the dismounted group and was silenced, unfortunately, with a Sten. The rattle of the machine-carbine completely gave the game away, and the bridge they had to demolish was on the other side of the town. "The only course now was to drop all precautions and drive at speed through Troarn," said Breeze. "All weapons were pointed outwards, Sapper Peachey being posted in the trailer with a Bren as rear gunner, and as we drove up the main street of the town, steady all-round fire was maintained. Apart from the movement of the careering jeep and bucking trailer, my memory is the sound of, and considering the cost of, replacing all the plate-glass shopwindows, so rudely shattered.

"Two German soldiers bravely emerged in front of us, to set up a machine-gun, but had to dodge into a doorway; then they re-set the gun in the road behind us, and opened fire after we had passed. Peachey returned the fire with our Bren, and because the road dropped down the hill towards the bridge, the German fire went over our heads. However, the bucking of the jeep and trailer, now nearly out of control with the speed down-hill, threw Peachey off, so that he was injured and captured. At the bridge, Serjeant Henderson and I covered the road back to Troarn while the charges were rapidly placed in the road over one arch of the bridge. Surplus charges were left in the trailer, which was also placed on the bridge, and the whole of the charges were detonated with a short safety fuse after an unnaturally short retirement distance."

After ditching the jeep because of the floods, and a conversation in "matriculation French" with a startled farmer's wife, who said either that there were 15 Germans about or that the Germans were 15 kilometres away, they swam a stream, saw two Germans, and reached Brigade HQ at Le Mesnil. As Lieutenant Breeze was settling into a half-completed slit trench, Brigadier Hill arrived at last, standing up in a jeep. "As he was some 6 feet 4 inches tall, his total and commanding stature was therefore some nine feet, from which imposing height he was clearly able to see directly into my trench. His very right and proper instruction was therefore that the sides of our trenches should be squared off, and boots cleaned thereafter." The Brigadier's upright position in the jeep was due to what had happened to him after his drop into the River Dives and the subsequent three hours of floundering through two miles of flooded countryside, consumed with anxiety lest his whole Brigade had been dropped as far off course as he had. "At this stage," he said, "I had gathered in some 40 stragglers who, like myself, had been dropped far from our target. They included two parachute sailors who had come with a radio set to help us fire the guns of the battleship *Warspite* and two cruisers, which were to support us, and also one of our Alsatian parachute messenger dogs. We were making good speed to where I reckoned 9 Para Battalion should be, when suddenly everything opened up; looking at my watch, I realised that the seaborne landings had started.

"Then there was a noise the like of which I never want to hear again. A large number of fighter aircraft were tearing towards us in tight formation at tree-top height, accompanied by a cloud of dust and an appalling din. Suddenly, we realised that they were carrying out pattern bombing and that we were directly in their path; we threw ourselves to the ground and into a ditch, as the bombs struck. Close on 40 good men died there, including the sailors and the dog, and after the aircraft had vanished, a smell of cordite and death hung in the air. My Defence Platoon Commander and I were the only ones surviving. After tending the very few who were still alive, but badly wounded, and giving them injections of morphia, we proceeded on our course. I had been winged in the backside, but was saved from worse by my waterbottle and spare clothing." Brigadier Hill was taken (on a bicycle) to Divisional HQ, for a minor operation, then the A.D.M.S. in person drove him to Le Mesnil. " On the way we saw a party of Germans crossing the road immediately ahead of us and, to my astonishment and concern, the good doctor pulled up his jeep and gave instant pursuit. However, they ran faster than he did, so he delivered me, instead of the Germans to my H.Q., where I found communications established, stage one of the battle over, casualties high and morale very good."

What the paratroops had to fear was immediate armoured counter-attack, before the seaborne troops could arrive with their heavier weapons. The blowing of the Dives bridges would prevent any immediate assault from the west, but there were very few anti-tank guns to bar the road which led south to Caen, behind which the tanks of 21 Panzer Division were waiting. What that division did during the next few hours would be vital, probably decisive, because they were near enough to intervene almost immediately. That part of the division which was at Cairon, nearest to the airborne landings, was ordered to move at once, as we have seen, and by 0330 was in action against 5 Parachute Brigade at Bénouville, overlooking the Orne and Canal bridges. They consisted of infantry and anti-tank guns; the tanks were south of Caen. Five hours after having been alerted, the tanks were still waiting, with the precious hours of darkness slipping by. At 0600 hours came the order to move, and they roared forward to the main Caen-Falaise road; and stopped again, strung out at intervals under trees. To the north, the sky was red; Caen was burning. Some drivers kept their engines running, because they expected an immediate advance, but nothing happened for another two hours, except that German vehicles from other units began to move past them towards the coast and a stream of refugees from Caen began to appear, going inland. Then, at 0800, their forward movement almost precisely synchronised with the arrival of the British and Canadians on the beaches the other side of Caen, they received the order: " March! "

CHAPTER THREE

THE BATTLE ON THE BEACHES

D.D. Tanks on D-Day—Juno Beach and
Sword Beach (I Corps)

All night, with half a gale screaming over their decks, dipping
their blunt bows with a crash into the waves, swept out of line
by the tearing force of the Channel tide, pitching and rolling
in the blackness, 5,000 ships and 130,000 men had been moving
remorselessly down the swept channels in the minefields which
would funnel them an hour after dawn onto the deadly beaches
of D-Day. " There was no faltering and many of the smaller
craft were driven on until they foundered," bleakly reported
Rear-Admiral Sir Philip Vian, commanding the British Eastern
Task Force. The weather, which had postponed the day and
nearly cancelled the entire operation, now provided them with
an additional, third element of surprise. They were expected in
Pas de Calais, and were steering for Normandy; they were
expected at high tide, and would be landing at low; they were
expected in calm weather, and not when the breakers were
roaring on the beaches. And they would have to pay the
penalties. The assault troops were sick and sleepless, their bowels
almost literally wrung out of them, before they had even stepped
ashore, let alone advanced inland ten miles. The unexpectedly
high tide, due to the gale, would wreck many landing craft on
the obstacles and seriously restrict manoeuvring room for
vehicles and guns on the beaches. And the launching of the
D.D. tanks as mobile pillboxes to cover the infantry in their
dash up the sand was in jeopardy.

On the British right flank, where Lieutenant-General G. C.
Bucknell's 30 Corps was to assault Gold Beach with 50 (North-
umbrian) Infantry Division, the decision was taken not to launch
D.D.s but land them direct from LCTs in the ordinary way.
" Rough seas were running and three LCIs, carrying the 2nd
Gloucesters, were circling round about three miles off the
Normandy coast," wrote a unit historian, describing the moment
of indecision. " Straining eyes pick out the coast line, and puffs

of smoke caused by bursting shells from the *Renown* and *War-spite*. After what seems an eternity of circling, the craft turn, shake out into formation, and make, with awful deliberation, for the beach. About 75 yards from the shore two LCIs collide, but down go the ramps, and the first man in the battalion to set foot in France, Major Goode, plunges into chest-deep water, trips over an obstacle, and disappears temporarily from view. Such was the anti-climax of our entry into real war." 50 Div was to take Bayeux, eight miles inland, by nightfall; but in fact were three miles short of their objective at last light. 2nd Essex took the town next day, at the cost of one casualty, Captain Hearne, badly wounded by a teller mine. The Gloucesters arrived in time only to be uneasy spectators of the lynching of ' collaborators ' by the French. This delay did not matter, as the role of 30 Corps was merely to protect the flank of the American landing at Omaha, which had broken down in bloody ruin, and by nightfall had barely got off the beaches.

The main, and extremely ambitious, British task on D-Day had been allotted to Lieutenant-General J. T. Crocker's I Corps: take Caen and the vital high ground of the Falaise road immediately to the south of the town. 6 Airborne Division had already dropped to clear and hold the left flank of the push; 3 Canadian Infantry Division with 2 Canadian Armoured Brigade in support were to cover the right flank by cutting the Caen-Bayeux road from Putot-en-Bessin to Carpiquet, the airfield of Caen; while the main thrust was to be made direct at Caen by 3 British Infantry Division with 27 Armoured Brigade in support. The scheme was ambitious because the distance to be covered was greater and because, while Bayeux was held only by a handful of German female typists, 21 Panzer Division was already established around Caen.

3 Canadian Div, landing on Juno Beach by Courseulles, were to be led in by the D.D. tanks of 6 Canadian Armoured Regiment (1st Hussars), while 3 British Div were to be preceded by the D.D.s of 13/18 Hussars (Queen Mary's Own) onto Sword Beach near Ouistreham. On the Canadian right, 30 Corps' D.D.s had not launched at all; further still to the right, off Omaha, the reckless Americans launched exactly as planned, to see all but three of the swimming tanks founder on the way in. No generals made

those decisions, nor did they elsewhere. They were made by comparatively junior officers, sometimes swayed by the feelings of their men. Indeed, Serjeant Gariepy's B Squadron of 6 Armoured Regiment launched in direct disobedience of orders from assault craft headquarters. There was divided command, the senior army and naval officers being supposed to agree a decision. Gariepy could see his troop leader on the bridge, arguing with the C.O. of the LCT; then he came to tell them that they were to be beached, not launched. The tank men began to argue. The troop leader said it was blowing Force 6 and suicide to swim the tanks, while the men replied that they would rather drown than be impaled on the beach defences. The landing craft circled to 7,000 yards, but the sea was still too rough, and at that point craft headquarters made their final decision not to launch. But at 3,000 yards the ' *down doors* ' bell rang for immediate launching. " The order had been given by the C.O. of B Squadron, who said his men would not have it otherwise," recorded the unit historian. First tank down the ramp was Serjeant Gariepy's.

Keeping afloat was his first preoccupation, and this was a matter of skill as well as bravery. With a freeboard of 24 inches, they had shipped a lot of water, and more was coming in; but the pumps more or less kept it in balance. The canvas boat structure and its supporting struts were fragile, however, and they had to go with the seas and not against them, or risk the collapse of the structure. Every other tank commander was in the same position, and therefore it was impossible to take up assault formation or even to steer for their particular objectives. " Out of 18 D.D.s which were to be launched, I could make out 14, no formation whatsoever," recollected Gariepy. " One LCT had its ramp hanging crazily, unable to launch its last two tanks; it was the one we had bumped earlier in the Solent, at the time thinking the damage negligible. Our own LCT was now going back to Blighty, facing hundreds upon hundreds of ships, all coming in towards the coast; on our flanks two huge warships were getting ready to bombard. I and three of my crew were non-swimmers, which helped a great deal in making us determined to reach the shore, in spite of the very adverse elements. Orders had been not to touch the beach before 0730 hours, no

matter what. It was then around 0600, but seeing the impossi-
bility of making any kind of formal approach, I decided to head
for land on my own, and some of the tanks began following
me." Thus began the seaborne invasion of France.

Although Field Marshal Rommel had warned that the enemy
might use " waterproofed and submersible " tanks, the defenders
had not been told what they looked like: not like tanks at all,
but canvas boats, insignificant among the great host of approaching vessels. Therefore, comparatively little fire was directed at
them. Gariepy came in crabwise, steering at an angle to the
waves, drifting steadily to the left of the blockhouse which was
his abjective, his crew strengthening the hard-tried struts with
fire-extinguishers, to prevent a complete cave-in of the canvas.
He could now count only 12 D.D.s, all having a hard time to
stay afloat; then great pillars of water began to erupt around
them as the German mortars opened fire. Where the tank of
Major Duncan, B Squadron commander, had been there was
now only a little group of men floundering in the sea, and trying
to board their bright yellow R.A.F. dingy which, because of its
distinctive colour, immediately became a target. "I was being
followed by two D.D.s about 200 yards behind and now the
quick staccato of machine-gun fire was very distinct on the hull
and the canvas was showing a multitude of holes, with the
water rushing in and our bilge pump working overtime. My
driver reported all was well down below, except that they were
sicker than ever. We were then approximately 2,000 yards from
the beaches and ahead of me was a midget submarine which
had surfaced.[1] There was a man standing up in it waving desperately at me to shift more to my right, but because of the
waves I simply could not. After several attempts at warning me,
he finally clasped his hands together over his head in a gesture
of ' good luck ' and I passed about 30 feet by him. I never saw
him again, but to me this was another of the unsung heroes of
the war. I will never forget the picture of this young sailor with
a white scarf flying in the breeze, standing like an avenging god
in the shallow water of Normandy with no weapons of any kind,

[1] Two midget submarines, X20 and X23, had been submerged for 64
hours off the beaches before surfacing at 0500 to act as lighthouses, erecting
radar beacons and flashing seaward the green light which signalled in the
leading waves of the invasion.

just simply directing traffic of the weird vehicles that were going in to fight a tremendous war machine." Behind them, a battleship was firing overhead, with the noise of a dozen express trains, its salvos of 15 inch shells; and as they came in towards the sand, the rows of low-trajectory rocket launchers known as ' hedgehogs ' and mounted on LCTs, opened up, firing by groups of 24 in rapid succession. The tracks of the D.D. met resistance, but Gariepy kept on going, in case they were merely on a sandbar. " Then, feeling sure we were all right, I gave the order ' deflate '; and there we stood naked like babes amongst the strong array of beach defences with which, from our briefings, we were absolutely familiar. It was exactly 0730 hours."

The machine-gun fire stopped momentarily, presumably because the Germans were so surprised to see a tank emerge from the waves, and Gariepy wasted no time on the beach, but drove up through the obstacles, and then moved to the shelter of the silent blockhouse which was his objective. Behind him at the water's edge were 9 D.D.s, with others still struggling through the broken water to shore. Ahead, the German machine-gunners and riflemen began to desert their positions and run back. Gariepy's machine-gunners engaged them but they could not advance further until the AVREs arrived to span the anti-tank ditch which lay beyond. The Canadians were glad of the respite, for they were physically and emotionally exhausted by their bout with the sea; in comparison, the enemy's opposition had troubled them little. The Germans, for their part, must have been momentarily shocked by the violence of the sea bombardment; the air bombardment, because of the bad weather, had largely missed the beach defences, falling well inland. " I ordered my crew to break open cans of self-heating ox-tail soup, and afterwards we opened a bottle of rum which I had kept for this occasion. Then we were lifted bodily off the ground by a great explosion. I thought for a moment we had been hit by a battleship. But, as I stood up in the turret, I saw the blockhouse gun recoiling: a huge coastal gun that belches a round that makes you feel you are standing in the mouth of hell, the shot generating terrific heat. We were exactly three yards from it, too close for either of us to fire. I held a conflab with my crew, and we decided to reverse down the beach and pelt the embrasure." Gariepy's gunner put seven rounds of H.E. through the embrasure, hoping to smash the breach mechanism, then they advanced, in time to see some of the gun crew leaving the block-house. They shot them down with machine-guns before firing in more H.E., to make quite sure of the gun, and then reported by radio to their C.O. that they had knocked out their first assigned target. There was no reply. Major Duncan had been sunk and no one had yet taken over from him. Only nine out of eighteen D.D.s had made the beach, and three of these had been swamped at the water's edge; which left six tanks to do the work of eighteen.

" By this time the AVRE was ashore and trying hard to fill the anti-tank ditch, but I told the serjeant commanding it that I could not get across. He asked me if I would risk going over his bull-dozer if he placed it at the bottom of the ditch. I agreed. The infantry were starting to arrive, and anything was better than just standing there and letting them go in bare without a tank. And once again, another Britisher just waved me good luck, for, picking up a Tommy gun, the serjeant simply walked away from his vehicle, while we drove on over it. He had served his purpose on the beaches. D-Day was full of these unsung heroic deeds; men doing the impossible and just walking away, feeling satisfied they had done their job." The Canadian tanks began to move inland across the dunes. The German machine-gun nests had been sited to hamper a landing; but a change of position was necessary to deal with invaders already at the top of the beach, and as the D.D. tanks had given the Germans no time to do this, the defenders simply adandoned their positions and retreated. Serjeant Gariepy found this interesting. " Why would a man run back, instead of coming forward to give himself up? Discipline in the German Army must be formidable."

The tide at Courseulles was coming up fast, and when Squad-ron Leader Hill's AVRE-carrying LCT arrived, the obstacles were already awash; the LCT went straight at them, crashed through, and lowered the ramp. " Can I come inside." Hill shouted to the commander of the leading AVRE. " No! If I stop on the beach to let you out, I'll get shot!" So Hill clung to the outside of the tank, as it splashed ashore, then dropped off dry further up the beach. Dumping his kit and bedroll by a hidden pillbox (from which, thirty minutes later, a Canadian serjeant flushed eight dazed Germans), Hill went for a stroll in the village, which was Bernières, just east of Courseulles. Canadians, Germans, and a few French were milling around; he noticed particularly a nice-looking girl arm-in-arm with a very tall German holding a dog on a lead. Then he went back to the beach, and sat patiently on his shooting stick, to wait for the landing craft carrying his barrage balloons and to discover that, as his C.O. had been wounded, he was now in charge of all the balloons on all three beaches. Waiting to advance under cover of the sea wall was a French-Canadian regiment which had lost heavily crossing the exposed beach; they were to acquire a reputation, later that day, for having dragged a female collaborator round the village behind a jeep. True, false, or exaggerated, it was a fitting rumour with which to open the ruthless battle of Normandy.

Further still to the east, on Sword Beach, where 3 British Infantry Division was to land, was the extreme left flank of the seaborne assault. The Merville Battery, which covered it, had been put out of action by 9 Para Battalion ninety minutes earlier; but the area was under fire at longer range by heavy guns at Le Havre and Houlgate. Hill's balloons were subsequently hauled down here, because it was believed that the Germans were using them for ranging their artillery. The sea was rough and the wind Force 5,[2] and again a crucial decision had to be taken. But whereas the Canadian tank crews had virtually made up their own minds, the British obeyed orders. Captain Bush, R.N., for the Navy, and Brigadier G. E. Prior-Palmer, for 27 Armoured Brigade, agreed to launch the D.D.s of A and B Squadrons of 13/18 Hussars from a position closer inshore than planned. It was a courageous decision on both sides. The Admiralty had opposed the D.D.s originally because they were unseaworthy, and the Brigadier's first introduction to his command, a few months before, had been both unsoldierly and unseamanlike. He had set sail in a D.D. which had come to a dead stop, in the middle of Fritton Lake, in the middle of the night, in the middle of a milling mass of other D.D.s, because it had run out of petrol.

---

[2] On the Beaufort Scale, 19-24 m.p.h., " waves pronounced and long; white foam crests everywhere."

"To make matters worse," wrote the unit historian, " the motor rescue launch failed to start, and the Brigadier finally had to be taken off in a rowing boat, manned by four soldiers, none of whom had ever handled an oar before." Upon the quickly-gained competence of such raw amateurs, in a sea far rougher than had ever been contemplated, the fate of the main British assault on Europe now depended.

At 5,000 yards offshore, the anchors of the LCTs roared out, the ramps went down, and 34 out of 40 D.D. tanks crashed into the sea. One, having failed to engage its propeller, sank imme-diately. The remainder drove on in recognisable formation behind their pilot boats for the beaches; the warships opened fire; the ' hedgehogs ' poured in their rocket salvoes; the LCTs carry-ing the AVREs began to over-ride the struggling D.D.s, and as they did so, a rocket salvo falling short made some of them take violent avoiding action. Captain Denny's tank was rammed by an LCT, and rolled straight over on its side, sinking upside down, so that only he got out. The crew of another rammed tank were only 400 yards off the beach at the time, in shallow water, and all escaped. 31 D.D.s reached the beach, more or less at the same time as the LCTs carrying the flail tanks and AVREs, and ' hull down ' in the water, gave covering fire until their guns were awash. In 20 minutes, all enemy fire, except from small arms, had virtually ceased, the flail tanks were clearing the mine-fields, and the AVREs were dealing with the obstacles. Corporal Raymond Arthur Hill arrived a few minutes later with C Squadron of the Hussars, whose Shermans beached into four feet of water towing waterproofed sledges containing the ammu-nition reserve. C Squadron was to advance through the D.D.s and carry on inland, but the congestion on the rapidly narrowing beach was such that it was about 45 minutes before he got off it.

Their objectives for D-Day were in clear view up the slope to Périers Rise, a fortified battery position (code-name *Morris*) and the fortified underground H.Q. of Oberst Krug's 736 Regi-ment of 716 Infantry Division (code-name *Hillman*). As they drove inland, Lieutenant Eric Smith recalled (for the Regimental history) two vivid memories: " Firstly, the reluctance of my driver and myself to run over a dead German body lying pros-trate across the road, and, secondly, the bewildered and haunted expressions of the inhabitants, who must have thought that their houses would be completely destroyed, and probably doubted our ability to remain in Normandy for any length of time." Once these two objectives had been taken, 185 Brigade Group was to land and pass through for the lightning dash at Caen. But, already, confusion and congestion were developing not only at the beach exits but on the sand, so unexpectedly narrowed by the high tide.

The D.D.-carrying LCT in which was Petty Officer R. H. G. McKinlay of the R.N. 'P' Commandos, had been hit on the ramp before it could launch the tanks, and drifted, under fire and out of control, all the way from Courseulles to Ouistreham. After one and a half hours, they had had quite enough of that, and had wild thoughts of swimming ashore, when they were able to abandon the LCT and thumb a ride in on an obsolete landing craft. Instead of landing on Juno Beach with the Canadians, they were coming ashore on Sword with the British, and their careful briefings meant nothing, for each unit knew only its own particular task, or, as McKinlay expressed it, " most things were secret from one another, and the organisation was such that one half did not know what the other half was doing. Now we were miles away, out on the left flank somewhere, and although there was a Major on the beach, it seemed as though most of his officers were killed, because we saw three Army captains on the trot, all lying dead on the sand dunes. So we had to make our own way, and between us and our beach were the enemy, which made it a bit awkward." This was a gross understatement. Many isolated German strong-points were still holding out, and would continue to hold out, for days; but between 3 British Div and 3 Canadian Div, from Lion-sur-Mer to Luc-sur-Mer, the German beach defences were solid and unbroken. No troops were swarming ashore there; the Germans were still in possession. " Well, naturally, we had to mop up a few of these Germans," said McKinlay.

As a commando, McKinlay got the job of lobbing a couple of grenades into the first pillbox in the way, at which the rest were to up and charge. " I put the two grenades in, and up and charged; and then it seemed deathly quiet—there was not a soul behind me, I was all on my own. Although this was a battlefield, with thousands of troops around, I felt lonely; and I dug a hole quicker than any rabbit could." However, after a while they moved on, and McKinlay went down, revolver drawn, into a dark darkout to clear it, tense and cautious, ready to shoot first and ask no questions afterwards. A man with a gun in his hand came at him, so he pulled the trigger repeatedly in a blaze of fire—and the 'man' disappeared with the crash of splintering glass. It was his own reflection in a full-length mirror, fitted presumably for 'walking out' inspections. Then he came round a corner in the fortifications, and there was a real German; they stared at each other for a moment, tense with fear. " He seemed an enormous man, and I don't know which of us was the more frightened; but I prodded him with my rifle, and searched him, and he seemed quite happy to give in. But we had to crawl back to the others, and when we got up, a shot rang out, and this poor Jerry fell down in front of me with blood coming out of his stomach. One of our lads must have mistaken him. Well, I gave the poor bloke a couple of fags and went and got on with the job." After they had picked up some two dozen prisoners, but were losing men to snipers from the back of the beach, the party arranged the Germans in a screen round them and marched on. " We felt much safer this way, but as we were walking along the embankment, a German soldier came out, loading his rifle to fire. A split-second more, and we might have got it, but he threw down his rifle and said 'Kamerad' and all that sort of stuff. Covering us was a Canadian corporal with a Bren, and suddenly he and the German were speaking the same language. They were both Poles, one in the German Army and the other in the Canadian Army, and they got talking together and forgot the war and became buddies." McKinlay received the C.G.M. for his part in this affair, which involved moving two and half miles along beach held by remnants of 716 Infantry Division, until they reached Courseulles, where they should have landed in the first place. There, " the bodies were still flopping about in the surf—rather a morbid sight, you just had to close your eyes to it."

Stanley Green, brother of Serjeant Green of 10 H.L.I., still in England, landed that morning on Queen sector of Sword Beach with 6 Field Regiment, R.A. Eight tanks lay knocked out at the water's edge, and at the top of the beach was an emplacement holding the old field gun which had got them all. Behind, in newly-dug graves, the gun crew were already buried, marked only by a notice on a stick, reading "*Six Unknown Germans*". From their country's point of view, they had not died in vain; nor had any of the defenders that day. They had been unable to stop the British and Canadian landings, but they could, and did, impose a brake on the forward impetus of the invaders both by direct fire and by flank fire which forced the attackers to funnel through a few, narrow, comparatively safe gaps. Beach towns like Bernières and Courseulles became clogged with troops and vehicles inching forward; and on Sword Beach, the all-important 185 Brigade Group, intended to rush Caen by a swift drive to the south, was split in two by the traffic jams. By 11 a.m., the three infantry battalions were ashore and in their assembly positions, ready to push off, but the tanks were still trapped on the beach by a confusion growing steadily worse as the tide rose higher and the room for manoeuvre became less.

CHAPTER FOUR

A TASTE OF CHAMPAGNE

*The British Dash for Caen and the German Counter-Attack
to the Coast, 6 June*

Already, halfway through the morning of D-Day, the British
and Canadians were paying the penalty for their bad weather
landing: the air bombardment only partly effective, heavy
casualties among the parachutists, far fewer D.D. tanks reaching
the beaches than expected, congestion on the beaches and at the
exits, delay in passing through the fresh assault formations which
were to drive deep inland. Although General Montgomery had
talked of " knocking about a bit " on D-Day down at Falaise, 32
miles from the coast,[1] even the capture of Caen, ten miles inland,
had never been better than an outside chance, and Lieut.-General
Crocker, commanding I Corps, had instructed Major-General
T. G. Rennie of 3 British Infantry Division in realistic terms:
before last light on 6 June, Caen must be " captured or effectively masked." Rennie, a solid but slow-moving infantry
general, was unlikely to go beyond those instructions. Moreover,
his division was made up largely of conscripts, in contrast to the
natural ' soldiers of fortune ' who had succeeded so brilliantly
in the airborne operations and the volunteer soldiers of the
Canadian division, who were ruthlessly determined to take their
D-Day objectives.

However, the surprise effect of a bad weather landing was
immense, giving a gain probably greater than the penalties involved. Most of the German radar stations, except those picking
up a dummy invasion fleet off Pas de Calais, had been knocked
out or damaged, so that the indications of activity off the Normandy coast were too slight to be regarded as conclusive. If the
weather had been glorious, as in May, decisive action might
have been taken earlier; and certainly, neither Rommel nor the
other senior commanders would have been absent from their
posts, on leave or on duty.

[1] *A Soldier's Story*, by Gen. Omar N. Bradley, p. 241.

Military operations are an art, not a science, because they are conducted without full knowledge of the facts, most decisions being made on partial evidence only. And because ruses and feints are to be expected, part of that partial evidence may be false, designed deliberately to mislead. In commerce, it has been said, the business man who manages to make six correct decisions out of ten, automatically becomes a millionaire; Rommel had become a Field Marshal because he had what he called a ' finger-tip feeling' for the real situation, which enabled him to guess right, more often than not. In Paris, it could be deduced that the landing of parachutists on a large scale must indicate a seaborne follow-up, to prevent the sacrifice of the lightly-armed airborne troops; but whether this was to be another and greater Dieppe Raid, timed to put the defenders off balance, or the invasion itself, could not then be known. The two nearest available divisions of the strategic armoured reserve, held back as a counter-offensive force, were Gruppenführer[2] Witt's 12 S.S. Panzer Grenadier Division, composed of volunteers from the Hitler Youth, stationed 30 miles south of Lisieux, and General-major Fritz Bayerlein's formidably-equipped Panzer Lehr Division, 75 miles south-west of Paris. On Hitler's orders only, could they be moved. Nevertheless, without asking permission, Field Marshal von Rundstedt instructed both to advance on Caen; but at 0600 hours had this order cancelled angrily from the Führer's H.Q., on the grounds that the enemy's intentions were not yet clear and that Hitler had not yet made a decision. This sounded well, but what it really meant was that the Führer, like Churchill a late-night worker, had gone off into a drugged sleep which no one dared interrupt. When he did finally wake up, it was mid-afternoon and D-Day was more than half over. Both night and the morning mist and cloud were gone, so that his armour had to resume their advance, not only late, but under air attack. Consequently, the only armoured formation near enough to the landing area to counter-attack on 6 June was 21 Panzer Division, with about 120 tanks.

The West Wall defences covering Caen were manned by 716 Infantry Division, commanded by Generalleutnant Wilhelm

[2] Rank in the Waffen S.S. equivalent to General of Division in the Regular Army.

Richter, to whom Generalmajor Edgar Feuchtinger of 21 Panzer Division was subordinate. Richter wanted the parachutists mopped up at once and, according to standing orders, could commit some of Feuchtinger's infantry and guns on his own responsibility; but he could not commit the armour, which was part of Rommel's reserve—and Rommel was on his way back from Germany. Richter in turn was subordinate to General Erich Marcks of 84th Corps, while Feuchtinger was responsible also, in the event of invasion, to Geyr von Schweppenburg's Panzer Group West. Caught in this cat's cradle of command, Feuchtinger hesitated, waiting for the situation to clarify itself, and his division was lost. At 0200 hours, Richter ordered him to put in a full-scale divisional attack against the airborne landings east of the water barriers; had Feuchtinger complied immediately, the attack must have succeeded—for the two parachute brigades had been severely weakened by losses; their third, air-landing brigade, was not due to be flown in until evening, and there could be no early support from 3 British Infantry Division. If the parachutists blew the bridges, the Germans would have been unable to intervene quickly against the seaborne landing, but at the least, the left flank cover of the British dash for Caen would have been destroyed.

As it was, only those units of 21 Panzer Division to which Richter was empowered to issue orders actually moved. Among them was Oberstleutnant Rauch's 192 Panzer Grenadier Regiment, whose II Battalion was directed against Bénouville at 0200. Leutnant Hans Höller was commanding a section of 75 mm SP guns in the 8th Heavy Company of II Battalion. They had been dug-in at Cairon, well-placed to meet the thrust of 3 Canadian Div. Now, they drove eastwards across the area where 3 British Div. was shortly to advance on Caen, and fought their way into Bénouville, now held by 7 Parachute Battalion. The original 21 Panzer Division had been part of the Afrika Korps, but had gone into captivity in Tunisia. Höller was one of the few who provided some continuity; he had served in Africa with 15 Panzer Division and been evacuated with multiple bullet wounds. "We got involved in heavy fighting with a strong parachute unit," he said. "We managed to penetrate into half the village, but the parachutists fought bitterly and the exit leading to the coast could not be taken." Realising this, Höller went off with two men to look for good defensive positions for his guns. A large building overlooking the Caen Canal offered an obvious vantage point, so they dashed towards it and began to climb the stairs to the roof. Actually, it was a maternity home, and there instantly occurred a comedy of errors and misunderstandings.

The matron, Madame Vion, told the British that a German officer, a serjeant, and a private, had forced their way in, despite her outraged protests, that she had shown them up the stairs, and that there one of their own anti-tank guns had mistaken them and opened fire on the building.[3] This must have been Höller and his two men. but he had not the least idea that the building was a hospital, until he opened a door and found himself looking into a ward, " a disagreeable surprise ". Before he got there, while still on the stairs, he had been fired at by a German gun; but it was not one of his own anti-tanks, naturally. The fire came from a German naval vessel which was already under fire from the British and was fleeing up the Canal towards Caen, unaware that the front-line, such as it was, ran through the middle of Bénouville. There had been two of these ships, escaping from the sea-borne assault, which had just begun. They reached the bridge just as the commander of 6 Airborne Division, Major-General R. N. Gale, crossed it on foot.[4] One was put out of action and ran ashore, where it was captured by parachutists; the other passed upstream, returning fire with a 2 cm gun, shooting up the parachutists, Leutnant Höller, and the Matron. "Of course, we were not allowed to fire back," said Höller, " but this spook soon disappeared, without doing us any damage." Had anyone been killed, yet another atrocity story would have been born.

At this stage, both the British and the Germans were mixed with civilians, and hampered by them. Höller had put his three 75 mm guns and the mortar troop into a nursery wood bordering the village and the chateau, part of which housed the maternity home. Protecting them was a group of panzer grena-

[3] See *The Red Beret* by Hilary St. George Saunders, p. 163.
[4] Ibid. And *With the Sixth Airborne Division in Normandy*, by Gen. Gale.

diers. "About noon," said Höller, " a very old man came staggering towards us from the direction of the enemy positions.
He appeared, or was pretending to be, almost unable to walk.
He came to a dead stop directly opposite part of a hedge which
hid one of our guns. Then, he turned round and stumbled back
towards the enemy, while the men discussed whether or not it
was wise to let him get away." The British parachutists, similarly, were not pleased to be enthusiastically greeted by French
civilians, since it was rather like marking their positions with a
red flag and inviting the enemy to fire. That was thoughtlessness,
but the old man was probably deliberately brave, for, a few
minutes after he had staggered away, two British tanks appeared
and fired on the German gun which he had located. The Germans
fired back, knocking out one tank and causing the other to disappear quickly. Strict military logic had demanded the death
of the old man and the occupation of the maternity home; but
these were the first few hours of the very first day. Elementary
decency still prevailed over the instinct of self-preservation, in the
same way that butter takes a few seconds before it melts on top
of a red-hot stove.

Miles away to the west, Serjeant Gariepy's unit was advancing
inland towards Cairon, which Höller's unit had left only a few
hours before. They had been reduced to half-strength by the
beach assault, and B Squadron now numbered only nine tanks.
They received a call for help from infantry attacking Pierrepont,
and received an instant and bitter lesson which they did not
forget. Swerving off the road to the attack, they moved ten yards,
and lost five tanks. " I saw Lieutenant McLeod's tank burst high
in flame," said Gariepy. " The troop corporal's tank suffered the
same fate, and I saw several other tanks knocked out." Their end
was instantaneous and dreadful, for they had stacked the floors
of the tanks high with reserve ammunition, fearful that the chaos
of D-Day would prevent supplies getting through. The Sherman
burnt quickly when hit, almost instantaneously; the Germans
called them ' Tommy Cookers', grim but apt, and the British
called them ' Ronsons', because of the trade advertisement—
' Light First Time', also grim but apt. When full of ammunition,
they exploded like bombs. In addition to his extra ammo,
Gariepy was now only too well aware that he had 15 scrounged

sticks of dynamite aboard, and at that moment, he saw, 30 yards ahead, the muzzle of an 88 mm dual-purpose gun rising up from a hidden emplacement to fire, the barrel pointing directly at him. " I gave rapid evasive orders to my driver and told my gunner to blast him. He fired two rounds; the second scored a direct hit. I reported to 'Sun Ray' that we were now going in to liquidate the crew. He advised me against this, but I moved up to the gun emplacement and mercilessly shot all the gun crew of fourteen men who were cowering in the trench."

There were now only four tanks left out of the eighteen, and they were ordered to withdraw to Reviers, but Gariepy volunteered to go forward to Pierrepont and look for survivors. One only of the five tanks had not exploded, and from this two men had escaped; there were no other survivors. " I was called by an infantry officer, who told me to be cautious. There was a sniper in the village who had shot, that morning, the commanders of three D.D. tanks. Although the infantry had been in there for hours, the sniper had not shot at them; apparently, he was only after tank commanders. So I 'closed down' and moved slowly ahead, and when I neared the site where the other crew commanders had got hit, I wrapped my beret over my earphones and waved it cautiously above the turret. The shot, when it came, was from an attic window, but the infantry were unaware of it, and as they were scurrying all round that house, they made it impossible for me to fire H.E. into it. So I and my loader-operator jumped out, hugging close against the wall, and bashed the door open. We found an old man and woman, imploring us in German, but we could not understand what they were trying to tell us. We pushed past them, rushed up the stairs, and saw at the top a single door. We threw a heavy chair at it, and it opened.

" There was the attic window, and in front of it, holding a Mauser low, but pointed at us, was the sniper. It was a young girl of nineteen. I cut her down with a burst of fire from the Sten. Angry, irritated, probably scared, I could not hesitate. By now, the house was full of soldiers, and we learned from the old people that this girl's 'fiancee' had been shot by a Canadian tank that morning, and that she had sworn she would liquidate all crew commanders, a tall order." In retrospect, it appears to be one of the braver actions of D-Day.

"I was never questioned on this matter, but it did get around the Squadron that I would not stop at anything. Now, twenty years later, I feel this was the result of being a member of the Permanent Force, a professional. We had to go forward and assert our inherent militarism under the eyes of the officers. It was necessary to appear absolutely ruthless in every action, each incident a case of 'his life or mine'. I may have been wrong; but today I am alive and well, was never wounded, and although I lost four tanks (two of them in one day), of my crew I had only one missing at the end of the war, my co-driver, killed at Fontenay Le Marmion. Of course, because we won the war, we were blameless, but all the enemy were supposed to be cruel, savage beasts. I took many prisoners, but I never met a 'monster'; for the most part, they were poor simple Joes, just soldiers who happened to be on the losing side. Moving back from Pierrepont that day, I met a German soldier coming down the road, riding a bicycle. Fully loaded with haversack, suitcase, slung rifle, and 'potato masher' grenade at his belt, he came steering crazily past the line of Sherman tanks, under the impression he was moving 'up front', gloriously drunk. We confiscated his bicycle and sat him on the tank, then handed him over to an infantry officer for questioning, but it was doubtful if he could then speak intelligibly, even in German. He was so drunk he could not walk, and had to be put into a wheelbarrow in charge of an artillery corporal. I saw him wheeled out of sight, I heard a distinct Sten shot, and then the grinning corporal came back, trundling an empty wheelbarrow. I could not swear he had shot the man, but I would guess this poor Gerry never knew what it was all about."

* * *

"We saw Caen at the horizon as a burning, smoking town", said Werner Kortenhaus of 4th Company, Panzer Regiment 22, as the tanks moved off at 0800. "The march was slow and difficult, the roads choked by other units moving up and by refugees fleeing from Caen." Having been alerted at 0100, the tank element of 21 Panzer Division, the four companies of Panzer Regiment 22, had done nothing for some six or seven hours, while the situation was obscure and the commanders argued. Now, the seaborne troops were landing, and the situation was clarifying; but the order now being obeyed by the four tank companies was General Richter's original directive, for the whole of 21 Panzer Division to attack the airborne landings east of the Orne. At 1230, the delayed British advance on Caen began, and half-an-hour later, at 1300, Feuchtinger issued another order. The tank force was to be split. 1st, 2nd, and 3rd Companies were to attack the seaborne landings; 4th Company was to join Oberstleutnant Freiherr Hans von Luck's Panzer Grenadier Regiment 125, together with some of the division's artillery, mortar, and reconnaissance units, and attack the parachutists. The reason was that 21 Panzer Division had been transferred to General Marcks of 84th Corps, that Marcks realised that the main threat lay in the seaborne assault by 3 British Infantry Division, but that he had been told to expect no help from 12 S.S. Panzer Grenadier Division, still held back as strategic reserve, and that therefore he must contain the airborne bridgehead with what he had. As originally disposed, 21 Panzer Division had been well-placed to encounter both assaults: the infantry and anti-tank guns dug in as a screen between Caen and the sea, the armour held behind Caen, so that it could drive left or right of the water barriers, as the situation required. Oberstleutnant Rauch's Panzer Grenadier Regiment 192 had merely to stay where it was, north of Caen, to be effective; while Oberstleutnant von Luck's Panzer Grenadier Regiment 125 could have attacked the parachutists much earlier, had they been given permission. Richter's orders had had the effect of clearing the way for 3 British Infantry Division, for he had moved some of the infantry eastwards and some of the anti-tank guns westwards.

Now, 21 Panzer Division was no longer a balanced formation, capable of bringing all arms into play for mutual support; and its tank element had just arrived east of the Orne, when it was ordered to attack west of the Orne. Direction of march had to be reversed, so that the commander of Panzer Regiment 22, Oberst Oppeln Bronikowski, was now at the rear. The three tank companies rolled into Caen, but soon realised that the streets, choked with debris and fleeing civilians, were impassable. Driving at top speed, urged on by their colonel, they took the diversionary route through the industrial suburb of Colombelles, which wasted a great deal of time. Once across, they raced for the vital hills between Caen and the coast. The 25 tanks of the 1st Company and H.Q., commanded by Hauptmann Herr, reached the area between Lebisey and Biéville at about 1500; the 35 tanks of the combined 2nd and 3rd Companies, commanded by Hauptmann von Gottberg, heading further west, reached the foot of Periers Rise at about 1600; and further west still, the armoured cars and infantry of I Battalion, Panzer Grenadier Regiment 192, were ordered by General Marcks to press on towards the coast also. The main counter-attack of 21 Panzer Division was therefore to be mounted with only three tank companies, some armoured cars, and a single infantry battalion. Worst of all, of the two dozen 88 mms of the anti-tank battalion which had been stationed on top of Périers Rise, only three were still there, the remainder having been moved by Richter.

And as the Germans moved to the foot of the heights, the British tanks, pushing on from the coast on the other side, reached the top. They were barely in position when the German attack came in. The bad weather bonus, which was the fundamental reason for the delay and confusion on the German side, had affected the British similarly. 185 Brigade Group, consisting of the tanks of Lieut.-Colonel Jim Eadie's Staffordshire Yeomanry, the infantry of Lieut.-Colonel F. J. Maurice's 2 K.S.L.I., and the SP guns of 7 Field Regiment R.A., should have rushed Caen at once, the infantry riding on the backs of the tanks. But, as the tanks and guns were held up by the chaos on the beaches, at 1230 hours the Shropshires shouldered their packs and started to walk there, minus their heavy weapons and vehicles, and without the tanks. The lightning punch at Caen had been reduced to a few hundred plodding riflemen.

As they climbed up the heights, they were joined by their own 6 pounder anti-tank guns, a few 17 pounders, and two squadrons of the Yeomanry. The third squadron was called up just in time to meet the attack on Biéville by Hauptmann Herr's 25 tanks. "At first these tanks received no opposition," runs a German account.[5] " Then, as they moved up the hill, the English

[5] Compiled by Kortenhaus from the testimony of survivors from all three companies, including Hauptmann von Gottberg.

opened heavy defensive fire from both tanks and anti-tank guns. Their position was tactically well-chosen and their fire both heavy and accurate. The first Mark IV was blazing before a single German tank had the chance to fire a shot. The remainder moved forward, firing at where the enemy were thought to be; but the English weapons were well-concealed and within a few minutes, we had lost six tanks." Meanwhile, sweeping round to the left of Périers Rise were the 35 tanks led by Hauptmann von Gottberg; they attacked Point 61, held by a squadron of the Staffordshires. "The position was the same. The fire of the English, from their outstandingly well-sited defence positions, was murderous. This group also was soon repelled, losing ten tanks. Within a brief space of time, the armoured regiment of 21 Panzer Division had lost a total of sixteen tanks, a decisive defeat, from which, especially in morale, it never recovered.[6] The long wait in the morning, plus the diversion by Colombelles, had consumed fourteen hours and given the enemy time to build up a strong line of defence. The one and only chance on D-Day had been lost. Never again was there to be such a chance."

Nevertheless, this brief skirmish had settled the fate of Caen. The British position was already precarious, and appeared worse than it was. There was a wide corridor to the sea on their right, the German tanks were milling about in it, and the infantry and armoured cars of I Battalion, Panzer Grenadier Regiment 192, were already driving down it. But above all, the rising ground inland of the beaches was crowned by four fortifications of the 'West Wall', which held out stubbornly after being over-run and raked the advancing British in the flanks. The two outlying forts, 'Sole' and 'Morris', fell at 1300 hours, but 'Daimler', covering the British left, held out until 1800, and 'Hillman', covering the British right, was only partially subdued by 2015. This latter was almost entirely underground and contained the H.Q. of Oberst Krug, commanding 736 Grenadier Regiment of 716 Infantry Division. As the main body of 185 Brigade Group moved past it, to back up the dash for Caen, its machine-guns cut down 150 men of the Norfolks. To Raymond Arthur Hill,

---

[6] The British claim of 13 German tanks destroyed was therefore an underestimate; in strong contrast to the almost invariable exaggerations of air forces, and also of navies where submarines are concerned.

looking up at it from behind the sights of a Sherman's gun, 'Hillman' was just a concrete dome, with British air bursts exploding ineffectually above it. Then there was a stunning explosion beside the tank, his periscope shattered, and he found himself temporarily deaf; it was a near-miss from a shell or mortar, incapable of doing more than shake the tank, but frightening the first time. Then, with other Shermans of the 13/18 Hussars, he moved up the rise and drove right on top of the dome, spraying everything in sight, and hoping to get nothing in return. Down below, in the underground galleries, bitter fighting was going on between the Germans and the Suffolks, with the pioneers using heavy explosive charges to destroy the stubborn defenders. At 2000 hours, the mechanised infantry of I Battalion, Panzer Grenadier Regiment 192, reached the sea between Lion-sur-Mer and Luc-sur-Mer, a few miles to the west, and linked up with the Germans still holding the coast there. The Hussars were pulled back from 'Hillman', to take up defensive positions on the skyline, and warned to expect a counter-attack from 21 Panzer Division. On the other side of the Orne, Werner Kortenhaus was with the Battle Group Luck at St. Honorine, waiting to counter-attack the weakened parachutists, and Brigadier Hill was organising his H.Q. staff at Le Mesnil as a fighting unit.

At about 2300 hours, they were all witnesses of what appeared to the Germans to be a lightning reply to 21 Panzer Division's thrust, but was in fact the planned fly-in of 6 Airborne Division's airlanding brigade in gliders with heavier weapons and equipment. "No one who saw it will ever forget it," declared Kortenhaus. "Suddenly, the hollow roaring of countless aeroplanes, and then we saw them, hundreds of them, towing great gliders, filling the sky." They came down in various landing zones, and on both sides of the Orne, some passing directly over Leutnant Höller's anti-tank guns, still holding on at Bénouville. "An uncanny silence seemed to descend upon everything and everyone," he recollected. "We all looked up, and there they were just above us. Noiselessly, those giant wooden boxes sailed in over our heads to land, where men and equipment came pouring out of them. We lay on our backs and fired, and fired, and fired into those gliders, until we could not work the bolts of our rifles anymore. Our 2 cm flak troop shot some down and damaged many more, but with such masses, it seemed to make little difference." These gliders, landing apparently behind the Germans who had reached the coast, caused the immediate abandonment of the counter-attack west of the Orne; another group of gliders, landing east of the Orne, bumped down directly in the path of the Battle Group Luck, not more than 100 yards from the 17 tanks of 4th Company, Panzer Regiment 22. " It was a unique opportunity," said Kortenhaus, " but there was a wait before the order came crackling in my earphones: *Tanks advance*. And then the air was alive with calls of: *Eagle to all, Eagle to all, come in, please*! Engines roared into life, flaps clanged shut, and we rolled in cautious tempo and attack formation towards Herouvilette. But before we had even fired a shot, darkness had fallen over the rolling tank formations, and then warning lights shot up—we were attacking positions held by our own panzer grenadiers! Baffled, the men shook their heads. Obviously, an advance into empty space. And that was all that we, a strong tank company, achieved on this decisive day."

The gliders had barely finished landing, before part of 185 Brigade Group, the Warwickshires, came pushing into Bénouville to relieve the parachutists and take over the attack on Höller's unit. They should have been in Caen by now, but they were only half way. First crack, they lost the Forward Observation Officer's tank and the officer with it, so that they could not call for artillery support. The first tank Höller saw rolled into view opposite a house 60 yards away across the park, directly in front of the muzzle of one of his 75 mm SPs which was camouflaged as a bush. But the muzzle could not be depressed sufficiently, and to start up the engine would have given the game away, so they put their shoulders to the gun and rolled it forward to the slope. " The suspense was dramatic," said Höller, " but we managed it, and without being seen, either. Then Corporal Wlceck cranked the gun handles frantically, until the muzzle bore. Meanwhile, the English commander had got out of his turret, and walked up to the house to talk to the occupants; obviously, he hoped they would tell him where we were. The end of the tank was instantaneous. As our first shell hit, the petrol and ammunition exploded with such violence that the house beside the tank collapsed in ruins. Clearly, the English still hadn't a clue as to where we were; they fired wildly, at extreme range, and in all directions except at the ' nearest nearness ', and under cover of the uproar, we were able to start up and get away." They only withdrew to a safe distance for the night, cursing their lack of tank support; with only a few tanks, they felt, Bénouville and the bridges could have been taken, and there would have been something to show for their efforts.

Their bitterness must have been matched by that of Lieut.-Colonel Jim Eadie, for at dusk his leading tanks had advanced six miles from the beaches and were on the summit of the wooded hills around Lebisey, looking down at their objective, the burning town of Caen, but without infantry support. The presence of 21 Panzer's tanks on their open right flank was the deciding factor, and they withdrew to Biéville. " Many weeks of desperate fighting were to elapse before the Regiment again stood on that high ground," wrote a Brigade historian. Similarly, Panzer Regiment 22 were taking stock. The front had been ripped open by the British, the static positions of 716 Infantry Division taken or by-passed; there were no infantry reserves, and the tanks of the counter-attack force must dig in and hold a defensive line instead. In those few hours, the fate of Caen had been decided. Not to fall easily, but to be taken, to be ' martyred ' or ' murdered ', according to one's point of view. Already, the inhabitants had guessed at part of the truth, whereas in the morning they had been innocent and naive.

" Early in the morning," wrote a nun at the Bon Sauveur convent, " the planes had dropped tracts telling that Caen railway station, electrical depot and other buildings would be objectives for attack." They believed it. They did not realise that, in the bitter logic of war, the best way to deny a communications centre to the enemy is to blow the buildings into the streets, and that the buildings of Caen, constructed mainly of stone blocks, were uniquely suitable for that purpose; and that to save the lives of men, often enough, men, women and children must die. " Not even the most pessimistic imagined the horrors we witnessed. At 3 p.m. there was a violent raid, killing and wounding many students and boys at St. Mary's Seminary and School. The Holy Family Convent and School were likewise destroyed. Refugees and wounded began to pour into our convent, we made hurried preparations to convert the wings of the vacant mental homes into temporary hospitals. Just after Vespers, three vast buildings of our Mental Home were hit, with nuns and patients buried beneath the debris. The wounded became panic-stricken; they would not remain in bed, but struggled down to the basements. And to add to the poignancy of the scene, the poor mothers from the maternity home appeared, clinging to each other for support, their babies clasped in their arms, crying pitifully. We heard the screams of terror and the roar of gunfire, and above it all, a voice raised in prayer to God for protection. We could see fire bombs drop and huge buildings blazing; we could see the planes swoop down, then rise up, having done their deadly work; hear the bombs and the sound of machine-guns. At midnight, 400 nuns of the Order of Our Lady of Charity, and as many girls, sought shelter with us. Their Convent and Home had been burned, sixteen nuns had perished in the flames. Almost every convent in Caen had been hit." The ' power stations' and the ' railways' were for the history books and the memoirs; the blood of the nuns was for reality, and a few hours delay to the Panzer divisions, which was vital but would not read well.

21 Panzer Division had been delayed; and 12 S.S. Panzer Grenadier Division was also to be delayed; but the greater part of the delay, in both cases, had been imposed by Adolf Hitler, not by the R.A.F. 12th S.S. Panzer Grenadier Division had been ready to move in the morning, but did not get the order until the afternoon. Then there was counter-order —and disorder. Eventually, a Battle Group commanded by Kurt Meyer and based on his S.S. Panzer Grenadier Regiment 25, moved off from the area of Lisieux—a town connected with Bernadette Soubirous—towards a dark cloud on the horizon, the stain of blazing Caen. " Once more into the breach . . ." His thoughts were very like that.[7] Poland—the Fall of France—the Balkans—the East Front—and now, once again, France! The wheel turned full circle—from the Wehrmacht in the years of first and overwhelming victory, to the Wehrmacht in defensive

[7] Based on his own account in *Panzermeyer: Grenadiere* (Schild Verlag, 1957).

battle to decide the fate of the world. Once again, the fleeing refugees, but this time moving back, flowing past the armoured hulls of the fighting vehicles that throbbed with menace and power; moving back and behind them. And this time, the enemy held the sky. No longer the screaming stukas under the high-flying gaggles of 109s. General Dempsey had asked, at 1100 hours, for air interdiction of the highways leading into Caen from the south and south-east. And he had got it. Meyer's command vehicle growled past a burning French omnibus, and even above the roaring of the flames and of their own motors, they could hear the screaming from inside it. A corpse hung in shreds of broken glass, blocking the door; and the passengers were being burned alive. Above, no stuka staffels now, but the fighter-bombers of the R.A.F., circling in the 'cab rank' for another target. *"Drive on! No halting! Do you want to be a magnet? Keep the cavalcade rolling!"* Ruthlessly, 35-year-old 'Panzer' Meyer drove them on; and ruthlessly, the Spitfires of the R.A.F. came roaring to the attack, their cannons winking a brief tattoo, their rockets screeching in fiery thunder into the roadway; a drum-roll snarl of engines, as they flashed overhead, and then they were gone. An old Frenchman came staggering along the road, screaming, crying out to the advancing German might: "Murder! Murder!" A bundle of dirty rags sprawled in the roadway was a German grenadier, and the flames leaping high ahead were their next petrol-point, where they should have re-fuelled. Thus, in their different ways, the armour of Britain and Germany came at last within sight of Caen.

And as they did so, the refugees fled not only to the Convents but to the great Abbey of St. Etienne, built by William as Duke of Normandy, in which he was buried as the Conqueror, King of England. The Normans remembered the prophecy, but the English did not: that if the cathedral was destroyed, England would fall.

> *" William, we did not come to take you back*
> *Having forgotten you were here; unaware*
> *Disturbed your dust and sent*
> *The evil smoke shouting in the air.*
> *Since then—*

We have surged across the world,
And now return
To wake you with the torrent of our guns;
To claim your dust within the Abbey,
Long within the Abbey,
With the dark blood of our sons."

At midnight, Kurt Meyer reached the battle headquarters of Generalleutnant Wilhelm Richter, deep underground, walking along the underground corridors lined with wounded men of two divisions. Richter told him he had no news. None of his positions were reporting. No despatch riders had been able to get through. The situation was still totally confused. And then the telephone rang, at last, having being silent most of D-Day. Faintly, they could hear the tinny voice at the other end of the line. It was Oberst Krug, former commander of 736 Grenadier Regiment, speaking from his headquarters a few hundred yards away from Corporal Hill's tank, but deep under the scarred concrete dome of ' *Hillman* '.

" The enemy are on top of my bunker. I have no means of resisting them, and no communications with my men. What shall I do?"

Meyer, Feuchtinger, every man in the room looked at General Richter, who hesitated, then spoke slowly into the instrument. " I can give you no more orders. You must make your own decision now. Goodbye." The receiver fell into place with a click.

*   *   *

But neither the English, nor the Germans, nor the Americans, the Americans least of all, could be satisfied with the first day of the invasion of 1944. Of all the land forces engaged on 6 June, one unit only had reached its set objective, and not merely reached it, but gone beyond it. This was Serjeant Gariepy's unit, the 6th Canadian Armoured Regiment, spearheading 3 Canadian Infantry Division as flank cover to the assault on Caen. Lieutenant McCormick's troop of C Squadron had got on to the final objective, the Caen-Bayeux highway, and pushed on through Bretteville l'Orgueilleuse without orders almost to Carpiquet, the airfield of Caen, ten miles inland. But the infantry had been unable to keep up, and the tanks had been forced to withdraw for the night to the infantry positions, which ran through Pierrepont and Fontaine-Henry. Soon, Kurt Meyer's grenadiers were to be in Carpiquet, and it was to take the Canadians more than four weeks to drive them out. Static warfare was to set in, but no one knew it then.

At 0200 hours on D plus 1, A Company of the French-Canadian Régiment de la Chaudière heard the rumble of an armoured column approaching their 'all round defence' position. As the armoured cars came to a halt and the bone-weary men got out, the Canadians concluded that this must be a newly-landed unit coming up from the beaches, hopelessly lost—a more than ordinarily dangerous proceeding, as there was no 'front line' to speak of. The ground between their 8th Brigade around Fontaine-Henry and the 7th Brigade around Pierrepont to the west, was not held by anybody. Somewhere in front was the 9th Brigade, which had passed through the positions taken by the 7th, and gone on towards Caen. To the east, was the German corridor to the sea made by part of Panzer Grenadier Regiment 192. It was all very untidy, as the Canadians realised when they heard their new reinforcements talking German. Instantly, the night erupted with the whine and whip-crack of bullets, the slow soft rhythm of the Brens contrasting with the rapid, irregular, red-hot zylophone noise of the Spandaus, the flat pop-popping bursts of the machine-carbines, and the single bang of the rifles. A haystack caught fire, and in its lurid, orange glow, the German vehicles began to back out, a target for the two 6 pounders of the Support Company. The German commander changed his mind, and advanced. The two anti-tank guns fired until both crews were dead, then the armoured cars ground through the position. Dawn on 7 June revealed seventeen wrecked armoured cars, a trail of German dead and wounded towards the south; and heavy Canadian losses, including fifteen prisoners. In effect, it was the close of the D-Day operations, the final recoil of the German drive towards the coast which was to split the beachhead; symbolic alike in its unexpectedness, confusion, and lack of satisfaction to both sides.

At 0645 on 7 June, Oberst Krug came up to surrender with three of his officers and 70 men. As he came up, Corporal Hill went down, past the sprawled bodies of German soldiers. "Reasonable supply of champagne down there, the first time I'd tasted it. The first time I'd seen dead bodies, too, puts one off a bit."

Across the Channel, the presses were already rolling to announce the fall of Caen, and the complete success of D-Day. "Allied invasion troops, surging into France in non-stop waves, have fought their way into Caen, a town ten miles from the coast. Heavy street fighting is going on," reported the *Daily Express*. The *Daily Mail* had the same story: " General Montgomery has struck for the town of Caen, ten miles inland, which dominates roads and railways radiating all over Northern Normandy. Our troops are officially reported to be fighting in its streets." Where this news came from is anybody's guess. General Montgomery's seaborne H.Q. had no idea what was happening; the communications centre was hopelessly jammed with a twelve-hour backlog of undecoded messages. With the over-rated implements of modern science at his disposal, he knew less than Wellington did on the field of Waterloo. In the U.S.A., Roosevelt had announced, on the evening of D-Day, that " Only two U.S. destroyers and one LCT have been sunk, according to a noon despatch from General Eisenhower." In Germany, the presses were rolling, too. "At last it is over, they are here at last! But the German soldier was alert, the entire coast awake. Death reaped a terrifying harvest. Inferno belched from German weapons, manned by men who felt that they had a special debt to square with the enemy for his criminal air warfare. Mountains of dead lay on the beaches, where criminal madness had sacrificed them for the conquest of the European continent." Although the style could be faulted, it was nearer to the reality of Omaha Beach than Roosevelt's heartening message. The war of the public prevaricators had begun. There was not to be street-fighting in Caen for another four weeks; and the Battle of Normandy was to last for two and a half months. D-Day was merely the overture, the first 24 hours. The great movements of men and material into battle had still to come.

CHAPTER FIVE

THROW THEM INTO THE SEA!

The German Two-Panzer Division Counter-Offensive
7 and 8 June

The (12 S.S. Panzer Grenadier) Division will attack the disembarked enemy together with 21 Panzer Division, and throw him back into the sea.

Gruppenführer Fritz Witt, 7 June 1944

" IF ONLY . . ." is the theme of much German debate on the first 24 hours of the invasion, rivalling in bitterness the French reaction to Waterloo, or the British view of Jutland. Undoubtedly, national pride plays a part, and therefore some discount must be made. And, of course, it is always easier to fight a battle correctly after it is over than during the actual events. However, in the case of Normandy, the German view is virtually cancelled out by an equal and corresponding view from the opposite side, covering a somewhat longer period. " I am convinced that the way was wide open for exploitation during the first few days," said Stanley Green, " but the Germans were allowed to re-group and rush up reinforcements which, with our air supremacy, should have been impossible. Utter confusion existed all round, with seemingly no one knowing what was going on and no one prepared to advance further than their original objectives." The debate is further complicated by the fact that the British and Canadian operations were basically a feint; what General Bradley called a " decoy mission."

The Germans were bound to be sensitive to any threat to Caen, real or apparent. From Caen to the Seine was 50 miles; from Caen to Paris was 120 miles; from Caen to the Siegfried Line was 300 miles. Above all, while much of Normandy was difficult country for tanks, the terrain south of Caen was ideal. But, as General Bradley pointed out, " when reckoned in terms of national pride, this British decoy mission became a sacrificial one, for while we tramped around the outside flank, the British were to sit in place and pin down Germans. Yet strategically it fitted into a logical division of labours, for it was towards Caen that the enemy reserves would race once the alarm was sounded."

And this was exactly what happened. Panzer division after panzer division was directed to the Caen sector, in the hope of mounting an armoured counter-offensive which would drive through to the sea; and in each case, when the battle smoke had cleared away, the British and Canadians were in much the same place as before, but the remnants of the panzer division had been incorporated in the German defensive line and was no longer a mobile reserve. Sometimes, the Germans were able to pull out a division here and there, for a refit, but almost always it was sucked back into the fighting again by a renewed threat to Caen. This was the planned British task for the Normandy battle, planned to last only two or three weeks; but because the Americans were late in breaking out, it lasted almost to the breaking point of the armies, British, Canadian, and German, engaged around Caen. And that is why this battle was waged on such a scale, and with such ruthless desperation, as to have no parallel in the Normandy Campaign, or indeed anywhere outside Russia.

D plus 1, 7 June, saw a renewed attampt by 3 British Div to take, or at least close in, on Caen frontally, while 3 Canadian Div came down on their right flank, driving south-east. Both divisions were, of course, supported by their respective armoured brigades, each roughly equal in tank strength to the single armoured regiment of a panzer division. Already landing behind them, on the I Corps front, were 51 (Highland) Infantry Division and yet another armoured brigade, both destined for the battle of Caen. Far to the right, 30 Corps was strengthened by the landing, 12 hours late, of 7 Armoured Division, with 49 (West Riding) Infantry Division and still another armoured brigade following up. The convoy carrying most of 7 Armoured Division had been shelled off Dover on D-Day by the German cross-Channel guns, and the Liberty ship *Sambut* had lurched out of the line, on fire and sinking, after two direct hits; part of an L.A.A. Regiment destined for Caen therefore did not arrive. But, apart from the night raids by the Luftwaffe on the beaches and ships anchored off shore, the Germans were almost powerless to affect the steady build-up of the Allied forces in Normandy.

The German reinforcements, on the other hand, were moving up under continual air attack, which caused losses and delays; Panzer Lehr had not yet arrived, and part only of 12th S.S., the Battle Group commanded by ' Panzer ' Meyer. The German plan was for Oberst Oppeln Bronikowski's Panzer Regiment 22, of 21 Panzer Division, to attack out of Caen in line with the whole of 12th S.S., when they had all come up and deployed. At the same time, the Battle Group Luck was to counter-attack 6 Airborne's bridgehead east of the Orne. The roads radiate from Caen like a fan, or the spokes of a wheel, and all these attacks —British and German—were taking place simultaneously this day, surging up and down the roads leading to Caen. Many German strongpoints were holding out well in rear of the British and the beachheads were not yet solidly linked up; the situation was ' fluid ', affording opportunities to both sides for bold and decisive action. But to succeed, the German counter-stroke would have to be lucky as well as bold, for the British and Canadian tank forces already ashore had a distinct numerical superiority, quite apart from the British artillery superiority, upon which they relied for the breaking up of German tank attacks. In the past, in similar circumstances, the opportunist Rommel had nevertheless won victories over British armies, when his opponents had fumbled the ball. The attack towards Caen by 3 British Div this day was a possible example.

The Warwicks were ordered to take Lebisey Ridge and village; in the event, their remnants had to be rescued from the Germans by the Norfolks. First, the Warwicks were delayed, so that the heavy artillery bombardment, by three Field Regiments and a cruiser, had also to be postponed. But two companies reached the start line, and, communications having broken down, attacked on time without artillery support. They had a thousand yards of open ground to cover, and their colonel, seeing them advance unopposed, committed the remaining companies. The Germans, of course, were not so foolish as to open fire at 1,000 yards; undisturbed by any barrage, they were able to wait until the last moment and make certain of their aim. The few British survivors were pinned down. At this point, the Battalion's carriers and anti-tank guns, which had been sent by a different route, drove into Lebisey Wood, assuming that it had been taken,

73

and were similarly dealt with; none of the vehicles got back, but some of the men did.

While this abortive attack was going in a mile or so to the west, Hans Höller, with Oberleutnant Braatz's 8 Heavy Company of 21 Panzer Div, was able to withdraw to Lebisey almost unmolested. They had pulled back from the park at Bénouville under cover of darkness and at dawn were drawn up on the road in column of march, covered by a thin screen of infantry. The only significant British interference with this delicate operation was a single tank which broke through the bushes onto the road 20 yards in front of the muzzle of Lance-Corporal Wlceck's 75 mm SP gun, and spoilt his breakfast. He dropped the piece of bread which he was buttering, cranked the gun to bear on the point where he expected the tank to appear, and when it did so, brewed it up with his first shot. The unit then withdrew to Lebisey and finally took up positions on the favourable high ground covering the bridges between Hérouville and the Caen industrial suburb of Colombelles, which they were to hold during the next four weeks. They discovered that the 'garrison' of Hérouville consisted of a girl interpreter who would not leave her office until officially relieved by the anti-tank gunners.

While 3 British Div were making their small advances that day, west of the Orne, 6 Airborne Division, supported by Commandos, were supposed to enlarge their bridgehead east of the Orne. This was in preparation for a drive to outflank Caen from the east which would begin in a few days when the units of 51 (Highland) Division had been brought up. In order to forestall this threat, the Battle Group Luck put in a spoiling attack. "After a restless night, which the men spent near Escoville either crouching in their tanks or lying underneath them, the day broke grey and overcast," said Kortenhaus. "This attack was supposed to make up for the failure on the previous evening. Our tank company, supported by panzer grenadiers in half-tracks, were to advance on Ranville, the H.Q. of 6 Airborne Division, the elite troops of the enemy. And so we rolled forward in attack formation, which we had practised so many times; but this time towards a real enemy. St. Honorine was empty, so some tanks went through it while others went round to the right up a hill to where the gliders had come down the previous day. Suddenly,

74

the enemy artillery opened up. The grenadiers were halted and began to dig in, the screams of their wounded mingling with the ceaseless detonation of the shells. Even inside the tanks, we ducked, surprised by this unexpectedly strong defence. But we drove through the fire, on and up the hill to the glider field, where we met such a hail of shells that the tanks turned off to the left towards Longueval. Now, prisoners began to appear and when we sprayed the tree-tops, wounded Englishmen fell out of them. Unsupported by our own artillery and infantry, we were in the middle of enemy anti-tank and infantry positions, where every hedge and ditch spat fire, their occupants determined not to be over-run. This was a difficult and dangerous position for tanks to be in, and we began to retreat down the hill."

As they retired, tank 431 was hit in the turret, causing the driver to stall his engine, so that this tank was momentarily left behind. Leutnant Hoffman, the company commander, ordered tank 435 to go back and look for 431; "a suicide order for a single tank," commented Kortenhaus. The commander of 435 replied: " *Understood—ready* ". Then, all guns blazing, he burst through a hedge to his doom. The Mark IV shook from a hit, turned quickly out of the line of fire, gun swinging round to reply. It was hit again, and only two men bailed out. Tank 432, out on the left flank, saw this happening but were unable to intervene in time, although they marked the positions of the British anti-tank guns and destroyed two of them before they, in turn, were hit. "It was a clear victory for the enemy," said Kortenhaus. "Our 4th Company had had its baptism of fire, but had not passed the test. The shock to morale of a first, unsuccessful attack over terrain unfavourable to tanks, was very serious for the younger men of eighteen or twenty. We moved back to a quieter position, but no one was able to sleep, in spite of the nervous exhaustion which followed the attack. What would the next few days bring? we wondered. What chance was there of survival, when one seemed almost certain to be hit? Where were our reinforcements? Where was our artillery? What had happened to our air force? It was a very lonely feeling."

In fact, the attack had caused considerable repercussions in the area of 3 British Div on the other side of the Orne, being reported as a break-through by Tiger tanks and an infantry battalion, which would have been a serious threat indeed.[1] While the fire of 76 Field Regiment directly supported the parachutists, reinforcements of anti-tank guns, tanks, and infantry were switched from the attack on Caen to the defence of the Ranville-Bénouville bridges, and even the Engineers engaged on throwing Bailey bridges across the waterways were called on to take up defensive positions. "There was obviously no great hope for any decisive success from these counter-attacks which my Battle Group made frequently after 6 June," stated Oberst Frieherr Hans von Luck. "The only time when there might have been a chance was during the early morning of 6 June, but I had no permission to advance then, and, as far as I know, the H.Q. of my Division had no permission either. Thereafter, we had to take as our main aim the containment of the bridgehead east of the Orne; by counter-attacking, to prevent the British expanding their bridgehead, and at the same time enabling us to build up defensive positions in our rear. This British bridgehead was thought to be very dangerous, because a breakthrough here would go deep into the flank of the German forces and on into open country. That we were right to fight for time in which to organise defences was later to be demonstrated by the events of 18 July, during Operation ' Goodwood '.

*　　*　　*

The operations of the Battle Group Luck, which consisted of Panzer Grenadier Regiment 125 and 4 Company of Panzer Regiment 22, plus supporting arms, were local counter-attacks with a limited purpose. But the main German operation of 7 June, planned for noon, was a counter-offensive designed to split the beachhead and drive the British and Canadians into the sea. The three remaining tank companies of Oppeln Bronikowski's Panzer Regiment 22 were already in position. When 12 S.S. Panzer Grenadier Division came into line, they were to

[1] The Mark IVH was a good, mechanically reliable 23-ton tank which, with its new ' long ' 75 mm looked not unlike the Mark VI, the Tiger, which, weighing about 60 tons and carrying the deadly 88 mm gun, was so formidable as to be a bogey already, even before a single specimen had been identified in Normandy. Most ' Tigers ' reported during June must in fact have 'been Mark IVs or Mark Vs, the 45-ton Panther. The Sherman weighed 30 tons and the Churchill 40 tons. Later, they were to meet the 67-ton Tiger II, or ' Royal ' Tiger.

attack together. The latter division consisted of the two armoured battalions of S.S. Panzer Regiment 12, and the 25th and 26th S.S. Panzer Grenadier Regiments, plus the normal reconnaissance, engineer, and artillery elements. Leading their march to the front was Kurt Meyer's battle group, based on his S.S. Panzer Grenadier Regiment 25. Meyer was a young and dashing leader who combined energy with an acute tactical sense, dubbed already throughout the division, which he was soon to command, ' Panzer ' Meyer. 12th S.S. was officially designated the ' Hitler Jugend ', or ' H.J.' Division, nicknamed by German propagandists the ' Baby Division' because most of the ' men ' were actually ' teenagers '. It had been formed after the catastrophe of Stalingrad had caused a manpower crisis in the German Army, and had been recruited largely from under-age youths. Like most of the Waffen S.S., they were volunteers.[2] And like the British ' gladiator ' units, such as the paratroops and commandos, and the entire Canadian Army, they were in a sense picked men; because they had ' picked ' themselves. The ' boy scout' aspect of Hitler Youth training made them especially suitable as soldiers from the fieldcraft point of view, and the ' political' indoctrination, such as it was, had given them not merely a ' cause ' and a ' hero ', but more important, a belief in the ' destiny of youth ' which resulted in a conscious feeling of superiority amounting to arrogance, no bad armour against the unspeakable shock of war.

But this was not 1940. Meyer had barely selected a forward command post in the tall buildings of Ardenne Abbey, with the division not even on the start line, but strung out behind him for miles along the Caen-Falaise road, when he saw that it was the enemy who were attacking. Ignoring the lagging 3rd British Division, who should have protected their left flank, 3 Canadian Division was driving confidently and aggressively for Carpiquet airfield. The leading infantry of 9 Brigade were already in Authie and the Shermans of 27 Armoured Regiment were

---

[2] ' Waffen ' means ' armed ', in the sense of bearing arms in defence of the state, and does not include those branches of the S.S. not composed of fighting soldiers. Recruitment was by no means confined to Germans. In effect, the Waffen S.S. was Hitler's International Praetorian Guard, a sign of his mistrust of the personal loyalty to him of the regular armed forces of Germany, the Wehrmacht.

moving by country lanes into St. Contest, less than two miles from Caen. These men, too, were volunteers, individualists, many of them bred to the use of firearms since boyhood, unlike the townsmen who form the bulk of conscript armies; they were as well-equipped as the Germans, and they came on with the over-confidence of inexperience. Meyer's field glasses brought the leading tank so close that, when it stopped in an orchard, he could see the commander appear, take out a packet of cigarettes, light up, and blink momentarily at the smoke. He was 200 yards from Meyer's nearest unit. Then the bulk of the Canadian armoured force appeared in Buron, making for Authie to support their infantry, the North Nova Scotia Highlanders. Their axis of advance would shortly expose to German fire not the heavily-armoured front of the tanks, but their lightly armoured sides. Now, the German Army showed why it had achieved such an awesome reputation. Complete fire discipline prevailed; not a shot was fired at the tempting targets. The Canadians had no idea that they were advancing into an accidental ambush. And Meyer, young, bold, and resolute, seized his opportunity without bothering to argue or ask for orders, although he was only a Regimental Commander taking part in an Armoured Corps operation. On his own initiative, he issued the order 'hold your fire' to the anti-tank guns, made a rapid plan to counter-attack immediately after fire had been opened at the most favourable moment, and sent a despatch rider to tell the divisional Commander what he had done.

It worked, as it was bound to do; but not as in 1940. The Canadians were driven pell-mell back from Authie and Buron with heavy tank and infantry losses, their own operation ruined. But they did not then disintegrate. They held, and called for fire and tank support. With a noise like express trains passing overhead, the ton-weight shells of the warships lying off the beachhead began to fall into the German positions. Meyer himself took cover in one of their enormous craters, as did a young officer cadet, Kurt Misch. " Our counter-attack won good ground because the Canadian units were so completely surprised," said Misch. " It was brought to a standstill mainly by the artillery of the invasion fleet. Because of this concentrated fire, such as I had never seen before on any European battlefield, both officers and men became demoralised and were forced to dig in. For perhaps an hour I lay in a giant shell crater together with some Canadian prisoners, and saw that they were just as demoralised by their own fire as we were, although these prisoners belonged to an excellently trained unit." And that was as far as the two-division armoured offensive got. Meyer had started the battle rolling, but he could not keep it up unsupported. On his right, 21 Panzer Division had been halted at Epron; and on his left, the tanks of 6 Canadian Armoured Regiment, spearheading the drive of 7 Canadian Infantry Brigade, had broken clean through the remnants of 716 Infantry Division and were in sight of Carpiquet, actually behind Meyer's battle group.

At first light, 6 Armoured Regiment had supported the Regina Rifles into Bretteville l'Orgueilleuse, then turned left towards Caen. " Practically no resistance was met on this drive," said Gariepy. " Small pockets of machine-gunners, with no cohesion in their defence, without field officers, mostly non-coms and junior lieutenants. We were amazed at the facility with which we were taking them. Their casualties were high, ours were negligible, few prisoners were taken. It is a problem for such groups to give up. First, they had to brave their own troops, then to face the opposing force, not always clear on their intentions. They come forward aligned down the muzzles of enemy guns, and a single shot fired by one man can cause thousands of others to follow suit. This was not yet ' savagery ' or ' revenge ', it was ' SNAFU ', or ' organised confusion '." Nevertheless, men going forward to surrender were shot down, and this could easily be, and most probably was, misinterpreted as deliberate ruthlessness on the part of the Canadians.

" We came very close to Carpiquet, so close that we could easily see the tarmac; yet a few days later, we were to fight bitterly to occupy this sector. Reports kept pouring in over our wireless that much fighting was occurring on our left flank, and we moved back to a new harbour at Secqueville-en-Bessin; at midnight, news leaked in that 9 C.I.B. was taking a terrific shellacking, and we moved to Bray cross-roads as mobile reserve force. We had been awake for 48 hectic, fatigue-laden hours; all seasickness had disappeared, but the men were still weak from it; we had been issued ' bennies ' to keep awake, and the haggard look they gave the men made us appear like 'zombies'; and all through the night reports came in of increasing enemy effort, with an armoured attack imminent. But it never came off, and we ran about for several days and nights at various reported 'Tiger' apparitions. The men believed these hide-and-seek tactics were all part of a well-organised plan to make the Germans think we were there in strength, and that nothing less than a large-scale counter-attack could dislodge us."

What had actually happened was that more of 12th S.S. had come up 8 June, found Carpiquet airfield and its enormously strong defences deserted, the Luftwaffe having flown and the Canadians having neglected to occupy it when they had the chance; and having dealt with 9 Brigade already, had turned to deliver the same treatment to 7 Brigade. Using Panthers as well as Mark IVs, they re-took Bretteville l'Orgueilleuse and Putot-en-Bessin, destroying the forward companies of the Regina Rifles and the Canadian Scottish. Putot changed hands again that evening, when 7 Brigade counter-attacked and drove out the S.S. But casualties were very heavy and the formerly 'fluid' situation was beginning to solidify, almost unopposed dashes being succeeded by the desperate pendulum of limited, local attack and counter-attack. The British had failed to take Caen; the Germans had failed to throw them into the sea.

But 8 June, D plus 2, was a wonderful day for German Intelligence. At three widely separated points, they received three priceless gifts from the hands of the dead. From a water-logged landing craft, a derelict of D-Day, which had drifted ashore on the German-held Vire Estuary between Omaha and Utah, Cossacks of 439 East Battalion took a beachmaster's copy of the American VII Corps plan and time-table, giving information also about forthcoming operations by V Corps and the British 30 Corps; these made clear that the American landings were not a diversion, but were intended to take Cherbourg, although they did not reveal the really vital information that the major break-out was to come in the American sector, nor that Normandy was the main point of Allied effort. From a Canadian armoured car, containing a dead lieutenant and driver, which had been knocked out while advancing from Putot-en-Bessin by an anti-tank gun of III Battalion, Panzer Grenadier Regiment 26, the Germans took a special code map of their own defences; sheer chance, because the gun had accounted for two vehicles, and the first had burned, together with everything and everyone inside it. And from a Canadian tank similarly knocked out near Authie, the Germans took a copy of the Wireless procedures and codes. The two latter discoveries were complementary, and they were brought to Hubert Meyer, then the Ia, or chief staff officer (operations) of 12 S.S. Panzer Grenadier Division, and no relation to Kurt Meyer.

"When we came to look at the map," he recollected, "we were astounded at the accuracy with which all the German fortifications were marked in, even the weapons, right down to light machine-guns and mortars, were listed. And we were disgusted that our own intelligence had not been able to stop this sort of spying. We found out, later on, that a Frenchman had been arrested who admitted that he had spied for years in the Orne sector, appearing every day with his greengrocer's van on the coastal road. We could clearly see on this map the result of his activities, and that of other spies also. What was useful for us, now, was that all the place names had been substituted, for instance, the Orne was marked as ' Orinico ', and that the enemy continued to use these cover names in his wireless transmissions for quite a while afterwards. At the same time, this glimpse of espionage, in which we had become involved, seemed to us much more exciting than even the most sensational and breath-taking fiction, because it was real and important. Taken together with the wireless codes also captured, we were able to understand much of the enemy's radio traffic, which helped partly to make up for the advantages he enjoyed. As we were in a foreign country, we could not expect any co-operation from the population, whereas the enemy could; and because of his supremacy in the air, it was practically impossible for us to do any tactical air reconnaissance. So that all that was left was to form special recce units to do radio listening work, and so on; and in this we were repeatedly successful. In effect, it was espionage by radio."

CHAPTER SIX

JERRY'S ON THE RUN!

*The German Three-Panzer Division Counter-Offensive and the
British Double-Envelopment of Caen
9 to 12 June*

The British head-on drive for Caen had been halted. The
German two armoured division drive to split the beachhead
had broken down. As a direct result, on 9 June two conferences
were held. General Geyr von Schweppenburg, commanding the
now-operational Panzer Group West, came to Meyer's H.Q. at
Ardenne Abbey, just outside Caen. He cut short the S.S.
General's report with, " My dear Herr Meyer, the war can only
be won now by political means." But there was to be one last
major effort to break through to the coast with three armoured
divisions. 21 Panzer was to attack out of Caen, on the right, with
12th S.S. in the centre, and Panzer Lehr on the left, near
Bayeux. The operation would begin as soon as Panzer Lehr had
reached the front and deployed. Win or lose, the three divisions
would be ' burnt out ' afterwards, and there could be no repetition.

Montgomery, Dempsey, and the American General Bradley
met in a field near the fishing village of Port-en-Bessin, and
studied a map spread out on the bonnet of a Humber staff car.
Montgomery was wearing ' image order '—faded bush jacket,
turtleneck sweater, corduroy trousers, and black beret. As 21
Panzer and 12th S.S. had now dug in, on the defensive, around
Caen, they were to be encircled simultaneously from east and
west. A ' left hook ' out of the Airborne bridgehead east of the
Orne was to be made by 51 (Highland) Division and 4 Armoured
Brigade, with Cagny as their objective; the more powerful ' right
hook ' was to be delivered from Bayeux by 30 Corps, with 7
Armoured Division leading, towards Villers Bocage and Evrecy.
When the tips of the two ' pincers ' had reached Cagny and
Evrecy respectively, the British 1 Airborne Division was to be
dropped between them, thus completing the encirclement of

Caen. The Americans were to attack towards Caumont, parallel with 30 Corps. The intention was to enlarge the beachhead and to divert attention from the major American effort to take Cherbourg. The operation was to start next day, 10 June, and a day or two afterwards the Canadians were to advance, keeping pace with the left flank of the 30 Corps drive.

The British and German plans were in mutual opposition therefore, and with timings virtually identical. 7 Armoured Division was to advance from Bayeux to take Villers-Bocage; and simultaneously, Panzer Lehr Division was ordered to advance from Villers-Bocage to take Bayeux. At the other end of the line, 21 Panzer Division was to advance into the Airborne bridgehead; and simultaneously, 51 (Highland) Division was to advance out of it. And in the centre, 12 S.S. Panzer Grenadier Division was to advance north of the Caen-Bayeux road; while shortly afterwards, 3 Canadian Division was to advance south of the road. There was bound to be a head-on confrontation all along the line, unlikely to give unrelieved satisfaction to either side, but which would certainly serve to divert attention from the major Allied objective—Cherbourg.

Already, on 9th June, the Battle Group Luck was putting in a spoiling attack towards Escoville, while 346 Infantry Division attacked the airborne bridgehead from the opposite direction, through the Breville gap. After a 90-minute artillery bombardment, the tanks of 4 Company rolled forward. " Escoville was but a stone's throw away," said Kortenhaus, " and from there to Ranville, not much further. Between us and success stood only two battalions and some anti-tank guns." But it was difficult country for tanks; they were forced to advance nose to tail and then deploy in full view of the parachutists, who were positioned in a ditch forward of an innocent-looking hedge which in fact concealed a heavy stone wall, part of Escoville Castle. " We rolled through the gap one after the other, the panzer grenadiers storming on behind us, weapons at the ready, trying to shelter behind the tanks as they deployed into broad-front formation on the other side, for the attack which was to steamroller us into Ranville. The firing began when we were only 30 yards from the hedge, and the first wounded grenadiers dropped groaning to the ground. Tank 432 was hit, and lost a track. Thirty seconds later, Tank 400 was hit and our company commander, Leutnant Hoffmann was staring in horror at the bloody mess which had been his leg, while Tank 401 exploded, blowing open the hatches and literally flinging the crew out. We had seen three tanks, including the leader's, destroyed in a few seconds. Then, simultaneously, both Tank 422 and Tank 423 were hit, the former in the turret, and the artillery of 3 British Division began to deluge with fire our already faltering attack. The other tank drivers began hurriedly to reverse, under cover of a hail of fire from their turret guns and M.G.s. Terrified, they watched the exploding mushrooms of earth and smoke shoot up around them, and saw too late the dead and wounded grenadiers lying along the road of retreat; some were squashed by the tanks. Perhaps six minutes had passed since we had rolled through that gap, and now the tanks were piling up there again, crashing into each other. We had been reduced to 12 tanks, had lost 32 men, and were retreating in panic. The 23-year-old company commander was too inexperienced, and wounded too early, to stand even a chance of succeeding; and anyway, I think the point of attack itself was absolutely wrong. Certainly, it will never be forgotten by the men who survived."

That same day, in the evening, 6 Canadian Armoured Regiment had their first, long-dreaded encounter with the panzers; not Mark IVs, but Mark Vs, the formidable 45-ton Panthers. The first real test of an untried unit is always critical for morale. "For a while it was nip and tuck," said Gariepy, "but finally the great apprehension we felt about the superiority of the enemy in tank warfare was destroyed; the hard work on the ranges in hitting bulls-eye, paid off." Lieutenant G. Henry, commanding a 'Firefly', a Sherman equipped with a 17 pounder, took up an ambush position, and from a flank, with rapid, accurate fire, accounted for six Panthers with seven rounds. "Such scores made the enemy hesitate about forcing the issue, and boosted our morale as well as that of the infantry. We found our Shermans were much more manoeuvrable than their clumsy, low-slung tanks, and we could traverse and fire with much greater rapidity. True, they could out-range us by far, but if you were fortunate enough to see him before he saw you, you could easily work circles round him. We could fire three rounds to his one, and in any given position, stopped or going full speed, forward or in reverse; but he apparently had trouble to fire on the run. We saw that we could not only take it, but dish it out, and this we did that day with gusto."

None of the plans laid on 9 June came off tidily or quite on time: they were spoiled by the fighting already in progress. Enemy pressure tended to force the Germans to commit units prematurely and in the restricted Norman countryside the British found that they had insufficient infantry to protect their tanks, due in part to miscalculation and in part to the number of German strongpoints holding out in their rear which required infantry to reduce them. One such stronghold, in the caves of Fontaine-Henry, fell to the Régiment de la Chaudière as a result of a parley over Canadian wounded in a previous unsuccessful attack, who were now lying out in front in the path of their own barrage. A group of Canadians went forward with their hands up, shouting: "We have come to look for our wounded!" Not a shot was fired while they located and retrieved the wounded; then a German came forward with a Red Cross flag, asking for an officer to accompany him. Captain Michel Gauvin chose to go, and was taken to a quarry honeycombed with caves in which, by the flickering light of candles, he could see some fifty wounded Germans and Canadians. The German doctor in charge asked Gauvin to remove the Canadian wounded, as some would not live if they did not receive proper attention immediately. Gauvin replied that all the wounded would be taken to a hospital if the German garrison would surrender; a few minutes later, the Germans agreed to do so.[1]

This was a case where strict military logic would have forbidden mercy. Quite different were two cases concerning 12th S.S. On 8 June, a group of Canadian prisoners were executed by the Germans, and on 9 June, before the morning conference at Ardenne Abbey, Meyer was shown the bodies of a similar group of German prisoners, who had obviously been lined up and shot through the head by the Canadians.[2] Meyer was later held nominally responsible for the murder of the Canadians and his

[1] See *Le Geste du Régiment de la Chaudière*, by Majors Ross and Gauvin.
[2] See *Panzermeyer: Grenadier*, by Kurt Meyer and Hubert Meyer.

judge was the former Brigadier H. W. Foster, who had commanded the Brigade which Gariepy's unit was supporting; no Canadian general officer was ever held responsible for the murder of the Germans, or any explanation tendered for a notebook entry found by the Germans on a Canadian captain on 7 June, to the effect that prisoners would not be taken.[3] The death sentence on Meyer was commuted by the Canadian G.O.C., General Crerar, despite protests by the Canadian Legion and others who were ignorant of the background. Serjeant Gariepy took the grim but logical view common to most regulars. " I am grateful to General Crerar for this. The German sub-division commanders had very little choice at the time about what kind of war they were going to fight. We had the initiative, and we called the shots. Their position was very precarious, they were being pressed by the Allies who had everything they lacked. We had co-ordination, we had equipment, we had an overwhelming superiority in weapons, air cover, and tactical advantages. We were fighting in ' friendly territory', they were not. Their troop deployments were restricted, they could only commit their troops piecemeal, this was their downfall; had they been able to concentrate, they would have pushed us back into the sea any time up to five or ten days after D-Day. We were then hacking at their reserves, and their commanders must have been crazy with the impotence of their high command. Can you imagine a young officer asking, ' What about the prisoners, sir?' You can imagine the reply: ' To hell with the prisoners, do what you like with them.' So it gets handed down to, perhaps an N.C.O., and he is not too happy, or feels the pangs of revenge, or wants to show his determination for the Fatherland, and decides to erase the problem the easiest way. And that was that. To place the blame on the Div commander is pathetic. I deplore the deaths of these men, but it was no more monstrous than the destruction of Monte Cassino. War is not pretty and the soldier cannot ask

---

[3] There is a case for ruthlessness, based on the self-preservation principle and the fact that most ' atrocities ' occur in situations of misunderstanding. There is a case for mercy and chivalry, but any chance of re-establishing such a code was forfeited by Nuremberg, where justice was one-sided or absent entirely, *e.g.* the case where Russian judges helped to try Germans for a massacre of Polish officers for which in fact the Red Army had been responsible.

for any special privileges." Such actions do tend to snowball, however.

On 10 June the Battle Group Luck and the 346 Infantry Division again attacked east of the Orne, before 51 (Highland) Division and 4 Armoured Brigade had assembled. " With the events of the previous day still fresh in our minds," said Korten-haus, " we fired with bitter determination until all our ammunition was exhausted." Some ground was gained by the tanks, but infantry losses were heavy, one battalion being reduced to about 100 men, further cause for bitterness. The attack of the Highland Division was effectively spoiled, however, for it was sucked into battle piecemeal. 5 Black Watch went into their first action on 11 June, and lost 200 men. During the day, " a very ugly thing happened," according to the Divisional historian. " Some men far out on the flank had been captured. Their captors shoved them up against a wall and shot them in cold blood. All were killed but one man, who feigned death, and later was able to get away and tell the story, a very different story from that con-cerning the chivalrous behaviour of the German 90th Light Division in Africa." A Serjeant Aitkenhead of 5/7 Gordons, who was also taken prisoner this day, killed his guard with a knife, and returned to his unit. " Is that you Serjeant Aitkenhead?" said the first Highlander he met. "Aye, I ken't they could never kill *you*." The Germans continued their attacks until 16 June, failing to gain an outright decision, but forcing the British to commit the Highlanders as reinforcements to the hard-pressed men of 6 Airborne Division, and thereby preventing the British from mounting their drive to outflank Caen from the east. The Black Watch, for instance, were put under 3 Parachute Brigade, and Brigadier Hill, an experienced airborne soldier, was im-pressed by the severity and intensity of the conflict; there were many dead to be seen, and much hand-to-hand fighting, both unusual occurrences in the rather loose conditions of modern war in Europe and Africa. The physical and nervous strain, accentuated by lack of sleep, was considerable, and, said Briga-dier Hill, " the point that impressed me most was the staying power of the chaps during fourteen days of such continuous fighting."

The most the Highland Division could do was to mount a

Brigade attack with two battalions up on 13 June, which met the Luck Battle Group head on, both sides recoiling eventually. The British lost on the start line three out of the four tanks supporting them, and 4 Company of Panzer Regiment 22 was reduced now to eight tanks, less than half strength. " The men had come to the end of their tether," said Kortenhaus. " The fact must be faced," wrote the historian of the Highland Division, " that at this period the normal very high morale of the Division fell temporarily to a low ebb." Stalemate was near.

On 10 June, the proposed advance of 30 Corps on the opposite, western end of the front was disrupted by elements of Panzer Lehr Division coming into line and attacking; and when the British advance did get going, it went slowly. That evening, Panzer Lehr began a night drive towards the coast, which quickly ran into trouble. Particularly unfortunate was Light Flak Unit 98, equipped with 20 mm automatic guns mounted on armoured half-tracks, and manned by the Luftwaffe. " It was our task to pretend that our half-tracks were actually tanks," recalled Kurt Erich Groetschel, one of the gunners. " This was possible under cover of night, but when we arrived at the farm which was our objective, we found the courtyard full of enemy tanks, real ones, and had to turn and beat it, for against them we were both powerless and unprotected. Firing on a tank with a 20 mm gun, we called ' knocking ', for that was all it was. Another Troop, in which my uncle was serving, lost half their men as prisoners that night. Weeks later, my uncle wrote to me from Canada, that the P.O.W. camp compared so favourably to life in wartime Germany, that when he sat down to his first lunch, he thought he had been invited to a wedding! A day or so afterwards, yet another Troop was similarly shot to bits in a British tank attack and the Battery medical orderly taken prisoner. But they let him go again, because he was a First Aid chap, and perhaps also because he was an Austrian, as most of us were. He told us that an English officer had said farewell to him with the words: ' We'll meet again in Warsaw, when we both line up against the Russians.' The reaction to this event was enormous. All who had Austrian nationality got an English-speaking comrade to write for them on a slip of paper: *I Am An Austrian*. But after Falaise, not many were left alive who carried that piece of paper in their pockets."

In the centre, on 10 June, there was a change of plan. 3 Canadian Infantry Division and its supporting armour was ordered to prepare to advance in 48 hours time, to step up the pressure on the left of 30 Corps. Serjeant Gariepy's unit, 6 Armoured Regiment, was given 20 replacement tanks, bringing their total to 76 tanks, and told to get some rest; they were dog-tired, some had not shaved for five days, and all were fed-up with living all that time on iron-hard Army biscuits. The rumour flashed round: *Jerry's on the run*. Next morning, they received a string of orders: at 0400, the attack will start in 24 hours from now; at 0800, the attack will start at 1300 hours *today*. That left five hours to plan and organise the attack, assimilate the new, replacement crews and tanks, and get them in battle-worthy condition. As a matter of course, they were modified. Spare tracks lashed on as extra armour; studs fitted to the sides to take camouflage; turret-flaps cut away, to give the commander all-round vision; seats re-modelled to enable the loader-operator to move easily; turret-baskets removed, to give easier bail out. Every commander had his own ideas on how to ensure his tank got off the first, decisive shot, and the Regimental C.O. encouraged such modifications. "'O' Groups went fast and furious," said Gariepy. "Speed, speed, and more speed, with the result that little information was passed on to the tank crews; there was no time even for an artillery barrage, but we were not told that. First objective was: seize and hold Le Mesnil-Patry, then push on to Cheux. Order of march was: B, C, R.H.Q., and A Squadrons. So when at noon the order to 'roll' came, I led off as 'point' tank of B Squadron, followed by my troop officer. It was a beautiful sunny day, warm, with hardly any wind, the men in high spirits and planning on teaching the 'rookies' how to behave themselves in action.

"When I reached the start line, the Caen-Bayeux railway near Bretteville, it looked as if we were moving up on a 'piece of cake'. Our infantry, the Queen's Own Rifle Regiment, had been allowed to climb up on our tanks for the ride into action, and were having the time of their lives, smoking, talking, enjoying the trip. Near the railway line we detoured a knocked-out Panther

which aroused the looks of the many new men in our squadron
—they had never seen an enemy tank before. Then we were
told of another alteration—the start line had been changed to a
spot near Norrey-en-Bessin. But this didn't affect us, for we'd
passed it already, and were going across the road south of Norrey
towards a spacious wheatfield lying just before Le Mesnil-Patry.
All this time, I could hear the comments of an officer over the
wireless. *We are now approaching the railway. We are now
nearing dead enemy bear.*[4] *We are now near the schoolhouse.
We are now moving into the wheatfield.* The affair had such an
air of ease that no efforts were made to caution him. But it made
me sick to listen to it, so I switched off my set, which may have
been wrong, for otherwise I would have heard the order to
withdraw."

As his Sherman rolled through the corn, Gariepy had his head
out of the turret, looking downward for any sign of mines. He
found himself staring directly into the eyes of men lying in the
wheat; they wore the helmets of the panzer grenadiers. Simultaneously, a heavy artillery shoot began, the shells rustling and
screaming over towards Bretteville. Momentarily, he thought it
must be a Canadian barrage; but it wasn't—those were German
guns firing. He switched on his set again and reported being in
the middle of a heavy concentration of enemy infantry. " By
that time we had by-passed a strong contingent and were being
fired upon from rear as well as from the front. Pendemonium
broke loose, our own infantry jumping off the tanks to avoid
getting shot, and the German infantry desperately trying to get
away from under the tracks of the Shermans, which kept on
coming. But on the air now, no orders for deployment, nothing,
not even a commentary, just dead silence. Knowing that A and
C Squadrons were coming up behind me, I gave my driver the
order to speed up and, ignoring the German infantry, pushed
on for Le Mesnil-Patry. Our own infantry were all mixed up in
battle with the Germans in the cornfield behind, so B Squadron
headed on, blazing away with machine-guns at various pockets
around."

They had not yet drawn heavy fire, but as the Shermans
reached a slight rise in the ground, at the edge of Le Mesnil-

4 ' Bear '—code for tank.

Patry, they exposed their left flank to hidden German guns; six tanks blew up in rapid succession. Meanwhile, C Squadron moved to high ground on their right and began to open covering fire; but they were immediately engaged by anti-tank guns of 50 (Northumbrian) Infantry Division, part of 30 Corps. Under attack now by a German division on the left, and a British division on the right, the Canadians were unable to hold their position and withdrew, flying recognition signals and replying only to the enemy fire from the left. They had to retire, as they had advanced, through and not round Norrey-en-Bessin because of a minefield laid in their path by their own Canadian infantry; and their retreat was further hampered by the debris caused by the German artillery bombardment, and particularly by the church, most of which was lying in the street. An excellent example of what the Canadians called a ' FAFU ', or ' SNAFU ', the inevitable result of too much hurry and too many orders and counter-orders.

B Squadron, cut off and alone among the enemy, was destroyed to the last tank. An S.S. officer who engaged them said, " I led three tanks in a counter-attack on the right wing of our line and re-established our old positions. A tank battle had already started in the orchard of a large farm and we put out of action all the enemy tanks which had broken through here. The infantry lay out in the cross-fire, and there were losses on both sides." Or, as the British official history primly puts it: " Touch with the leading squadron was lost," a superb understatement. It was the squadron which was lost, not the touch. Serjeant Gariepy's Sherman was probably the last to go. In the ' point ' tank, he arrived first, and has the distinct impression that the Germans were not in defensive positions, but were themselves forming up for attack. He saw in rapid succession three of the half-tracks which the Germans used for bringing up their panzer grenadiers, lined up side by side, with Germans milling around in confusion. Then some thirty tanks, also tightly aligned; a battery of 88 mm guns, still limbered up; and then more half-tracks, with men jumping out of them. Firing on the run, he accounted for three of the half-tracks, before his Sherman was hit and set on fire. This probably saved them, for it was only their bedding rolls and some spare belts of m.g. ammunition, all slung outside the tank, which were blazing. Pouring out clouds of dense, billowing black smoke as it ploughed onward, the Sherman must have appeared doomed. " Reverse! " he called out to his driver, and trailing behind them a long plume of smoke, they backed 600 yards through the cornfield, with panzer grenadiers jumping up and hurling potato masher grenades at them, their own guns firing, and the spare ammunition crackling away. Then they bailed out and crawled for the shelter of a ditch. " Our ' old faithful ' D.D. was burning brightly, quite some distance from the rest of the squadron. It was sad to see the old wreck which had carried us from England, and through the invasion, finally come to an end in the middle of a wheatfield; everything we possessed was in that tank." By wriggling along the ditch, over dead Germans and Canadians, they finally got back and reported to Major Marks who, bare-headed, was looking for his flaming squadrons in the distance, and trying to make out what had happened.

37 tanks had been lost, 95 officers and men killed, apart from wounded and missing. No officers came back, and only three N.C.O.s. On that one day, 11 June, the Regiment suffered almost one-third of all their casualties in the European campaign, and ever after, any man who had been at Le Mesnil-Patry was pointed out to the replacements with the encouraging words: " There is always a possibility that you will survive." In the evening, there was a moment of mercy. "At dusk, with the lessening of the artillery bombardment," recollected an S.S. officer, " several ambulances drove out into the open from the enemy lines. Men sprang out of them, waving Red Cross flags, and started to pick up their wounded. For a moment, we were stunned; then came the shout, ' Cease fire, Red Cross! ' For the next few minutes, not a shot was fired and both sides collected their wounded and their dead."

Infantry of the Régiment de la Chaudière and tanks of the Fort Garry Horse were rushed up behind the shattered 6th Armoured Regiment and dug in between Bray and Rots, in case 12th S.S. should take advantage of the confusion and roll through to the coast. For the Chauds, it was their first meeting with the Waffen S.S., and not a happy one. From their first patrol into Rots, only a few wounded men returned; the grenadiers had let them walk right up, before firing. Later in the evening, the crack 46 Royal Marine Commando assaulted Rots against the picked youngsters of the Hitler Youth. " They fought like lions on both sides, so that the dead lay corpse by corpse," wrote the historians of the Chaudière, who went into the village next morning. " We searched every house, every courtyard, to avoid ambush. And here is the confirmation of how ferocious last night's battle must have been. The Commandos lie dead in rows beside the dead S.S. Grenades are scattered all over the road and in the porches of houses. Here we see a Commando and an S.S.-man, literally dead in each other's arms, having slaughtered each other. There, a German and a Canadian tank have engaged each other to destruction, and are still smouldering, and from each blackened turret hangs the charred corpse of a machine-gunner. Over here, are a group who ran towards a wall for shelter, and were shot down before they got there. And then, near the church, as the advance guard of C Company and the carriers turn the corner, there are three Germans. Only three. But one of them instantly draws his pistol, and hits one of our men. A Bren gunner kills two of the three S.S.-men, but the survivor does not surrender; he dodges us, and gets away. Now, we understand with what kind of fanatic we have to deal."

Gariepy's unit was suffering from the same sense of shock. " The morale of the men was very low indeed. So many of the long-time comrades had stayed behind on the battlefield, the battle itself had been so savage, so furious, that every man felt that the 12th S.S. Panzer had a personal grudge against our tanks. Silently, grimly, we were looking at each other, knowing exactly what was in the other man's mind. They simply lay there, not sleeping, eyes opened, just staring into space. A poet or a writer would have found the proper words to describe this vacant look and what was going through their minds, but other than a few comforting words from the Padre, Major Creelman, not much was said. Mostly, everyone was rather vindictive, and silently swearing revenge. Had they met 12 S.S. Panzer again, immediately, they would have been very hard to control. The Padre did his best to get this feeling out of them, but was not too successful. Had any young subaltern said the wrong thing that day, the men would have been up for court-martials, they were in such a mood."

Because 12th S.S. were the Hitler Youth Division, courage, skill and determination were dubbed 'fanaticism', and ascribed to a political creed. But politics entered into their morale only in the broadest sense: they were told that they were fighting an evil thing which would destroy their country, and mostly believed it. "The little episode of the Red Cross at Le Mesnil-Patry shows that our hatred was not directed against the soldier, the individual human being," commented an S.S. officer. The Waffen S.S. and the regular Wehrmacht were rivals, not always on good terms, so perhaps Leutnant Höller's testimony may be as unbiased as can be expected in the circumstances. "In Caen, the 'Hitler Jugend' were always our neighbours on the left; they fought bitterly for every yard; the help of one comrade for another was so spontaneous and unselfish that it was unequalled; and although you yourself have only heard detrimental facts about them, I can speak of experiences of a most humane nature."

"On 14 June, while we were still reforming and absorbing new crews, two more men missing since the 'hell' of Le Mesnil-Patry came back," said Gariepy. "They had, they said, escaped from the Jerries; they talked of seeing some Hussars who had given themselves up being shot in the back after being taken prisoners. The old grim look of revenge was revived, and we began to look forward to our next engagement. Up to now, there had not been any particular viciousness on either side; sometimes our fire, or that of the Jerries, strayed a little, to allow the crew of an enemy tank to get out. Looking back on it now I think, rather cynically, that these yarns brought back by men who escaped or played dead, were not always the truth; or the truth was twisted in the mind of the teller. I cannot now stomach all the atrocities attributed to Kurt Meyer's Div. I don't deny there has been the occasional martinet, we had them on our side, too. I once shot two Canadians out of a tree, on orders from a young infantry officer who had mistaken them for German snipers. These things are unavoidable. The medieval 'After you, my dear Alphonse' is not the pattern. The modern method is not to teach the recruit to die for his country, but to make the enemy soldier die for his; for in that attitude lies success. I do not condone the extermination of the Jews, nor the execution of political prisoners; I am talking about incidents in a theatre of war.

"But I must admit that these alleged atrocities served, as good propaganda at this time, for the news got around fast that the panzers were taking no prisoners. '*Act with that in mind*,' we were told, and there was actually an order-of-the-day published saying that we must not take prisoners. This created quite a furore and the officer concerned was called to the carpet; but to give him the benefit of the doubt, it was stated that all he meant was that tanks should not take prisoners but leave them to the infantry. This got him off the hook, but I still smile. I don't think he was fooling. It made the Canadians all fighting mad, a very good point in battle, almost a necessity to a green man. We often saw cases of men actually hesitating to shoot an enemy; a certain natural reticence at pulling the trigger point-blank on a human being. This is a normal reaction for the first time; after that, it's easy."

After Le Mesnil-Patry the offensive drives by both sides in the Canadian sector petered out, in the same pattern of mutual exhaustion as was occurring east of the Orne. The Padre and Serjeant Gariepy were able to get out to the tanks they had lost on 11 June in order to identify the dead. "In some cases the bodies were indistinguishable from one another, simply a mass of cooked flesh welded together in the great heat; we had to sift through this for identity tags. Each tank told the same story —broken legs, broken arms, open-chest wounds, and so on, had trapped many, so that they had burnt alive. The screams I thought I had heard during the action had not been imaginary after all." The horror of all this, under a summer sun, in the ripening corn, seemed a blasphemy to British and German alike. "During the next few weeks we lay in a sport stadium close to the outskirts of Buron," said Kurt Misch, an officer-cadet of 12th S.S. "I remember the unselfish actions of our own medical staff, and of French civilian doctors also, in treating all those in need, without any distinction of friend or foe. In daylight, I have seen Allied fighter-bombers dive on any vehicle which moved, including even despatch riders, and literally hunt them down the road. Reliefs took place by night, and even the bringing up of rations involved a trip of life or death. One particular night I most vividly remember. My wireless operator and I were moving up to relieve the team in our Forward Observation Post, and we took always as our land mark in the darkness a gigantic crucifix, nearly twenty feet high. Lit by the flashes of artillery fire, lonely yet comforting, it stood among the corn in this blood-soaked field. That night, it was gone, destroyed by a direct hit; yet we reached unharmed our forward positions."

Only on the right flank did the British offensive achieve, momentarily, a deep penetration in the effort to encircle Caen. There, the fruitful earth of summer burst into flame, as the attackers, with dread in their hearts, got up out of the corn to go forward and expose naked flesh to the savage whine of shell-splinter and tearing bullet.

CHAPTER SEVEN

WE'RE GOING SWANNING!

*The 'Right Hook' round Caen—the Twin Tank-Battles of
Villers-Bocage and Caumont
10 to 18 June*

7 Armoured Division began to advance through 50 (Northumbrian) Infantry Division on 10 June, supported by some independent infantry and tank brigades. This was the 'right hook', the drive to encircle Caen from the west, and it had far more weight behind it than the abortive attack out of the Airborne bridgehead east of the Orne, or the pacing Canadian advance in the centre. Even so, it was extremely ambitious, for even when Panzer Lehr Division had been identified, it was still thought possible to encircle them and perhaps compel their surrender. The 'Lehr', or demonstration division, was the most formidably-equipped armoured formation in Normandy at that time, and was led by Generalleutnant Fritz Bayerlein, Rommel's former chief-of-staff in Africa. Its fast, reliable Mark IVs were backed by a heavy tank battalion of Panthers and Tigers, and by much specialised armour.

On the other hand, 7 Armoured Division had brought back from the Mediterranean a nickname ('the Desert Rats'), a good fighting record; and very little else. Their tanks, vehicles, and guns they had left behind them in Italy. In place of the Shermans, they were now using Cromwells, light 'cavalry' tanks, ideal for a fast pursuit, but unsuitable for the Normandy bocage. In the uninhibited atmosphere of the B.A.O.R., the Division's first anonymous historian could afford to be really scathing in his comments on the horrible collection of unsuitable vehicles and equipment to which the Division was hurriedly converted in England, and particularly in regard to the inadequacy of ranges and training areas. Of the enemy's heavy 'infantry' tanks, he had this to say: " The Panther and the Tiger were both more heavily armoured than our own tanks, and mounted a gun which, in the case of the Panther, was the equal of our 17 pounder, with the additional advantage that it could fire H.E., and, in the case of the Tiger, superior to any tank or anti-tank gun we possessed. In the Normandy fighting their heavy armour and armament amply compensated for any disadvantage they might have had due to their lack of speed, though this latter factor, coupled with a lower standard of mechanical reliability, was to tell heavily against the enemy during the great advances."[1]

Panzer Lehr had started to come into action opposite part of the Canadian sector, but the reception there was so hot that Rommel ordered the Division to side-step left and attack up the long, straight road to Bayeux. Part only were in the line on 10 June, a number of units being still on the long road to Normandy, leaving behind them the burnt-out, bullet-riddled wrecks of many vehicles, including Bayerlein's own staff car, victims of the R.A.F. Nevertheless, they had driven to within three miles of Bayeux until ordered to halt as a result of the battle of Le Mesnil-Patry on 11 June. The German infantry, caught there massed in the cross-fire, had suffered heavy casualties, and the armoured reinforcements which the Canadians had at once brought up seemed to the Germans a serious threat to this weak point, the junction between Panzer Lehr and 12th S.S. Therefore, Lehr were ordered to go onto the defensive in the Tilly-sur-Seulles area, the line to be thickened up as the lagging units arrived one by one, and as a result the 30 Corps drive went in against a part of the line which was being reinforced continually. By 12 June, it was clear that the 'right hook' had not even started to swing; Panzer Lehr had blocked it at the shoulder. The British were being altogether too successful in their 'decoy' mission of pinning down the German armour. "By the evening of June 12," wrote General Bradley, "we had celebrated our first week ashore without a single threatening counter-attack on the American beachhead." On the right of 30 Corps, the Americans were reporting almost no opposition to their advance on Caumont, twenty miles inland; and it was this tempting ease of advance, in contrast to their own experiences, which suggested to the British a shift westwards of the whole offensive, moving

[1] *A Short History of 7th Armoured Division*, B.A.O.R., 1945.

the attack on Caen further away from Caen, towards the American sector. There, a maze of apparently undefended secondary roads and tracks led round the flank of Panzer Lehr towards their original objective, the high ground behind Villers-Bocage.

As 7 Armoured Division moved off on 12 June, the word spread: We're *going swanning*. This was more like it! The Desert Rats did not enjoy being tied down in the close country-side of the bocage, its tiny strip fields bordered by deep ditches and high thick-banked hedges, their roots as firm in the Norman earth as if set in concrete and impassable to most tanks. The enemy was literally within speaking distance, concealed even at the moment when his guns fired. As a Yankee soldier who fought at Caumont told a relieving British unit, " We reckon it's rough here. You can reach through the hedge and put the safety-catch on their Spandaus." While 50 Div tried unavailingly to push back Panzer Lehr, 7 Armoured sidestepped to the west, and drove through three-quarters of a great circle, first into the American sector, then south through the gap in the German defences, and, when abreast of Caumont, swinging eastwards again to come in behind Panzer Lehr at Villers-Bocage. By the morning of 13 June, the armour of 4 County of London Yeomanry (the ' Sharpshooters '), backed by the half-tracked infantry of 1st Battalion the Rifle Brigade, were moving up the centre-line into the town of Villers-Bocage, without opposition; although the flank units, 8th and 11th Hussars, were slowed down by contact with the enemy. They were six miles behind the German lines.

A Squadron of the Sharpshooters, accompanied by A Squadron of the Rifle Brigade, forming a composite group of armour and armoured infantry, drove clean through the town and dashed for the vital high ground to the east, Hill 213, where the national highway led straight to Caen. Bunched up, in order not to slow the advance of the rest of the division, coming on behind, they roared forward, cheered by the civilians; a compact mass of Cromwell tanks, light Honey tanks, two de-gunned O.P. tanks, half-tracks, and Bren carriers, including R.H.Q. of the Sharpshooters. Unknown to them, Hill 213 was occupied by 2 Company of Heavy S.S. Tank Battalion 501, commanded by Obersturmführer Michel Wittmann, a tank ' ace ' from the

Russian front with 119 victories to his credit. They had just arrived, after a long and arduous drive from Beauvais, and only four of their Tigers were operational.

Immediately available to him, to block the breakthrough of an entire British armoured division was one Tiger—his own. From the corner of the wood where his gigantic fighting vehicle was hidden, Wittmann fired one shot from his high-velocity 88 mm gun. One of the leading vehicles in the British column, a half-track of 1 Rifle Brigade, slewed in blazing ruin across the road, effectively blocking the British advance. Then the Tiger, shrugging off its cover, rolled ponderously forward to the road and turned down it towards Villers-Bocage, presenting only its massive front armour to the British guns. Half-track after half-track went up in flames, the evil smoke helping the survivors to hide from the Tiger's machine-guns. Then it encountered a tank, the Cromwell commanded by Major Carr, second-in-command of the Sharpshooters. The Cromwell's gun fired point-blank and, for all the apparent effect it had, it might have been a pea-shooter. The Tiger stopped, the 88 mm steadied, then the menacingly long barrel thundered. The Cromwell was instantly wrapped in flame and the dense, welling smoke of a ' brew up '. Steadily down the road clanked the Tiger, like some impervious dinosaur out of pre-history, belching poisonous flame, which consumed its victims. First, the vehicles which composed R.H.Q. of the Sharpshooters; then two of the R.H.Q. tanks; then a third R.H.Q. tank, commanded by Captain Dyas, which had unwisely attempted to stalk the Tiger from behind, the comparative weak spot, at this range, of the rolling steel fortress. But the wily Wittmann was not victor over 119 Russian tanks for nothing. The move was seen, the great turret swung ponderously round, the 88 spoke. And Captain Dyas, too, was bailing out of a wrecked Cromwell. In a brief five minutes, Wittmann is believed to have accounted for 25 British armoured vehicles. The full loss, after R.H.Q. and the leading companies had been surrounded by the rest of Wittmann's command and infantry from Panzer Lehr, totalled 25 tanks, 14 half-tracks, and 14 Bren carriers, according to the British official history. The spearhead of 7 Armoured Division had been annihilated.

The Germans rolled on into Villers-Bocage, but the British

did not retreat. Small parties of infantry, with Piats, and supported by 6-pounder anti-tank guns, began to stalk the Tigers. One 6-pounder was run into position inside a house; a Tiger rammed the wall, and the house fell down. Another Tiger took cover inside a shop and was fired at by a Cromwell lurking round the corner of a sidestreet. Wittmann's own Tiger had a track blown off, and the ace of the East Front bailed out. Two other Tigers were hit by Piat projectiles and no one bailed out; the bomb was designed to funnel its charge through a tiny hole in the plating and spread the occupants all over the inside, like jam. The Tigers burned, and the local fire brigade, the Pompiers, joined the battle on the side of the S.S., trying to put out the fires in the German tanks.[2] The town was untenable and unrelievable, the divisional commander[3] decided, and those who could do so began to retreat about nightfall.

One factor was the failure of 50 Div to get forward at all that day to their support. Another was the staggering shock inflicted by the legendary Tigers, which resulted later in the formulation of a general rule: if 1 Tiger is reported, send 4 Shermans or 4 Churchills, and expect to lose 3 of them. The third, and weightiest factor of all, was the arrival of the leading elements of a new, and totally unexpected, armoured formation —Generalleutnant Heinrich Freiherr von Lüttwitz's 2nd (Vienna) Panzer Division, which had made a rapid march from the Abbeville-Amiens area without being detected. Now, they were beginning to fan out: north-west for Caumont, north for Livry, north-east for Villers-Bocage. Had the planned seaborne reinforcements of armour and infantry reached the British at this time, they might have decided to hold on; but the build-up had now fallen two whole days behind schedule and the units which might have tipped the scales were still in their ships. Instead of encircling Panzer Lehr (which had not budged, but was stubbornly beating back 50 Div from Tilly), the lightly-equipped 7 Armoured Division was likely to be crushed between two superior armoured formations. But although their spearhead had gone, the British did not immediately withdraw the shaft;

[2] See *The Desert Rats*, by Major-General G. L. Verney.
[3] Then Major-General Erskine, who was succeeded by Major-General Verney two months later.

instead, as if by desert instinct, the Desert Rats contracted into a compact defensive box which the troops nicknamed the 'Island'. And on 14 June, the Germans began a general attack upon it from three sides.

7th Armoured rapidly discovered that this was not the desert. Because of the close nature of the country, only G battery of 5 R.H.A. was able to engage, and with only one Troop at that —four self-propelled 25-pounder guns. " We had heavy casualties, because we were tightly packed into a defensive box," said Arthur H. Markham, acting Quartermaster of G Battery. " There was a vehicle to every ten square yards. The first shell to arrive was American, which was off-putting, and that was followed at once by German shelling; and the first German shell landed on my own Q2 vehicle, ruining the engine, seriously injuring the driver, and forcing us into a half-completed slit trench for eight hours, except for a few dashes out to get at our Bren, which was buried under scrimmage netting in the back of the truck. We had never expected to use it. Now we were told we were cut off. The shelling became very heavy and we were told that German infantry were coming in to attack; they were now about half-a-mile away. The guns of our battery took them on over open sights, with air burst fuses, and halted them. We couldn't see much ourselves, but were told later that it was a classic piece of defensive fire and that not one German infantryman reached our lines." The attack of the panzer grenadiers had petered out 400 yards from the gun muzzles. In the bocage, it was very much easier to defend than to attack.

That night, under cover of an R.A.F. raid, 7th Armoured was pulled back seven miles and the first major attempt to encircle Caen had failed. " It was the only defensive battering that the 5 R.H.A. had had to take, all the way from Alamein," said Markham. " Only now did we lower our colours, so to speak. But the loss of my Quartermaster vehicle came in handy; when anything was found deficient later on, the excuse was: ' Oh, we had that on Markham's Q2, and we lost that at Villers-Bocage '."

*   *   *

Faced now by four German armoured divisions, General Montgomery reported that, as he was not strong enough to carry out simultaneous offensives at both ends of the British front, he intended to go over to the defensive in front of Caen and put on pressure in the area of Caumont. But already the left battle group of 2 Panzer Division was advancing on Caumont; by nightfall on 13 June they had forced the British off Hill 174, near Cahagnes, and had nearly cut the road between Caumont and Amaye-sur-Orne. Thus, momentarily, the battle for Caen moved away from Caen.

One of the men who took part in this advance was Ober-feldwebel Hans Erich Braun, a senior N.C.O. of a tank-hunting unit, Panzer-Jäger-Abteilung 38 (Sf). The German ' SF ' had the same meaning as the British ' SP '—it stood for self-propelled.[4] But while the 1st and 2nd Companies had a dozen 'long' 75 mm guns, each mounted on the chassis of a Mark IV tank, Braun's 3rd Company was equipped with nine 75 mm anti-tank guns drawn by half-tracks. " On the 14th of June ", he said, " the battle area south-east of Caumont was still covered in thick mist. The night had been quiet, apart from British artillery fire on the back areas, and the new dawn came slowly. At 5.30 a.m., approximately, the English stopped firing. Possibly they took their morning coffee at that time.[5] We, too, drank a kind of coffee at this hour, a brew which not even by smell, let alone taste, deserved the name. Only the previous day we had snatched a British patrol near les Bruyéres, and, lacking anything better, had offered the four flabbergasted Tommies a sip of the so-called ' Muckefuck ' from our field-flasks. Never shall I forget their horrified faces! They took one sip, shuddered (as though we had offered them hydrochloric acid), and immediately spat out the raven-black, unsugared concoction, before apologising with an ' I'm sorry ', for their only too understandable reaction.

" This early in the morning there were no enemy Jabos (fighter-bombers) in the air; only the ' Iron Tommy ', their artil-lery observer, who was already in his plane and spooking about in the sky. Under these conditions, it was soon to be almost

[4] In wartime, in most armies, most words are officially abbreviated, both in correspondence and conversation: *e.g.* ' Reinforcements ' was written ' Rfts ' and pronounced ' Rufts '. ' Division ' was always ' Div ', 'Infantry' always ' Inf.'

[5] One British formation, when requesting fire from ships of the Royal Navy, never thought to ask for it at ' pink gin time ', unless the enemy was absolutely hammering at the gates.

impossible for us to move by day. Most of our division were living as if on a platter held out under the eyes of the enemy, for his inspection. From Caumont, especially from one of the town's highest towers, the enemy could see everything, and fired at the slightest movement in the forward area, usually with several batteries combined. However, the three 75 mm anti-tank guns of my Troop were so well dug in and camouflaged, in the orchards and by the field paths which ran to the north, that it was impossible for anyone who did not actually know that they were there to spot them from a distance of twenty paces. The thick, rather wild foliage of the bocage helped a lot. We felt at home in this landscape with its rows of hedges, over-grown stone walls, and deeply-sunken roads, where one could see for only fifty or a hundred yards. And we had been in action so many times before, that whenever there was a halt, even if only for a few hours, we instinctively seized our spades and dug as deeply as possible, in order to disappear inside the protective earth. Things like field-of-fire, cover, and camouflage had become a habit with us, and we had become masters at them all. Several times, during those first few days in Normandy, we allowed enemy patrols, tanks, or armoured cars to come so close that our sudden fire overwhelmed the British. Their infantry fell and their supporting tanks went up in flames, before they had a chance to hit back.

"We very soon found out that the enemy had previously fought in the desert and fought more than shy of an encounter at such close quarters. For us, however, it was different. So often in Russia we had fought hand-to-hand, busting up a Russian infantry attack with pistols, hand-grenades, even spades. We were used to those witches' cauldrons at close quarters, those battles in the woods, with their bushes and dense undergrowth. Sometimes for months, we had known nothing else. So here, at first, it was battle experience and better nerves which counted, and not just superiority of weapons and equipment.

"Often, we were accused of fighting fanatically, but we had long since learned the lesson, that one thing alone counts in war: to fire first, by a fraction of a second, and kill; or otherwise, be killed oneself. Apart from that, in this sixth year of the war, we Germans knew what was in store for us. But because we were in reality defending our homeland, our parents, our wives and children, who had already suffered unspeakably from the attacks of the enemy night-bombers, we were determined, if necessary, to fall by our guns before we would let the enemy advance a step further.

"And now, as the sun slowly rose that morning of the 14th, the mist began to disappear. The 'Iron Tommy' droned lower still overhead, and men who had been moving about, covered by the mist, began to vanish into the ground until finally all was quiet and there was nothing to be seen, not even in the slit-trenches of the grenadiers a bare thirty to sixty yards ahead of us. By 6.30 a.m., it was clear, the British gunners had finished their breakfast. For fifteen minutes there was a continuous howling and shrieking in and around the orchards. Shells thunder-clapped, throwing up clouds of smoke and dust; red-hot splinters, lumps of earth, shattered branches, and splintered tiles from the farmhouse roof behind us, flew round our ears at each detonation. But this was only the beginning. Minutes later, after we had just carried two of our wounded to safety in the farmhouse cellar, it seemed that the very earth around us was going to burst.

" Hundreds of shells of all calibres literally ploughed up the gardens. Dozens of hits shook the walls of the farm and set its roof on fire. Thick smoke clouds as bitter as gall, from the high explosive, made breathing difficult and irritated our throats so that we developed a dry cough. A hurricane of fire raged through the countryside, wrapping everything in grey smoke and dirt; only once before, in the great battle near Orel, had we ever experienced anything like this. Then, suddenly, it stopped.

"In the strange quiet, we heard the high-pitched hum of aero engines, which rose to a growl, and then to a terrifying, whining fortissimo, punctuated by the rattling of machine-guns. But the growl of engines grew louder still. Like the rabbit in front of the snake which it knows is about to strike, we stared from our holes into the morning sky. Through the thinning mist we could dimly see swarms of British Typhoons circling us like hawks. From my trench, which I had dug beside a stone wall five yards from our gun position, I noticed a group of seven Jabos break away from the great formation and begin to fall like thrown stones onto a grenadier position 200 yards to our left. Flashes of light rippled along their wings as they fired. It was as though a deadly sewing-machine was stitching up the bushes and the gardens, stabbing and tearing at everything in its path. Instantly, several of our vehicles, parked out of sight in a sunken road, went up in flames, marking our positions for the enemy with columns of jet-black ascending smoke. We could almost hear the pilots calling down their comrades onto us. And then they came.

" Hell broke loose. Machine-gun bursts mingled with the screeching of rockets. Some of the Typhoons were still diving, firing down into our trenches, when their noses were only a few yards above the tree-tops. We lay huddled here, pulses beating, while the ricochets went chirping through the bushes, or hit with a crack against the stone walls. Through the roaring, whining engine noise drilled the mechanical Pappappappapp Drtdrtdrt-drtdrtdrt of their cannons and machine-guns and the Pfiupfiu-pfiupfiupfiu of the bullets. Then the bombs came whistling down, nearly bursting our eardrums, and men, weapons and fragments of shattered vehicles were thrown into the air. Explosive rockets came howling away from under the wings of some of them. They burst on the ground, brightly-glaring as a lightning flash, leaving behind a spray of a thousand splinters. For an eternity of minutes, the screaming of my wounded comrades, and the terrified roaring of mortally-wounded cattle which had been grazing in the fields, was mingled with the chaotic sound of the low-level air attack. There were cattle lying in pools of blood, and others were battering their heads against walls and fences as though they had gone mad. When the last pilot pulled his machine back into the sky, then already the ' Iron Tommy ' was hovering overhead, to direct another fire-hurricane by the British artillery, which in violence left nothing to be desired."

In fact, American as well as British artillery were involved, in close liaison. There were code names for various-sized concentrations of guns. The American code for their specialty, which could only be ordered by a General, was, aptly enough, ' Pandemonium '. One British commanding officer who put in a request for ' Pandemonium ', and got it, to spoil an expected attack by infantry of 2 Panzer Division, rather suspected that the ammunition expenditure caused telegrams of protest from

Washington. Nevertheless, the right-hand Battle Group of 2nd Panzer attacked next day, 15 June, and took Launay and St. Germain d'Ectot, although with heavy losses; and on 17 June, the left-hand Battle Group attacked northwards against le Quesnay.

"By now", wrote Braun, who was with this latter group, "the breath of decay and destruction lay heavy over the bocage. For days the carcasses of cows and calves killed by the enemy's fire had lain in the fields. Bloated to bursting point like swollen balloons, their legs sticking up stiffly towards the sky, or with sides ripped, torn, and covered by a myriad of blue-shimmering flies, they exuded an indescribable smell and made life anywhere near them almost impossible. Some of the animals which were still alive were almost mad. You could tell that by their protruding eyes and foam-covered muzzles. Now and then they would go bucking and raving, tails up and heads down, bellowing and roaring, into a gallop against the heavy fences, snorting and charging until their horns broke off. This gruesome game was continually repeated, until they broke down and died, rattling in the throat. Only now and then would one of the soldiers rise up in his slit-trench to make an end of the suffering animal with a well-aimed bullet, for every time a soldier took pity, the stench only became worse.

"In spite of the enemy's strength in artillery and in the air, our left Battle Group assembled early on the morning of 17 June for yet another attack towards the north. In our Company we had five operational anti-tank guns left; their task was to follow close behind the attacking grenadiers, down roads or paths, or across the patch-work of fields. At the start, I was with the two remaining guns of my Troop, in support of Panzer Grenadier Regiment 304. Overhead, as we assembled, shrilled and whispered the protective barrage from Artillery Regiment 74. Our grenadiers rose up from their trenches and went forward, firing their machine-pistols and machine-guns from the hip as they advanced. In this way, and with some close combat, they got into the outskirts of le Quesnay. We pushed our guns forward, muzzle first, straining and heaving, to keep up with them.

"We entered a sunken road with high hedges on either side, and tree branches overhead, which led to a small stream near the south-west corner of le Quesnay. After we had advanced 200 yards down it, shells exploded in the branches above our heads and there was a rain of splinters. I felt a heavy blow on my right heel, and simultaneously heard several comrades call for aid. I got up, and saw that a splinter had torn away half the heel of my boot. That was luck, for now I could help the wounded men. Three of our unit were lightly wounded, but two of the grenadiers who had been helping us to push the guns were dead—the splinters had even penetrated their steel helmets. While we were still bandaging the wounded men, we heard a very loud sound of engines, and there was a shout of, *'Anti-tank guns—forward!'*

" I told the crew of the first gun to get it forward at the double, then ran along the sunken road in front, followed by my messenger, Obergefr. Graef. Up there, it was thick with grenadiers, lying behind their panzerfausts and covering every arc of fire. To one side was an overgrown stone wall, through which a gap led out onto a broad field. Several Englishmen were lying in the gap, gun in hand, where they had been shot down. We got hold of their feet and quickly pulled them to one side. Meanwhile, the roar of heavy engines had become even louder and now we could plainly hear also the clatter of tank-tracks. With his machine-gun spraying and his gun firing explosive shells continually, directly to his front, the enemy tank hoped to shoot his way through us.

" But now, at last, my gun had arrived. It was already camouflaged as a bush, so we ran it directly into the gap in the stone wall, while shells and bullets screamed overhead and ricochets cracked around. Frantically, the gunner cranked the hand-wheel, and slowly the barrel swung round to the left, where at any moment the enemy tank would appear. A hail of mortar bombs forced us to duck for cover, and it was clear that there were British infantry nearby, for we could hear several of our fast-firing German machine-guns in frenzied action. Then the enemy tank came into sight, 130 yards away, half-left. Obviously, it was in another part of the sunken road, for we got no more than a glimpse of the top of its turret, before it vanished behind the next bulge of the hedge. From the noise, there were several other tanks following on behind it. Finally its turret and upper hull rode into sight where the stone wall was so low that the overgrowth could no longer hide it. It was a Cromwell, its gun pointing half-right; that is, past our gun to the right. I gave the command: 'Fire!' Simultaneously, some of the grenadiers let fly with their panzerfausts (which only tore holes in the ground short of the tank), and my gunner pulled the trigger.

" Bright-red flame: a terrific detonation: a violent blast of air. The shell screeched away towards the Cromwell, hitting the sloping top of the turret, and shooting straight up into the smoke-obscured sky, hissing and spitting. Unfortunate. The British gun began to swing in our direction, as the turret revolved. My crew re-loaded with solid shot, and fired again before the enemy gun could bear. The shell went straight through the turret and, thinking that the enemy gunner was now probably out of action, my crew recommenced firing with the appropriate ammunition, this time into the lightly-armoured side. Immediately a deep blue flame, surrounded by a bright flash, leapt up from the tank; there was a terrific explosion; and the Cromwell literally burst apart. We dived for the ground. Heavy armour plating and the complete turret of the ' steel box ' flew in an arc through the air, howling and whistling, to land with a series of crashes in the bushes or the treetops. There was one more explosion, as the petrol tank burst, and then a dense, black cloud of burning petrol welled up.

" But this also alerted the Jabos who were circling overhead, trying to identify us, and they immediately attacked, so that we could hear the angels sing in heaven. Over to the left, another Cromwell had been knocked out, this time by two grenadiers with Panzerfausts. And eventually we got into le Quesnay, fighting house-by-house, cellar-by-cellar. In sixty minutes, the grenadiers lost 9 men killed and 26 wounded, but the British, too, left some of their feathers behind, for everywhere, in the road, on the paths, in the gardens, lay their dead and wounded, but there was no time to stop just then. We were supporting the grenadiers by firing explosives point-blank into the houses.

" We had started at 4.30 in the morning. At 7.30, in addition to our losses in the sunken road, earlier, the commander of my first gun, Corporal Berger, was killed and two of the crew seriously wounded. We carried them into the nearest half-ruined house for shelter, and would have run into trouble but for the fact that some of the grenadiers who were helping us push the guns had searched the cellar of it a few minutes before. They fetched out two Britons armed with machine-pistols, whom they had found hiding behind some cider barrels. They seemed suspiciously gay and jolly, and not a little confused—perhaps because of the German fire and the surprisingly swift assault. Anyway, although a grenadier lieutenant told them to get busy helping their own wounded who were lying in the road outside, they seemed, or pretended, not to understand. However, accompanied by a medical orderly of the grenadiers, they at last went out to bring in to shelter their wounded comrades.

" In the north part of the town and in the adjacent orchards, the British infantry were still fiercely holding out. Here we cleaned up a shed, after pushing our gun through someone's backyard. At the first shot, a number of Englishmen, some wounded, came out to surrender. This was lucky, for we had only two rounds left. Eventually, we were pulled back to regroup, and while sorting ourselves out, found a Bedford truck in the bushes. We tossed out tins of beer, lemonade, tinned pineapple, whole boxes of corned beef, and any amount of the excellent Navy Cut cigarettes. The men at the gun were as happy as little children when they saw these luxuries, of which they had been deprived for a very long time. Then we got down to digging in, for the forecast was ' iron ' air. At the moment, the British artillery and air force had no idea which part of le Quesnay was held by our forces, and which by theirs; but they would know soon. So I decided to take that opportunity to go back with my messenger, Gräf, to find out what had happened to the crew of my second gun. I hadn't seen a single one of them since the destruction of the Cromwell tank.

" We worked back cautiously, keeping 100 yards clear of the road, which was under mortar fire, until, as we were passing a farm where a number of vehicles were blazing, the British artillery opened up again; the flashes leapt from the ground around us and the detonations whirled debris through the air, as we dived into some abandoned British mortar positions. Now came another drumfire, raging through the countryside, and the Typhoons joined in, flashing down on le Quesnay with rattling guns and hissing rockets. We became hidden in thick, evil-smelling smoke. Burning houses. Burning vehicles. Burning rubber. And perhaps also a Pioneer lorry was on fire, for thick, white, bitter-scented smoke poured over us, obscuring the sky. We heard tank-guns behind us, the clatter of tracks and the growling of heavy tank-engines. Was a British counter-attack coming in?

"Now, the British artillery fire began to lift, and to search further back, apparently to prevent us bringing up our reserves, so we pulled ourselves together and ran wildly from cover to cover, across dead British and German soldiers, jumping over bomb craters, keeping close to the stone walls bordering the fields, when we could. With racing pulses and hammering hearts, we at last reached that sunken road from which we had destroyed the Cromwell. We had no sooner got there than we had to take cover in a trench, for the British began to lay a 'fire-roller' on the southern outskirts of le Quesnay, and this rolling barrage was moving steadily towards us, rending the ground with prehistoric violence. At moments like these, when death seems so close and certain, one is incapable of thought. So close to the earth do you lie, that you feel as thin as a pancake. Every muscle is tensed, all breathing stops. The heart beats madly and the nerves are taut and vibrating. Waiting for the terrible pain, the tearing of the body; the impact of the razor-sharp, red-hot shell splinters. Cramped fingers claw the soil; perhaps a prayer, or the name of a loved person far away is pressed from between tight lips—or even an animal-like scream which relaxes the lungs through a mouth thick with earth. This is what happens under this hell thought out by humans.

"With an almost mathematical exactitude the fire-roller destroys the countryside yard by yard. Close in front, a shell screamed down and exploded, throwing earth and stones over us. Then another detonation sent a heavy body flying through the air, to thump down on the right of my trench. A putrid stench made me want to vomit. Despite the roaring fire, I lifted my head and with suddenly-opened eyes saw not an arm's length away the rotting insides of a cow, crawling with maggots. My stomach turned over and I began to retch. I had meant to shout out to Gräf, who was behind me, that I was still all right, but my stomach was still revolting against the stench, and I could not do it.

"At last, the fire-roller was gone. Drunkenly, I stood up, and looked for Gräf. He lay a few yards behind me, still pressed close to the earth. As I went towards him, he did not move, and I then saw the two sharp-edged, blood-soaked splinter holes just below one shoulder-blade. Gently, I turned my comrade over. His dusty face, with its stubble of beard, was pale already with the pallor of death. Thin little rivulets of blood from nose and mouth were the infallible sign. His broken eyes were blood-shot, the whitish-yellow eyeballs turned inward. I closed his eyes and then, suddenly, something burst inside me. I screamed and raged like someone possessed. I cursed the war and our damned fate, I blasphemed God, who allowed all this to happen, and I made a vow, to make the enemy pay bitterly for all this.

"A call for help quickly brought me to my senses. Over at the sunken road the half-track which towed my second gun was blazing. I left Gräf and ran as though driven by furies across the cratered field. Between the tracks of the flaming vehicle, which was loaded with ammunition, lay two badly wounded men from my Troop. A third wounded man, Corporal Dempf, was trying to pull the two men out from under the vehicle. I joined him, and together we extricated L/Corporal Kneur and Mehringer, the Oberschütze. Thinking Kneur was still too near the half-track, I was running back to it when a hissing flame shot vertically upwards from it, and as I flung myself to the ground, the ammunition exploded.

" The half-track disintegrated, its parts raining down over a wide area, and from where it had stood, stifling clouds of black smoke welled up to foul the air. When the last fragment had fallen, I raised my head and looked for Kneur. Mehringer was all right, we had taken him round a bend in the sunken road, but Kneur we had laid down quickly, in the shelter of our knocked-out second gun, 20 yards from the half-track. The blast from the explosion had done for him; it had rolled the gun backwards across his body.

" Then the first waves of retiring grenadiers began to pass us, and we could hear the roar of enemy tanks above their artillery and mortar fire. The British had forced their way back into le Quesnay, and cut the line of retreat for the German half-tracks and lorries. It could have been a catastrophe, but energetic officers and N.C.O.s stopped the panic and the British attack was halted. At the end of the day, we were back precisely where we had started from. But next morning, our depleted companies advanced once more against le Quesnay, took it, and pushed on to Briquessard; and all our abandoned tanks and weapons fell into our hands again in good order, even to the single remaining anti-tank gun of my platoon. But what had we gained? A little ground, laughably unimportant, exchanged for irreplaceable manpower. When I sat down that evening of 18 June, in the cellar of a ruined farm house, and looked at the few remaining men of my platoon, I saw in their faces the knowledge that this war in Normandy was lost for us. Behind them lay the campaign in Poland, the breaking of the Maginot Line, the taking of Boulogne in 1940 from the stubborn British. Then the New Zealanders in Greece, the great tank battle of Wjasma in the Soviet Union, the advance towards Moscow in 40°C. of frost, so that, as the vanguard division of the German Army, they came to within 23 kilometres of the Kremlin. Then the defensive battles, Gsatsk, Kursk, Orel. You need a large map of Europe to point out the graves of our dead during the Second World War. Privation, strain of battle, and fear of death had marked their faces; but they faced with courage the three alternatives of the future: a grave, disablement, or a prison camp."

CHAPTER EIGHT

SMUDGER, YOU'LL NEVER GET TO 'EAVEN

Death on the Beaches—Mine Clearance—the Sniper—the
Bayeux Tapestry—the Normans—the Priest—the Convents
at Caen and Pont L'Abbe
8 to 18 June

Life, for the man who carried a rifle in Normandy, where battalions lost 200 men in a day, was not long. The path of the advance was marked by the rifles of the fallen that summer, stuck, bolt-less, muzzle-down into the red earth, with a tin-hat aslant on the butt, and perhaps on the raw mound a battered can, with a little water and some wilting flowers in it, placed there by some unknown villager. Identity disc, sometimes, or a crude board inscribed *Unknown Scottish Soldier*. Sometimes, a specific name: *Wolfgang Dietrich, 27th S.S. Regt., Panzer Grenadiers*. Or, sometimes, more hurriedly interred, no headboard at all; just a clawed hand reaching through turned earth for the sky, or the toecap of a mildewed boot. And some were not buried at all, until found the following year, ruined things much closer then to earth. But they are gone now, in Normandy, gathered into disciplined legions where the crisp white headboards stand in stiff, drilled ranks, as if the dead rose up to be counted; and the Germans and Austrians stand up shoulder to shoulder with the British and the Canadians, in line together for the final parade. It would take long to count them all, even so meticulously aligned as they are. We thought it would have been better to leave them where they fell, by the wayside tended by some village girl, in individual graves. For there, they were no longer an army, but men like you and I.

Not all were fighting men, or ever struck a blow before they died. Where the tanks had ground to white powder the roads that ran between the white-walled cottages of Norman stone, and the signboards shrieked *Dust is Death,* there the Military Police, the once-hated, the once-despised, stood impeccable at the cross-roads, ranged to a yard on the German maps. They fell like flies that summer, to be instantly replaced by another just as immaculate in red cap and white webbing, until he too fell, a bundle of red and twisted rags face-downwards in the deep white dust. The battle, the final purpose of the journey, lay at the end of those dusty roads, signposted *Forward Area—Straight On.* There, the long lines of trucks groaned in low gear towards chaos and where, on the verge of the maelstrom, the trim ranks of guns thundered into the smoke. Beyond, death was anonymous, without face or name. Whoever spoke of the ' heat of battle ' never referred to this. There was nothing to see—not in flank, nor in front. There was only an area where nothing moved, and yet the breath was quick with tension. Only the defeated were visible: the dead, the wounded, the bloated cattle. The burning farm, the dust, the flies, and the summer breeze blowing the acrid smoke across the corn. Corn is life and now, among the corn, there was so much death. Jagged, unexpected. The bullet-whine the soldier never heard. The treachery of mine and booby-trap. The shell that screamed for a second before it thunder-clapped amid the grass; the hot fragments that whined away out of the black smoke. The Panther that rode out from behind the farm, massive, invincible, with its distortedly long gun and hot, watchful eyes behind the Spandaus.

Behind, the sea was a roadway that never wore out—a living bridge of ships from England to Normandy. They moved along the swept channels in the minefields like some vast conveyor-belt out of a madman's imagination; a supply line held in place by the destroyers and corvettes, their stained hulls rising to the slow swell, their guns raking the horizon with each lift and fall of the sea. Normandy was the focus of the world that summer, and by summer's end, more than a million men had come by sea to Normandy; approaching stealthily in the night-time while the bombers raced across the moon and the fiery gouts of tracer poured up from ten thousand guns; until the burning day began and the landing craft turned in for the shore, to where the sand dunes ahead erupted with the smoke and crack of exploding mines.

*   *   *

When Corporal Harry Bloodworth Smith went ashore at Queen Beach on 8 June with 23 Bomb Disposal Company, R.E., he saw the bodies of two young civilians, hanging from the branches of a tree, side by side, eyes bulging, heads aslant. A Frenchman approached the group of newly-landed soldiers and asked if he might have the hanged men's boots. "We assumed the Germans had done this," said Smith, adding as an after-thought, twenty years later, " of course the Germans got blamed for everything in those days." With him, 'Smudger' Smith had five men. There was an air raid that night, and in the morning he buried two of them. When the main body of the unit arrived, his squad was made up to strength again and ordered to clear a path up the cliffs, along which was to be laid the first sub-marine cable connecting London with Normandy. The cliff was a ruin, pocked with bomb and shell craters, sown with Teller and 'S' mines "like grass-seed", and flecked with fragments of bomb and shell casing which started the detectors ticking for a false alarm. The mechanical gadgets, which weirdly resembled vacuum cleaners, were blind; a mine, an old tin can, or a shell splinter were all the same to them. So when the ticking started, the sapper had to stop and dig around the suspicious object with his hands, very slowly and carefully. After a time, at a buzz which seemed weak, there was the temptation to think, ' *Oh, that's only a nail* ', and walk on. But if it was not a nail, but a Teller, there would be a blue flash and nothing after evermore. If it was not a Teller, but an 'S' mine, both legs would be amputated and the man might survive; but if he was not a father already, he had lost his chance. Most men preferred the Teller, but some, thinking of Douglas Bader and his two tin legs, did not.

After working for 23 hours, six teams between them had cleared only half the path up the cliff. In terms of nervous strain, they found, five hours mine-lifting was equal to five days with an unexploded bomb. As work ceased, 'Smudger' Smith's best friend stayed behind for a few minutes, marking up the cleared area with white tape. Suddenly, he called: "Smudger!" Smith saw the man standing unnaturally still, and began to climb towards him. " I've had it, Smudger." The words were spoken slowly and carefully, as a warning; and now Smith could see the three prongs of an ' S ' mine under the soldier's boots. He went back to a distance, as he was trained to do, and when he had reached safety, his friend made an effort to end the suspense and cheat the mine. There was a dull, thudding bang. " We put his remains in a groundsheet," said Smith bitterly. " There wasn't enough meat there to make a meal. We buried it, and I said a prayer over his grave. The others cut a piece of wood from a wrecked boat, and made a cross; and I put his name and number there and left it."

On the following day, his squad was reinforced by another team of five men under Corporal Taylor: and because the job was urgent, Taylor went into the minefield himself which, as an N.C.O., he should not have done, and Smith went up behind him. Almost instantly, the cliff vomited dust and smoke, there was a thud like a double-barrelled shot-gun being fired, and the remains of Corporal Taylor hurtled down the cliff, landing at the feet of Smith. Taylor had lost a leg from the knee downwards, and there was a gaping hole in his back, but he was still living. Using a ladder as an improvised stretcher, they got him down off the cliff and into a First Aid Post. That day, as the cable-ship had arrived off the beachhead, but the pathway had not been cleared, it was decided to lay the cable at another point which had been so thoroughly plastered by H.M.S. *Warspite* that there were hardly any mines left unexploded. And here it finally was laid, without casualties.

A few days later, another of his friends, Corporal Reg Beaumont, came back with nine German prisoners—one old Serjeant-Major with twenty years service, the rest youngsters. They had been cut off for days, sometimes able to hear English voices around them, but at first they had taken Beaumont prisoner before he was able to convince them that they ought to surrender to him. " I think if Beaumont had had his way, he'd have shot the lot, and I would have, too," said Corporal Smith. " I'd lost two uncles in the first world war, it'd been bred into me that the Germans were inhuman, and I'd just seen my best friend killed. But I didn't do it, because these chaps seemed to us to be fair; and one of them even had a leave pass valid for the Monday, when he was to have gone home. But still, I did shoot a German in the back around this time.

" I think it was about five days after our landing, so it must have been near Tracy-sur-Mer. We were billeted in a farmhouse, and the people there told us that a sniper had been bothering them; he'd been sheltered by a Frenchwoman. I saw her taken away, she was about fifty. He'd killed two or three people that day, so Corporal Dick Verling, a Scots boy from Motherwell, and I, decided to get him. The firing was coming from the top of the church, and it seemed quite an easy climb to me. Verling gave me a leg-up onto what looked like the roof of a boiler-house, and then I went up using my toggle ropes on those silly heads—what do you call them, gargoyles? There were rows of them, eight inches apart, all up the wall. It was no trouble, after I'd climbed the first two or three. The steeple or tower was about 50 feet high, on top of the main building, so the height I had to go was 80 feet. I picked out a window up there, a slit it was, really, and this was the chancy part. If he looked out, he could pick me off. All I had was a bayonet, as I couldn't have done the climb with a rifle. The window turned out to be bigger than I thought, and I knew at once I could get through. There was nothing much to be seen out of this window, so I knew I'd be coming in behind him. I couldn't hang on forever from the gargoyles, but I didn't rush it; I waited my chance, listening, then peaked over the sill. The chap had moved across to the other side, about 6 or 8 feet away, and I went through sideways, one leg first, straddling the sill. He had his back to me. I came through onto the floor, making no sound at all, because obviously he must be a very good soldier, and I went for him quick and put my bayonet into his back. He gave a little grunt, and then he was down, dead at once; and I saw he was S.S. So it seemed a great thing to me, something I'd never done before. It was interesting, I'd enjoyed doing it, and although it was murder, I'd no regrets.

" I went to the window and shouted to Dick to come on up, and I'll never forget the look on his face as he saw this bloke with the blood running out of his back. We never thought either of us was capable of this.' You wicked bastard, Smudger, you'll never get to 'eaven! ' he said.

"We slung him through the window and the French people undressed him, took off his boots and socks to wear. But not in a bad way; the French were very reverent to the dead, and besides, they thought the Germans would come back, and then people who'd helped the Allies would be shot; so they were not very helpful to us. Of course, they'd not much to thank us for. Later, I saw wounded refugees marching through the battle, and in Villers-Bocage, just a desolation, all massacred; and in Tilly they were living like animals, in sickness, poverty, and hunger, so much it made you cry. But the oddest thing was when we were sitting in Bayeux Cathedral, playing cards for Black Cat cigarettes beside eighteen coffins. We saw the tapestry, and were puzzled why such a valuable thing was left there (not knowing then it was only a reproduction), and we were struck by the parallel with us." Many British soldiers after them were to gaze at that tapestry in amazed recognition:

> " They are marching to the ships—the knights,
> Crossbowmen, the brown-burnt men of Normandy.
> Conquerors these. These twisted streets
> Ring their re-echo to their tread—
> The sisters of Arlette are brave, bright-eyed,
> Though this one weeps: they wave on
> These dark faces; their laughter
> Rings brittle, like arrowheads on mail.
>
> The Public Relations Outfit did a good job
> On that tapestry. It is, you might say,
> A graphic portrayal of the campaign—
> Here are landing ships in process of construction,
> And here the supply services are bringing up the beer
> In hogsheads. This depicts
> The invasion armada in mid-Channel
> (Observing radio silence), and here
> Assault landing craft are unloading war chargers
> On the beaches. This might be the Beachmaster,

And over here you see that the armour
Was committed shortly after D-Day,
Losses being heavy; and the campaign
Went badly for a time. But they broke through—
Here—and history began."

What they did not know was that the Conqueror's tomb was in the Abbey at Caen, and that his birth-place was in the Castle of Falaise. The twin names of Normandy—the beginning, and the end. And that they were to take those places, as they had taken Bayeux. But, at the moment, many were bewildered at their equivocal reception by the Normans they had liberated. "The first people we saw were jubilant at just being alive," recollected Leo Gariepy. "I personally lived this phenomenon quite often, especially after some hard action. The civilians were not any different in this respect. But when the cooling after effect took place, it was different; they were taciturn. The Normand is by nature a dour individual, more like the Scots farmer than the typical Frenchman; we have many French-Canadians who are the descendants of Normands, and they are just the same. So, after the first few hours of rejoicing at seeing battledress instead of the field-grey uniform, they naturally went about their routines. Now we naturally curtailed all traffic—pedestrian, bicycle, or cart—and this they did not like. They told us in no uncertain terms that even the German occupying forces allowed them some freedom. Like farmers the world over, they were stubborn, but we would not deviate, in some cases to the point of immediate execution. It was when this was realised that we became most unpopular. They were put out, too, by the fact that we would not barter with them for eggs, butter, etc., of which they appeared to have a very ample supply; they said they did this constantly with the occupying force and it was rather profitable. Furthermore, we would not allow them to go to the nearest towns, such as Caen, to sell their supplies, some of which were perishing. We often heard them call the Canadians: 'Savages', 'North American Indians', 'Trappeurs', 'Courreur de bois', 'Natives of the North', etc."

Patrick Walsh, who served in Normandy with the Royal Canadian Military Police, and later with the French-Canadian

Régiment de la Chaudière, noticed other reasons. ' Some of the farmers were bitter because their wheatfields had been mined by the Nazis and were not *immediately* cleared by us. But, on the other hand, there was the frantic search of all and sundry for that ' new drink ' Calvados; many of us under-rated the potency of it. A cause of bitterness especially was the smashing of the traditional narrow-necked bottle containing a pear, which was kept for the first son when he got married; our lads hadn't been told about the Normandy farm traditions."

" Being fluently bilingual, I had many calls to interpret in these cases ", said Serjeant Gariepy, " and in one case, it was a priest. He was a man of about forty, had a loaf of bread under his arm, and was calmly walking through our forward posts without paying any attention to the frantic calls of an infantry officer. Somehow this father pretended he could not understand what was being said, and kept lifting his hat, saying he was sorry, he did not understand. I jumped off my tank and went over to him, telling him in French that walking through our lines was absolutely prohibited. He was amazed that I spoke French, then began telling me the tale of an old widow who had lost three sons in the war and was sick, ' she lived just over the hill ', and it had been his God-ordained duty to give her his own loaf of bread every day, the poor creature was bed-ridden. I sympathised, but explained the danger to our troops of allow-ing a man who could describe our positions and their armament, to get across to the enemy. He was flabbergasted that we should think he would say anything to the Germans, and began a tirade about the terrible oppression of the Boche, etc. I told him to re-peat it to AMGOT[1] once they got established. He said that, even at the cost of his life, he must carry out the ' will of God '. I trans-lated that to the group of officers we now had around us, and they told me to tell him that under no circumstances would he be allowed to proceed, even if we had to arrest him.

" The good father smiled, lifted his hat, and said he was going on, we could do what we wished. I then told him that if he took one step forward, I, a French-Canadian, would shoot him

[1] AMGOT—Allied Military Government. Composed of the quasi-military Civil Affairs detachments, responsible for bodies, and Town Mayors, respon-sible for buildings, billeting, requisitioning, etc.

down cold, in the back, if necessary. He reddened a little, but was unyielding, and started to walk away. I fired a Sten burst at his heels, and told him the next shots would be in his back. He turned around and cursed me for all he was worth, but proceeded to the rear. A field officer then decided to arrest him, feeling he could not be trusted and was unusually insistent simply for a loaf of bread. I never heard afterwards what happened to him." Spy, or genuine priest, he was certainly a brave man; probably a stubborn Norman determined not to let earthly irrelevancies like the Second Front interfere with his daily routine.

" I was once singled out by an officer of our higher formation, 2nd Canadian Armoured Brigade, for the purpose of knocking down church steeples in Normandy ", Gariepy continued. " This was because I was a Roman Catholic, and it was necessary to have someone, French if possible, and Catholic also, in case, as the liaison officer explained, some of the troops interpreted this as defamatory action against the R.C.s. I found that very funny, but had no qualms. To me, these churches were enemy observation posts, part of his equipment, and so I knocked them down, telling the infantry regiment lying about (they were French-Canadians most times), that the spire was an enemy OP and must come down." In this way, many a 12th century guide-book item, from Norrey-en-Bessin in Normandy (where the road-sign ' Merveille du XII. Siècle ' still stood, but the church was a stump) to the commanding height of Hochelten on the Rhine, ceased to have much interest for antiquarians; and for the inhabitants, the theoretical difference between an ' enemy ' and a ' friendly ' shell was rendered entirely academic—both of them could kill you.

* * *

On 8 June, with more than 1,800 wounded crammed into the great buildings of the Bon Sauveur convent in Caen, two French volunteers did a very brave thing. "At the risk of their lives," wrote one of the nuns, " they cycled across the city to interview General Montgomery. He received them very kindly, and when they told him of our position, advised us to place Red Cross flags on the roofs of the principal buildings. He also assured the two volunteers that the Allies would spare us. So we worked hard that day making huge Red Cross flags." On the same day, M. Cacaud, the prefect, and A. Detoile, the mayor of Caen, signed an evacuation notice: " Owing to the murderous bombardments which are making our city a city of death, we strongly advise those who have no official or administrative charge to evacuate. Our heartfelt sympathy goes out to the people in this time of terrible suffering." But the convent, with its mass of wounded, sick, and mentally ill patients, could not evacuate through a battlefield, and consequently had to remain on it.

The British official report on the convent, made to the Bon Sauveur foundation in Wales, and signed by Brigadier H. Price Williams of G-5 Division, Displaced Persons Branch, Supreme Headquarters, Allied Expeditionary Force, recorded: " On 6th June, 1944, approximately 1,800 wounded were cared for in the Institution. Since 6th June, the buildings and grounds received no less than sixteen direct hits by shells, mortar or aerial bombs. Three wings of the building group were demolished, three fires of severe intensity were put out. Three sisters and two doctors in the Hospital were killed during the performance of their duties. Two operating rooms were hit at a time when operations were in progress. The staff have done a magnificent piece of work, have shown great courage in the face of indescribable danger, and in spite of these harrowing experiences throughout the early days of the invasion, they have carried on in a truly splendid manner. A further report will follow."

On 17 June, one of the nuns wrote: " Today it is rumoured that everyone must leave Caen. Our poor wounded were greatly alarmed. Where can they go? All seek excuses to remain with us. In St. Etienne's Church nearby[2] a great number of people have taken refuge. Caen is a dead city. Heaps of rubble everywhere and buried under it the bodies of unfortunate victims. At every turn one hears refugees exclaim sadly, ' I don't know what has happened to my people. When the bombs fell we were together, but there was no trace of them when we cleared the debris '. Or, ' I am the only one left of my family '. On 22nd June we buried the dead, and it was time, for the building which served as a mortuary was becoming unapproachable, with sixty dead bodies.

[2] The Abbey of St. Etienne, containing the tomb of Duke William.

Impossible to get coffins, so the dead were wrapped in sheets, and failing that, in paper. Certainly God will have accepted the sacrifice of human lives. We could not take them to the city cemetery, for Germans were reported to be hiding there, so we buried these poor victims in our courtyard until such time as the bodies can be taken up and re-interred in the cemetery. People are burying their dead in gardens and on the roadside. The city seems to be one huge graveyard and the worst is yet to come." This terrible prophecy was, within two weeks, to be fulfilled.

The reason why Caen was not yet totally destroyed was due to Montgomery's decision at the conference of 9 June, to strike south from Bayeux with the British 30 Corps, the American V Corps from Omaha conforming on its right; and further still to the Allied right, the American VII Corps from Utah driving towards its ultimate aim, the capture of Cherbourg, by way of St. Mere-Eglise, which led them directly to the other Bon Sauveur institute in Normandy—that at Pont L'Abbe. Consequently, during the period from the 6th to the 18th of June, the 1,000 sick, deaf-mutes, and mentally ill patients at Pont l'Abbe were at first in the middle of the German gun area; then, when they tried to flee, they ran straight into the fighting; and finally wandered into the right flank of the advancing British troops of 30 Corps. The poor lunatics became involved in the operations of three armies fighting desperately.

On D-Day, the out-buildings of the convent were bombed, but only two people were hurt, and there were rumours of British troop landings by sea and air, which were denied. On 8 June, the Feast of Corpus Christi, the nuns assisted at Holy Mass and received Holy Communion. Then, wrote one of them in her diary: "At 11 a.m. a German soldier came to tell us that they expected a very heavy bombardment in another hour. On hearing this, our doctors said that it was not possible this soldier could know what the Allies were doing. During the course of our simple meal there were three alerts and the noise was fearful. Reverend Mother asked us to make the sacrifice of our lives, and we repeated that beautiful prayer, 'Into Thy Hands, O Lord, I commend my Spirit'. But nobody really wants to die, and each of us added fervently, 'Sacred Heart of Jesus, I place all my trust in Thee'."

The crisis came on 11 June. In the calm lines written by the nun, one can see the frightful truth. The sick were frightened, the mad people in such a state of terror that the handful of nuns could hardly control them, as the continuous sound of shells passing both ways screamed and wailed overhead, or thunderclapped nearby, and buildings began to burn from incendiary bombs. Father Belloir, with a presentiment of deadly danger, advised evacuation into the fields if necessary; but the doctors opposed him with logic. " How can we persuade 1,000 people, many of them insane, and most mad with terror, out of the house and into the open fields, and keep them together? And where could we take them, and how could we feed such a host?"

" For a few hours there was a lull," wrote the nun, " then the bombardments recommenced with such ferocity that the sad truth dawned on us at last—our Convent and hospitals were the objectives of this attack." The patients were guided somehow by the handful of nuns to safety in the basements, but by 5 p.m. the buildings above their heads were on fire, and even the chapel was blazing. The Chaplain ran into the flames to rescue the Ciborium, which he gave to his assistant, Father Belloir, who gave it to a nun for safe keeping. " The joy of that chosen soul was indescribable. In that hour she had been entrusted with the Ciborium, and all horror was forgotten in that knowledge. Jesus in the Blessed Sacrament was in her keeping. Moreover, the Chaplain had taken the large Host, and when the sad exodus began that day, he headed one of the escaping groups of nuns and patients, and so, in spite of bombs, machine-gun fire and every danger of death, there was a procession following Jesus in the Blessed Sacrament on that Feast of Corpus Christi, a procession such as we had never dreamed of, but a most fervent one, because our faith burned with a greater intensity as blindly we stumbled along, beseeching His Mercy and trusting implicitly in His protection."

The nun who kept a diary went with one group of refugees, some 500 in all, of whom 350 were mental patients, led by Father Belloir, striding along in front. They walked straight into the battle. "Americans and Germans were fighting desperately from hedge to hedge. Only one thought was in our minds—to save our patients. Some kept rushing madly into danger, others, help-less, were wheeled along in wheel-barrows, or dragged on mat-tresses. All around was stark, staring ruin—houses blown down —and a deafening noise—and fires raging everywhere—and bombs and bullets raining down on every side—and some of the roads were impassable, where German troops occupied them. Humanly speaking, we had not the ghost of a chance to make a way out of that inferno. But we slowly struggled on, stopping to get under hedges and ditches. Meeting German soldiers, we implored them to spare us and our unfortunate charges, some of whom were trying to escape, thinking in their madness that safety lay in flight." The patients, many of them old people, including eccentric old women and half-wit girls, were very hard to control, dashing this way and that, either back down the road, or forward into the machine-gun fire and the mortars. The nuns themselves did not really know where to go, but looking at it on the map afterwards, it can be seen that for some days they wandered along the fringe of the fighting, from Pont l'Abbe northwards to Gourbesville, then north-east towards St. Mere-Eglise, taking shelter each night with some kindly farmer, who would give them shelter in his barns and outhouses, and supplying food to the multitude. M. Rolland, their first benefactor, could only give them milk, and for two days they all lived on this frugal diet.

All this time, they were in the forward area, by day and by night. " The battle raged around us, shells and bombs fell like hail on every side, while overhead planes machine-gunned savagely. Father Belloir told us to make an act of contrition. " It will be a miracle,' he added, ' if we get safely out of this '. But how we dreaded the night! Bombing and the sound of terrible conflict always, while we crouched on the stone floor of our stable lodgings, and prayed for peace and the protection of heaven." Father Belloir was out always, collecting meat, pota-toes, and butter from the charitable, to feed the patients. Other nuns came in, telling how their patients had run straight into the German lines. On the 14th, their poor lodgings were shelled, and when the Reverend Mother went to the door to see if there was any chance of escape, two patients followed her, running out blindly into the open. A shell fell between them, killing one old woman but leaving some life in the bleeding body of the other.

" We could not remain. We went through fields and meadows, crawling through hedges, carrying our most helpless patients, and also the poor wounded women. Some of our mental patients, thinking we had brought on all this suffering, in their delusions gave us untold trouble; others, however, became almost lucid, and did their utmost to help us, and to cheer their companions. We reached a little house owned by Madame Esdart, who invited us to shelter there, but we were anxious to reach ' Bethany ', a large house some distance away which belonged to the Institution. Hearing us say this, a gentleman instantly volunteered to go through the lines to the Americans, to ask if we could pass through safely. Wearing a Red Cross armlet he set off, but soon returned, informing us that we could not pass for at least two days." Eventually, two days later, on 16 June, the pathetic procession of the sick, the mad, and the wounded, shepherded by the nuns, and led by the Reverend Mother and the Chaplain, carrying the Host, set off across the battlefield.

" Preceded as usual by the Blessed Sacrament, we set out on the saddest journey we had ever made. The sights were horrible beyond belief, and to be seen at every turn of our journey. Houses in ruins, meadows and gardens torn up, but worst of all, American and German soldiers, lying close together, cold in death. Tears fell freely as we prayed for their souls. May God console the poor, saddened hearts of those who mourn for them. Only a short while before, they had been full of life and vigour." Many of the refugees were old and ill, their lives behind them; but the dead soldiers were young, boys who had died before they had ever lived, the saddest sight of all.

As they plodded painfully on, they came to fields newly turned into cemeteries, on each grave a rough wooden cross, with the dead man's helmet aslant on top of it, to show the nationality of the boy who lay there in foreign soil. Then they came to living American soldiers, who were so filled with pity for the old, and the sick, and the wounded, that they fell in with the procession, helping those who could no longer walk. Convoys of American trucks thundered along the road, when they came to the back areas, but these invariably halted to let the tragic procession pass. "Go to St. Mere-Eglise," they advised," that's a safe place." There, the American Commandant supplied them with 150 blankets and also provisions; but, best of all, he greeted them with cheerfulness and encouragement, qualities they needed even more badly than material assistance.

On 18 June, their worries seemed over. They reached 'Bethany' that day, a convoy of American lorries later bringing in all the missing patients and sisters who had become scattered during the flight from Pont l'Abbe. Indeed, there were so many of them now, that 'Bethany' was not large enough, and the Reverend Mother rented a large house nearby which accommodated the overflow of nearly 100 patients and nuns. And then the British Army arrived (but perhaps it was only AMGOT). The desperately fighting, hopelessly out-numbered Germans had not harmed them in any way, indeed had even accepted the risk of letting a Red Cross volunteer (who could describe their positions) cross through their lines to the Americans. The Americans had greeted them with open-handed and open-hearted generosity, accepting the responsibility for the situation they had created. But the first thing the British did was to throw the nuns and the mental patients into the street. "Scarcely had they settled down in the rented building near 'Bethany' than the British arrived and took it over," wrote the nun in her diary, simply and without recrimination. These cannot have been fighting troops, compelled to a distasteful duty by the imperative needs of the battlefield; but a rear area unit waging war without risk and determined to have it as comfortable as possible, even if it meant evicting sick and wounded lunatics.

"There was only one thing to do," wrote the Nun. "Reverend Mother decided to send some nuns back to Pont l'Abbe and lodge them in the wing of the building which had escaped the flames. So we returned, and what a heart-rending spectacle met our eyes! Smoke-blackened ruins stood where our Convent and Church, Schools, Hospitals, and Home had been. The part which had escaped total destruction was a wreck; doors were torn down and smashed, windows were gaping holes, and amidst all this destruction our provisions were being carried off. Not even our presence there stopped this looting.

"In 1937, we had celebrated the centenary of the Pont l'Abbe foundation, and looking at those ruins today an unbeliever would exclaim: ' There goes one hundred and seven years of devoted labour, to deaf-mutes, mental patients and the education of children, wasted, blown to atoms or burned to cinders '. Not so, do we think."

The terrible contrast of Normandy, between pity and pitilessness in the same person, is most pithily illustrated by General Bradley's order: " If it becomes necessary to save time, put 500 or even 1,000 tons of air on the place and take the city apart." And when he saw what he had done: " For more than four years the people had awaited this moment of liberation. Now they stared accusingly at us from the ruins that covered their dead."

CHAPTER NINE

THE MOST FAMOUS GALE
SINCE THE ARMADA

*The Battle of the Build-up—the V.1 Bombardment Begins
—the Führer Confers—Montgomery Orders a New Attack
on Caen—but the Gale Intervenes—the 'Oyster' Mines—
Death of a Regiment
13 to 24 June*

There was deadlock in Normandy. Only substantial reinforcements, on one side or the other, could break it. If it was broken, the German Army, slow-moving, dependent on horse-drawn transport and harassed from the air, would be at a fatal disadvantage. If it was not broken, the Allies would be pinned into a tiny strip of French territory, their communications affected and possibly imperilled by the pounding of winter gales on the vulnerable beaches and artificial harbours. Above all, the pretence of threatening Pas de Calais with a non-existent army of which General George Patton was the only bona fide member, could not much longer be maintained; then the Germans would feel free to transfer many infantry divisions from there to stiffen the Normandy front, now crying out for infantry. Because of this imaginary threat, and also the activity of the Allied air forces, the flow of German reinforcements to the battle was neither so great nor so rapid as it might have been; but it was taking place. The planned build-up of Allied formations in the beachhead was taking place, too, but already it was 48 hours behind schedule; largely because of the weather, but also because of the inherent difficulties of landing men and vehicles and stores over open beaches. To interfere further with that build-up, but above all in order to force Allied decisions at a very high level, Hitler now began a futuristic bombardment of London, and especially the dock area, the like of which the world had never seen before. It was, truly, a foretaste of Things to Come.

On 13 June, when the bombardment began, men and material were being sucked towards the furnace of Caen from all over the face of Europe. Far away in the east, the two formidable armoured divisions which made up II S.S. Panzer Corps were entraining at Lemberg. As their troop trains began to roll from one end of a continent to the other, towards the Normandy battle-front, so the British formations of the 'Follow Up' Force were moving into London Docks to exploit the gains already made by the Assault Force. On their first night encamped in the Marshalling Area near the docks, the men of 43 Reconnaissance Regiment, the spearhead of 43 (Wessex) Infantry Division, were disturbed by an air raid which seemed to have no end; it just went on and on, in contrast to the 'in and out' tactics used by German bombers in the recent 'Baby Blitz' on London. The crash of the guns was punctuated by heavy explosions and the patter of shell fragments falling into the tented camps; and among the men there were fitful discussions concerning the unusual engine-note of the hostile aircraft. But it was not until 16 June that the newspapers were allowed to set their screaming headlines: "Pilotless Planes Raid London!" No one yet knew what to call these weird, sightless weapons, but they were one reason why Hitler was so sure that the Allies would land in the Pas de Calais. His V (for 'Vengeance') weapon sites were grouped there, and had been under concentrated Allied air attack for many months already; he felt sure that the British must either see London destroyed, come to terms with him, or assault the Pas de Calais. The divisions of the German 15th Army must remain in their fortifications; and Normandy must look after itself.

On 16 June, the Battle Group Luck made their last attack. St. Honorine had fallen once more; it was to be re-taken. 4th tank Company led the advance, with Hauptmann von Gottberg in command. How many commanders have they had now, buried in their shallow graves beside the Orne? The German artillery thundered, drenching with fire the British positions. And the British artillery replied, thickened up by the salvos of the battleships, monitors, and cruisers lying offshore. The infantry went to ground, the Mark IVs rolled forward alone and engaged Sherman tanks. But without infantry, they could not break through. The head of the attack was crushed, and the 4th Company retired, now seven strong. " The men know that the battle is lost already," wrote Kortenhaus. " There's not a chance anymore. Not even the first V-weapons which thunder across the night skies towards England give them any hope. The enemy gets stronger every day. One can feel it. The 4th Company has received not a single replacement since D-Day: not a man, not a machine, to replace our losses. With other units, it is the same. The troops are bled to death. The survivors are completely exhausted, for they have been fighting continuously since the 6th of June. We go on to the defensive, and even though they are still in the line and under fire, the men regard this literally as a holiday. Now, our task is simply to hold the enemy; no longer can we attempt to drive him back."

That same day, it was thought safe enough for His Majesty King George VI to land on Juno Beach and visit the British and Canadian troops. On the following day, 17 June, Hitler arrived in France for a ' conference ' to be held at that command post which he had ordered constructed in 1940 for the invasion and conquest of England. History had now turned almost full-circle. Neither Rommel nor von Rundstedt believed that the Normandy front could be held; they wanted permission for a withdrawal; and they were prepared to hint to Hitler that he should end the war. Hitler's reaction was necessarily violent, for who would make peace with him? While the talk was going on inconclusively, above the deeper under-currents which intuitively alarmed Hitler, news arrived of an American breakthrough at Carentan which threatened to cut off the Cherbourg peninsula at its base, and this was followed by an erratic V.1 diving to earth nearby. Half convinced that this was part of a plot to kill him, Hitler at once flew to his mountain refuge at Berchtesgaden.

Next day, 18 June, 20 Allied divisions were ashore, facing 18 German divisions, most of which were under-strength, the line in some cases being held by clerks, drivers, and storemen. Believing that there was a chance that it might crack, if pressure was applied quickly, General Montgomery ordered the capture of Caen and Cherbourg. The ' pincer ', or double-envelopment method, was to be repeated as far as Caen was concerned; but the drive would take place much nearer to the city on the west and was there to be conducted by the new 8 Corps, which was just landing, 30 Corps having this time only a supporting role. This would be a much greater battle launched with far larger resources, and it was planned to start on 22 June, by which time the follow-up formations should be ashore. One of the divisions intended to take part, 43rd Wessex, was embarking at London Docks that day. The men of the reconnaissance regiment, burdened with counterfeit-looking French currency, lifejackets, and what the Q.M. designated as ' *bags, vomit* ', struggled up the gangways under heavy packs, clutching a fist-full of documents; in 1944, in order to invade France, the soldier had to have both an embarkation and a disembarkation card, which he handed to the appropriate official at the appropriate place, a refinement not dreamt of by William the Norman, whose pre-fabricated castles for defending his beachhead had been surprisingly up-to-date and forward-looking. 43 Recce Regiment had been stripped down otherwise to ' Light Scales ' and numbered a little over 500 men. Because of the shortage of shipping, the remainder would follow later. Yet so little did the Germans understand the realities of amphibious operations, that Hitler's arguments at the Margival conference the day before had included a repetition of the theory that the V.1 offensive would force the Allies to destroy the remainder of their forces in a head-on attack from seaward against the ' Rocket Coast ' of Pas de Calais. But there were simply not enough ships or specialised landing craft for this to be possible. In any case, the V.1 bombardment, although severe, was mostly failing to do damage of military importance, let alone drive the British Government to desperation, although it did cause a great exodus of civilians from the capital.

One of the few really serious ' incidents ' occurred this day when, at 11.15 a.m. a billow of smoke in the shape of a waterspout rose to 1,500 feet above central London. It was a direct hit on the crowded chapel of the Brigade of Guards, ironically, on Waterloo Day. In the dust-reeking ruins, the text of a mosaic given by Queen Victoria stood intact above the slain. " *Be thou faithful unto death and I will give thee a crown of life.*" A few yards away lay the bodies of the worshippers, men, women, and children, who a few seconds before had been listening to the service. Heaped together like grey logs were 121 dead and dying, and 68 wounded. Unlike shell, bomb, or rocket, the V.1 did not waste most of its force cratering the ground; almost all the blast went sideways. A few hours later, Winston Churchill arrived to watch the rescue teams working in the debris; he stood there silently, tears pouring down his cheeks.

At that moment, 43 Recce Regiment had been embarking at Tilbury, a few miles away. Next day, they were anchored prosaically off Southend Pier, while yet another Normandy convoy gathered. Bombers coming back from France passed overhead in streams and two of them, American Flying Fortresses, crashed into the water alongside their ship, M.T. 41, the *Derry Cunihy*. They sailed at evening on the 19th, passing through the Straits of Dover about midnight. From Cap Gris Nez, invisible over the black water, yellow flashes began to wink; half a minute after, heavy shells came plunging down upon the ships with a thunderous rumbling roar. Water reared up white beyond the tops of the masts and red-hot splinters clanged against the iron sides of the transports. One ship reeled out of the line and was run ashore near Deal.

The morning of 20 June was brilliant with sunshine, too coldly brilliant, perhaps. It was the beginning of a change in the weather which was to disrupt Montgomery's offensive plans and save the Germans. " I reckon this will be the most famous gale since the Armada," said one witness, as the white-caps began to foam on the beaches. By the time the *Derry Cunihy* had reached the Normandy coast that day and dropped anchor off Ouistreham, at the extreme eastern end of the beachhead, the sky was covered by grey clouds. " The sea was turning rough," said Major A. C. Packer, then Captain and Adjutant of 43 Recce Regiment. "An array of ships rode wallowing and plunging at anchor while Naval vessels, including the giant battleship *Rodney*, fired thunderous salvos inland and enemy guns replied. Occasionally, a ship changed anchor hurriedly when shells arrived uncomfortably close; while the stunned and dying fish that rose to the surface were retrieved by the men with basket and bucket, a welcome change in diet from ration packs. It was the start of a storm which held up landing operations on any large scale for several days and, indeed, endangered the success of the invasion; but it is difficult to be dramatic about it. It did not seem to me to be unduly severe, but, of course, LCTs and other such craft used for invasion were fair-weather boats and pretty uncontrollable in any sort of high sea."

"As for the gale, most of us were well prepared," said Petty Officer McKinlay, who was now working with a beach group. " It was very similar to an exercise we had done with DUKWS in winter near Berwick. The landing craft would come in to beach, and as the sea took charge of them so would the beach groups take charge of the sea, men up to their necks in water with their backs as fenders, keeping the craft straight and taking a pounding at the same time. Our main trouble was when a craft broached to, *i.e.*, was swept sideways onto the beach. She was immediately at the mercy of nature, but in all seriousness I don't think we lost a craft on this beach in this gale."

Squadron Leader Hill, also stationed on Juno Beach, in charge of the barrage balloons on all beaches, agreed; but pointed out that the pattern was not the same everywhere. " On the beach just west of where I was at Juno, there was utter chaos; literally hundreds of small craft were washed ashore by the gale at high tide and lay on the road which traversed the beach, rather like a cargo of timber logs." He had now found out that his cousin, Brigadier Hill, was only a few miles away across the Orne, and took this opportunity to visit him. Wearing khaki, but driven by a batman wearing blue R.A.F. uniform, he crossed ' Bulford Bridge ' near Bénouville; this struck him as odd, because his grandfather had owned the real Bulford Bridge back in England, and most of the surrounding land as well, where the airborne troops had trained. After driving about for some time on the other side, searching for H.Q. 3 Parachute Brigade, he came at length to the sand-bagged position where his cousin was. The harassed look he saw on the Brigadier's face was due to the fact that their jeep had been in full view for some time, driving merrily along a road which nobody held because it lay between the British and German positions. Not a shot had been fired, because no one, British or German, could make out whose jeep it was. One of the men wore khaki, but the other was dressed in R.A.F. blue which, under its coat of dust, resembled German field-grey. A German with a British prisoner? Or an Englishman with a German prisoner? None of the hundreds of men looking at the speeding vehicle from behind rifles and machine-guns for one moment imagined that it was merely a social call; indeed Brigadier Hill's men had almost made up their minds that both men in the jeep were Jerries, when at last the vehicle took the right turning. It was very quiet now, for the fighting had died down; " the most terrible moment they experienced in the airborne bridgehead while I was there was when a tent was pitched on a wasps' nest," recollected Squadron Leader Hill.

For three days, the breakers roared ceaselessly on the beaches; " no such June storm had been known in the Channel for over forty years," wrote the British official historian. But, in fact, only occasionally did it even reach gale force. To disrupt the delicate mechanism of an amphibious operation, it did not have to. The big transports lying off-shore could not tranship men and vehicles to landing craft for the actual run-in to the beaches; they were in no danger, but unloading, as far as they were concerned, was at a standstill. The build-up had stopped. The landing ships and smaller craft, designed to beach, did so; but the rate of unloading was slowed down, so that a backlog of these very vulnerable and uncontrollable craft were compelled to remain at anchor. Some took shelter inside the ' Gooseberries ', protective arcs of sunken blockships laid in place with this very contingency in mind; but there was not room enough inside for them all. Some beaches were more exposed than others, either by reason of their alignment in regard to wind and sea or because there were no natural underwater protective features, such as reefs or sandbars, to act as early, invisible breakwaters; and off these beaches, very often, anchors could find no holding ground, in sand, with that sea and tide running.[1]

But by far the most serious aspect of the bad weather was that it had come at a critical time in the erection of the artificial " Mulberry " harbours, both of which were incomplete. Further, many of the component parts were actually being floated across the Channel when the storm blew up. If the landing craft were vulnerable, these were defenceless. The ' Phoenix ' caissons, for instance, were great slab-sided rectangular boxes of floating con-

[1] The present author once had the job of going down 18 feet, holding his breath, to ' dig in ' the anchor of a motor-boat which was going steadily backwards; and found himself chasing the anchor madly along the bottom until he ran out of puff. The wind was only Force 4.

crete, hundreds of feet long, whose walls acted like sails. They just went drifting down Channel with the wind, sank, or broke up. The 'Rhino' ferries, low, floating platforms for conveying vehicles ashore, were little better. But most delicate of all was the 'Whale' equipment. Some $2\frac{1}{2}$ miles of this floating, articulated steel roadway was being towed across the Channel when wind and sea turned angry; almost all of it was sunk or cast ashore. Nevertheless, the British 'Mulberry' harbour survived the storm; not intact, and not by any great margin, but it was still there when the wind began to die away on 22 June. Of the American 'Mulberry', off unlucky Omaha, nothing but wreckage was left. "When on June 22 we went down to the beach to survey the damage," wrote General Omar Bradley, "I was appalled by the desolation, for it vastly exceeded that on D-Day." And that was saying something, for Omaha had been the bloodiest beach of them all, by far.

Bradley was left with only a three-day stock of ammunition in his dumps, which seriously affected his offensive plans. That meant that the planned breakout in his sector would be delayed, and that meant in turn that the British must continue trying to fight the bulk of the German Army in Normandy to a standstill for longer than had been originally contemplated. And because of the delays caused by the gale to their own build-up, the British were, when the storm abated, short of three divisions which would otherwise have been ashore. And that again meant a further delay in the new offensive against Caen which Montgomery was planning; and it meant also that there would be more German divisions in the line to oppose it, when finally it did go in.

By the evening of 23 June the storm was clearly over, and the men who had been cooped up for days in the transports lying off the beachhead were told that they would be landing next morning. During this and the preceding nights the Luftwaffe was active, laying off the Normandy coast a weapon which Hitler had mentioned at Margival—the new pressure, or 'oyster' mine. These were deadly, because they were unsweepable by any known method. The pressure change caused by the movement of a ship's hull through the water made them 'live', after which the normal magnetic and acoustic fuses would fire the mine;

there was no way to counterfeit the pressure change at a safe distance, and so explode the mine prematurely. Already, on the 23rd, Admiral Vian's flagship *Scylla* had fallen victim to a pressure mine; and during the period 22nd to 29th June they accounted additionally for four warships sunk and seven damaged, plus four other vessels sunk.

The 500 men of 43 Reconnaissance Regiment slept late on 24 June, as usual; to fit in with ship's routine, reveille had been set back to 0830 hours. Most of them were in the after holds of the *Derry Cunihy*, stacked up in layers like living sandwiches, with only a foot or so between one man's head and the canvas bunk above; and so on up to deckhead level; and with only narrow gangways between the packed sleepers. Their armoured cars, half-tracks, and lorries were mostly in the forward holds of the ship, but some were stacked in the open on deck. Major B. V. J. Vigrass, the Quartermaster, was well organised; his morning cup of tea usually arrived at 0700, the time at which, punctually, he woke up. This time, there was no tea, because the ship was about to move to a safer anchorage for unloading. He could hear the Chief Engineer routing out his staff from the cabins nearby with a shout of, "Come on, we're going to start the engines!" A few minutes after, he heard the engines start. Somewhere on the seabed directly under the keel of the transport, the acoustic fuse of a deadly cylinder closed the circuit.

The *Derry Cunihy*, with her load of 500 soldiers and all their vehicles, was blown clean in half. Astern, almost simultaneously, a British destroyer was likewise split in two by another violent underwater explosion, and began to sink rapidly. The afterpart of the transport, containing the tight-packed troopdecks, went almost instantly from sight under the cold sea. Probably, as the riven afterpart went down, the heavy vehicles on the well-deck above collapsed through on top of them. Few got out. Serjeant-Major W. V. Critchley, from a vantage point on the forepart of the wreck, saw one or two heads in the swirling water, fortunate men who had been blown through the sides of the troopdeck. Serjeant Pavey's awakening was something out of a nightmare; he found himself under the sea, unable to breath. But his bunk was near the edge of the hold, and he was able to haul himself up to the surface and safety, a few seconds before the stern half of the ship vanished from sight. Struggling near him in the waves was Trooper Meikle, whose 'reveille' had been almost equally shocking. He had gone to sleep the night before inside one of the half-tracks which were lashed to the top of number four hold; and was woken up by the noise and movement of the vehicle as it slid off the deck into the sea. Both men were picked up.

The forepart of the ship was settling, but still afloat. Major Vigrass removed a radiator which had fallen on top of him at the moment of the explosion, and heard the Chief Engineer's shout to the engine-room staff, " Come on out, it's hopeless! " He heard their footsteps as they ran past his cabin, and then the man who normally brought the 7 o'clock tea put his head round the door and shouted, " Come on, sir, the ship's sinking! " When he got on deck, the bows were rearing in the air and the number four hold, which held the bulk of the Regiment's transport, was blazing fiercely; and as the ammunition in the vehicles began to explode, patches of burning fuel began to spread out on the waves alongside what remained above water of the *Derry Cunihy*. There were pitifully few swimmers in the sea, and absolute quiet, apart from the popping and spitting of the ammunition exploding in the fires.

" The first thing that impressed me was the calmness and discipline," recollected the Reverend J. E. Gethyn-Jones, M.B.E., Padre of the Regiment. " There was no vestige of panic and very little noise. It was as though all realised that every breath was needed for the hard and difficult task of getting everyone to safety. ' Self ' was forgotten, and I saw badly wounded men rising above pain and struggling to help less fortunate comrades. For that time, they became supermen, not bound by the normal limitations of the body. One saw such bravery and forgetfulness of self in those few minutes that I was amazed that human nature could rise to such heights. One example is enough. A little man, clad in vest and pants, his one arm useless, his head bleeding and he himself nearly unconscious, struggling to support an unconscious comrade. He was gripping him by the hair and holding the lad's head above water, until they were both handed to safety. And the second impression I had was of the promptness and whole-heartedness of the Navy's aid."

First alongside the stricken transport was the naval launch HMML/BG 204 in which L. A. Bridge was serving in the engine-room. During the night they had heard the mines hitting the water, the sound being transmitted through the fresh-water tanks in the bilges. Now, looking through a scuttle, Bridge was witness to their effect. "I recall looking straight into the after hold of the *Derry Cunihy* and seeing men in their underwear trying to scramble through the tangle of twisted metal to safety," he commented. "I also saw, at very close range, that little man clad in vest and pants holding up a comrade's head. He was standing partly under water on the shattered deck, calling for help. I do not think his comrade survived, as he had a terrible wound. Our deck-hose was turned on to try to stem the flames licking out of the great split in the ship's side. Ammunition from the burning trucks was popping all round and almost raining down on our decks. Our small crew worked frantically to get the badly injured away first, this being made difficult by the tearing decks, as the afterpart of the ship settled very quickly. Soon we were absolutely packed out with survivors, many gravely wounded and burnt. When we pulled away at last, our main-engine fuses suddenly blew. Our rather portly 'Jimmy', still clad in blue-silk pyjamas, cap and seaboots, started to run to the engine room, but slipped in the blood and fuel oil, and fell flat on his back. Then, even the survivors had to laugh."

The forepart of the *Derry Cunihy* finally came to rest on a sandbank, with just the bows rearing out of the water, a strange and ominous seamark for those who came to the beachhead later. Meanwhile, the survivors were transferred to a former French luxury liner, the *Cap Tourain*, and on the evening of the 24th of June the adjutant, Captain Packer, called the roll. "Only then," he said, "was the full extent of the Regiment's tragic loss revealed." Over 500 names were read out, and most of them were answered by—silence. Three hundred and thirty times, Captain Packer called out a name, and only the gulls replied. 180 were dead, 150 were wounded, and of these three did not recover.

A Regiment had died.

CHAPTER TEN

THE BIRTH OF THE 'BUTCHER BEARS'

Prelude to 'EPSOM': The Battle of Fontenay
25 June

After heavy fighting on the severely weakened left of the 12th S.S.
Panzer Division and right of Panzer Lehr Division, attacks by
successive waves of enemy troops, supported in the air by continuous
enemy sorties, succeeded in tearing open a gap 5 km wide and 2 km
deep.

Log of German Army Group 'B'

Some battles are easy to describe, others difficult, a few impossible.
The next British offensive to take Caen, ordered by Montgomery
on 18 June, for 22 June, but delayed until the 25th by the gale,
comes into the latter category. Its code name was 'Epsom'. When
a later attack on Caen was code-named 'Goodwood', some
civilian German commentators assumed that the implication
that it would all be just a happy day's racing was behind the
choice of name. In fact, code names are chosen haphazard deliberately in order not to give away the least hint as to their
subject. It is far more likely that these racing terms were suggested by the name of a village near Caen, which every British
soldier who went through it saw with surprise and remembered
—St. Leger. Another apparent—but only apparent—coincidence
of names was that the village of Colleville, near the Odon, which
was to be taken during 'Epsom', fell to a battalion commanded
by Lieut.-Colonel Colville. And of course, one of Duke William's
leading military commanders had been Roger de Montgoméri.
More coincidental was the name of a village near Villers Bocage,
Jerusalem; but, coincidence or not, this was the title of the
song (in fact, Blake's bitter poem set to music) which a great
many British soldiers in Normandy took up as a favourite;
it expressed exactly the depth of their feelings, after the first
dreadful shock of battle experience. The horrible current top of
the top ten 'pops', an American import called "*Mairzy doats*",

died in its tracks under the Spandau fire. Some of the divisions from the Mediterranean theatre preferred German or Italian versions of "*Lili Marlen*"; and, while the official anthem of 15th Scottish Division was "*Scotland the Brave*", the more popular unofficial tune was "*I'm nae awa' tae bide awa'*". Oddly, two American discs also hit off the current mood: "*My guy, come back*", and "*Long ago and far away*". This strangely assorted, apparently haphazard string of tunes had a red thread running through them; as sung or played, they were nostalgic, deeply melancholy; laments for dead friends, from those about to die.

In the roll of battle honours, long afterwards, this operation is simply called "The Odon"—for its purpose was to establish an armoured bridgehead across that small stream. Its nickname, in the regimental and divisional histories, is "The Battle of the Scottish Corridor"—for that, in fact, is what it became.

In outline, the battle plan is easy to grasp. It was just a repetition of the double-encirclement of Caen, which had recoiled at St. Honorine and Villers-Bocage when tried by the battle-experienced divisions. As originally conceived, the main thrust was to have been on the left, out of the Airborne bridgehead, and part of 15th Scottish was actually moved there. But General Dempsey, commanding the British Second Army, soon realised that a major attack by large forces out of that area would be almost fatally constricted by the sheer lack of space, as well as being vulnerably exposed to enemy fire from the heights on two sides. Therefore, he decided to make the 'right hook' the major effort. In intention, this also is easy to grasp. The object was to drive round Caen, starting on the west, cross two rivers, the Odon and the Orne, sweeping round to the left until Bretteville-sur-Laize, due south of Caen, was reached. This would establish a strong force in rear of the city, cutting or dominating all roads leading into it from the south. The 'left hook' might, with luck, cut some or all of the remaining main roads which ran into Caen from the east and south-east. The Germans would be literally ' squeezed ' out of Caen.

The timing of the plan is also easy to understand. Those troops on the British right would have the furthest distance to cover in this circular movement to the left; therefore, their attacks were to go in in that order. The battle would start on the right, and then run rapidly from right to left, until the whole British front was ablaze, and wheeling round Caen for the final encirclement of the city. Three Corps were involved; reading from British right to British left—30 Corps, 8 Corps, and 1 Corps. On 25 June, the 49th West Riding Division (30 Corps) was to seize some vital high ground—the ridges of Fontenay and Rauray. This secured, the divisions of 8 Corps in the centre were to make the main thrust for the crossings of the Odon and Orne—one division following after the other. 15th Scottish were to lead, aided by 31 Tank Brigade and 4 Armoured Brigade; the mopping-up behind them was to be done by another infantry division, the 43rd Wessex, and 11th Armoured Division was to advance also, ready to break-out for the lightning left-wheel round Caen from the bridgeheads secured by the infantry divisions and the tank formations directly supporting them. While that was in progress, the Canadians further to the left were to move up on Carpiquet airfield, and the 51st Highland Division (also 1 corps) was to break out of the Airborne bridgehead to come round Caen from the other side.

Now it will be seen why the operation as it actually developed is impossible to describe in any connected narrative: the 15th Scottish was to leapfrog its battalions forward on a narrow front, one relieving the other at short intervals; with the battalions of 43rd Wessex close behind, and mopping-up; and 11th Armoured Division moving with and through the advancing infantry. It looks like a recipe for organised confusion, and it was; with everything going up the centre-line, through ruined villages, immovable traffic jams occurred. As far as the fighting was concerned, the countryside was bocage mixed with some cornfields —average range of vision 100 yards. And plenty of cover for the defenders. A hundred, a thousand, small-scale fights developed; a soldier's battle, not a general's. It was summed up by Serjeant H. Green of 10 Highland Light Infantry: "I feel that my writings may be of a disappointing nature—on reflection, I don't seem to know very much about the battle considering the fact that I was in the middle of it." This, in spite of the fact that he was with the Intelligence Section of the battalion, and wrote a very detailed narrative in 1945, when the events were still fresh in his mind. Even so, Serjeant Green's story is exceptional, in that he knew where he was, and on what date.

There are two points of difference with the earlier abortive double-envelopment plan which should be remembered. This offensive was very much greater in scale, because many more divisions had now been landed. 8 Corps alone, attacking in the centre, numbered 60,000 men, 600 tanks, and 300 guns, with additional support from 400 guns firing from the two corps to left and right of it, plus the guns of three cruisers and a monitor lying off the beachhead. The planned air support was also on a very large scale. The other point of difference was that these divisions were untried in battle; only 49 Division had been engaged at all in Normandy, and then not as a division. Whereas the formations which had failed at Villers-Bocage, Tilly, and St. Honorine had been battle-hardened veterans of the Mediterranean theatre. This selection of unseasoned troops was said to be deliberate. The earlier failure had resulted in many generals receiving their ' bowler hats ', in the ruthless Monty way, but it was being whispered that the real reason for failure lay not with the command, but that the men had ' crosssed too many start-lines '; were tired and stale. Indeed, the official historian made a point of mentioning that 8 Corps was " fresh from England and eager for battle." Ironically, Serjeant Green had written long before, in 1945, that: " Future historians will in all probability show us as being elated at the prospects of getting to grips with the enemy after a wait of four years, but this will be far from the truth. The prospect was too grim for even the super-optimist to be elated. We faced the thing as a dirty job which had to be done, with the thought, ' the sooner we get into battle, the sooner it will be over '. After the first excitement, the hidden fear of the unknown sobered even the brightest spirit and there were more grave than happy faces to be seen." So 15th Scottish Division, and so, too, 11th Armoured, each man secretly wondering: ' How will I stand it? Will I let the others down?'

*　　*　　*

"An optimistic picture was painted for the infantry", wrote the historian of the Gordons. " They would receive the strongest of air and artillery support and need not expect to encounter a very stout resistance. As some remarked, ' It sounded good '." And indeed it looked good for the British, particularly if the map you were studying was that which lay in front of Hubert Meyer, the operations staff officer of 12 S.S. Panzer Grenadier Division. It showed the line held by 12th S.S., now very much understrength, as running from Fontenay-le-Pesnil, where 30 Corps were due to attack, through the area of St. Marvieu and Cheux, opposite the build-up of 8 Corps, as far east as Carpiquet airfield, which was an objective of 1 Corps. One decimated division of ' teenagers ' stood wholly in the path of 8 Corps, and partly in the path of the other two Corps. On their left, they would have to face 49 West Riding Division, with some help from their flank division, Panzer Lehr; on their right, S.S. Panzer Grenadier Regiment 25 would have to face the Canadians alone, outnumbered five or six to one· But in the centre was the gravest threat, for there elements only of S.S. Panzer Regiments 12 and 26 would face the entire weight of 8 Corps—15th Scottish Division, 43rd Wessex Division, 11th Armoured Division, 31 Tank Brigade, and 4 Armoured Brigade. 60,000 men, 600 tanks, 700 guns—against a few thousand teenagers.

Meyer knew that this was where the main blow would fall. " Through our wireless reconnaissance we realised that, during the period 22-25 June, strong enemy tank units were massing in readiness in the area west of Norrey-en-Bessin. As a counter measure, we moved up our II Heavy Tank Company behind the main battlefield in the sector of II Battalion, Panzer Regiment 26, as a movable tank defence, excellently camouflaged." These dispositions were to be thrown out by the attack of 49 West Riding Division on Fontenay; the German reaction in turn affected the plans of 49 Div; and that, in turn, affected the main blow by 8 Corps and, in effect, created the " Scottish Corridor ".

The task of 49 Div, supported by 8 Armoured Brigade, was to take the commanding ridges of Fontenay and Rauray, from which the Germans could sweep the right flank of the 8 Corps advance to the Odon. The heights were to be in their hands by evening of 25 June, so that the main 'Epsom' assault could be launched next day, 15th Scottish leading. 49 Div had served as the garrison of Iceland, and their divisional sign was the Polar Bear. They included a number of Scottish battalions, but most of the men came from Yorkshire, or thereabouts, and they were therefore twice connected with 15th Scottish Division, the Highland Brigade of which was partly recruited from the highlands of England, the rest mostly from Aberdeen and Glasgow, the Gorbals contingent bearing distinctive razor-slash badges.

At 0400 on 25 June the guns began to beat away, and the people in Caen heard the distant drumfire along the Odon. " The artillery preparation was immense", wrote a historian of 11 Royal Scots Fusiliers.[1] " Looking back behind me, the sky was lit with flash after flash, increasing rapidly in tempo until the skyline was outlined almost in one continuous glow, as mediums, field guns and heavies joined in. The continuous whistle of shells passing low overhead, the stubborn rumble of the guns behind and the roar of the bursting shells ahead." Immediately to the right of the R.S.F. on the start-line was the Hallamshire Battalion of the York and Lancaster Regiment, with the Lincolns on their right. For them, it was: 0415 hrs.—Zero hour! " Company commanders and platoon commanders shouted to their men to advance", wrote a historian of the Hallams.[2] " Though their voices were drowned in the noise, the long line of men in extended order instinctively moved forward at a steady pace behind the creeping barrage—pausing every now and again as they got too close. Then the unexpected happened. As the two forward companies advanced down the slope through the cornfield they were swallowed up into a dense mist—a mist so thickened by fumes that it was impossible to see more than a few feet in front of one. Companies, platoons, sections, and even men—deployed for daylight action—began to rapidly lose touch with one another. Soon the lateral road at the bottom of the hill was reached and from there onwards enemy opposition could be expected. It came in the form of a machine-gun firing blindly down the road. A quick dash, however, got them over without a casualty, but C Company on the left bumped into and by-passed a Tiger tank sitting on the road junction."

Heavy German defensive fire took toll of the attackers at first, but then, as the historian of the R.S.F. wrote, "Germans and British became inextricably intermingled in the fog and

[1] & [2] Various issues of " Polar Bear News ", 1945, the descriptions being written in all cases by participants.

bitter hand-to-hand fighting developed where no quarter was given on either side. By midday a foothold had been firmly established round the Calvary in the west end of the village of Fontenay. We like to think that it was to some degree as a result of this action that 49 Division came to be known in enemy circles as ' The Polar Bear Butchers '."[3] On right of the R.S.F., B Company of the Hallams was now on its objective, the high ground south-west of Fontenay. Of the approximately 120 men who had set out that morning, 2 officers and about 30 men were left. As they began to sort themselves out, and position the 6-pounder infantry anti-tank guns against counter-attack, they heard the roar of heavy tank engines.

Acting as Bren gunner, covering the anti-tank guns against infantry attack, was Cecil Heald, who now lives in Winnipeg, Canada. " We had reached a road junction to the east of Fontenay church on the Caen-Bayeux road," he recollected, " and were covering the road coming from Caen. A short distance away was a bridge which crossed a stream. Then we heard tank engines and saw three Tigers approaching from the direction of Caen." These were certainly from 12th S.S. Panzer Grenadier Division, probably I Heavy Tank Company, which was supporting that part of the front; but the tanks may well have been Panthers and not Tigers, the two frequently being confused. " The detachment commander, L/Serjeant Thompson, called the gun crew to action stations, then we waited until the first tank was on the bridge, when the order to fire was given. L/Corporal ' Taffy' Williams then fired, destroying this first tank on the bridge, thus blocking the approach from Caen. The second tank turned to the left, exposing its tracks, and ' Taffy' fired again, blowing off the track; his second shot destroyed it completely. By now, we were under heavy fire from the third tank, which reversed to the rear and to the right. ' Taffy' was wounded and we carried him to a nearby farmhouse." This third tank was eventually knocked out by a Sherman carrying a 17-pounder gun, which the C.O. of the Hallams borrowed from the Lincolns for the occasion. "After a while we received orders to evacuate

---

[3] After this battle, 49 Div referred to themselves, not without pride, as the " Butcher Bears "; and when they eventually arrived in Germany, requisitioned a beer hall which they re-named " The Butcher's Arms ".

our position and to consolidate with the infantry companies, which had suffered heavy casualties," said Cecil Heald. " We dug in for the night in an orchard facing Caen, covering the left flank, which was exposed as the supporting battalion had not reached their objectives. We were on stand-to all night, as there was considerable enemy firing; and next day advanced in the direction of Tessel Wood."

The West Riding Division had failed, by a large margin, to take Rauray, which lay beyond and to the east of Tessel-Bretteville. When the Scottish advanced next morning, they would be swept by fire from those heights. Nevertheless, the 'Butcher Bears' had broken through the German defences, and alarmed 'Sepp' Dietrich, commanding I S.S. Panzer Corps, the headquarters controlling 12th S.S. and 21 Panzer Divisions. So, as Cecil Heald was settling down for an uneasy night on the Fontenay ridge, Dietrich was giving orders for the II Heavy Tank Company, the last mobile reserve which 12th S.S. Panzer had in the path of the main advance to come next morning, to move out of that area and counter-attack 49 Div. " The I Heavy Tank Company was already there ", recollected Hubert Meyer. " But on the evening of 25 June, I S.S. Panzer Corps ordered even this last unit to go into action the following morning, to clean up the break-through in the vicinity of Panzer Lehr Division on our left flank. We begged the Corps most urgently to withdraw this order, as we already expected an attack for the following morning by the enemy tank units which, we knew, were west of Norrey. They saw no possibility of complying with our request; perhaps they did not take our wireless-reconnaissance evidence seriously enough."[4] So, at 0500 on 26 June, the II Heavy Tank Company assembled for a counter-attack across the line Fontenay-Tessel-Bretteville, in the direction of Juvigny. That left S.S. Panzer Grenadier Regiment 26, unsupported, directly in the path of 11 Armoured Div, 15 Scottish Div, 31 Armoured Brigade, and 43 Div.

"At 7 o'clock on 26 June, this great British attack of about

---

[4] German generals could be just as critical of each other as the British and Americans, firm ideas and a forceful personality being necessary attributes. " Decent but stupid " was the verdict of the aristocratic von Rundstedt on Dietrich. "All he could do was stand on a tank and shout, ' I am the King of Africa,' " was Dietrich's own description of Rommel.

500-600 tanks on a breadth of 5 kilometres rolled over the Pioneers and the Panzer Grenadiers. Eventually it came to a halt only because our artillery fire separated the enemy infantry from their tanks. Several pockets of resistance did considerable damage. The battle headquarters of the Panzer Pioneer Battalion 12 under Sturmführer Siegfried Müller had been made into a strongpoint which was to be held until well into the night; then the survivors managed to get out to the west of Le Haut du Bosc, and were picked up by some of our tanks advancing in a counter-attack. As late as 28 June, our operators picked up radio messages from British tanks attacking the remnants of 3 Pioneer Company which still held several strongpoints in the old front line between St. Mauvieu and Fontenay. We tried to convince I S.S. Panzer Corps that a well-planned counter-attack by tank units from the south-west might restore the original front, or at least, relieve the surrounded units, but fresh forces were not available."

CHAPTER ELEVEN

THE BATTLE OF THE 'SCOTTISH CORRIDOR'

'Epsom'—the Drive to the Odon and Hill 112
26 and 27 June

On 25 June, while the 'Butcher Bears' were fighting for Fontenay, the infantry of the 15th Scottish Division were marching to their assembly areas behind the start-line. Clouds of fine white dust enveloped the sweating, heavily-laden men. Now they appreciated the purpose of all those seemingly meaningless, endless route marches they had cursed so much in training. Their eyes took in those signs which showed that this was no exercise —piles of rubble which had once been villages. Bretteville l'Orgueilleuse, Norrey-en-Bessin, le Mesnil-Patry. Piles of discarded equipment, a holed steel-helmet, the blackened hull of a Sherman. Serjeant Gariepy could have told them what had happened here, barely two weeks before. No sound came from the marching files, except the slush of boots through the dust. There was no singing, for this was the time before battle. The generals of a previous century had known what they were doing, when they supplied bands to play the Regiments into action. A man needs war-drums at such a moment. A motor-bike went blaring down the column, with roaring exhaust, trailing a banner of dust. The rider was searching the faces of the infantrymen, red and hot under a cake of white dust, streaked with rivulets of sweat, like war-paint. His gaze passed unseeingly over Serjeant Green, anonymous among the burdened men; but Green recognised the set of his head and shoulders as he rode by, and shouted out after him, " Stan! "

" My brother had never seen me in marching order before ", recollected Sergeant Green, " only on leave together. He had heard of the 15th Scottish attack, when the plan was given out to his battery, and had set off to find me. We had a talk, then he gave me a lift on his motor-bike to the head of the column,

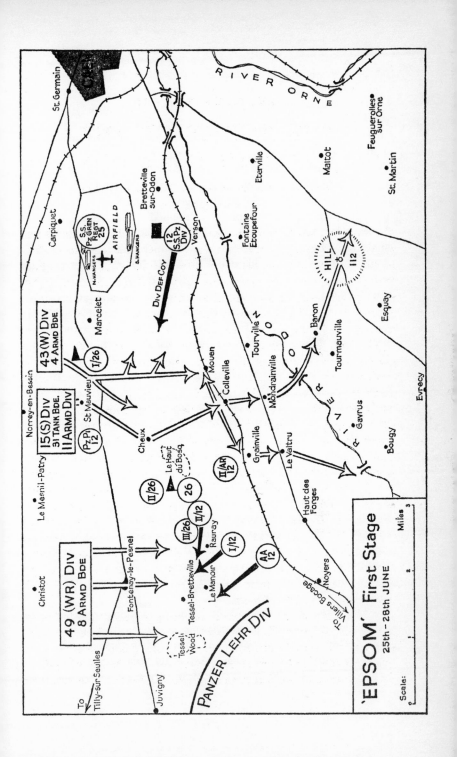

'EPSOM' First Stage
25th - 28th JUNE

which had stopped for the inevitable wait. We had ten minutes or so together, but the parting was one of the worst moments I was ever to know and I never expected to see him alive again. We were an unhappy pair, for every cross we saw from then onwards had us looking in dread of the name we might find there."

Up to now, even the 'I' Section had not known the plan of attack, but that day they struggled with a sand model of the battlefield, while the guns of Fontenay thundered ceaselessly in the distance. "How impressive seemed those plans," wrote Serjeant Green. "The Jerry defences were to be hammered mercilessly by 250 bombers and a 'Monty' barrage, until they cracked; then we could pour through the gap, sweeping all before us. Our flanks were to be secured by 49 Div, who promised faithfully to capture Rauray prior to our attack. Our plan was for 46 Brigade to capture the village of Cheux, 44 Brigade to clear St. Mauvieu. Then my brigade, 227, would take part. The main objectives for 227 Brigade were the crossings over the River Odon, which were to be captured by the Argylls after 10 H.L.I. had prepared the way on the right by the capture of Grainville-sur-Odon. The Gordons on the left were to clear Colleville and exploit forward. The crowning blow was to be made by 11 Armoured Div, who were to crash through the gap we would make and race for the high ground at Baron and Hill 112, before turning east and seizing crossings over the River Orne. Pity the Germans who were to try to withstand it."

That night, as if the guns had been thunder, it began to rain; huddled under the miserable shelter of trees, the tired men dozed fitfully, the rain-drops falling on their faces; and then the drizzle became a downpour and there was no more sleep. Stiff and chilled, long before dawn, they were walking about or stamping their feet to get warm, and waiting for a mug of tea and a mess-tin full of bacon and biscuit. Four years' training— for this.

Then 700 guns opened fire from the fields around them, with a savage, deafening concussion which stunned the ears and dulled the mind. As they went forward through the drizzling rain, through ruined villages, the few inhabitants gazed at them sullenly and silently; perhaps it was pity for the doomed men of the division. But the soldiers did not understand it and were disconcerted by this contrast with war films and propaganda. "All ranks had heard much of the sufferings of France under the Occupation, also many tales of the French 'Resistance'," wrote the Gordons' historian, " but these Normans seemed unimpressed by the turn of events. In our few days ashore, we had gathered that some of the women had married German soldiers, and there was a general air of caution—a reluctance to accept the presence of the invaders as a change for the better. 'The Boche had said that he would be back in three weeks', we were told. A Gordon officer who wanted the use of a barn to shelter his men was told by the farmer that it could not be permitted as the farm was the property of the Third Reich. Food was abundant and it seemed that in Normandy the German behaviour had been 'correct'."

As they marched up the road to Putot-en-Bessin, under the continuous moaning and wailing of the shells, there was ahead a new and uneasy sound. The continuous rippling noise of machine-guns, a high-pitched rattle quite unlike the slower, regular beat of the Brens. But the advance was going slowly, there were many hours spent waiting by the roadside. After Putot-en-Bessin they came to the first signs of battle—two Churchill tanks blown up in a minefield short of the Caen road, their crews laughing and joking with the 'Jocks' as they passed, over-excited at their escape from both death and battle. Then a dead 'Jock', huddled up, rifle at the ready. Another halt was ordered, just short of the Caen road. "A threat to our right flank was developing from Rauray, where 60 tanks were reported. Our friends of 49 Div had failed us; so had the bombers we had been so faithfully promised. Both flanks 'up in the air', we had to go on. Cheux was cleared, St. Mauvieu taken, and so our time had arrived," wrote Serjeant Green.

" It was late afternoon when we were ordered forward in extended order across the Caen road towards Cheux, every man keyed up and searching each fold in the ground for snipers, though as yet not a shot had been fired at our leading troops. When within fifty yards of the road, a young German in a camouflaged uniform rose up from the long grass almost under the muzzle of a Sten gun which killed him instantly. This was purely a nervous reaction on the part of the owner, and the only case I was to see of a German being killed for no reason. But it started a sniper scare and a lot of indiscriminate firing took place in all directions. The rain now came down with teeming ferocity and the darkening sky portended a wet and dreary night. The orchard area of Le Haut du Bosc was reached without incident, and we had left behind the forward troops of 46 Brigade, but the rain and lowering sky made control difficult, direction was lost in the orchards, and then we struck trouble. Machine-guns opened up at the leading companies which, shocked by the suddenness of it, went to ground. Our supporting tanks replied, the tracer ricochetting in all directions, a source of fear to all and sundry, Scottish and German. Each time the leading companies tried to advance, they were met by heavy fire, and the advance petered out."

As the attack had lost direction and gone astray, the C.O. decided to re-group in Cheux, before advancing once more through the orchards of Le Haut du Bosc towards Grainville. " When we had first entered Cheux that day," recollected Serjeant Green, " the only dead to be seen were two R.E.s on the pavement. A mortar shell, bursting at their feet, had blown them open like peeled oranges. This must have happened only minutes before, because the bloom had not yet left their faces. Yet as the day progressed, I was to pass them many times, lying obscenely exposed to the mounting layers of dust which slowly covered them. I never got used to seeing them, but as Cheux was slowly pounded into rubble, someone got them away before they were buried under the falling masonry."

Cheux was rapidly becoming a bottle-neck, jammed with rubble and wrecked vehicles, with two divisions and two brigades trying to pass through one narrow street. 31 Tank Brigade, with its slow-moving but heavily armoured Churchills, some of them equipped with flame-throwers, went forward with the infantry. As soon as they had reached the Caen road, which ran parallel to the front between St. Mauvieu and Cheux, 11 Armoured Division was to advance, with its 29th Brigade leading. In the usual ' two up and one behind ' style, 23 Hussars and 2 Fife & Forfar Yeomanry advanced, followed by 3 Royal Tank Regiment as reserve.

'C' Squadron of 23 Hussars by-passed Cheux to the east, although the remainder went through the village, and working their way through difficult country supported the advance of 2 Gordons on Colleville. 'C' Squadron was therefore separated from the rest of the regiment by the Cheux traffic jam. The greater part of 2 Gordons, including Battalion H.Q., were likewise held in the jam, and only two companies attacked Colleville—'A' and 'B'. 'A' was pinned in a cornfield by mortar fire, but 'B' Company, quite alone, actually got into Colleville. The rest of the Battalion were miles away, motionless in the traffic hold-up.

Eventually, 'C' Squadron of 23 Hussars was joined by 'B' Squadron, and they tried to help the infantry forward. The Churchills in close support were clearly having a very bad time. "As soon as one of them showed itself over the crest it drew fire and there were already three or four in flames just in front of us", wrote a witness in the Regimental History. 'B' Squadron moved forward past the blazing hulks and 'C' went down the slope to aid the infantry. "As with the Churchills, so with the Shermans. As soon as the leading tank showed itself it was hit and set on fire. This was the first tank of the Regiment to be destroyed in action. Those who witnessed it will always remember the shock of seeing for the first time one of the Regiment's tanks go up in flames. One moment an impregnable monster, with perhaps a crew containing some of one's best friends, forging irresistibly towards the enemy: the next, a crack of terrific impact, a sheet of flame—and then, where there had been a tank nothing but a helpless, roaring inferno."

*　　　*　　　*

Much of the opposition met by 227 Highland Brigade and 23 Armoured Brigade in the evening, as they took the lead of their respective divisions, had not been there in the morning. Only a handful of Hitler Youth teenagers with rifles, machine-pistols, Spandaus and panzerfausts. The late afternoon report of a tank counter-attack coming in from still-untaken Rauray had been correct. On the morning of the 26th, not even Fontenay was completely clear and only half Tessel Wood had been taken. The two heavy tank companies of 12th S.S. which had been moved there, were helping to hold the 'Butcher Bears' and, against their opposition, an attack from Tessel towards Rauray that day broke down. A historian of 12 K.R.R.C., the British 'panzer grenadiers' helping 49 Div and its supporting armour forward, wrote: "The main enemy resistance between Tessel Wood and Rauray were some six to ten Tiger tanks, each with an attendant party of infantry well dug in. Progress was slow and the enemy picked off the '18' wireless sets of the leading platoons. Consequently the gunners could not support them properly. Barry Newton will not forget his visit to Le Manoir church. He was just discussing with his platoon serjeant its desirability as Platoon H.Q. when the church spire fell at his feet. Neither will Roger Green forget the sight which greeted him as he poked his head inquisitively round the end of the church—a Tiger tank at rather less than 40 yards! Hardly believing his eyes, he had another look. This was too much for the Hun, who removed his tin hat with a ricochet off the church wall. About this time the attack we were protecting petered out and the Battalion was ordered to withdraw under the cover of smoke to Fontenay."

These attacks south-east from Tessel, through Le Manoir, towards Rauray, were being driven back by elements of S.S. Panzer Regiment 12, plus the heavy companies. Convinced that the 'Butcher Bears' were being held, and that the Scottish breakthrough to the east was more serious, in the late afternoon units of Panzer Regiment 12 were ordered away from Rauray in a counter-attack designed to take the 15th Scottish and 11th Armoured breakthrough in flank and plug the gap which had developed there. The 8th Company was one of these units. "At that moment", recollected the Company Commander, " our Mark IV tanks were north-east of Rauray, re-fuelling in feverish haste and being filled with ammunition to bursting point. Since early morning, the enemy had been pushing with more and more force against our lines, and the men hardly took time even for a swig from their field-bottles. We had been in continuous action for 24 hours already, and the men's faces showed the strain. Then, as we were about to move, I was given a direct order by the commander of the Regiment in person, to take those tanks south-east of Cheux, where the enemy had just broken through on our right. 'Situation doubtful—quick action imperative—no infantry available to cover you '—that was the gist of what he said. But our engines were already roaring, and his last words were drowned in the rattle of the tracks as we moved off."

Almost instantly, they were in action against the leading brigades of 11th Armoured, 15th Scottish, and the supporting Churchills of 31 Tank Brigade. At the sight of the British armour pouring through, the Company Commander ordered a firing stop. " We engaged these visible targets, and the enemy armour began to pour out those well-known clouds of dark black smoke. Then, at top speed, taking advantage of the confusion our surprise attack had caused, we raced across an open plain to the cover of a little hollow, and pushed on from there, firing all the time. Our own artillery began to bring down defensive fire to help us, we contacted our troops on the left flank, who cheered our arrival, and spread out to the right, eastwards, to close the gap broken in our line. Finally, we were in position on the eastward, or enemy side, of Le Haut du Bosc, facing towards Cheux; and there we were ordered to stay for the night."

Almost simultaneously, the leading squadrons of 23 Hussars, who had just seen their first Shermans go up in flames, pulled back behind a hill for the night, which, as it was summer, was long in coming and short when it came. Re-fuelling, re-ammunitioning, essential maintenance, and a hurried meal, left little time for sleep before the next dawn lightened the few hours of darkness. They would be lucky to get two hours undisturbed. Under the trees of Le Haut du Bosc, a little way away, the men of 8 Company, S.S. Panzer Regiment 12, spent an even more uncomfortable night, for they had no infantry protection. " Darkness set in with more sheets of rain," wrote the Company Commander. " Slowly, the noise of the battle quietened down. Now and then a machine-gun barked and an occasional flare burst far away under the heavy, lowering clouds. Our gun-crews sat exhausted and dozing beside their weapons in the tanks, while the drivers and radio-operators kept watch outside. Ammunition and food were promised us, and I used this lull to make my report." Not far away, also sheltering miserably in the orchards of Le Haut du Bosc, was the 10th Battalion of the Highland Light Infantry. " We dug in for the night under intermittent mortar fire," wrote

Serjeant Green. " To add to our wretchedness, the rain still persisted, although we were already so wet that we scarcely heeded the downpour; the mortaring and the rain made sleep almost impossible. The attack was to go in again next morning, 27 June. When it came, breakfast was cold tinned sausage and the tea a muddy concoction."

The German artillery used the cover of darkness to alter their hasty gun positions to better-chosen sites, and the artillery commander in person made the rounds. At about midnight, he reached the tanks of 8 Company, and asked the Company Commander about his fields-of-fire. Ammunition and food supplies had just arrived, and one of the vehicles, in turning, had become bogged in the soggy ground. The little group of officers standing by the Company Commander's tank were about to join in the pushing, when dark figures rose up out of the bushes, and came crashing forward, firing from the hip, shouting " Hands Up!" The Company Commander dived straight at the nearest one, and they went down in a tangle together, the British soldier's Sten gun firing of its own accord as it hit the ground. He also had a bayonet or a knife, but he got the point entangled in the German's tank overalls, while the German tried to grab the Sten. " Help!" shouted his opponent.

" One of the man's companions shot at us immediately," recalled the Company Commander, " but hit him, his friend, instead of me, his enemy. The man groaned once, then collapsed. I jumped up, pulled my pistol, and ran after the second man, who was retreating. In my excitement, I emptied the whole magazine at his vanishing form. Above the noise of the shooting, I heard a weak voice calling in German. It was the Artillery Commander, who had fallen beside his vehicle, fatally wounded and covered in blood. I just had time to pull him under the cover of his car and send a warning to the tank nearest to me on my right; then as I turned the other way, towards the nearest tank to my left, about 80 yards distant, I saw to my horror two dark shadows on top of it, pulling at the entry flaps. In English came a shout: " Hand grenade!" An explosion rent the night and hell broke loose around our tanks. In the darkness, everybody shot at everyone else. Grenades burst all around and I pressed myself against my tank, to get some cover on one side.

"Suddenly, the noise stopped and there was a deathly silence. I no longer felt the rain. Pressed hard into the soaking earth, straining with every nerve to tell friend from enemy in the surrounding blackness, I could hear nothing but the mad beating of my heart. Then, with a scream, the engine of my leading tank started up, the gears crashed, and it began to move. I was just about to throw myself at it, assuming it to be in enemy hands, when it moved back to the spot where the attack came from, turned 90 degrees, pushed itself towards me, stopped and cut the engine. Again silence, seconds like long minutes. At last, I got up, ran forward, threw myself flat on the slippery ground behind the tank, and listened. No movement. With my empty pistol, I knocked on the metal, prepared to defend myself with the pistol butt. The flap lifted a little and a German voice from inside called out politely, 'Pardon?'

"Obviously, the enemy had gone. My men were unhurt, but the gunner of my own tank was missing; the darkness, and the fear of another and stronger enemy patrol, made it unwise for us to go out to look for him. But soon after, he came back on his own and reported to me, 'Sir, I have been taken prisoner.' Unarmed, he had made for the tank on the right, and walked straight into two of the enemy. They grabbed him and bundled him away towards their own lines. From their voices, he judged them to be Americans. Then a burst of machine-gun fire sent them all diving for cover. Rolling over and over, on his side, he had been able to move a little distance away into the darkness, until he splashed into a small stream, where he lay motionless. When the firing stopped, he heard the two men searching for their German prisoner, then go off, trailing a series of 'God Damns'.[1]

"This aggressive patrolling by the enemy made it likely that a large-scale attack would come with the morning, and I reported the incident to the C.O. of our II Battalion, the unit on our left flank. But he had no reserves to send me to cover that open flank

[1] A number of young Canadian officers were seconded to British infantry battalions under a scheme called 'Canloan'; the accent, the words, and the absence of Americans anywhere in the vicinity, make it almost certain that these men were Canadian officers.

on my right. After talking to him, I walked back in the dawn to my tanks, the earth steaming with moisture, passing on my way the over-tired young grenadiers of the II Battalion who sat huddled under tarpaulins in their slit-trenches. I said a few encouraging words, but had hardly reached my own Company, to give the tank crews their orders, when the first enemy shells screamed overhead. Fountains of earth spat a hail-storm of clods and stones; trees were bodily uprooted. Luckily the whole lot was falling behind us, and for half-an-hour the enemy artillery did not alter their range. Then the infantry, strengthened by about a dozen tanks, started the expected frontal attack. A rising mist hid them at first. We heard only the roar of advancing engines and the ceaseless banging of gunfire. The tank shells were not yet reaching us; but these were the standard tactics of the Allies, to ' plough up ' the ground in front of them as they advanced. Then the first figures materialised in the mist. Behind them, with the second wave, rolled the heavy tanks. Range about 2,000 yards—still much too far." The 10th Battalion of the H.L.I. came on, through the standing corn and under the deadly trees in the orchards.

The defensive fire of the German artillery was already taking its toll. " Our leading troops were caught in a heavy barrage before they could cross the start-line, and shells bursting in the trees caused heavy casualties," wrote Serjeant Green. " Gone was the ' scheme ' complex, this was war at its bloodiest; the cry of ' Stretcher bearers! ' took on the soul-rending tone of human beings in mortal agony." But still the tanks of 8 Company waited for the order to fire. " We were positioned in the shadow of the trees, behind a slight incline, which hid the hulls of our tanks," said the Company Commander, " with young trees and bushes tied to the turrets to complete our camouflage. So I let them come up close, and when I gave the first order to fire, it was with the machine-guns only. Surprise was complete. Those who did not fall retreated in panic. Then I ordered the tank guns to fire on the enemy tanks which were in the rear, advancing with the second wave. Again, we stopped the advance, without any casualties on our side."

" Struggling forward through chest-high corn, the Jocks were cut to pieces by dug-in Panther tanks firing at close range," wrote

Serjeant Green. "Frantically they went to ground, but mercilessly the enemy mortars plastered the cornfield. Training had taught them much, but could never teach the horror of seeing their friends torn to pieces before their eyes. One minute, a strong, virile young man; the next, a useless hunk of flesh. The gaps were filled as the reserve companies were pushed forward, but the attack was failing against strong opposition and was rapidly becoming completely stuck. The Regimental Aid Post was working at top speed to ease the pains of the wounded, but as rapidly as they were driven away others took their places, until the procession seemed never-ending. Jeeps and carriers were pressed into service and never stopped in their journeys back and forward from the Casualty Clearing Station. A 1 Echelon were caught in the open, the men who had failed to take cover paying with their lives."

" I sent back a short report asking for ammunition," said the Commander of 8 Company, " and, if possible for reserves to cover my open right flank, where I could see the enemy concentrating. That compelled me to bring my tanks out of their safe cover and move to where I could deal with this threat. The inferior cover just had to be accepted. Through my glasses, I watched a group of enemy pioneers, about 1,500 yards away, dragging heavy explosive charges. The tank on my left fired just one shell, which burst right in the middle of them. In an unimaginably violent explosion, human bodies flew high into the air, flopping to the ground again like sacks. The sight took my breath away."

" The whole area was infested with snipers," wrote Serjeant Green, " and the intermittent crack of their rifles kept breaking in on the duller roar of the mortars. Every gun in the vicinity was turned on them. The few that were captured proved to be very young. We were amazed at their youth and their arrogant attitude; to have shot at soldiers from corn in such a manner and then to expect mercy was almost beyond belief—the fact that they were spared at all says much for our men. These were the only German soldiers we saw, but five Panther tanks broke into the orchard and menaced the whole position. The Battalion anti-tank gunners stuck to their guns and a duel developed, with the Regimental Aid Post and Battalion H.Q. in the middle, between two fires. The Panthers' shells were chipping lumps from the top of the wall sheltering the wounded, as all and sundry grabbed stretchers and hurriedly got the casualties away, crouching low behind the wall to avoid the heavy fire. The anti-tank gunners won the duel, and five shattered Panthers bore testimony to their shooting. But the road leading back to Cheux was becoming impassable, even for the wounded, packed with the tanks of 11 Armoured Division, small consolation now that the climax of the battle had been reached and passed. When we had needed them most, we had looked in vain for their mobile fire power."

"At about 11 o'clock we began to go forward," wrote a historian of 23 Hussars. " It was not long before the enemy reacted. Some Tiger tanks seemed to be trying to work in from the flank from the direction of the Haut du Bosc feature. 2 Fife & Forfar Yeomanry, who were on the right flank, also engaged them." Almost certainly, this was the move to new positions by 8 Company of S.S. Panzer Regiment 12. In the first attack, their hull-down Mark IVs were reported by 10 H.L.I. as dug-in Panthers; and now they were in the open, they had become Tigers. But, as yet, there were very few Tigers in Normandy.

" Soon after we had moved to the right, the expected enemy attack came in," said the Commander of 8 Company. "Again, we let them come close; and again, the same success. The retreating infantry had heavy casualties and more than a dozen burning tanks exploded in the distance. One only of them managed to break through near our position. I could see him on my right flank behind the crown of a tree some 600 yards away; my gunner could not get at him, because there were too many branches in the way, and even I, from my higher vantage point, could see only the top of his turret. But I was sure he had not spotted us, and was not particularly worried. It was the next concentration of enemy troops, forming up for yet another attack from the hill in front, which took all my attention. And it was this murderous material superiority of the enemy which made our desperate struggle a stark necessity. We had no glory to defend, but we meant to fight to the last for all we had left: that bond of comradeship and unconditional mutual help, regardless of rank, which bound us completely together. We did not hate the enemy soldier, the individual human being, but, as our much-admired commander wrote in his book, when he knew that this sacrifice of young life was useless: ' I begin to hate the war! '

" When the third enemy attack started to come in, I had half an eye on the chap on my right flank, but he made no move. Then, as the enemy in front began to get close, I had to concentrate ahead. Shell after shell left the barrel of our gun; each one a hit. We fired so fast that the ventilators could hardly cope with the fuming gases. My eyes, pressed to the periscope, were burning and blinking as I watched the effect of each shot and searched for new and dangerous targets. Abruptly, the ground in front of us appeared to explode—a tank shell fired from the right flank! One look over there was enough. The lone enemy tank had changed position and was 400 yards away, firing at us. Before we could even swing the gun round to bear, he hit us. Flames blew up around us and escape hatches flew open.

" Through the left hatch, the gunner bailed out, his clothes flaming; through the right hatch went the gun-loader. I could not get out through the turret hatch, so tried to follow the loader; and at the same moment, the radio operator had the same idea. Nothing for it but to go back into the flames. My head spun and I felt weak to fainting-point. With eyes tight-shut against the fire, and with my last effort, I pushed the radio operator bodily through the hatch and tumbled after him. And then I found myself in mid-air, hanging down the side of the tank, with machine-gun fire rattling against the plating. In my mad rush, I had forgotten to unplug the wireless lead which was fastened round my neck by a metal band. But after a desperate struggle I got free, fell to the ground, and rolled out of the line of fire.

" When I got under cover of the trees I found my badly burned crew trying to smother the flames which still smouldered in the clothing of the gunner. I threw myself on top of his moaning body and stifled the last glimmer of flame; but he did not survive, nor did my driver, who found his grave inside that tank. I felt no pain from the burns on my face and hands just then, because the enemy attack was still rolling on. My other three tanks had not even noticed what had happened to us; completely absorbed in the battle, they were firing shell after shell. Helpless, I stood between the fire-spitting monsters, and then, to my delight, saw that once more the enemy was retreating. The turret-hatch of the nearest tank opened, and a pair of tired eyes in a thin, smoke-blackened face stared at me in horror. I knew then that I must be a dreadful sight. In fact, my face was burned and swollen—the shape and colour of a boiled potato. So I handed over command to the senior tank commander present, and took my badly wounded comrades back to the Regimental Aid Post in the vehicle which had been abandoned during the attack by the enemy patrol. The steering wheel was like burning metal to my tortured hands, so I put my foot down as hard as I could, to get some relief to our wounds from the cool wind of movement. Even while I sat in a chair, giving my report to the Regimental Commander, the doctor was giving me a morphia injection. So I was out of it. But think—this wilderness, this fury of war which I have described, it covered barely 24 hours of a conflict which lasted years; and of the millions who took part, how many really wanted it?"

* * *

Through the gap on the right flank of the remnants of 8 Company, the Argyll & Sutherland Highlanders of 227 Infantry Brigade reached that day the unblown bridge over the Odon River at Tourmauville, and were followed across by 23 Hussars of 29 Armoured Brigade. The command tank of the Hussars was taken as a target by German guns and the Regiment were amused to hear their Colonel, in the middle of a battle, come on the air with a startling order: "*Get behind me, Sixteen Charlie, there's some bastard shooting me up the dock!*" Probably the Germans grinned too. Certainly, Hubert Meyer's radio spies were following the course of the attack with an interest which was rapidly becoming personal. "On 27 June, the British, having advanced through Grainville, took a bridge over the Odon near Baron," said Meyer. "And that afternoon, our W/T intelligence heard an enemy tank unit asking their superiors: '*Are you still interested in the quick settlement of Operation Verson?*' Our Div H.Q. at Verson was only 4 kilometres from that river crossing. Our Defence Company was not available; it was already in the fighting, north of Mouen. So all members of the staff who could possibly be spared were put on a hill to protect H.Q. from the south. This sort of self-defence was nothing new. Only the day before, several British tanks had broken through as far as Verson and two had been destroyed by staff orderlies with Panzerfausten. But we never heard the answer to that interesting radio question; and no attack on Verson took place." 23 Hussars, leading 29 Armoured Brigade, were actually wheeling in behind Meyer's H.Q.; not merely south of Carpiquet, but south of Verson itself. The thinly-held German line had been ripped wide open, and the dominating height of Hill 112 lay ahead. As they roared down to the Odon near Gavrus, the Hussars' tank met head-on a civilian car, driven by a German, bowling along the road from Esquay and the heights looming ahead. He was still going merrily when, at 20 yards range, Corporal Essex put a 75 mm armour-piercing solid shot straight through the vehicle. " Surprisingly, the driver managed to get out," wrote a witness, " and though pursued by Corporal Hoggins with a Sten gun, got clear away and was last seen going very fast in the direction of Esquay."

On the approach to the river, the tank commanded by Lieutenant Weiner was knocked out; and his captors were 12th S.S. If the rumours spread by the Canadians about the S.S. were even half-true, a British officer with a name like that was a goner. But he survived to tell his story, " a remarkable one ", according to the Regimental History. " Narrowly escaping summary execution at the hands of his captors, who were about to shoot him when a less brutal officer intervened, he was borne away past rows of Panthers waiting to counter-attack our bridgehead. He had been slightly wounded in the leg and was taken to a hospital in Rennes where he received the usual primitive treatment. One day, the noise of guns was heard; the Americans were arriving, and in due course they liberated him. He duly ' escaped ' from their insistent offers to send him to England, and arrived back with the Regiment, still in Normandy."

CHAPTER TWELVE

THE COUNTER-ATTACKS
COME IN

'Epsom'—the Panzer Divisions Gather Round the 'Corridor'

28 June to 2 July

The containment mission that had been assigned Monty was not calculated to burnish British pride in the accomplishments of their troops. For in the minds of most people, success in battle is measured in the rate and length of advance. They found it difficult to realise that the more successful Monty was in stirring up German resistance, the less likely he was to advance. By the end of June, Rommel had concentrated seven panzer divisions against Monty's British sector. One was all he could spare for the U.S. front.

General Omar N. Bradley

The situation on the morning of 28 June was that 8 Corps had taken the first objective, the crossings of the Odon River, well behind schedule; and in doing so, had tied themselves up in knots. Nowhere could the enormous weight of men and material be brought irresistibly to bear. A 20th Century army consists in the main of a mass of vehicles, equipment, and stores, with a comparatively small number of men up the 'sharp end', actually in contact with the enemy. It is a potential two-way traffic jam of immense magnitude. Because the bulk of the vehicles are wheeled, not tracked, the decisive factor in battle is the number and quality of the roads leading in the right direction. But the bottleneck which built up in Cheux was inexcusable. Apparently, no-one even bothered to control it, let alone bulldoze roadways through the ruins or build by-pass tracks round it. No-one even directed the tracked vehicles to go round the village, possibly because of the minefield which had caused casualties to the Churchills and AVREs on the first day. But minefields not covered by fire are made to be cleared. So the bulk of the tanks which should have supported the infantry sat firmly in Cheux, holding up the advance, closed down against mortar and artillery fire, and, bitterly complained the infantry, "deaf to all appeals".

The German artillery commander had come forward in person

on the first night, to make sure his guns were properly sited; admittedly, he had been killed doing it. A little more of that spirit on the British side might have made all the difference. Then again, unlike the Canadians, the British infantry and armour were insufficiently integrated; they did not really know one another. And, finally, the sniper fire all over the area, greatly intensified by wildly-aimed retaliation in all directions, was not recognised for what it was: not snipers at all, not a thin screen out in front of the main German battle line; those scattered shots, with the occasional burst of machine-gun fire, *was* the main German position—all that was left of 12th S.S. Panzer Division on that front, a handful of determined teenagers, toughly arrogant at the havoc they were causing. A band of brothers fighting for all they had left now—pride in themselves and in their comrades.

But this situation could not, and would not, last forever. While 8 Corps writhed against the choking constriction of Cheux, struggling to convert a six-mile breakthrough into a breakout that would sweep around behind the entire German front in the Caen sector, rushing the Germans to ruin, the Germans were reacting. Already, on 27 June, reinforcements were near. On that day, 4 Company of Panzer Regiment 22, 21 Panzer Division, were on the road from the Airborne bridgehead where they had fought so long, to Caen. Werner Kortenhaus was still with them. By evening, they had reached Verson, the H.Q. and base area of 12th S.S., commanded now by the energetic young general, Kurt (' Panzer ') Meyer. "It was a restless night," recollected Kortenhaus. "The enemy were so close, we could hear their voices. Next day, 28 June, a hastily-formed Battle Group of 12th S.S., supported by the last tanks of our 4 Company, and some S.S. Panthers, attacked along the railway embankment towards Mouen. The astonishingly young grenadiers of this unit were indescribably brave. We broke through the forward enemy, in a battle that lasted for hours, advancing through a wilderness of abandoned equipment and dead British soldiers."

"We had remained dug-in around Le Haut du Bosc until the morning of 28 June", wrote Serjeant Green. "Then we moved off down the road to Colleville—also choked with tanks and vehicles of all descriptions. The Battalion had been ordered to clear the area around Mouen; little resistance was expected, and orders for the attack were brief and sketchy. I was with Battalion H.Q. We were to follow behind 'A' Company on the left flank, and so we moved forward into the corn. 'A' were in extended order, and H.Q. in two files a few yards apart; and as the barrage screamed overhead, we were only faintly apprehensive, in view of the fact that we had been told that the area was clear of Germans. We were well into the field when the enemy, who had let us get very close, opened up with machine-guns firing on fixed lines which swept the ears off the standing corn. The leading section of 'A' Company tumbled like wheat before a scythe, but the right-hand sections, and part of H.Q., dashed forward before they were enfiladed, and broke through into the cover of a small copse. The rest of us, officers gone, lay doggo in the field, pinned down. To the left, a Sherman tank went up in flames.

" I was in the lead of the left file of Battalion H.Q., with Serjeant McNeil behind me, followed by the rest of the Intelligence Section. When the rippling fire began and the section in front hit the ground, we also went to ground, the fire whipping overhead, clipping the corn, as the machine-guns traversed the field. We lay head to foot in the furrows of Panther tank tracks, and began to crawl along them; they screened us and there was no betraying corn to give away our movements by waving about. The machine-gun fire was still sweeping overhead, and the clipped-off ears of corn kept pinging down on to our steel helmets. I pushed my shovel, blade uppermost, over the back of my neck (we carried them under the small pack), to get what protection I could. One of 'A' Company was screaming with pain and shock, crying out with horror at the sight of his shattered forearm—blown open by a burst of fire which had exposed the bones and sinews. We had to bully him to get back control of himself. I timed the crawling, so that we moved when it had passed into the distance, and stopped when it began to come back again. Serjeant McNeil got impatient at this, and said we would get along faster on hands-and-knees. As he rose up slightly to show me, he was shot in the back by a single round fired from a line of trees on our right. His momentary appearance made the enemy concentrate his fire on where we were, and I was glad to get a spurt on and crawl forward. The thundering roar of an approaching solid shot was also a frightening experience; it went by only a foot or so overhead, and destroyed the Sherman tank which was on our left flank.

" When I reached the edge of the corn, I was horrified to see a wide stretch of open stubble between us and the trees where we had hoped to find cover. The piled-up bodies of 'A' Company were marked by the white hair of L/Corporal McCloy—now vividly blotched with blood. Clearly, we would never get across that stretch. We seemed to be quite alone, so I decided to strike back and to the left, along a convenient tank track. I bumped first into Serjeant Corbishey and some of his platoon and then came across the knocked-out Sherman, one of my section helping a member of its crew to bandage his shattered knee-cap. Eventually, the fire seemed to fade away, and we stopped for a smoke, and said to hell with the Germans. By now, it seemed worth making a dash for the cover of the trees where we could see some of rear H.Q. There we found the C.O. riding up and down in his Bren carrier trying to urge on the attack over the R.T. set —one of the operators was shot through the head by a sniper and was pitched over the side—and the C.O. was frantic in his desire to urge on the attack. From what I could gather, ' D ' Company, attacking on the right, had been cut to pieces, and the C.O. was unable to give them any help. He asked me what the situation was in the forward corn and was scornful when he heard that 'A' Company were pinned down. He wanted to know why we had come back, but he knew that the ' I ' Section had never been trained to fight. We were too glad to be out of the cornfield to care what he said. Anyway, we found that our task in a real battle was so different from training that we had to start and re-learn our functions under fire.

" Meanwhile, the leading platoon of 'A' Company had been able to break through the cornfield and into the enemy positions beyond, with no quarter asked or given. For two days, the Jocks had been hammered by an enemy they had not seen; their pals killed and wounded from a distance. Now they had real men in front of them, they meant to repay the agony of the last two days, and their ferocity appalled the Germans, who fell rapidly to bullet, bayonet, and grenade. They retired in panic, leaving over fifty of their dead to bear testimony to the fury of 'A' Company's attack. The remainder of the tanks also had better luck than that first Sherman—they chalked up two Panthers and four Mark IV tanks."

"Round about 1700 hours, the Mark IV tanks of our 4th Company found themselves in a triangular field bounded by the railway line running between Mouen and Cheux," recollected Werner Kortenhaus. "It was a dangerous position, and when the enemy attacked we found ourselves engaged in a bitter battle with enemy tanks and anti-tank guns. Tank 413 had a track broken by a shell, but the crew repaired it, covered by their 'little brothers' of the S.S. Grenadiers. Then the commander of tank 421, standing up in the turret, had his head blown off by a shell; the crew were so horrified that the driver reversed abruptly and broke part of the track-mechanism. Both these two crippled tanks retired, moving very slowly. Tank 422 was the next to be damaged; its turret jammed by a hit, it reversed into a sunken road to carry out repairs. Tank 425 first had its engine put out of action, then its gun; immobile, it lay in the middle of a close-quarter fight between S.S. Grenadiers and enemy infantry. All its commander could do to help our men was to chuck hand-grenades out of the turret. It was hit again, and caught fire. Finally, Tank 412, the leader's machine, went up in flames. We had lost two tanks and had three seriously damaged." Korten-haus was wounded in the fight and spent three weeks in hospital. When his division was finally withdrawn from the line to reserve at Emieville, it numbered about 40 tanks.

*   *   *

If the track of one Battalion alone, say 10 H.L.I., was plotted for the 'Epsom' operation, it would resemble a cross between a geometric design and a crazy doodle; they went to and fro, up and across, backwards and forwards, east, north, south, and west. When, finally, south of Cheux, the centre line of 11 Armoured Division was directed to intersect and cross that of 15 Scottish Infantry Division, the traffic pattern became a real old bundle of knitting. Partly, this was because the offensive was being launched 'against the grain' of the prevailing road pattern. But when 43 Wessex Infantry Division was sent in to follow up, mop up, and then hold the eastern flank of the 6-mile deep and 2-mile wide ' Scottish Corridor', 8 Corps was virtually strangling itself to death, even if for sound military reasons.

The Wessex Division, which actually was recruited from that old kingdom, from the counties between Hampshire and the Bristol Channel, consisted of untried troops also; many had not even the slight preliminary baptism of fire afforded by air raids. Their immediate introduction to war, in the division's first operation, was as grave-diggers. " I had never seen dead people," said William Biles of 4th Wiltshires. " But we were sent up to a village, not yet clear of snipers, which had been taken the day before by some Scottish Light Infantry. I went up a very narrow lane with about four houses on one side and a couple of barns on the other. Hanging out of windows and from doorways and lying in the roadway itself were about sixteen Scottish infantry-men. The first chap I picked up was a Corporal who had been wounded in the stomach. We laid them all down in the small cemetery, and then the padre told us they were not to be buried there; we would have to dig graves for them outside the cemetery wall. In manoeuvring the Corporal over the wall, the gascape he was wrapped in fell off and half his insides fell out."

On 29 June, the day after 10 H.L.I. had been pinned in the cornfield at Mouen and Kortenhaus' 4th Company had lost two tanks in the field by the railway line, 1st Worcesters took the village, the first unit of the division to fight. Next day, L. Upping-ton, sent to them as a signals reinforcement, started life as a slit-trench dweller in the very field where Kortenhaus had been wounded. " It must have been some battle ", he remarked. " The orchard and the railway and the fields around were a real charnel house. The embankment was littered with German dead. There was one long ditch with a number of dead Monmouths, who had tried here after the Scottish, before the Worcesters finally secured the place. The area of the ditch was peppered with mortar-bomb holes and it looked as if they had been taken completely by surprise. One or two had blankets over them, as if they had been sleeping at the time. Just beyond, the gun barrel of a knocked-out German tank had thrust itself through the hedge, still managing to look menacing. And behind my foxhole, on the far side of a hedge, were nine dead Monmouths and another knocked-out German tank. Dead bodies everywhere, in fields and hedgerows. We were forbidden to bury our own men, the reason given being that a padre should see them first. At the end of a fortnight, no padre, and the British corpses blackened and bloated and still lying there, when eventually we pulled out. However, we had already buried the dead Germans and the cows and parts of cows that were lying around the railway embankment and in the fields and orchards. Quite a work of art, burying cows. A hole had to be dug alongside the dead animal and the depth judged accordingly. Consequently, when the hole was filled in, the hooves or horns would be protruding above the ground. And many a German's toe-caps were pointing skywards after we'd buried him. But in the village itself, there were still civilians, pushing barrows, prams, and anything else that would hold their belongings.

"With typical Army logic, H.Q. Company were dug in on one side of the railway crossing, and the field kitchen was situated on the other side. You had to take a chance and dash across for food and dash back again, in between being 'stonked' by mortars, particularly the 'Moaning Minnies', which sounded just like a lot of women sobbing their hearts out. The noise would start in the distance and get louder and louder, almost to a scream, and then down would come six 6-inch mortar bombs. A mess-tin with tea in it would be nearly empty by the time you'd got back to your fox-hole after taking a dive or two to earth. Another thing was the canned food. The labels were often missing. You'd look forward to a nice tin of hot soup and find, on opening the tin, that it was treacle-pudding. The tea always had a sort of purple hue and tasted of chloros or something like that."

No breakout. Static warfare. What had gone wrong with the great encirclement of Caen? Principally, the timing. The timing as planned had been correct. The timing as achieved was 24 hours too late. By 29 June, it was already too late. In their first reaction to the great gap torn in their lines, and the mass of tanks, led by 29 Armoured Brigade, pouring out of the Odon bridgehead gained by the infantry, the Germans had thrown in anything that was immediately to hand and, in spite of Allied air supremacy, they had moved a lot faster than 8 Corps. One example had been the intervention by the elements from 21 Panzer Division, drawn from the other side of Caen, plus anything that could be scraped together from H.Q. 12 S.S. Panzer Grenadier Division. Very weak forces, but in the circumstances, just enough. Another example, and this time of a unit brought from the other side of the 'Scottish Corridor', was the rush move of Luftwaffe Motorised Flak Unit I/53, equipped with the deadly dual-purpose 88 mm guns. Their high velocity shells, travelling at 1,200 yards a second, had virtually no trajectory and were unaffected by wind; the shells simply went in a straight line to the target. Aim was unerring, deadly accurate.

At the start of 'Epsom', this unit had been stationed on the hill above Gavrus, protecting the workshops of 12th S.S., but under command of Panzer Lehr, the left-flank division. The Austrian gunner, Kurt Erich Groetschel, who had previously been with Light Flak Regiment 98, had been transferred to the 88s a few days previously, just in time to see a low-flying attack carried out by twin-motor bombers on the workshops. As soon as the bridge at Gavrus was taken by the Argylls, the 88s went into action against it; then came the menacing drive of 29 Armoured Brigade towards Hill 112, which dominated the south-western approach to Caen. For 12th S.S., Gavrus was a minor crisis, but Hill 112 had all the makings of a major disaster. As the Shermans of 23 Hussars roared up onto part of Hill 112, Motorised Flak Unit I/53 was already in movement to deny them control of the summit.

"It was our job to repel the attacking British tanks", said Groetschel, "and also to relieve one Battalion of the 12th S.S. Panzer Division 'Hitler Jugend' on the hill. We moved in shortly before mid-day, losing one of the gun-towing tractors to enemy tank fire. The ground was stone and chalk—almost impossible to emplace the guns. To one side lay the village of Esquay with all its farms. We had expected to relieve an entire S.S. Battalion on the hill, but to our surprise found that they actually consisted of only half a Company of exhausted young soldiers, worn out by the hard fighting there. They told us that, the previous day, an 18-year-old boy had destroyed five enemy tanks at close quarters, using Panzerfaust or 'stovepipe' equipment. For the last one, indeed, he had only used a pistol. He climbed up on it from the

173

back, knocked with his pistol on the turret hatch, and ordered the crew to get out. My brother-in-law now, who was not my brother-in-law then, also belonged to this troop.

" We wasted no time in finding positions for our guns, then sent the tractors down behind the hill, to shelter in a wood at the foot of it. We were in action right away, for already enemy tanks were pushing forward among the houses in the little village below us, trying to shelter behind the walls, and only visible now and again. I saw one tank come forward from behind a house, I saw the turret-hatch fly open, and the commander appear. He raised field-glasses to his eyes, and looked straight at us, scrutinising the ground carefully. I felt as if I could touch him, for I was using a superb telescope designed for really long-range use against aircraft. Our guns began to fire. The first shell missed the tank, but hit the house. Before the tank commander could reverse, the second shell hit the turret. This first encounter was over almost before it had begun, for the tanks down there realised that they could not deploy among all those buildings while under rapid fire from us. They put up smoke, and withdrew.

" Next morning we were twice attacked by low-flying aircraft and beat them off, helped by 2 cm flak guns. But in the early afternoon, came the end. About a dozen tanks were rolling towards us, when two formations of twin-engined Lightnings attacked. Where to fire first? At the planes or at the tanks? In the confusion of the air attack, the tanks opened fire at us. Gun after gun was knocked out, and the crews with them. Only one thing to do—withdraw! We blew up the 2 cm guns and one of the 88s, then, with the machine-gunning planes continuously circling us, we crawled back like seals, on our tummies. I don't know how many tanks we got; but the last one was destroyed by Panzerfaust during our withdrawal. We re-assembled in the wood where the gun-tractors were hidden, and in the early evening were ordered to retrieve all the 88 mm ammunition which we had been forced to abandon on Hill 112. This order did not exactly make us jump for joy.

" Just before midnight, we moved up the hill in three trucks. To our surprise, we found the hill free of enemies, not a tank anywhere. Even the S.S. men who had been put out on sentry-duty were sound asleep. So, feeling bold, we crept forward to those houses where, the previous day, the British tanks had been. Inside them, all was quiet and still. But as I was walking down a passage towards a room, I heard something. From the doorway, I suddenly picked out, over in a corner, the shape of a man. Strange noises were coming from him, and at eye-level, something glittered. I called out to the shadow, first in French, and then in English, but got no reply. I had no torch with me, and was getting nervous. So I tightened the grip I had on my machine-pistol and fired a burst straight into the shape. There was a thundering of boots in the passage as my comrades came dashing to my aid, and then we all stormed into the room. But the shape in the corner was not dead, for it was an old grandfather-clock.

"We were sure now that the enemy had withdrawn, and we brought down from that hill five or six hundred shells and some refreshing cider from the cellars of the houses. I have not been back since to Hill 112, but if there are any broken 88 mm guns still there, then they are ours."

29 Armoured Brigade withdrew from Hill 112 on the night of 29 June. The last unit to retire, the 23rd Hussars, were moving back by 0300 on 30 June. They had not been driven off it by the exhausted remnants of 12th S.S., or the reinforcements hastily flung in, although they had been held by them. The cause for the abandonment of that hard-won and vital height was much more far-reaching, and came originally from Russia.

*　　*　　*

In April, the Red Army's spring offensive had been broken by a powerful armoured reserve—II S.S. Panzer Corps, commanded by Paul Hausser, and consisting of 9 S.S. Panzer Division 'Hohenstauffen' and 10 S.S. Panzer Division 'Frundsberg'. Then they had gone into Army Group reserve in the area of Tarnopol. On 13 June they entrained at Lemberg for their move to Normandy, switched from one end of Europe to the other; from facing in the East attacks by a horde reminiscent of Ghenghis Khan or Attila, to a highly mechanised, modern enemy in the West. When the Russian summer offensive broke on Army Group Centre a month later, the lack of this heavily armed and mobile counter-attack force led to collapse on the central front; and the

Russians began flooding into Europe, a 'human sea' of ragged soldiers plodding across country on foot or sweeping forward on horseback, with little transport except farm carts and American Lease-Lend lorries, and living off the countryside. The long-range consequences of 'Epsom' were momentous, for this Russian invasion, coupled with the desperate, indeed hopeless, situation in Normandy led four weeks after to the 'bitter end' of the German Resistance groups.

Normally, the move of an armoured corps by rail a thousand miles and more across Europe presented no problem to Twentieth Century communications; this had been Germany's great advantage for the first four years of war, when she was fighting on one major front only at a time. But with the 'Second Front' in being, the situation was very different. "Substantial parts of both divisions had to de-train in the Nancy area", recollected William Bittrich, the general commanding 9 S.S. Panzer Division. "In their wheeled vehicles, they went on by road, only the tanks and tracked vehicles continuing by rail. Even so, the massive destruction of key railway installations by the enemy bomber fleets was so great and so widespread, that continuous detours were necessary. Enemy control of the air space over France made daylight movement only occasionally possible, so the rail and road movements were mostly confined to the night. The concentration in Normandy of both divisions was delayed, but particularly that of 10 S.S. Panzer Div. Nevertheless, we were required to conform with the previously planned timing of our attack—which was to begin on 29 June."

By itself, this would have been bad enough. Hausser tried to get a 48 hour pause, to allow for proper assembly of his force, but his senior, General Dollmann, commander of the 7th Army, was already under pressure from Hitler and dare not allow it. Then, that morning of 28 June, Dollmann had a stroke, and died. Hausser was appointed to succeed him, and at mid-day, in the middle of a conference at which the orders for the following day's attack were being given to the senior officers of 9 S.S. Panzer Division, William Bittrich was told to take over Hausser's former appointment as commanding general of II S.S. Panzer Corps. He, in turn, was forced to appoint a successor as commander of 9th S.S., the choice falling naturally on the senior Regimental Com-

Field Marshal Erwin Rommel inspects 21 Panzer Division a week before D-Day–and is not pleased. The divisional commander, Generalmajor Edgar Feuchtinger, is on the right, with hand upraised.

ABOVE, left :
Oberfeldwebel Hans Eric
Braun in 'walking out' d

ABOVE, right : Radio
operator Heinz Trautma
on duty in Tiger 134.

LEFT : Leutnant Hans
Höller on D-Day, during
the battle of Benouville.

A 75mm SP gun of 21 Panzer Division dug-in at Cairon, just before D-Day.

Leutnant Höller with one of his 75mm anti-tank guns disguised as a bush.

Churchill tank at Maltot, in the shadow of Hill 112, D. Blyth, of 11 Armoured Division, reports that the picture was taken by the only war photographer he ever saw during the war!

British infantry on the start-line, waiting to attack.

ABOVE : Heinz
Wittmann's Tiger 134
after a hard-fought
action in Normandy.

RIGHT : A tank of 7
Armoured Division
'brewing up' after
being knocked out by a
Tiger of S.S. Heavy
Tank Battalion 502.

Grenadier of 10 S.S. Panzer Division digging in under a knocked-out Sherman, to get overheard cover.

Teenagers of 12 S.S. Panzer Grenadier Division 'Hitler Jugend' on the march heavily laden.

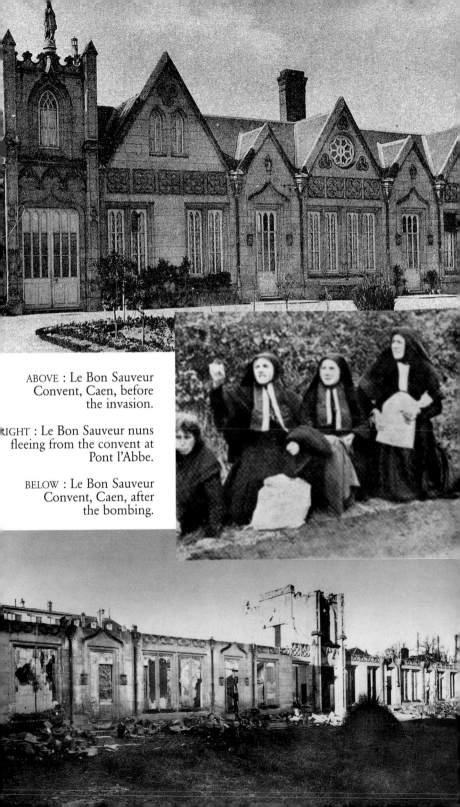

ABOVE : Le Bon Sauveur Convent, Caen, before the invasion.

RIGHT : Le Bon Sauveur nuns fleeing from the convent at Pont l'Abbe.

BELOW : Le Bon Sauveur Convent, Caen, after the bombing.

Sherman tanks in battle order firing on the enemy near Cheux during the Odon offensive.

Shermans of 13/18 Hussars in 'harbour'. Serjeant Raymond Arthur Hill on extreme left.

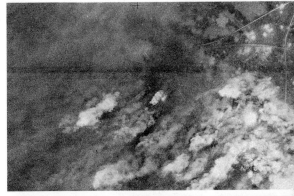

ABOVE : The strong-point village of Sannerville before 'Goodwood'.

[R]IGHT : Aiming Point picture of Sannerville taken from F/Lt. Linacre's Lancaster, 18 July.

[B]ELOW : Sannerville after the bombing. Note close, even cratering of the area.

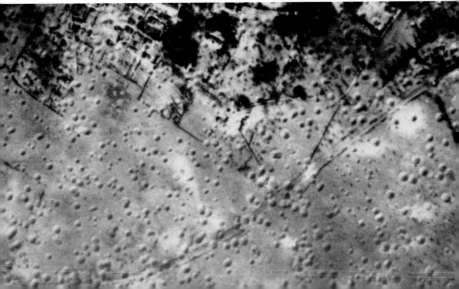

Young German sniper, captured during the Odon battle, is urged on in no uncertain matter.

British soldier takes cover by a knocked-out German tank and a dead sniper. The Odon, 28 June.

One of Wittmann's Tigers, knocked-out in Villers-Bocage during the June battle, photographed after the 'liberation' of the town two months later.

Unspoken eloquence. An Allied soldier gazes dumbly at the ruins of Caen.

HERO'S REWARD
Serjeant Sears of 23 Hussars, who has just knocked-out a Mark IV in Le Beny Bocage, 1 August, accepts his due.

HERO'S GRAVE
Canadian Scottish soldier supervises a POW burial party (the 'ghoul squad').

mander, Oberst Müller. So, at the critical moment before an extremely critical attack, the command structure was re-shuffled. But this was not all; there was one more blow still to fall.

The orders given out were for a full Corps attack on the 'Scottish Corridor' from the south-west, 10th S.S. striking at the Gavrus bridgehead over the Odon and at the flank of 11th Armoured on Hill 112, while 9th S.S. attacked in line northward against le Valtru and the bottleneck at Cheux, aided by yet another S.S. formation—2 S.S. Panzer Division 'Das Reich'—and Panzer Lehr. The opposite flank of the 'Corridor' was simultaneously to be attacked by 1 S.S. Panzer Division 'Leibstandarte Adolf Hitler', which was arriving from Belgium, aided by the battered remnants of 12 S.S. Panzer Grenadier Division and 21 Panzer Division. Never had there been so many S.S. divisions in so small a space. Yet, although none of the new divisions had completed its assembly, what had arrived was, without fail, to attack on the morning of 29 June. Even this was delayed by Allied air action, and an officer of 9th S.S., out early reconnoitring routes leading towards Cheux, was captured by 15th Scottish, complete with the plans of the coming attack.

This gathering of all the armoured power of the German Armies in the West around the 'Scottish Corridor', pushed nearly six miles deep into the German positions but still barely two miles across, caused the British to switch to the defensive and pull back their armour, now 'out on a limb' on Hill 112. In terms of ground, 'Epsom' had been no more than half a success; in terms of lives, it had been extremely costly, roughly a quarter of the infantry having been killed or wounded; in terms of strategy, it had been a two-fold triumph. The task of Second Army was to engage and pin-down the bulk of the German armour, in order to allow Bradley's U.S. First Army easy passage and a break-out in the Cherbourg peninsula; and of the eight panzer divisions now in Normandy, seven and a half were being engaged by the British. But Montgomery's strategy also envisaged creating threat after threat, first on this sector, then on that, to force the Germans to react to him, never to allow them time to mount, not the limited, local counter-attacks they had been putting in up to now, but a massive offensive of their own, designed to split the beachhead in two. He had succeeded. First, the intended three panzer division drive by 12th S.S., 21 Panzer, and Panzer Lehr had crumbled into mere 'line holding'; then 2nd Vienna Panzer Division had been similarly sucked in to the front-line dogfight; and now, the great strategic reserve of armour, intended to come under command of Gehr von Schweppenburg and his planning staff of Panzer Group West, was being similarly committed, piece-meal, to the battle in a desperate reaction to the British drive. In 1940, the French Army had been destroyed for lack of such a powerful, mobile reserve; in 1944, the German Army had a formidable reserve, but it was being destroyed by the British and Canadian armies.

So the British immediately went on to the defensive to meet the attack, taking no risks, and knowing by bitter experience that in the bocage particularly, the attacker was at a disadvantage and must suffer losses exceeding those of the defender by three or more to one. Now was the time, not to advance, but to put the German strategic reserve through the ' mincing machine ' and cripple it for further operations. All day on the 29th, in the drizzling rain, they awaited the massive blow, the Wessex lining the eastern side of the ' corridor ', the Scottish facing west towards II S.S. Panzer Corps, those formidable divisions which had brought the Red Army spring advance to a stumbling halt. Up to now, most of the ' Panthers ' and ' Tigers ' they had met had been Mark IVs or SP guns. Now, many of the ' Panthers ' and ' Tigers ' really would be Panthers (there were still very few Tigers in Normandy: that was soon to be remedied).

For 10 H.L.I., it was a " quiet day ", said Serjeant Green. " To all intents and purposes, we were out of the battle. Heavy fire from the direction of Le Valtru caused havoc to the trucks of A 1 Echelon, which carried the most urgently needed supplies, and when a heavy German attack developed against Le Valtru itself we could see two German flame-throwing tanks in action and machine-gun fire was incessant. Walking wounded came streaming back along the embankment, and our Battalion stood by to seal off any penetration, but gradually the position was restored and the fire slackened. A nasty situation had been developing, but despite being over-run by enemy tanks, the infantry held firm and the Germans were driven out." This attack was delivered by 9 S.S. Panzer Division, as was another to the north, some tanks getting into Cheux; but there was no retreat by the infantry, they stayed where they were, and the German tanks behind them were eventually destroyed. At the southern end of the ' corridor ', 10th S.S. pushed forward near Esquay and Gavrus.

But, for both divisions of II S.S. Panzer Corps, used to facing an enemy air force so tenth-rate that its aircraft were a joke and the fire, sometimes heavy, but unco-ordinated, of the Russian field artillery, their attack on the Scottish part of the ' Scottish Corridor ' had been something of a shock. " The firing power of a British division can hardly ever be compared to that of a Soviet armoured division," said Walter Harzer, then the 1a, or Chief Operations Staff Officer, of 9 S.S. Panzer Division, " because the British support by aircraft and artillery was far superior to any-thing the Soviet could ever offer us. Now, if the Luftwaffe had been able to deal with the Allied navies and also stop the accurate bombing of certain targets, I think that the British-Canadian landings would once again have ' fallen in the ditch ', as they say. As it was, our counter-offensive broke down under air attack and artillery fire, particularly the heavy guns of the battleships. They were devastating. When one of these shells dropped near a Panther, the 56-ton tank was blown over on its side, just from the blast. It was these broadsides from the warships, more than the defensive fighting of the enemy's troops, which halted our divi-sion's Panzer Regiment."

While, on 29 June, the first attacks were going in, carried out by those units which had arrived first, the remainder were struggling towards the front, the urgency being such that move-ment was being risked in daylight. 9th S.S. were moving up through Villers Bocage, scene of the old defeat of 7th Armoured, and then taking cover in the woods north of Noyers. It was here that the ' heavies ' of Bomber Command took a hand, putting in an accurate and effective attack. Panzer Grenadier Regiment 20 had been given the task of taking Cheux. Had that traffic jam fallen into German hands, there might have been a minor Falaise for the British. " The III Armoured Grenadier Battalion of our Regiment were lying in a forest near Bas des Forges, preparing to take Cheux, when the bombers got them," testified Lothar Greil. " The raid was by about 100 Lancasters, and was most effective, because it delayed the attempt to take Cheux. Whereas the bombing next day seemed to us, at the time, to make no difference."

*   *   *

"All aircrews are to report to the briefing-room for a lecture immediately!" blared the tannoy on the base of 115 Squadron, at Witchford, near Ely. It was just after lunch on 30 June, and F. R. Leatherdale, now a Squadron Leader, but then the navigator of a Lancaster III, was dozing in the hut he shared with his pilot, another Canadian, Flight-Lieutenant D. C. McKechnie, D.F.C. From the charts which he had pasted together that morning, plus the loading of the aircraft with incendiaries and the full petrol tanks, he had already deduced that the target they were to attack that night was some major town in Bavaria; which one would not be known until the evening briefing. " Never before had the sequence of events been altered," recollected Leatherdale. " On bicycle and on foot, we sped to the briefing-room, filled with curiosity; of one thing we were certain, there would be no lecture. As soon as we were all gathered, the Station Commander announced the amazing news. Rommel was moving a panzer division to repel the sorely-pressed Allied armies trying to break out from their beachhead in Normandy. The battle had reached a critical stage, for the bad weather had prevented us from landing all the supplies and troops that had been planned. An attack by a veteran panzer division could well tip the scales against us. Field Marshal Montgomery remembered that the bombing of Cassino had so torn up the streets of the town that his tanks could not pass through it. Between the front and the German panzers was the small town of Villers Bocage. If that could be torn apart by our bombs, the panzers would be stopped long enough for British armour and field guns to be brought up to join the battle. Accordingly, he had sent a signal to H.Q. Bomber Command, asking for every available bomber to be thrown into the battle. This was the situation the Station Commander quickly outlined to us.

" Unusual indeed for crews engaged in strategic bombing by means of carefully planned raids. The briefing which followed was even more strange. ' Navigators remain to receive your charts and weather report. All other crew members, go at once to your aircraft; help the armourers take off the incendiaries and bomb-up with H.E. Take off as soon as your plane is ready. If possible, fly in formations of threes for mutual fire protection. There will be Halifaxes going in 1,000 feet above you, to give you the added protection of their extra machine-guns in the mid-upper turret. Low level fighter cover will be provided by Spitfires of 2nd Tactical Air Force, high level escort will be provided by Thunderbolts from the U.S. Army Air Corps. Good luck.' We had not operated in daylight before and everything was out of keeping with the methods we had been taught. But excitement was high. We were all pleased to take a hand in the land battle and help our brethren on the ground.

"At 1755 hours, our Lancaster lifted eleven 1,000 pound bombs into the Cambridgeshire air. There was still no sign of cloud and the Luftwaffe was still a force to be reckoned with. We were not optimistic about our chances of returning to base; but nor were we frightened, for we realised that, if shot down, we would be able to get back to the British lines. All around us there were groups of Lancasters climbing up from their bases. Being one of the crews detailed to act as leaders, we fired our Verey lights and soon had other planes on either side; then we headed for the Isle of Wight. There were none of the usual route-changing tactics to avoid enemy fighters; our bombs were needed on target as soon as possible, and so our route was nearly a straight line to that Normandy town.

" While I was busy calculating the details of our flight, into my ears came the excited chatter of our air gunners and bomb aimer. Never had they seen so many aircraft in the sky before. Everywhere they looked there were Lancasters and Halifaxes converging slowly on our track. Then they saw some Stirlings— another surprise, for this was an obsolescent bomber. We droned out over the Channel and below us, in the clear, sunny air, was spread out the invasion armada: some vessels headed north, their job done, but most were headed towards the French coast. Now, our amazement knew no bounds, for we were overtaking planes of even older vintage than the redoubtable Stirling. Here there were Blenheims, there an Anson, and way below, a few Oxford trainers. And there were several Wellingtons. Truly, ' Bomber '

Harris had dug deep to unearth such planes. Then the French coast loomed up and we could see that we were getting near the front of this massive bomber fleet. We got in position below and a little behind a 'gaggle' of Halifaxes, keeping clear of their bombs, but taking some comfort from their superior fire power.

"Now we were passing over the green French fields, and anxiously I checked my wind finding, to pass the most recent and reliable wind to Ken, our bomb-aimer. Had I found the right target? Anxiously, I stood behind the flight engineer, checking our path from my map. Below, we caught an occasional glimpse of a Spitfire sweeping round in an arc; and on the ground, some signs of the battle raging there—columns of smoke, occasional vehicles. I think we were about 12,000 or 14,000 feet, a good height for accuracy and too high for the light flak really to worry us. Then, in the evening sunlight, we spotted Villers Bocage. It looked a very neat town. It did not sprawl out into the green patchwork of the fields around it; its edge was abrupt, as if it was a walled town, perhaps a relic of medieval France. As I began to wonder about it, the bombs from the leading wave of aircraft erupted across the town in long sticks. Huge spouts of reddish smoke shot upward. I wondered why the smoke was red. I scanned the sky for enemy fighters, but saw none; only a few puffs of black smoke as two or three 88 mm flak guns opened up. As we began the run-up, I looked at the target once more. Then the reason for the red smoke struck me—it was brick dust. Villers Bocage was being pulverised. Such is the price of war: a neat, pleasant town whose only crime was that it lay in the path of Rommel's panzers.

"Our Lancaster lurched as the bombs left their slips and went down to add to the havoc. Then we were through the flak and starting our slow turn to the west and the flight home. The tension eased, as we realised that even if the expected fighters arrived and shot us down, we should surely be able to glide to behind our lines. Suddenly, way down below, I spotted a battery of guns firing northwards; they were drawn up in a field, from which appeared puffs of smoke in quick succession. I looked to the north, and there I could clearly see a rather similar line of artillery firing, but to the south. I feel sure these two opposing batteries were engaging each other. Our bomb aimer said how much he wished we had even one bomb left to aim at that German gun position. The desire to help our soldiers was great in us all.

"I think I remember seeing a Halifax spiralling down, pouring out smoke, but I am not sure now after all these years, which is strange, for the raid was so spectacular and is today still vivid in my mind's eye. Certainly, the fighters never appeared and our losses were negligible. Three hours and ten minutes after take-off, we landed back at Witchford to discuss excitedly and at length what had been for us all the most moving experience we had ever had. How many planes were used on that raid I do not know; but if it was not the largest raid of the war, it must surely have been the raid on which the greatest variety of aircraft were used. Had Villers Bocage suffered in vain? We were told that it had not, and that the frustrated panzers could not join the battle at the critical stage."

"I can speak of that air attack from personal experience, for I was in the near vicinity when it took place," recollected General Bittrich, now commanding II S.S. Panzer Corps. "The bombardment fell on the Panzer Battalion of my former command, 9 S.S. Panzer Division, which was strung out along the road towards Villers Bocage, and it was hit there. But, in spite of casualties and damage, the Battalion continued its march through the ploughed-up little town into the assembly area allotted to it."

* * *

At dawn on 30 June, the day of destruction for Villers Bocage, 10 H.L.I. were ordered to move south from Colleville to reinforce the Argylls, who were being hard-pressed in the bridgehead over the Odon near Gavrus by elements of 10 S.S. Panzer Division. The men were got out of their trenches and closely grouped for orders in one of those deadly orchards which the officers had not yet learned to avoid. The men began to grumble. "Just asking for casualties," was the muttered comment from all sides. Prompt to the second, as if on cue, a salvo of mortar bombs came screaming down to burst overhead among the branches; out of the clouds of dust and smoke came cries of "Stretcher bearers!" And among the wounded were the Commanding Officer and his Second-in-Command. "If matters had been chaotic before," commented Serjeant Green, "they became even more muddled now. It was not until a Major arrived from the Argylls to take over the Battalion that we had any idea of what was to happen." Eventually, the idea of going to Gavrus was abandoned, and the H.L.I. marched instead to Mondrainville, hearing the heavy fire from Le Valtru, where the Seaforths were being attacked again.

" The Battalion found a defensive position around a small wood and began to dig in. The ground proved to be both marshy and stony, which made it very difficult. But how we had progressed in the short space of four days! Was it but a week ago that digging a slit trench was considered more work than it was worth? Now, the shovel had become a mighty weapon of war, a treasure to be hoarded carefully, lest it be snatched up by some pilferer; being without a shovel left one feeling as naked as a man in Piccadilly without his trousers.

" The ground on the far side of the River Odon was visible from some of our positions, and the German counter-attacks which developed against the Argylls' bridgehead could be seen quite clearly. The rush of figures across the open ground—the sudden fire of machine-guns and the shells bursting among them —then the figures streaming back in disorder. We felt like spectators at a football match, with a guilty feeling that we were not taking our share of the battle."

On the night of 1st/2nd July, advance parties of a newly-landed formation, the 53rd Welsh Infantry Division, arrived to take over from the Scottish. Their presence in the beachhead was a great secret, but the build-up was still three divisions behind the time-table; there had been no way of catching up on the delay caused by the gale. " 53 Div were as yet ' unblooded ', and they regarded our slit trenches with disapproval. They demanded that we deepen them from 2½ feet to 4½ feet, otherwise they would not accept them. They looked around with the same ' rookie' air with which we had greeted our own first action; our dirty, unkempt condition, and the way everyone stuck to their trenches, seemed to them unnecessary. We made an attempt to deepen the trenches, but because of the stony, root-infested ground and our physical exhaustion, we had not much success. Finally, because the C.O. was anxious to hand over the area as clean as possible, we spent our last few minutes there picking up paper and empty tins, diving to cover from mortar fire every few minutes, but cleaning up the battlefield before we left! The language used almost drowned the noise of the shells."

By dawn, 10 H.L.I. were marching through St. Mauvieu towards billets at Norrey-en-Bessen, stumbling under their loads, eyes smarting with fatigue, and now, at last hungry. "We went 24 hours at a time on a few biscuits," wrote Serjeant Green, " but the urgency of battle produces a tightness of the stomach and a dryness of the throat which rejects all feelings of hunger; bless those boiled sweets with which we were so abundantly provided." At Norrey, they settled in an orchard near a ruined farm, among the smell of decaying cattle; and because they were by now apprehensive of the red-hot splinters which showered down from above when an orchard was mortared or shelled, they dragged out furniture from the shattered farm to provide head-cover over their slit trenches.

No sooner had they done this than an old woman arrived at the farm, which seemed to have been used previously by the Germans as a strongpoint. She soon discovered that it had been ransacked by the Jocks to improve the safety of their slit trenches. Serjeant Green heard the uproar, and saw her ranting along the road, waving her arms, and screaming: " Worse than the Boche! Worse than the Boche! Worse than the Boche!" over and over again. The Scots, sentimental towards a woman old enough to be their mother, rather pitied her, and their replies were consequently of a moderate nature.

" Och away, yer bluidy awd hen."

" Shoot the old bastard."

" Worse than the Boche! Worse than the Boche! "

" Think yersen bluidy lucky it's still stanning."

"Allez, yer bluidy awd hag, afore somebody shoots thi."

" Worse than the Boche! Worse than the Boche! "

" Och awa'."

During this period, their C.O., who had been wounded, returned to the Battalion and had all the N.C.O.s gathered in a barn for an address by him. They waited for him to begin, expecting a certain amount of praise and a tactical lecture. " Instead," wrote Serjeant Green, " they were treated to a verbal attack on their lack of ability to carry out orders—their cowardly efforts during the attacks which had left so many of them alive—

if they had been doing their jobs properly, most of them would have been dead or wounded; that they were here at all was proof of their cowardice. The N.C.O.s began to murmur ominously, and the R.S.M. had to wave his stick and threaten them. This quietened the gathering, but did not improve their morale, for they knew that this would inevitably reach the ears of the private soldiers and still further lower their confidence in their commanders.

" But the C.O.'s anger could be understood. The Battalion's record in the battle had been dismal—not one successful attack —abject failure to gain even the start-line during the most vital attack of all, the first, which resulted in almost a 12-hour delay in momentum and over 200 casualties, with nothing to show for them. Most of the Battalion had not even seen a German— dead or alive—and to the ordinary soldier life had been one glorified muddle in which he had been mortared, shelled and sniped by an enemy he never even saw. Our first action was nothing to be proud of and no one realised it more than the Jocks themselves. But they had stood up to all the enemy fire without flinching, and that *was* something to be proud of. However, there had been a vagueness about the whole thing which puzzled us all at the time; no one had seemed quite sure what they were supposed to be doing from one minute to the next."

* * *

The Germans were not pleased, either, for General Bittrich was now convinced that Hitler's advisers at the Führerhauptquartier " had no clear vision of the enemy. Their ideas were based on a faulty appreciation of our own forces and also those of the enemy; they underestimated him, probably the most dangerous of all mistakes. An attack such as this one, unprepared, hurriedly mounted, under the most difficult circumstances, required as a minimum condition control of the air space over the battlefield. But we could not even get information on artillery targets because, apart from the Home Defence fighter force, the Luftwaffe was now non-existent. In these conditions, our attack should never have been made during the daytime. Only a night attack might have stood a chance of limited success. I deeply regretted that the commander of Panzer Group West,

General Geyr von Schweppeburg, had to give up his command at this time due to personal conflicts with the high command. Under his leadership I, as a divisional commander in France in 1943, had been able to study the mentality of our English adversaries. By means of various war and planning games, he had prepared the crop of tank leaders for the coming invasion, making full use of his detailed knowledge of the English way of thinking and acting. A large part of our conversations concerned night attacks with tanks. I had carried out such attacks on the Eastern Front with great success and therefore knew the methods—small mixed squads, of storm infantry with a few isolated guns, penetrated the enemy lines during the night; and behind them tanks and infantry in armoured carriers to widen and deepen the breaks at dawn. But thorough reconnaissance is vital, by aerial photography if possible. As it was, our hasty, rushed attack broke down under the enemy air force and the increasingly rapid fire of their artillery. In spite of excellent training, our losses were high, particularly as the area consisted of rocks covered with about 8 inches of leaf mould, which made it impossible for the troops to dig in. The fact that there were, from time to time, breaks in the flow of reinforcement and supply was not a decisive factor. The haste prevented the troops from obtaining results of any importance, except a halt of a few weeks of the enemy's attempt to reach and cross the Orne. Even this small success was not made use of by the High Command; the tank troops merely became worn out and so useless for mobile operations."

The failure of ' Epsom ' was to force the British to reconsider their slow, orthodox, costly, and conventional methods in principle, as well as in detail; and, eventually, to produce a totally different type of attack, very similar to that which had already been discussed by von Schweppenburg and Bittrich, but tailored to the masses of tanks, aircraft and guns available to them. At the moment, this solution did not occur, because they lacked any equivalent to the fully-tracked armoured troop carriers which had enabled the Germans to avoid the road-block at Villers Bocage, simply by going cross-country round it; except when on their flat feet, the British infantry were road-bound. That the Allies at any point were inferior in equipment to the Germans would have been the last thing to occur to any German soldier, however. Prisoners taken both by 49 Div and 15 Scottish Div at this time were said to have asked to see the new British wonder-weapon: the belt-fed, multibarrelled 25-pounder gun. " Veteran Germans with battle experience of the Russian front asked with reverence to be allowed to see this weapon," said Serjeant Green in particular; " they refused to believe that the colossal weight of shells to which they had been subjected could possibly be fired by ordinary field guns."

CHAPTER THIRTEEN

NO PRISONERS ARE TAKEN THAT DAY ON EITHER SIDE

The Bitter Canadian Battle for Carpiquet
June/July

While the sullen drumfire of the Odon battle was turning the shallow stream of that name, flowing between steep-sided hills, into what the soldiers were beginning to call 'Death Valley', the rest of the front was held by the tension which precedes the breaking of the storm. The Canadians were poised to take Carpiquet, and when that had fallen, with the British they were to assault Caen head-on; the flare up of the front, which had started at Fontenay, was planned still to roll in succession, sector by sector, from west to east, until finally Caen fell. Unaware, Madame Luce Triboulet set out on 22 June to traverse the British-Canadian front from west to east, and enter Caen. She and her husband, Raymond, had five children and one of them, Francois, was in hospital at Caen. She intended to remove him from danger and bring him back to their home at Sainte-Croix-Grand-Tonne, near Bayeux. Her husband could not accompany her as, on 14 June, he had been appointed sub-prefect of Bayeux by General de Gaulle, who had landed in France that same day at Graye-sur-Mer. All he could do was to obtain for her from M. Piéplu, Mayor of Blainville, documents explaining and authorising her journey. But shells and bullets cannot read.

Riding a bicycle, she crossed first the area where the Canadians had been engaged in the first few days after the landings, and where 8 Corps were assembling for 'Epsom'. She spoke to the parish priest of Secqueville, whose congregation totalled eight persons, some of them refugees from nearby Bretteville l'Orgueilleuse. " God be with you," he said in farewell, as she rode away. But the roads were packed with guns and tanks and transport, tearing the surface to shreds and kicking up blinding clouds of white dust; often, she had to dismount and push the bicycle.

From the hill beyond Colomby-sur-Thaon, near Fontaine-Henry, she saw " a thousand bright specks shining in the direction of the sea, the silver balloons which protect the ships against aeroplanes." A few miles beyond, she began to traverse an ominously quiet wilderness. " I crossed a completely deserted plain, in that silence which is peculiar to the front line. An English motorcyclist stopped and asked me for wine, but I had none; and finally I came to Blainville, where the houses were intact and lived in, but shaking to the concussion of the English guns firing on the other side of the Caen canal. There I met Madame Tresarieu, who was also going to Caen, to see her sisters, and we travelled together. We had not gone 200 yards when we found the road barricaded with coiled wire and a notice reading: Mines '. We went into the fields, to get round the barricade, and were questioned by some English soldiers. They asked where we were going, and when we told them, replied that it was very dangerous. We got back onto the road, and another 200 yards further on, found that it was covered by round, black canisters— mines. We lifted our bikes onto our shoulders, and stepped very carefully over them. 100 yards ahead was yet another minefield. At the chateau of Beauregard, we stopped to tie white handkerchiefs to the handlebars of the bicycles, and went on, pushing the bicycles now, because we thought there might be Germans in the park who would fire on the road. Then we came to a shellhole in the road and an area where the telegraph posts and wires were down; and just after that, we had to re-mount and cycle fast, because shells were passing overhead, though they burst on the other side of the canal. And then we came to Hérouville, completely evacuated, the houses ruined, with tattered curtains fluttering in the shattered windows. Rounding a corner, we saw some Germans in a lorry, but they paid us not the least attention." And the two ladies had not the least knowledge of what they had done.

There were two groups of bridges spanning the River Orne and the Caen Canal, between the city and the sea: those between Bénouville and Ranville, taken by 6th Airborne on D-Day and held ever since; and those between Hérouville and the Caen factory area of Colombelles, which had been held by 21 Panzer Division since 7 June. " My three 75 mm self-propelled anti-tank

guns were standing in Hérouville, protected by houses against
the almost ceaseless fire of the enemy's land and naval artillery,"
recollected Leutnant Hans Höller. "The main battleline ran
behind thick stone walls along the road in Hérouville some 200
yards from the Canal bridge, and across the two roads running
parallel with the Canal in the direction of Lebisey. The area up
to the chateau (at Beauregarde) was no-man's-land, and the scene
of frequent patrol actions. About the middle of June, a strong
party of Tommies had even penetrated into Hérouville as far as
the stone wall along the road, but were thrown back by the loss
of their officer." Madame Triboulet and her companion had
advanced from the British lines under the muzzles of Höller's
three guns, carefully concealed among the ruins of houses, and
manned by men expecting trouble.

But no one stopped or questioned them until they came to
the square of Saint-Gilles, in Caen. "We were halted by a
German sentry, who asked where we were going, then advised
us to return that night. Caen itself presented a scene of horror.
In the port area, there seemed to be nothing left standing. When
we got into the city, we found places where no house stood
higher than a yard off the ground; and the entrance to the Rue
Arcisee-de-Caumont, where my son was, we found blocked and
impassable by the ruins of its houses. But eventually I found
where Francois had gone to—the Convent of the Sisters of the
Sacred Heart—and we were re-united. The house where he had
been living was destroyed on 6 June, I learned, and at the school
he attended seven children, a sister, and a teacher had been killed
the same day. Madame Tresarieu was not so lucky as I; she
found no trace of her relatives."

Madame Tribulet set off at once to re-cross the lines with her
son. They had no trouble getting through Hérouville, still held
by Höller's troop, but bullets began to fly overhead when they
took the road west to Lebisey. There, they came across a few
German soldiers lying in a ditch with a machine-gun—in fact, a
forward position of 21 Panzer Division. These men would not
let them pass, so they returned to Caen. A few days later, they
tried again, this time taking the Bayeux-Cherbourg road, detour-
ing into the fields at one point to avoid the Carpiquet cross-
roads. They were now in the area held by Panzer Grenadier

Regiment 25 of 12th S.S. Division. The Hitler Youth were masters of camouflage, and although Madame Tribulet could hear German voices in the fields of corn through which she passed, the only visible sign of the presence of German soldiers were some half-dozen graves, marked by wooden crosses. On the horizon was the Abbaye d'Ardennes, ' Panzer ' Meyer's old headquarters; Officer-Cadet Kurt Misch was at this time using the tower for his Artillery Observation Post. British guns were in action, but when Madame Tribulet and her son came out onto the main road again, everything was quiet. "Ahead of us was a barricade where soldiers were lying on their stomachs behind machine-guns. I told them that I was only taking my son back to Sainte-Croix, and had begun to step over the barricade, when a German officer rose up from his hidden position about 100 yards away, and began to yell at us." Once again, mother and son had to turn back. They were trapped in Caen.

" There, our life was very simple. We had to queue for water, the queues often being dispersed by shellfire, and we would eat at the convent; then I would queue for milk, and Francois would break some wood to make a fire on which we could boil the precious liquid. In the evening we would both go to the service at the splendid church of Saint-Etienne, which was packed with refugees. Each family had staked out a little private territory, marked by lines of chairs; inside they had straw, sometimes beds, sometimes even their bicycles. Everything smelt of disinfectant. Each night there was a sermon, often by the priest Pelcerf. Then we sang with all our hearts, recited the act of contrition, received general absolution, followed by communion for those in danger of dying." And now, irony was reaching towards a supreme climax.

The building of Saint-Etienne was begun by William the Conqueror in 1066, and dedicated in his presence in 1077; a modern plaque marks the place, below the altar, where he was eventually laid to rest in the heart of his native Normandy. Now, refugees were encamped on his tomb, sheltering from English guns. The gunfire was incessant, as the Odon battle rolled to its climax, and on 29 June evacuation was ordered. But, as II S.S. Panzer Corps counter-attacked, and stabilised the situation, the people were merely urged to leave the city, if they could. The Germans, however, were beginning to pull out all their base units. Even the convicts from the civil prison were set free, and put on the Paris road. In the first week of July, it was plain that the Germans had abandoned all hope of holding Caen. The officials of the Kommandantur evacuated, and, most significant of all, the Gestapo. Only the fighting soldiers were left, and they were mostly outside the city, holding the northern outskirts and the factory area on the heights of Colombelles to the north-east, where part of Höller's unit was dug-in, covering the bridges by Hérouville.

The British bridges, further downstream, between Bénouville and Ranville, had always been a thorn in their side, and at this time the Germans were planning to blow them and so cut the communications of 6th Airborne Division and prevent any attack being launched on Caen from the British bridgehead east of the Orne. Both the British bridges and the German bridges had been repeatedly attacked from the air by the other side, without the least success; they were too well-covered by flak. What aircraft and artillery had failed to do, a handful of underwater swimmers would accomplish. "At the end of June," recollected Höller, " some frogmen came to Colombelles to be initiated by us. One put on his suit, took a torpedo into the water, which he towed behind him on a lead, and without a sound swam off in the direction of the enemy. However, he was soon back, with the torpedo, having found his way barred by an obstacle. There was then some talk about a simultaneous operation in both the canal and the river, with the frogmen entering the water further upstream, which would lengthen the distance they would have to swim. And this was how it was actually done. Both bridges at Bénouville were to be blown at 6 a.m. on either 3rd or 4th July, and when the time arrived, we were all anxiously looking at our watches. Dead on time came an enormous detonation from downstream, and then our own bridge at Hérouville, 100 yards from my dug-out, blew up in our faces. A very special sort of surprise. One of the frogmen, because he had got into the water so far upstream, had overestimated the distance he had covered under water and tied his torpedo to the wrong bridge. At any rate, a single German had succeeded, where all the British had failed. . . ."

*　　　*　　　*

From their rest area near Norrey, 10 H.L.I. could see the village of Carpiquet perched on a hill just west of Caen; southward, the hill sloped down to a plain on which the airport, with its hangars and control buildings, was situated. It was supposed to be strongly-held—" enemy-infested " was the story Serjeant Green heard—and its defence was so bitter and successful that ' Carpiquet ' became a legendary name, identified with the most fanatical sort of fighting. " Information brought back by patrols, plus Intelligence reports, confirmed that the airfield of Carpiquet, the last bastion of the Caen defences, was the strongest and best we had so far encountered," wrote the historian of the Régiment de la Chaudière. " Most of the defending troops had been identified as belonging to the 12th S.S. Panzer Division. We were going to fight the cream of the German Army."

In Operation ' Windsor ', both village and airfield were to be taken by the 8th Canadian Infantry Brigade (North Shore, Chaudière, and Queen's Own Rifles of Canada), plus another battalion, the Royal Winnipeg Rifles, loaned from the 7th Infantry Brigade; and they were to be supported by the tanks of the Fort Garry Horse, plus flail tanks and flame-throwing ' Crocodiles ' from 79th Armoured Division. A heavy concentration of ground artillery was laid on, 428 guns, backed by the fire of warships, including the nine 16-inch guns of the battleship *Rodney* and the 15-inch guns of the monitor *Roberts*.

In terms of man-power, this was quite ridiculous. Carpiquet was held by 150 teenagers of the Hitler Youth, drawn from Panzer Grenadier Regiment 25. About 100 were on the airfield, about 50 in the village; the latter being the objective of the Régiment de la Chaudière, who therefore outnumbered their opponents by about 18 to one. When it became obvious to Hubert Meyer and the staff of 12th S.S. that an attack on Carpiquet was impending, the armoured reinforcements they were able to send to this vital sector consisted of two or three tanks which were moved into the hangars on the south side of the field; in the anti-tank gun reinforcement line, they were slightly worse off—they had to borrow an 88 mm gun from the air defence of Caen, which they sited in an anti-tank rôle on the western approaches to St. Germain-la-Blanche-Herbe, covering the main Caen-Bayeux road which runs just north of Carpiquet. To these shifts was now reduced that counter-attack force which, as originally planned, should have thrown the Allies into the sea within a day or so of the landings. The grim battle of attrition for Caen was not merely holding the German armoured forces where Montgomery had intended to hold them, it was literally burning them away in the fires of war.

Nevertheless, the Canadian attack failed, and with " relatively enormous loss ", as the historians of the Chaudière wrote. The German defence was in fact much stronger than would appear merely by counting heads or the weight of shellfire. " The panzer grenadiers defending the airfield had the advantage of sitting in very well-built underground blockhouses, which were connected by passages," recollected Kurt Misch, who saw the whole affair from the tower of Ardenne Abbey. His British opposite number wrote: " The Canadian attack on Carpiquet lay in full view of 43 Div observers in the houses and from the church spire of Fontaine Etoupefour—first, the spurting, dusty smoky barrage as it crept across the green open space; next the Canadian infantry, small black dots moving steadily forward. They were reminded of a carefully rehearsed tattoo, the only difference being that, when the first attack failed, no drums rolled, no searchlights flashed, nor did the men lying so still get up and walk away."

The other special factor favouring the defence, said Kurt Misch, was that " our Radio Intelligence Section was in possession of the key to the codes used by the Canadian command, so that we were well informed about any plans made by the other side." Indeed, Hubert Meyer's service was working overtime. " On 3 July, intense patrol activity disturbed the Carpiquet sector," he recalled, " and our wireless intelligence noted a lot of R/T traffic between enemy armoured units. No mention of any definite intentions, but we concluded that a large concentration of tanks was taking place east of Norrey and St. Mauvieu. It seemed an attack was being prepared. A breakthrough on our south wing would threaten the whole front north of Caen from the rear and make the city impossible to hold." It was then that a few tanks and a single 88 were moved up. Much more important were the arrangements made for defensive fire from artillery and mortars, although this was hampered by lack of ammunition. This was the final, and probably decisive, factor—reading between the lines of the Canadian account, which makes an interesting comparison with Meyer's. Neither, of course, is completely accurate, because the enemy situation can rarely, if ever, be known with absolute exactitude at the time; and rarely afterwards, because the standard military historian believes that he has done his duty if he chronicles with thoroughness the doings of one side only. To be fair, this is all that his specialised public demands. Of the two witnesses here, Meyer was in much the better position, because he could, to a quite large extent, ' read ' his enemy's intentions.

Meyer: " We concluded that a large concentration of tanks was taking place east of Norrey and St. Mauvieu." He was not supposed to know this, and considerable pains had been taken to mislead him. Majors Ross and Gauvin, historians of the Chaudière, wrote: "At approximately 0330 on 4 July, there was feverish activity in St. Mauvieu. The streets of the village were choked with tanks, carriers, half-tracks, and infantry moving in Indian file silently towards the start-line at Marcelet. The noise of the vehicles was covered up by the continuous bombardment of our 25 pounders. It was a great war machine which now began to move forward against the fortifications of Carpiquet."

Meyer: " In the early hours of 4 July the enemy R/T traffic increased, pointing to preparations for an attack. We suspected their assembly positions to be in the forest east and south-west of Marcelet. By experience, we expected the attack to start at 0700. To destroy, or at least disturb, their assembly, we brought down two artillery and mortar bombardments at 0600. The Regiment from 7 Werfer Brigade under Oberstleutnant Böhm and the S.S. Werferabteilung 501 under Major Müller fired two ' shoots ' each. Listening to the enemy R/T, we knew he had been badly hit."

At this point, the two accounts cease to ' mesh ' perfectly. The Chaudière historians wrote: " H-Hour had been fixed for 0500, and at that time exactly the two assault companies of the Regiment, ' D ' (Major G. O. Taschereau), and ' B ' (Major J. F. L'Esperance), crossed the start-line behind the artillery barrage, which lifted and moved forward 100 yards. Everything went according to plan until the moment when the Germans began to lay a barrage 100 yards behind our barrage in order to make us believe that our shells were falling short and so cripple the advance. Our barrage continued to go forward, but we were held back by the enemy's barrage, which became more and more intense."

In the first phase, the Chaudière were to advance on the right of the road to the village of Carpiquet, the North Shore on the left of the road, both with tank support. The Chaudière, " after relatively enormous losses, stifled the resistance of the enemy and the assault companies established themselves near the first buildings in the village, while 'A' and ' C ' Companies advanced through them. In a dug-out, Lieutenant Miller found two disguised Germans, one in the uniform of an English captain, the other in the uniform of a British soldier. Realising the consequences of such an offence against the laws of war, the two S.S. men resist to the death. No prisoners are taken this day on either side."

Meyer: " Carpiquet village was defended by about 50 men of Panzer Grenadier Regiment 25, and was attacked by the Régiment de la Chaudière and numerous tanks. Eventually, after hand-to-hand fighting in the ruins of nearly every house, the village was lost. The advance of several tanks past the village and further south over the airfield was stopped by the fire of the 88 mm flak gun and the counter-attack of a few tanks. We heard the O.C. of the Régiment de la Chaudière report to his Brigade the taking of the village. He gave his position as the centre of it, and was ordered back. Our mortars and artillery held him there. Every time he tried to retreat, we stopped him. So it went on until evening."

"At approximately 1400 hours, after eight hours fighting, we held our position in the village under a shelling that became more and more intense each minute," wrote the Chaudière historians. " The mortars, the rockets, and artillery never stopped, and for the next five hours Carpiquet was an inferno. There was not a piece of ground as small as a man's thumb which had not been touched. The bombardment was so continuous that hardly anyone dared venture out of the trenches and dug-outs. Under it, the Queen's Own Rifles of Canada who, in the second phase, were to have taken the control building on the airfield, were unable to do so. In the evening, we attempted to put down a minefield along our front, but the bombardment caused us so many casualties that we had to leave it until the next day. And the next day, it was the same."

Meyer: "Next day, 5 July, we fired at the village with 50 kg mortar bombs which were part-explosive, part-incendiary. They had been part of the airfield defence long before the landings, and when our Werfer Regiment got them ready for action, they obviously caused considerable casualties. The enemy kept very quiet here for the next few days; even during the great attack on Caen, they stayed on the defensive. However, our own attempt to re-take Carpiquet from Franqueville failed."

"At approximately 0700 hours on 6 July," wrote the Chaudière historians, " the Germans counter-attack with tanks and infantry on the positions held by 'C' Company and take prisoners. In spite of this, the counter-attack is repelled and Lieutenant B. Dorion succeeds in escaping from the Germans and regains our own lines. In the evening, we succeed in putting down that minefield."

So far, so very good. So close an agreement between historians of opposing sides is rare indeed; but then, these historians actually took part in the events they describe. But eye-witness historians do not always tell all of the truth, particularly when publishing very soon afterwards (the Chaudière history was printed in Holland just after the war); and if they publish long afterwards, documents may be missing and dates and times perhaps not quite accurately remembered. But out of one counter-attack by 12th S.S. at Carpiquet came a whisper. " You will not read it in any official document," said Serjeant Gariepy, " but you ask anyone who was there, and he will tell you, in a hush-hush tone." It even got into the *Daily Telegraph,* in a sort of back-handed way, and was reprinted in *The Maple Leaf Scrapbook,* which headed the article (by H. D. Ziman): " Canucks fight like dervishes, writes Englishman ". What the *Daily Telegraph's* Special Correspondent actually wrote was: " It is no wonder the German troops believe Nazi propaganda about Canadian soldiers being savages with scalping knives. Many of the captured enemy are quite surprised to find that these Canadians who have fought like wild dervishes are really quiet, civilised, calm and well-disciplined when one meets them after the battle."

"I witnessed a real carnage of infantry troops (Germans) in a field close to Carpiquet," wrote Serjeant Gariepy. "The Germans had succeeded in infiltrating the advance post of the Régiment de la Chaudière, tough, rugged French-Canadians who brawl on weekends for divertissment, at home. We were very close by when the alarm sounded at around 0400 hours. The Régiment de la Chaudière scurried in the semi-darkness and actually slit the throats of most soldiers they found, wounded as well as dead. This horrible carnage I actually saw from the turret of my tank at first light. These boys were actually crazed by some frenzy at being caught napping; the officers of the Regiment had to draw their pistols against their own men to make them come back to reason. This was shortly before the so-called 'massacre' of some Canadian prisoners by the S.S. Are you surprised?"

This 'massacre' or a very similar one took place within the hearing of Madame Corbusson-Fleming, when a Canadian patrol penetrated into Caen along the road from Carpiquet to the suburb of St. Germain-la Blanche-Herbe. "This was in July, I think, and the most extraordinary 'fireworks' were going on: continuous noise, shelling, machine-gun fire, air attacks, and so on—what we called the 'Military Band'. We were all living on our nerves, and thought of release, but unfortunately it was a mere dream—we learned that some Canadians had come close to our residence (we heard the machine-guns), but they were taken prisoners, executed and buried in the grounds of a nearby farm in St. Germain-la Blanche-Herbe."

For the first few weeks after the landings, there had been only a few sporadic, isolated incidents; regrettable but not typical. Looking back on it afterwards, it is clear that the change took place at the Odon; to be precise, at Fontenay on 25 June, where the reputation of the 'Butcher Bears' was born (they may have been influenced by Canadian stories). However, from then on, variations of the phrase, "No quarter given on either side this day", toll through the individual narratives, the Regimental histories, and even the Divisional histories. Spoiling the pattern is the fact that witnesses from other units were equally emphatic in declaring the opposite: they had never witnessed the deliberate execution of prisoners—deliberate, as opposed to accidental shootings or misunderstandings, but even here there were sometimes border-line cases, open to misinterpretation by any enemy who witnessed them. The men responsible were under extraordinary strain and tension, knowing that you had to shoot first in order to stand even a slight chance of staying alive. Major H. Wake, M.C., contributing to the history of 2 K.R.R.C., wrote: " I was riding up in a tank on 15 August to see 4 Platoon, because the ground was impossible for our wheeled vehicles—you never saw such a fox-hunting nightmare in your life—when four Germans wearing steel helmets suddenly emerged out of a wood in front. The gunner of the tank opened up, quite rightly, and shot two of them. However, instead of being a German bazooka party, a rather worried Rifleman Hyde appeared behind the Germans, complaining that one bullet had gone through his hair, another into his arm, and would we mind leaving his f.....g prisoners alone! Lesson: Always remove a Jerry's helmet and, in spite of undergrowth, insist on them keeping their hands up."

Arthur Knight, also of 2 K.R.R.C. (the ' panzer grenadiers ' of 4 Independent Armoured Brigade) was emphatic. " There was no shooting of prisoners by our unit, except one probably not necessary case. We were on an embankment when we saw two Germans walking up. A Serjeant called on them to surrender: they seemed surprised, one put his hands up, but the other didn't obey quick enough. So the Serjeant fired a mortar bomb which landed between them and killed one. I think myself, with a little more patience, the slow one might have surrendered; but that's just an impression." This scene, witnessed from a distance, might easily have been interpreted in a different way, as could another witnessed by an anti-tank gunner of 59 Div during the Falaise fighting. " We'd gone out to get some snipers, I think from 12 S.S. Panzers, mostly 16-17-year-old boys. Some of them surrendered, then, as we were herding them along, another Nazi stepped out of a trench and let go with an automatic rifle. One of our lads had half his head blown away, and his pal went crazy with the bayonet among the prisoners." This was the more usual pattern: snipers who would pick off two, three or four men of an advancing platoon, then as they came to close quarters, stand up and surrender. The men whose friends had just been shot by him did not always feel inclined to let the killing stop at that point.

By August, said a private of the South Saskatchewan Regiment, "the Germans weren't too eager to surrender. We Canadians never took any S.S. prisoners now, and sometimes dealt with Wehrmacht formations in the same way. One German came in covered all over in Red Crosses, to make quite sure we wouldn't shoot him. And other Canadians told me: "When the Jerries come in with their hands up, shouting ' Kamerad ', we just bowl them over with bursts of Sten fire." A witness from 15th Scottish recalled how, in the beginning, they had taken prisoners, and while their Serjeant Major was removing their valuables from a fresh batch, a Canadian with a Sten came wandering along the road. Apparently, his unit had suffered lately, for he muttered ' bloody bastard Germans,' and emptied the magazine into the row of prisoners, hitting the Scottish Serjeant Major in the stomach. " But any German who tries to surrender nowadays is a brave man; we just shoot them there and then, with their hands up. There's nothing to choose between the British and the Germans as regards atrocities . . . ." Evidence of this trend, from the German side, is almost impossible to obtain, because any such admission could still lead to a war crimes trial, a hazard not faced by Allied soldiers. The evidence has to come from the British side. In his narrative of the battle of Mouen, L. Uppington of 1 Worcesters had concluded by saying: " In those days, no quarter was given by either side." Asked to elucidate, he replied : " I noticed that when the enemy met us, whoever had the advantage of surprise or position, it was nearly always shoot first, regardless of whether or not a man could be taken prisoner. None of this ' Hande hoch ' business; see the enemy, and let loose with Spandau, Bren, Sten or Schmeisser; get in first, no matter if the other fellow was a sitting duck or not. That, of course, is ninety per cent instinct of self-preservation. But what of the other ten per cent?

" There was the incident after the crossing of the Seine. The Germans had been trying to infiltrate into our position. One of their dodges was to take off the jackets and helmets of the British dead and wear them whilst moving through the woods. This was quickly spotted. A party of eight or ten Germans were coming towards our positions, not knowing that they were walking into a cross-fire of Bren guns. Now, they were 'sitting ducks'. But no one called out and told them to put up their hands. The Brens fired and their heads simply disintegrated. In the same action, a German on a push-bike came tearing down the hill towards us and the river. He was unarmed and it was obvious that he wanted to be taken prisoner. But no such thing happened. Our men were either side of the road and as he came down the hill, opened up and shot him off the bike. Now, he was no threat to them, and he was unarmed, but he was still shot down.

" Then there was the Serjeant with six of our men who moved on ahead of us across a field. They were nearly across, when a Spandau opened up from behind them and shot them all down. The Germans could have taken them prisoner, as we found out afterwards. As for German prisoners being pushed under tanks, I never actually saw it happen, but there were certainly a lot of churned-up German bodies where our tanks had been. Of course, they might have been dead before they were run over."[1]

There were, in Serjeant Gariepy's words, " many tales twisted in the mind of the teller ", which helped whip nerve-strained men to the ultimate fury. At one end of the scale was sheer annoyance at the stubborn refusal of the enemy to give in which caused the historian of 43 Div (who was commanding a Brigade in it at the time) to comment on the Hitler Youth: " The young S.S. troops were detestable young beasts, but, like good infantry, they stood up and fought it out when over-run." At the other end, was the cautious comment of the Gordons historian: "In one unpleasant incident some Germans displayed a white flag from the turret of a disabled tank and then shot the Gordon corporal who went forward to take the surrender. That this was deliberate treachery was open to doubt, for shots may have been fired by our own men who had not seen the flag. The Highlanders on the spot held their own opinion."

But Uppington's analysis is the most complete. He summed up: " The feeling on either side seemed to be the utter destruc-

---

[1] The historian of 43 Div accused the Germans of deliberately running a tank over a wounded man at Cheux on 27 June. It may be so; but it will be remembered that Kortenhaus' unit ran over their own wounded grenadiers by accident; most infantrymen do not realise how restricted is the immediate view out of a tank.

tion of the other. I think this was brought about by no single specific reason, but by a blending of several. Firstly, the war in France was different altogether to the fighting elsewhere. Normandy was a war of sunken lanes, thousands of hedgerows, fields of tall, waving corn; cities, towns, and villages, one after the other. Street by street, house by house. Dirty warfare. Grenades in trees, booby-traps in foxholes, mines under the cobbles of the village streets, where you least expected them. A war where you were in close contact with the enemy nearly all the time. And you had a feeling that you were fighting in your own back-yard; you weren't more than a stone's throw from England, as it were. I suppose subconsciously, there was a desperation about it all. That it was now or never. That our whole existence depended on routing the enemy; pushing them back from our own land. We'd waited a long time to start it, and get it over and done with. To the German mind, it was much the same. They were crack troops, hard troops, who had had everything their own way all over Europe. They had a new empire to lose and if they lost that, their homeland would follow. When they were gone, the ones that were left weren't of the same calibre; these saw the writing on the wall.

" Then again, the tendency is to fight fiercer and harder when cornered or frightened, and the S.S. troops could be very awe-inspiring, especially to the younger element in our troops. The S.S. stood for everything alien to our way of life; they were the troops met early on in Normandy, and the most hated. They had to be exterminated, and they were. But as the fighting moved northwards and the bulk of the S.S. and the cream of the German Army had been despatched, there was little animosity towards the ordinary German soldier. Him, we could feel sorry for; he was going through the same misery as us. A sort of kinship, especially from the P.B.I.s point of view. The bottled-up feelings of the years of being bombed and blockaded and getting the worst end of the stick, exploded in Normandy; but gradually diminished when the cream of Hitler's troops were defeated. Once a foothold on Europe had been secured and the danger of defeat was over, a happier frame of mind developed and replaced the animosity of earlier days."

In fact, the tragic irony of war: that the recipe for understanding is to fight each other; that hate is wiped out by the experience of mutual butchery. But only so far as the front-line soldiers are concerned. The mass of the peoples at home, bombarded by enemy weapons and their own propaganda, yet unable to relieve their feelings by fighting, end a war with a feeling of frustration, emotionally ready for a repeat performance in due course.

But it is clear also that the tales told about 12th S.S. by the Canadians, from the time of Le Mesnil-Patry onwards, had had their effect. " We knew before the Odon battle of the 12 S.S. Panzer Div reputation for shooting prisoners," wrote Serjeant Green, " and this did not encourage us in our first attack to surrender—rather the reverse, I am afraid. However, I have discussed the shooting of prisoners with my brother, who was in the artillery supporting the Canadians from D-Day onwards, and he is unable to vouch for the truth of any of the rumours; he heard plenty, but did not actually see anything of that sort happen."

Although all these specific reasons are undoubtedly valid, there was a further and deeper factor, made absolutely plain by the facts behind the butchery with knives at Carpiquet. Battlefield atrocities are rarely acts of brutality committed in cold blood by ruthless men. The contrary. They are rooted in the twin springs of fright and fury. In shock, and horror, and revulsion, and the overwhelming impulse to hit back; to assert the naked human personality in the screaming wilderness of bombardment. And once so asserted, the pent-up nerves are momentarily eased and relaxed. In these circumstances, killing becomes an act of macabre pleasure, having no moral, and certainly no political, significance. It is so very easy, with all restraint removed. And every one of us is capable of it.

* * *

Even in their rest area near Norrey, spectators of the struggle for Carpiquet, the men of 10 H.L.I. could not relax; the tension, and the memories of battle, were with them yet; perhaps for always. " Hourly we expected the sudden call, ' panic stations ', which would send us once more into the horror of sudden battle," wrote Serjeant Green. " Timidly, we clung to the immediate vicinity of our slit trench. For a whole week, we had learned the hard way that to stay above ground invited sudden death; such instincts are not lost in a day—to be honest, I doubt if any man could say that the shadow ever left him. Gradually, however, the quiet began to ease our distorted nerves and, like children first learning to walk, we day by day wandered further away from our havens of safety, but with one ear always cocked for the scream that would denote an approaching shell. Were these the young soldiers who but a short week before had been inoculated into the most horrible ways of dying ever devised? Watch the group over there. Creep up and listen. Are they laughing at some smutty joke? Boasting about their latest female conquest? A few words drift over.

' There was Smudger coming across the field with his dinner in one hand, when over comes a Moaning Minnie. What does he do? You know what Smudger is like when it comes to grub! He puts the dinner down carefully, then high-dives like a sack o' tatties into a hole. When the dust settles, out pops Smudger, looking for his grub, and the ruddy Moaner had blown it to bits.'

" You can see Smudger grin sheepishly, and hear his reply.

' If I could have caught the baskit what fired that ruddy gun there'd be another good Jerrie in the world! '

" They are laughing over what were tragedies but a short few days ago. In the midst of death, the Jock had found life. Now, he was able to hold his own in any company. Had he not faced every form of death and survived? Why, back in England, when a man had a driving accident, he had to face a battery of Courts of Enquiry. And now? Listen to the voice.

' Remember that bloke on the motor-bike who stopped one in Cheux? Before he hit the ground, they were shouting: " Get that bloke out of the way, he's holding up the traffic! "

" The sudden shock of losing one's best friend, his life snuffed out like a candle, was getting to be as casual as lighting a fag. Not that we didn't recoil with horror and stomach revolting, but we were getting used to not thinking about such things; hiding them in the recesses of the mind, to be remembered for ever, but never aloud. Vividly, we individually recounted the way ' old Shiner ' or ' Taffy ' had caught a packet; a moment's silence as each story ended, for unspoken thoughts. Were we callous? Who may judge? No man, however he may talk, has the remotest idea of what an ordinary infantry soldier endures.

" Then one day came the unique opportunity of watching another battle, as spectators this time. The Canadians were attacking Carpiquet aerodrome on our left, and too well we appreciated the task they had been set. How we cheered as the drone of engines set us gazing aloft, to see the specks coming nearer until an unending stream of Lancasters came into sight and began to unload their bombs with shattering devastation. ' That's the stuff to give 'em! " we howled in unison, the smoke and dust billowing up till the sky was black with man-made clouds. How could anyone be left alive after that? we asked ourselves; but there were still Jerries holding out, there always seems to be."

But Carpiquet was still untaken, for this was the evening of the 7th of July. The bombers' target was not Carpiquet airfield, but the city of Caen itself, a few miles distant. The greatest single atrocity of the Normandy campaign had been committed.

CHAPTER FOURTEEN

WE WERE MEANT TO DIE IN CAEN!

"Charnwood"—The Bombing and Battle of Caen
7 to 9 July

Le communiqué nous annonce ce matin (8 juillet) que 450 forteresses sont venues bombarder des objectifs militaires dans le région de Caen. Nous en savons quelque chose!
The Caen Diary of Prof. René Streiff

Evidently the complete destruction of Caen—or what is left of it—had been decided upon. *The Caen Diary of a Bon Sauveur Nun*

It was obviously a bloody good raid. Tremendous concentration. Aiming point dead on. *F/Lt. G. D. Linacre, D.F.C., Pathfinder Force*

Caen had paid a tragic price, great areas having been ruined by the preliminary bombardment and many people killed or injured.
Col. C. P. Stacey, Canadian official historian

The troops themselves were entirely unaffected by this attack.
Kurt 'Panzer' Meyer

Investigation showed the tremendous effect of the heavy bombing on the enemy. *General B. L. Montgomery*

. . . just a waste of brick and stone, like a field of corn that has been ploughed. The people gazed at us without emotion of any kind; one could hardly look them in the face, knowing who had done this. These were the people we came to free, and this is the price that freedom cost. *The present author, in his Normandy Diary*

You will not find in any British history, official or othewise, or in any British general's memoirs, and most certainly not Field Marshal Montgomery's, any mention of what actually happened in Caen on the late evening of 7 July, 1944. On this subject, they remind one of the British wartime propaganda motto: " Be like Dad—keep Mum." They have a bad conscience. They tried a great experiment in the technique of war, and found that they had committed mass murder for nothing; no British lives were saved. Their embarrassment matched that of 2nd S.S. Panzer Division ' Das Reich ' who, to avenge the death of one of their officers at the hands of the Maquis, burned the offending village to the ground, together with most of its inhabitants; and then discovered that it was the wrong village. A minor mistake of war, which numbers so many, the corpses of the men, women and children being counted only in hundreds. In Caen, they were to be numbered by the thousands. And, a small point perhaps, at any rate to the propagandists of total war, while the Germans were after all only killing their former enemies, the British were murdering their former friends.

There were equally embarrassing technical errors, so that the British histories may be searched in vain for the true story; they reveal no more than a number of inaccuracies and evasions. Having tried many times the technique of 'indirect approach' to the city, it had now been decided to make a head-on attack from the north, once Carpiquet had been cleared. For once, a typical Monty 'set-piece' battle—three divisions numbering 115,000 men were to assault on the morning of 8 July, supported by the usual terrific artillery barrage backed up by the battleships, monitors and cruisers of the Royal Navy. But it was known that the Germans had turned the villages on the northern outskirts into linked fortresses and after one-and-a-half companies of panzer grenadiers had shown their ability at Carpiquet to hold up the attack of one-and-a-half Canadian infantry brigades, using to the full the advantage of concrete strongpoints, it was perfectly obvious that a similar defence of the Caen outskirts would prove prohibitive in life and time to the attackers. General Dempsey, commanding Second Army, therefore decided to try on a grand scale what had already been tried out in miniature—the intervention of the Strategic Air Force on the battlefield—a task for which it had been neither designed nor trained. The attitude behind this had been crudely but effectively put to General Collins by General Bradley a few weeks before: " If it becomes necessary to save time, put 500 or 1,000 tons of air on Carentan and take the city apart. Then rush it and you'll get in." For Caen, the British were going to use 2,560 tons " of air ", but entirely neglected Bradley's brisk injunction: " Rush it and you'll get in."

General Montgomery wrote afterwards that " owing to the weather forecast " the bombing was timed for between 2150 and 2230 on 7 July, with a gap of some six hours before the ground operations began next day at 0420. The official historian, however, writing still later, examined the R.A.F. records and actual weather forecasts for both days and found that " this was not so."[1] The Germans were downright contemptuous. " This attack on Caen was preceded the evening before by a preparatory bombardment by about 500 four-engined bombers flying in two waves at 2,500 metres," recollected Hubert Meyer. "A camouflaging of the start of the attack was therefore not possible, although the wireless discipline of the enemy had improved." It ought not hurriedly to be assumed that the British failure to integrate the two components of their attack was due to stupidity, for it was to happen again at Caen, with much larger forces involved. The plain fact seems to be that the sheer enormity of the bombardment power suddenly at their disposal made for an emotional feeling that nothing whatever could stand against it. The mighty force which had gutted the great cities of the Reich would surely sweep away the German defences like some enormous broom wielded by the Lord on High. Anyone who has ever at any time worried about the world being blown up by ' The Bomb' has experienced precisely this emotion; and may be perhaps equally in error.

But one very obvious flaw there was. Air Chief Marshal Sir Arthur Harris, who knew his men, demanded a safety margin between the British forward positions and the bombers' aiming point of 6,000 yards. This was accepted, and the target area, on paper and in theory, was a rectangular box which took in the northern outskirts of Caen, but left entirely alone the main German defence positions, as these were far too close for comfort to the British front line. In theory, they were to be neutralised or knocked-out entirely by artillery fire. Therefore, all that could really be hoped for from Bomber Command was some disruption during the night of German back area communications. And so the scene was set for tragedy.

* * *

" We were airborne from Downham Market, south of King's Lynn, at 8.20 p.m.," said Flight Lieutenant Linacre of 635 Pathfinder Squadron. " Our task: Visual Backer-up to the Master Bombers." Caen was to be done in style by standard Bomber

[1] *Victory in the West*, p. 313.

Command methods, tailored to Berlin and Hamburg by night, but with a comparatively rigorous regard for accuracy, particularly against the distressing tendency of all such bombing to move rapidly back from the aiming point. If it did that, on this occasion, Lieutenant-General J. T. Crocker's I Corps would collect the better part of 2,500 tons of ' air ' on its assembly areas. Linacre's sole job was to prevent precisely that happening. The reason for it happening at all was not technical, but purely psychological. " No one's anxious to die, except perhaps a few cranks, and no one wants to take a risk, except for a friend ", explained Linacre. " So the bomber crews were quite detached from their target, with self-preservation uppermost. All the way from base right up to the target, we were working, as we put it, for the Government. But once the bombs were gone, then we were working for ourselves. So the final run-up time on ' Government business ' was critical, with everyone feeling: ' If only we can get over the next three minutes, I stand a good chance of getting home.' There was a tendency to bomb at the earliest possible moment, particularly if you got flak up the backside at that point. ' That's near enough—let 'em go!' Then nose down and go like hell for home. With everyone doing that, naturally, the aiming point of the entire bomber stream tended to drift back. So now we had this method where the Master Bomber marked the target, flew around and observed results; then called in the Deputy Master Bomber to either ' back up ' (if the aim had been correct), or correct the markers (if the aim had been off a bit). Then, as the main stream bombed, there was a tendency for their bombs to blow out the markers or obscure them with dust or smoke. The job of the Visual Backer-up was to keep those markers going. He flew over, therefore, after the raid had started and he only dropped his bombs and target indicators if he could see the aiming point. And with Bennett as leader of the Path-finder Force, you brought home aiming point pictures—or else. You never knew if he had taken out his pet Beaufighter and was kicking around himself, watching you; just as likely as not, you'd find the gaffer breathing down your neck. He was demand-ing, but first-class, and didn't agree with ' Butch ' Harris, who was indiscriminate. Harris would send them out for the sake of sending them out, regardless of whether results were possible or not. This time, we knew our troops were only a short distance from the aiming point, so the briefing stressed: ' For God's sake, don't let them drop back at all '. And as we came up to the aiming point which this time was Caen, the town itself, we could hear the Master Bomber for once shouting it out: ' Back up the reds! Back up the reds!' (or whatever the target indicator colour was, I forget)."

That was the cue for Linacre at his bomb-sight to add his load of markers to the target indicators already growing faint amid the boiling, spurting smoke and flame which was Caen. " I wasn't bothered much with impressions at that moment: I was looking through the bomb-sight, feeding information into it quick, and hoping to God it was right. I was looking ahead and down, but got odd snapshots of what was going on round about, too. Although it was getting dark, I could see some of the other aircraft. The flak was intense, more than I'd ever seen before, even in ' Happy Valley', the Rhur. Don't understand how the Germans managed it. And down below in the fields, I saw troops, and I thought: ' poor bastards, you're stuck with it, but we go home to bed.' "

And the troops, down below, gazed up in awe at the majestic, roaring array of heavy night bombers driving unswervingly into the flak in the last of the daylight. West of Carpiquet, the men of the H.L.I. were shouting in unison: " That's the stuff to give 'em, that's the stuff to give 'em!" Somewhat further away, Arthur Knight of the K.R.R.C. was scribbling in his diary: " Colossal raid on Caen by R.A.F., marvellous and awe-inspiring sight. Terrible to watch. I saw no bomber shot down. Dust obscured the sun." But they were being shot down. Directly in front of Caen, in the centre seats of the grandstand, were the men of the newly-landed 59th Staffordshire Infantry Division who, next morning, were to be centre division of the three-division attack on the city. A Gunner Officer serving with them wrote home next day: " The R.A.F. are terrific—I have never seen anything like it—I take off my hat to those heavy bombers sailing into an attack in the face of a wall of A.A. fire, as steady as Destiny." And Lieutenant John F. Brown, of the 6th North Staffordshire Regiment, recalled: "As we lay close up by the start-line we were heartened by the sight of 500 heavy bombers streaming in from the coast in a long unswerving line straight over the city. They completely ignored the heavy flak and we watched the bombs come streaming down. One aircraft disappeared completely in a huge white flash, another tilted over and spun down, losing a wing on its journey, but a third—obviously in trouble—flew lower and lower in a large circle and as it passed over us I could see that all the fabric covering the tail and rudder had been shot away. We marvelled at how it kept on flying, and eventually it appeared to come down well behind our lines. Soon, the whole target area became obscured by smoke and dust, rising high in the air, but still the bombers roared across. This was a terrific morale booster for us, but had little effect on our immediate objective, the village of La Bijude, which was well outside the target area."

In Caen, from near the Lycée Malherbe, directly opposite the great abbey of St. Etienne, René Streiff looked up and saw them come, to the crash of the anti-aircraft fire. " Hundreds of four-motor bombers passing over the city in Indian file . . . an awful spectacle . . . the sky is covered with the black and white bursts of the flak . . . it explodes beside a bomber . . . the bomber is on fire . . . there are the parachutes. . . ." Madame Tribulet and Francois, her son, were lying in a cellar, with pillows over their faces to protect their eyes from broken glass. " The two children of M. Le Basle were blinded by that," she wrote, " and now the whole earth seems to shudder. It went on and on and on for fifty minutes, with a single break of five minutes." And at the great convent of San Sauveur, too, " the earth shook with the storm of falling bombs," wrote a Nun. " In the basement the 'Ave Maria' could be faintly heard above the diabolical fury of the bombardment. Evidently the complete destruction of Caen—or what was left of it—had been decided upon. Thousands of tons of bombs fell on one of the most historic cities of France. Refugees poured in, including Benedictine Nuns who had been buried in the debris of their Convent, yet miraculously escaped. St. Pierre is destroyed, many killed, two priests among their number."

Linacre's Lancaster came roaring in after the raid had started, with the Master Bomber's voice shouting it out on the R/T: " Back up the reds, back up the reds! "—and the target indicators were still glowing in the boiling, fuming volcano that was Caen, and he knew that he must not let the aiming point drop back towards the soldiers who would not be going home to bed tonight, but into battle tomorrow. " Crossing the coast, we could see that the aiming point was on," he said. " Obvious it was a bloody good raid. Tremendous concentration right on the markers. Most impressive. Flak was heavy, but we were still working for the Government. Then the bombs were gone, and we were working for ourselves." Five tons lighter, the Lancaster surged forward across the city, the labouring note gone from the engines; all they had to do was get home. A violent detonation shook them all, and the great bomber slewed over, one wing pointed downwards to the boiling inferno on earth far below. Each man checked his parachute in momentary panic, flinching at the expected shout: ' This is it: jump, for Christ's sake!' " You can't weigh up the damage at once, when you're hit by flak," said Linacre, " but the panic was over quick, for we were not hit badly enough to stop us getting home. A cakewalk, really. All over in about three hours. Not like the 5 or 6 hours to, say, Nuremberg—where we lost 94 aircraft out of 795, back in March."

Watching from the beach ten miles away was Squadron Leader Hill, who was being visited by his cousin, Brigadier Hill. " It was a beautiful evening, I remember," said the Squadron Leader. " We were not of course supposed to know, because it was not our job, but it was the general impression at that time that there were no Germans in Caen and that the raid was a waste." Within the shattered city, now a mound of smoking rubble, they knew it. " The bombardment of 7 July was absolutely futile," wrote Professor Streiff.[2] " There were no serious military objectives in Caen. All the bombardment did was to choke the streets and hinder the Allies in their advance through the city." And the Nun wrote in her diary: " They say that 5,000 are dead. I know that many hundreds are still buried in the debris, still alive. Everyone united in the rescue work, but we were so few, and the number of victims so many, that the task was beyond us. The piteous cries of those we could not reach will haunt us for a long time."

[2] *Ceux Des Equipes D'Urgence*, by Prof. René Streiff (Caen, 1945).

There was only one German unit of importance which by any stretch of the imagination could be said to be ' in ' Caen. This was the H.Q. of 12th S.S. Panzer Grenadier Division, which was being hunted round Normandy by the British artillery, from Verson to Louvigny and from Louvigny to Venoix. At Venoix, on 6 July, they were hit by heavy artillery fire and moved the same day, not into Caen, but to a barracks on the north side of the city next to the garrison church, actually in the area to be bombed. " Perhaps this spot was rather prominent," said Hubert Meyer, who watched the raid from there, " but we had several stories of a well-built structure above our heads. In the heavy raid, the church nearby was destroyed, but we ourselves had no casualties." Bomber Command, although a mighty power, was never designed to carry out attacks of pin-point accuracy such as had been successfully tackled on hundreds of occasions by the German dive-bomber force in the early campaigns, including the Battle of Britain. One squadron of stukas—9 aircraft—could and did on occasions wreck a British airfield, with no more than one or two bombs a few hundred yards off target onto nearby civilian homes. To lay down bomb-lines in a rectangle 4,000 yards long by 1,500 yards wide on the northern outskirts of Caen was, with the force available, no more than a pious expression of intention. In the circumstances, very strange to them, the Pathfinders and bomb-aimers generally did extremely well; perhaps too well. In their anxiety to prevent the aiming point moving back to murder their own troops, they may in fact have been moving it forward, creeping from the northern outskirts remorselessly across the city, the bravery of the men in the bombers blotting out the lives of the men, the women and the children helpless down below. The minimum damage was done to the Germans, the vital defence zone was left intact—but deliberately so, for it was not included in the bombing plan; it was to be smothered by artillery next day. And as the barrage fire opened on 8 July, and the infantry of three divisions began to advance, once more the Spandaus whiplashed the corn, the mortar bombs came screaming down, and the hidden 75s and 88s began to fire the high-velocity shells the troops never heard until they had arrived. 2,500 tons of ' air ' on Caen had had no observable effect. If any of the British commanders had ever thought that they could intimidate the

Germans by killing the French, they had been most gravely mistaken. All they had done was to alert every last German soldier to the imminence of a major attack.

*　　*　　*

Operation 'Charnwood', the capture of Caen, was to be carried out, in the centre, by the inexperienced 59th Division; the left flank of the attack was to be carried forward by 3rd British Infantry Division, who were to advance parallel to the Orne and take Lebisey and Hérouville, their original D-Day objectives; the right flank of the attack was to consist of 3rd Canadian Infantry Division, part of which was already in the line at still untaken Carpiquet. In addition to the 'funnies' of 79th Armoured Division, two Canadian armoured brigades were in support. One of these, 2nd CAB, included Gariepy's unit, which had not fought since the disaster at Le Mesnil-Patry. The two experienced divisions, on the wings, drove deep, outdistancing 59 Div. Gariepy, with the 1st Hussars, met severe initial resistance, and then they broke through. " The Germans were using elements of various formations, we even found paratroops in their very distinctive uniforms," he wrote. " Perhaps this was the reason why, after some very hard-fought duels lasting about 90 minutes, they relented and retreated; there appeared to be some lack of co-ordination. We eventually gained momentum and reached l'Ancienne Abbye and Cussy, after capturing Buron, Authie, and Franqueville." At last, the Canadians had avenged their early defeat there, and were now passing Carpiquet behind the backs of the panzer grenadiers, who still fought on against the Régiment de la Chaudière and the rest of 8 Brigade.

By now, 3rd Canadian and 3rd British had been fighting in Normandy for a month; they knew the 'form'. Not so the 59th. " We had spent the whole of the war in the U.K.", recollected Lieutenant Brown. " Most of the men were from the pottery districts around Stoke-on-Trent and, once I learned the dialect, I found them naturally light-hearted, yet also rugged and dependable. We were pretty fit and hard-trained, but the majority had no battle experience and it was with perhaps a little over-confidence that we approached our task in Normandy." Exactly the same could be said of every new division. Almost everything came as a surprise. The first Frenchmen Brown met, as so many did, was aged seven or eight. Inevitably, his first words were, "Cigarette for Poppa." Inevitably, he was given, not one, but a whole packet, followed by a box of matches. Disillusion was very rapid; in the case of Lieutenant Brown, almost instantaneous. "A few minutes after I saw the same little chap sitting in a farm gate-way, gaily puffing away without a care in the world." The farm was inevitable, and equally inevitable the bartering of army biscuits for bread, which was now found to be a luxury. And inevitably, the first curious questions about the Occupation, with 'Nazi Beast' propaganda in mind. And the standard reply: "The Boche had behaved very correctly, but nevertheless their hatred of him was deep and bitter." And the nightly air-raids. There was a Luftwaffe, after all, but it flew with the owls. And then, the first battle: and the same mass of new, tiny—but now life-and-death—facts to be grasped. After Caen, a Gunnery Officer of the Division, serving with 481/116 Field Regiment, was writing home: "Send me a couple of bits of khaki cloth with two cloth pips sewn on. I've got bored with being sniped. Jerry goes for an officer—or anyone carrying binoculars, map, case, etc. So we are all Gunners now—no N.C.O.'s even." And he added, referring to Caen: "A lack of realism played hell with us in our first engagement, unfortunately one of the biggest battles fought out here: too much of a holiday spirit and lack of a sense of responsibility. We are wiser now . . ."

Lieutenant Brown was second in command of the 6-pounder anti-tank gun platoon of 6th North Staffs., and was held back in the Reserve Pool as an immediate reinforcement. Nothing to do but wait in a ditch, until somebody got killed. "By mid-morning news began to filter back that all was not going too well, but it was mid-afternoon before I was sent for and with three others drove in a jeep down a dead straight stretch of road towards the battle. At Battalion H.Q. I learned that, after some pretty confusing fighting which had swayed first in our favour, then in the enemy's, we had captured La Bijude, then been pushed back by a counter-attack, but had eventually re-occupied the position. Another battalion had now advanced through us and was carrying the battle a little nearer Caen." This was the 7th South Staffords, which failed to take Malan, the next objective. " The enemy in La Bijude had been occupying a fantastic deep trench system, similar to those used in the 1914-18 war, with slits, dug-outs and dug-in Tiger tanks. In front of it all was a deep anti-tank ditch. Now we had to clear these dug-outs, and in groups we wandered through the trenches, making sure they were empty. The recognised method of doing this was to heave a couple of grenades into every dug-out, and if nothing came out, it was considered clear.

" I came across a still-smouldering Tiger tank; lying alongside was a boot with the foot and stump of a charred leg still attached. Over all hung a most appalling smell, from the grotesque carcases of bloated cattle and horses lying in the fields. Then I came face to face with a steel-helmeted German, head and shoulders out of a slit trench, rifle pointing straight at me. In sheer panic, I fired several times with my revolver; but, as there was no reply, advanced cautiously. I need not have worried, he had been dead some hours. The poor fellow's intestines were hanging from a gaping hole in his stomach. A mortar bomb must have landed alongside him.

" Over the inevitable brews of tea, we talked; and a couple of stories I heard that day come to mind. One officer had arrived at the brink of the anti-tank ditch, jumped down into it for shelter, and was confronted by a Spandau post dug into the opposite bank. He tried to fire his Sten, but that temperamental weapon refused to work, so, waving it above his head and screaming like a maniac, he ran at the Spandau post full pelt. Knowing this officer, he must have made a spine-chilling sight; anyway, the German machine-gunners never fired a shot and quietly consented to being put in the bag. Another officer, having been knocked unconscious, but otherwise unharmed by the concussion of a shell-burst, came to, found two Germans approaching him, and feigned ' dead '. One German turned the ' corpse ' over with his boot, but did not take his revolver. As they turned and walked away, so the ' corpse ' jumped to his feet and took them prisoner. A young Bren gunner, on his own and cut off, discovered that he was being stalked by two Germans intent on taking his life. It was cat and mouse for some time, until one German got close enough to lob a stick grenade over.

The lad fielded the grenade and threw it back before it went off, eventually escaping with only a bullet in the ankle.

" In the middle of clearing up the dug-outs, a light-coloured open car drew up on a narrow road which ran through the German trench system and in the back seat was a familiar figure wearing the famous black beret. We all made a dive towards the car to give General Montgomery a cheer. After a few encouraging words, he handed over several large cartons of cigarettes for distribution amongst the troops. The honour of receiving them fell to Major John Towers who beat me in the dash to the car by a short head."

Next day, 9 June, 6th North Staffords took Malan, another village turned into a fortress by trenches, dug-in Tigers and 75 mm anti-tank guns. Then they were withdrawn, never having got into Caen. In their first 48 hours in action, they had suffered 190 casualties, nearly a quarter of their strength, and this was not exceptional, but typical. And it could not be afforded indefinitely. Behind the British bombing of Caen, the over-optimistic attempt to get the city the easy way, lay a growing crisis in infantry reinforcements. For the British and the Germans, and for no one else, this was the fifth year of war. In Germany, women were being conscripted for the factories, the fields and the hospitals; in Britain, they had long since been so conscripted and girls were manning the guns of London as the V.1s came put-putting in. Other nations had either been knocked out of the war early, or been dragged in late; but of the original contestants, only these two still stood on their feet. But they were not as fit or as fresh as they had been five years before; there was nothing much left to give. Remorselessly, the stage was being set for the take-over of Europe by the peoples of two other continents. And given the leadership they both had, there was no chance of calling off the contest at a sensible hour.

Their military leaders were caught in a desperate trap, trying to solve technical problems and so save the lives of their men, their ultimate loyalty. General Montgomery was writing to General Brook at the War Office, " I would tell him of how I saw things, my hopes, my anguish when it became clear the Allies were going to win the war but were so placed that we were certain to lose the peace." The German generals, more desperate still, torn between the oath of loyalty they had sworn to their Leader and their deeper concern for Germany were even now, some of them, resolved to clear the log-jam at the top by literally blowing it away; but deadly afraid of the weight of propaganda-influenced opinion against them. It was as if the British military chiefs, in 1940, had planned to depose or assassinate Winston Churchill. Even Hitler's own generals, of the Waffen S.S., were becoming disillusioned. They had no objection to fighting for clearly understood and achievable objectives, and in the beginning, while there was still a chance to drive the Allies back into the sea and so score a victory which would be decisive for years, if not for ever, they were enthusiastic. But now, they were rebellious, loyalty to their men coming uppermost.

Caen was being held on their right flank by an infantry division, which had replaced the worn-out forces of 21 Panzer Division on 6 July, on the eve of the attack; and in the centre and on their left flank by the battered remnants of the Hitler Jugend division. Repeatedly, ' Panzer ' Meyer requested permission to withdraw to the river line which ran through the centre of the city, was shorter, and much more defensible. Again and again, he was referred to the ' Führer Order ' not to yield a yard of ground. " We were meant to die in Caen ", he wrote, " but one just couldn't watch those youngsters being sacrificed to a senseless order." On 9 July, without orders, and defying the Führer, he began to pull his troops back over the river barrier into the industrial suburbs of Colombelles and the Faubourg de Vaucelles, and back from the shell-torn airfield of Carpiquet. The battle of Caen was not over, but on that day, while 59 Division were still miles from the city in the north, 3rd British moved in from the east and 3rd Canadian from the west.

Already, on 8 July, the inhabitants of Caen had seen the writing on the wall. Shells, including the 16-inch projectiles from the *Rodney,* were still falling into the city; although only three divisions were assaulting, the artillery of five divisions was employed in the bombardment. And the bombers and fighter-bombers of the Tactical Air Force were still attacking. "At about 6.30 on 8 July there was an air of something about to happen," wrote Madame Tribulet. " Curiosity made me open the front door. The road was sinister, just one German soldier looking at the horizon, his rifle on his shoulder, as though he was going to shoot at the planes as if they were partridges. Opposite, a few men were queuing at the butchers—fifteen minutes later, they were dead. We heard the roar of an aircraft just over the roof-tops—Francois ran to the cellar, calling to me to follow him—then we were covered in falling plaster and rising dust—and Francois was bleeding from the head. A two-ton torpedo had fallen 13 yards away, destroying ten houses, killing 56 people. Wounded were crying and dying in the debris; those rescued had their faces covered in blood.

"I helped Francois towards the Lycee Malherbe and we reached the cloister under the shadow of the immense bells of the Abbaye aux Hommes (St. Etienne). More than a thousand people were huddled there. The badly wounded were being taken to the Bon Sauveur Convent, but the place for Francois was the emergency hospital in the monks' refectory. There, the marble tables were covered with wounded, and we waited in a queue to be seen. A boy was brought in, with his arm torn off. Others were already dead. A man sat at a table, keeping a record of the names, where they were known, but often the rescue teams could give only the street or the number of the house where they had been found. After Francois had been treated, we slept that night at the Lycee; but the night was long, the fighting was still going on, and the babies cried continually. Next day, 9 July, there were optimistic rumours, and I saw a wounded Canadian outside the Lycee, and then a little Canadian caterpillar tank. The firing went on, and we thought the Germans would take Caen again, but on the 10th the battle had died away; and the way was open for Francois and I to go home. Glad to be free at last, we hurried out into the country towards Sainte-Croix where, in September, 1944, I wrote these lines."[3]

At the Bon Sauveur Convent, a Nun wrote in her diary, under 9th July: " *Date of the liberation of Caen*. But liberation in part only, for we passed another month before tranquility was restored. This morning, we learned that the Canadians had arrived. We could scarcely believe it, nevertheless it is true. But

[3] *Pour Retrouver Mon Fils A Caen*, by Luce Tribulet (1960). Madame Tribulet's husband, M. Raymond Tribulet, is now a Minister in General de Gaule's Government.

the Germans are still in the city and are merciless. In the evening, we actually saw the Canadians, they were outside. Our refugees, eager to catch a glimpse of their liberators, climbed onto walls and peered through windows, even smashing those few panes of glass which still remained. This alarmed the Canadians, and they feared treachery. At once, they ordered the gates of the Convent to be opened, and some of the Resistance men obeyed; but the gate was heavy and had been damaged, it would not open easily. We heard the sound of machine-gun fire. Rushing out with other Nuns, I found that the Canadians had opened fire on the Resistance men, slightly wounding two of them. When the poor Canadians saw us, and realised that they had fired on a Convent, they were mortified and full of apologies. Then they entered, and were warmly welcomed."

" The folk of Caen have gone through hell in the past month," wrote an airborne soldier in the divisional newspaper. " So have we, but we had the comfort of knowing that our women and children were not exposed to such shattering danger. They are every bit as heroic as the people of London who stuck the blitzes with a joke on their lips. Perhaps even more heroic. For here there are no underground stations, no deep shelters. Hundreds of homeless families live herded together on the floor of the great Cathedral of St. Etienne, whose white stone pillars and crystal candelabra contrast violently with the improvised beds of straw or chairs. Surely this church, almost the only one not badly damaged, has never had a congregation more grateful for its protection!" But many of the people of Caen must have wished that Duke William had never conquered England.

CHAPTER FIFTEEN

'THE HILL OF CALVARY'

The Taking and Re-Taking of Hill 112
10 July to 1 August

" . . . and meanwhile the pot was kept boiling by a limited action
to hold the enemy armour in the east . . . The bridgehead south
of the Orne was to be expanded by the capture of Éterville and
Maltot and by the recapture of Hill 112."

Major L. F. Ellis[1]

In the middle of the first week of July, the midnight peace of
many sleeping villages south of Caen was disturbed by a metallic
roaring and rattling, beneath which the roads shook and the
houses trembled. Those who dared, peeped out and saw monster
tanks, like enormous hunched beasts, their long guns pointed
rearwards ' at 6 o'clock ', creeping through, lit by the eerie glow
of their panting exhausts. The real Tigers were coming. On D
plus one, 3rd British Division had been reporting Kortenhaus'
Mark IV as a Tiger. When the enormity of being ashore at all,
and alive, in Fortress Europe had worn off, it was mostly Panthers
which were counted as Tigers; an easy mistake, if one had never
seen a Tiger, for the Panther was a big tank, too, with a very
big gun. But the Tiger was a monster and its gun was the deadly
88 mm dual-purpose anti-aircraft/anti-tank gun with the high
velocity and flat trajectory. Its front armour, 7 inches thick, was
to all intents and purposes impenetrable to any gun the Allies
were likely to be able to oppose it with, short of sailing H.M.S.
Rodney up the Caen Canal, or putting the ' mediums ' in the
front line. It was, as a Canadian officer said feelingly, " a hell of
a tank."

A number of Heavy Tank Battalions had recently been
formed, and they went instantly into the line opposite the British
and not the Americans. Overall, the Montgomery plan was working. The bulk of the German armour was being pinned down
around Caen, frustrating his attempts to take the place, but still
leaving the door of opportunity open to the Americans. The

[1] *Victory in the West*, H.M.S.O.

great American breakout began on 3 July, spearheaded by General Middleton's VIII Corps, and by 14 July it had advanced 12,000 yards—or 1,000 yards a day. In addition to bocage, there were bogs and water obstacles, and although the largest tank they were up against was the Panther, they had no equivalent to the 17 pounder the British had fitted to a proportion of their Shermans.[2] And the longer the Americans stuck in the bocage, the harder the British would have to battle around Caen. The coming of the Tigers made their task very much harder. Heavy Tank Battalion 503, formed in Germany, came under command of 21 Panzer Division and went into the line at Troarn, northeast of Caen. Their first action was on 11 July, their 3 Company only being engaged against twenty Shermans. While 1 Company was equipped with the very latest model Tiger II (the Königs Tiger or Royal Tiger), 2 and 3 Companies had the earlier Tiger Is. But the Shermans gave 3 Company very little trouble. Of the twenty, thirteen were knocked out, two were captured intact, and the remaining five got away. There were no German losses. It was the Western Desert all over again, but with the sizes of the tanks and their guns scaled up. The British inferiority remained.

503 was a Wehrmacht unit, but the Tigers which were put in at once to oppose the British take-over bid for Hill 112 were from S.S. Heavy Tank Battalion 502 and they came under command of II S.S. Panzer Corps.[3] The Waffen S.S. men of 502 had assembled at Wezep in Holland from all over Europe: experienced drafts from tank and grenadier units serving on the Russian front, drafts from convalescent depots, and raw recruits from the training camps. The first category were wary ' old soldiers' of eighteen or nineteen; the second men who no longer believed they were ' bullet proof'; the third eager for action in an elite unit, anxious to prove themselves. A ' Battalion spirit' was quickly built up, led by the experienced East-fronters; but even they had no idea what was in store for them. The ' card ' of 1 Company, Baumann, was one of these. Whatever was lacking, wherever they were, Baumann could organise it. As they

[2] For full details, see Omar Bradley's *A Soldier's Story*, pp. 320/1.
[3] In the British official *Victory in the West* they are misprinted as 102; similarly, the wounded from the " Derry Cunihy " are misprinted as 105 instead of 150; there are numerous other errors of minor fact and figure, not normally found in expensive official histories.

moved towards Normandy, halting in the woods each day, it was Calvados and a party which he organised. ' Staff Baumann ', or the ' Baumann Organisation ', was the current nickname for him and his cronies. ' The Brotherhood of the Drunkards ' was what Heinz Trautmann, wireless operator of Tiger 134, called it. " But this ' landsknechtsmilier ', this hearty ' men-at-arms ' atmosphere, with its bawdy songs and private jokes," he wrote, " was not to last long. And in the early hours of 10 July, it was clear that we had almost arrived. I was on sentry duty once more—my seniors felt that I was virtually pre-destined to it, probably because of my hard Bavarian nut—and it became clear that something was ' on '. Of course, where, as they say, the front is the ' most frontest ', the clacking of the small arms never stops, even at night; but this night—or rather, very early morning—the MGs were rattling away and the thunder of the artillery rose minute by minute to a howling crescendo. And this ' schützenfest ', this firework display, seemed to be only a few kilometres from our resting place! "

The 43rd Wessex Division, plus 46th (Highland) Brigade, a brigade of 3rd Canadian Division, supported by 4 Armoured Brigade and 31 Tank Brigade, with artillery from three divisions and two AGRAs, had attacked at 0500. To ' keep the pot boiling ', Operation ' Jupiter ' had begun. Hill 112 lay midway between the Rivers Odon and Orne where they begin to converge before entering Caen. It was more than 1,000 yards across on top, with woods and wheatfields, and where the road from Evrecy to Eterville ran across the summit and was intersected by a track from Baron to the north, there stood a wayside ' Calvary ', the Croix de Filandrières. This, together with what was to happen there, prompted the Germans to dub Hill 112 ' Kalvarienberg '—the ' Hill of Calvary '—and what had happened there caused the 43rd Wessex in due course to erect a divisional memorial on the summit, which many years later was to be visited and photographed by Heinz Trautmann. Possession of the hill was vital for any force advancing from the Odon to the Orne; but once secured, it was never secure, because its summit was in plain view from the high ground, including Bourguebus Ridge, on the far side of the Orne. It had changed hands twice already during the Odon offensive. General Paul Hausser, who had succeeded Dollmann in command of 7th Army, considered that the hill was the key to the back-door of Caen, and therefore of Normandy also. South of Caen, the bocage ended and the ground was suitable for massed tank attacks; very much less favourable to the defenders. He gave his orders to General W. Bittrich, who had taken over command of II S.S. Panzer Corps, and so, eventually, the humble wireless operator, Heinz Traut-mann, found himself committed to days and nights he would never forget. In an effort to forget them, he wrote afterwards a long and detailed narrative, and even revisited that haunted place. For him, then, the wheel finally came full circle; the matter filed, forgotten, put away in a pigeon hole. At that moment, he would have been glad to meet his former enemies and talk it over, to find out how had it been for them. And so he took a photograph of their memorial, standing on the bare hill top.

Other men, unable to express themselves on paper and so release the horror, kept their memories corked tight inside them. One British infantryman had never spoken of the matter, even to his wife; she knew nothing of what he had endured. But, when interviewed by the present author, it all came tumbling out, a jumble of memories, devoid of dates or exact place references; once the logjam had been broken, this normally in-articulate man spoke for four hours without a break.

The British advance began in the morning, along the line of the old names in the valley of the Odon: Verson, Mouen, Baron. From what the British soldiers already called ' Death Valley ' to what the German soldiers were soon to call the ' Hill of Calvary '. " Why do you want to take the big words away from us? They are all we have," protests the pilot in Nigel Balchin's *Lord, I Was Afraid*. For the infantry, it was indeed all they had, as they stood up and began to advance through the corn, sprinkled with red poppies and the machine-gun slits of the Waffen S.S.; only khaki tunics between bare flesh and the bullets. Their objective lay well beyond Hill 112—the bridges over the Orne. In the first stage, 129 Brigade on the right and 130 Brigade on the left were to take the hill. In the second stage, 129 were to hold, 130 was to breakout to Eterville and Maltot. In the third stage, fast tanks and infantry in tracked vehicles were to make a dash for the Orne, hoping to get the bridges intact. 130 Brigade had never been in action; within a few hours they were to meet in Maltot the Tigers of 502, which had never been in action as a unit, although many of the men were experienced.

When, at 0500, Trautmann heard the barrage begin, he gave the alarm, the officers were roused, and the men hurriedly began packing up. They had been spotted the previous evening by aircraft, and at dawn the Typhoons attacked; white, feathery clouds trailing behind them as the rockets left the racks, the earth shaking with the thunder of explosions. " In any case, and in spite of all this, we were on our way to our stand-by position," wrote Trautmann. " We drew up in an orchard and began camouflaging the tanks. The enemy artillery opened fire as our eighteen-year-old recruit, Günter Hensel and I were packing all the blankets and coats into the 'Africa box'. Willi Fey, the tank commander, ordered everyone inside the Tiger, but Trautmann and Hensel were late in obeying. There was the scream of a shell and Trautmann, wounded in the thigh by splinters, saw Hensel go sprawling into a flowerbed, the back of his head torn open. " He lay there, curled up as if asleep. Günther, who had been looking forward to his first operation so keenly." Then came the order to move to Maltot. There was just time to bandage Traut-mann, who remained on duty, get a replacement for Hensel, and then they were off.

They must have arrived just after the British, although the 43rd Division's historian disagrees, criticising the 7th Hamp-shires and their supports, the 5th Dorsets and 44 Royal Tank Regiment, for having claimed the capture of the village, when " in actual fact, they had merely superimposed themselves on top of a very strong defended locality," adding, " many Tiger tanks lay concealed in the orchards and dug in on the outskirts. As the morning wore on, the situation went from bad to worse —how badly was not realised at brigade headquarters for some considerable time." No doubt that was how it appeared to Brigade. There was a tendency to regard every turret-down Ger-man tank as ' dug-in ', a permanent feature of the landscape, and there was little realisation of how rapidly, in fact, the Germans shifted them about, making a handful go a long way. In this case there was no doubt whatever. One Troop went to Maltot, roaring across an open field for the shelter of the first houses, then creeping slowly forward, not knowing what to expect, and with no field of fire, for the hedges and garden walls blocked all view of the enemy positions. "There," wrote Trautmann, "the magic begins. Anti-tank guns and tank guns, still invisible to us, put down a barrier of fire. If we stay here much longer, we shall be cracked like a nut." So they drove boldly forward through the hedge and found four British tanks in full view.

"*Panzer—halt! Tank far left—200—fire at will!*"

With the second shot, the British tank began to brew. The enormous gun swung steadily to bear on the next nearest tank. That went up. The third was simultaneously destroyed by the Tiger of the troop leader, as that too burst through the hedge. The fourth British tank reversed rapidly out of sight on the Eterville road. The Tigers moved off at once for St. Martin, to take part in a major counter-attack on the hill, half of which was now in British hands. They were confident there would be no more trouble from Maltot, and indeed the Divisional historian uses the words "desperate" and "hopeless" to describe the situation there; as the British pulled out, and the Tigers formed up for counter-attack on the front of 129 Brigade, the three British tanks, burning still in Maltot, "flamed like torches against the evening sky." At 2200 hours, the sixteen Tigers of 1 Company, supported by grenadiers of 9 S.S. Panzer Division, were to go up the hill and restore the situation for the Germans. Simultaneously, the commander of 43rd Wessex, Major-General G. Ivor Thomas, was planning to restore the situation for the British by committing his last immediately available reserve, the 5th Battalion of the Duke of Cornwall's Light Infantry. The British attack was timed for 2230, half-an-hour after the Germans planned to leave their start-line.

"With the speed and precision resulting from long-practised, much-hated drill, we all swung into our seats," wrote Trautmann, "for our Company was due to attack in a few minutes. The call, '*Net in*'. I tuned my receiver and put on headphones and microphone. The frequency scales begin to light up, the current hums. 2100 hours. Above our heads, the turret hatches clang shut. The driver starts the engine, and we move forward with a jerk. Through our narrow vision slits, we can see the bushes and branches we have tied on for camouflage, start to fall off. We make a half-turn to the right, our tracks screeching. In a long line, our sixteen Tigers move obliquely onto the road. All we can see through the slits are trees to left and right, and the stern of the tank in front. Then a short halt, as we reach the start of the slope, and fan out into a broad wedge-formation. There are thick bushes growing halfway up the slope, and that is where we must go to take up firing positions. The enemy won't show himself, let alone come out and fight, he just hails down his fire until, as we say, ' the coffee-water is boiling in our arses '; but as long as he only hits the countryside, we are safe from a hero's death. For our infantry, however, who had no armour plate, it was different; they couldn't fire a shot, they just crouched at the bottom of their trenches and waited." Then they met something new in tactics. Willi Fey, the commander of Tank 134, wrote: " Down came a barrier of defensive fire such as we East-Fronters had never known; the Russians had never as many guns as this, and they did not use them in this way; and then came a thick smoke screen. Our attack folded up at the foot of the hill, before we even got onto the slopes." The shells drove the grenadiers to ground, and, parted from the close protection of their ' little friends ', the Tigers found themselves enveloped in swirling white smoke, vulnerable to a single enemy soldier with a Piat.

One of the men directing the guns from the top of Hill 112 was Serjeant Green's brother, Stanley Green. They travelled in a half-track, transferring to an O.P. tank with dummy gun whenever enemy tanks were reported. The Major he had landed with on D-Day was a veteran of the Desert Campaign, and knew all the tricks—such as digging a slit-trench and then driving the half-track over it for head protection—and he had an instinct for trouble which had kept most of them alive until now. The very first time they were on O.P. duty, he had sent them inside the tank for cover the moment two German air-bursts blossomed overhead; he knew they were ranging shots. The crews of the other tanks they were with disobeyed his order and remained in the open, paying for their carelessness with heavy casualties a moment later. They drove up to Hill 112, selected a position, dug their slit-trench, and the Major stood up to direct the half-track over it. There was a faint whistle, and a mortar bomb exploded, killing the Major. Another officer was instantly sent forward to replace him. " He said he was lucky and that nothing ever happened to him, but he only lasted half-an-hour on Hill 112. This was reckoned the worst place in Normandy. The Germans had such wonderful binoculars and observation lenses that no one who was able to get hold of any ever used British binoculars again. These lenses gave the Germans perfect vision of all the British positions from vast distances, sometimes without the observer having to move from the lying position. The German method of ranging with air bursts was also considered far superior to our method; the Germans took two air bursts and then usually found the target. With us, out of a battery of eight guns, one gun did the ranging, and everything depended on the skill of the officer; some of them were liable to require twenty shells or so, by which time the target could have vanished. However, it was the supremacy of the 88 mm gun which was the over-riding factor which ruled the actions of the forward tanks—its shell, travelling absolutely horizontal, without any allowances for drift, trajectory, or range, made it impossible for any British tank to live in the vicinity of a Tiger. In contrast, the British anti-tank guns could not touch the German armour and were even reduced to trying to bounce the shells off the ground into the belly of the Tiger or Panther. These are facts which my brother tells me were with them every minute they were on O.P. duty."

The British reached to the line of the main road running across the top of Hill 112; and there 129 Brigade came to a halt, unable to advance over the crest to the road just beyond, holding barely half the hill. The entire Brigade was hard-pressed, but wrote the Divisional historian, " it was in the centre, on the front of 4 Somerset Light Infantry, that the fiercest struggle developed." At 2230, 5 D.C.L.I. advanced through the Somersets, followed by their supporting tanks, in order to " stabilize the battle ", and in a wood on the far side of the ridge, they met 1 Company of S.S. Heavy Tank Battalion 502 advancing again to the attack. Shortly afterwards, a small party from the reserve pool of the Somersets came up to replace casualties. They consisted of Captain Scammel, a Serjeant, and Corporal D. B. Jones, an ex-aircraft factory worker from Bristol (it was a reserved occupation, but he had volunteered). They had been told that they would find the position very easily—all they had to do was to walk in the opposite direction to the casualties coming back. " I found my platoon dug-in along the straight line of a hedge just this side of the ridge of Hill 112," recollected Corporal Jones. " Just beyond, was the road; and about 100 yards behind was a small wooded area containing our tanks. It was obvious that this platoon—7 Platoon, 'A' Company—had been under fire and tank attack for some time. However, Brigadier Mole and our own C.O., Lieutenant-Colonel C. G. Lipscomb, were sitting on their field sticks, apparently discussing the battle. They were deliberately trying to uphold the morale of the men before an enemy attack, regardless of personal safety. This instilled a respect and affection for both of them, which I imagine was unsurpassed in any unit. However, a machine-gun opened up immediately with tracer, the Serjeant I had come up with was killed, and that prompted me to dive for cover in the nearest slit. It contained the body of a dead comrade whom I was unable to identify as he was headless. Not wishing to stay there, I crawled forward ten yards to another trench containing Serjeant Brewster, my platoon serjeant. In a twinkling, my cigarettes and water were gone, as we were in the centre of the platoon area."

As Serjeant Brewster talked, Jones realised why the Brigadier and the Colonel had acted so nonchalantly. Just previously, that part of the Duke of Cornwall's Light Infantry which had been holding a position on the far side of the ridge, just forward and to the left of 'A' Company of the Somersets, had retreated in disorder. They had come running back in panic through the trenches of the Somersets. A wounded officer of the D.C.L.I. had been trying to prevent them; he had been hit in the jaw, so that part of his face had dropped, and he was waving a pistol and trying to shout, making horrible sounds. Eventually, these men dug-in behind the Somersets, but the morale of 7 Platoon had been badly affected by their frantic passing, and it was touch and go whether or not they, too, would run away. So Brewster, the ex-middle weight boxer of the battalion, had leapt into a sitting position on his slit trench, pointed his rifle down the line of his own men, and shouted that he would shoot the first bastard who moved. From what happened a few minutes later, Jones judged that it was this action by Brewster which alone had kept the platoon in their trenches at the crucial moment.

"A short while later, a German tank attacked. As it approached very close to our platoon position, so one of our tanks emerged from the woods behind us. There followed an interesting battle, with firing between the two tanks, until the German tank stopped, approximately 40 to 50 yards in front of us. I think it was a Panther, not a Tiger. Immediately the German tank stopped, the Germans got out of the tank and surrendered, coming towards us. But as they did so, some of our platoon began shooting at them, and the Germans swerved away to the right; I believe only one or two made our lines. I saw the faces of our men who were firing; their expressions exhibited their detestation of the men in the tank; they really wanted to kill; it was obviously impossible to stop them. I only understood this attitude later, when they told me that in a previous German attack, the tank gunners had used their big guns on infantry in trenches, with horrible results; and I was shown one man, half in, half out of his slit, with his back blown away. The first impact of war on a soldier shows him its disgusting cruelty, and this was obviously the first reaction of fighting men who'd not experienced it before. To me, it appeared to be a violation of the British soldier's concept of fair play."

" In the very early hours of 11 July, we made another attack," wrote the commander of Tiger 134. " The little wood on top of the hill is solid with anti-tank guns. Firing continuously, we roll on. The grenadiers of the ' Hohenstauffen ' and ' Frundsberg' Divisions take heavy casualties as they advance with us, and are eventually pinned down. We go on alone." Trautmann, the wireless operator of the tank, wrote: " This time we tried in a northerly direction, against the side which faced Aunay. The tops of the trees were being blown to pieces by enemy fire and our panzer grenadiers dared not lift their heads; many brave comrades were left dead on the slope. But in quick succession, we destroyed several Churchill tanks. The planned march to Berlin seemed to have suffered a delay by this. Knecht was badly bothered on two sides at once, and we tore along at 20 km per hour across trenches and earthen banks until we had the Tommy in our grip. On the extreme left of this little wood, a square pasture for cattle actually, we saw the enemy busily emplacing his anti-tank guns. Brave they were, no doubt, these Anglo-Saxons, but we were rapidly closing to point-blank range, so that their efforts were meaningless; they would never be ready to fire in time. Courage or madness? we asked ourselves. The brief battle was like a training exercise. The guns were literally dismantled, shields flying through the air, wheels hurled across the field. The Tommies screamed, throwing their arms in the air as they died, or somersaulted, horribly mutilated."

In the south-east corner of the enclosure, huddled behind and under the 'dead' Sherman, was a party of a dozen men of the D.C.L.I., led by Lance Corporal Gordon J. Mucklow. "We heard the roar of tank engines, first a tank on one side of us, then another tank on the other side. They couldn't be ours, we couldn't hear the tracks. Then all hell let loose, red-hot bullets were sizzling in the earth inches from our helmets," recalled Mucklow.

One of the Tigers firing at them was Walter Knecht's, with Rudolf Wüster as gunner. Three hundred yards away was another Tiger, but from 3 Company, also firing on the scattered remnants of the D.C.L.I. Then, to Wüster's horror, the turret of the other Tiger began to revolve until the muzzle of the 88 mm gun was pointed at him. It belched flame, and the shot roared overhead.

"Reverse!" ordered Knecht, fumbling for the Verey pistol.

"Permission to fire, sir!" yelled Wüster.

"No!" shouted Knecht, as another shot screamed overhead.

As the 3 Company Tiger fired—and inexplicably missed again for the third time, Gordon Mucklow saw two Verey lights rise up from Knecht's tank. "Was it one red, one blue?" he tried to recall afterwards. "It didn't seem important at the time, but I remember everything going quiet except for distant explosions." Mucklow had no idea that the shells roaring over him were aimed at anything other than the Sherman they were sheltering behind; and it was nine years before Wüster discovered that the other German gunner had made an error in sight-setting earlier on.

Then down came the smokescreen again, to cover the retreat of the D.C.L.I.; but this time the Tigers roared blindly into it, shells exploding around them, at the order for top gear: " *March —caracho—March!*" And then they were through. " *Panzer— halt!*" A hundred yards away, the Bren carriers and other vehicles were loading up with men and equipment, ready to retire, covered by two tanks. The tanks went up in flames before they had time to turn their guns round, and then the Tigers blazed away at the helpless carriers. But, over his headphones, Trautmann was listening to the instant recall signal from their C.O.: "*Withdraw at once, withdraw at once!*" Reluctantly, the Tigers obeyed. "A few scattered Englishmen stood up in their trenches and came towards us, without having been told to. Soaked in sweat, black as miners, horror showing clearly in their eyes and in their faces, pleasant enough under the hideous grime, they came staggering towards us. They had fought bravely, and we treated them accordingly." It was the end of the D.C.L.I., who had lost their Colonel and most of the officers; but some escaped under cover of the smoke. One of the Tigers was missing, its fate not known. "It was on this day and during this same attack that fate caught up with Endemann and his brave crew, lost somewhere in the smoke."

As the battered Tigers withdrew, their sides scarred by shell-hits which had failed to penetrate, so the British moved forward. "After this, things quietened down," said Corporal Jones. "We were ordered to move that night over the ridge of the hill. We did this and attempted to dig in approximately 30 yards down the hill from the road, using our spades from the sitting or lying position, because the German MGs were firing tracer on fixed lines onto the road. Other units of our battalion had also been ordered to move forward over the ridge on our left flank. In the darkness they moved too far forward, to a position which was untenable, and were ordered to withdraw. During this time, my platoon were digging in, covered by three Brens, the usual drill. The Bren gunners were lying down, in the open, covering our left flank. We had not been told about our units which had gone forward, and knew nothing about them. A very good friend of mine was manning one of the Brens. Very alert, he spotted movement ahead and then the faint silhouettes of approaching soldiers, four or five of them in a bunch, running towards him. Being an expert, he held his fire until they were approximately twenty feet away, then opened fire and killed them all. I was digging and didn't even see them, until the Bren started firing. I crawled over to it, and the gunner suddenly said to me, "God,

I think they were our blokes '. And then he burst into tears. I crawled out to them and ascertained that they were our own men and that none remained alive. I assumed they'd been ordered to retreat, but in their panic to get back over the road, had run in the wrong direction, not knowing we were there. In the circumstances, the Bren gunner had been right to shoot them all, and I tried to convince him of this. We were still digging in and defenceless; had they been Germans, we should have been overrun but for him. It was the safety of 36 men against the deaths of five. We stayed there a few hours more, until dawn, and were then ordered back over the road, through the woods and into a field containing heavy mortars, and there we dug in.[4]

" In this field, we were heavily shelled, just as the mid-day meal was being cooked. Only one man didn't dive for a slit-trench, but carried on by the roaring pressure-cookers which drowned the noise of an approaching shell. I knew him. He was a deserter. I'd had to pick him up in Bristol from the police; his wife had gone off with another bloke; and he'd deserted to sort out the other bloke. I watched him now with a very healthy respect, then I crawled over to one of our blokes who'd been hit getting into his slit. Blast wound in small of back—just as if someone had opened him like the flap of a tobacco pouch, not bleeding yet, although the muscles and ribs were showing. I just slapped the flap of flesh back in place, like shutting a door."

Another man who came up, like Corporal Jones, as a reinforcement during a night of battle, was William Biles of 4 Wiltshires which, with 5 Wilts and 4 Somersets, made up 129 Infantry Brigade. He had missed the previous fighting by being in hospital, and the only dead bodies he had seen so far were of the Scotsmen he had carried as one of the burial party during the Odon clear-up. " It was just getting dark as I came up with the food wagon," he said. "All I could see was blazing tanks, tracer bullets flying everywhere, screeching of shells. First time I'd seen battle conditions. I was directed to my Company Commander's

---

4 *Warning*: this story illustrates a chaotic situation which is reflected in all six narratives—three British and three German—and also in the Divisional History of 43rd Wessex. None of the narrators had any real idea of time or place, because so much was happening so quickly, and the present reconstruction is, at best, merely approximately accurate, the best which could be hoped for in the circumstances—proof of the severity of the struggle.

trench and my Company Commander, who was in it with his batman, told me to get my bloody head down or bloody well get out of it, and what the hell was I doing there? I told him I was just back from hospital and was looking for my platoon. He pointed out where he thought they were, but said, if I'd take his tip, I'd get into the nearest trench and wait for daylight: the Company had suffered heavy casualties and would probably be withdrawing in the morning. I jumped into a trench with two chaps in it, and they promptly told me what a hell of a time they'd had, and that they didn't know where my platoon was. In the early hours of the morning, the tanks that were up there started to withdraw. Half an hour after that, there was heavy shelling. I was really scared. Then we withdrew to a field about a mile away, and there I found my platoon, or what was left of them. As they had been waiting to attack, so our own shells had landed right in the midst of them. The chaps I'd done my soldiering with had been blown to bits, most of them. A Serjeant asked if I'd go up with him and bring their identity discs back: I don't know for why, but I couldn't bring myself to go up with him.

" The following day, we went back up on the hill and were there in slit trenches for weeks. Never moved out of them. Never washed or shaved, or took our boots off. Had to walk back at night-time to pick up food and take it back to our trenches. All this time, constantly shelled day and night, 88s mostly. Time and time again, I prayed, lying in the bottom of a trench. Never saw a German once. Thinking mostly about the next shelling. Hearing blokes scream and cry, when trenches around were hit. Used empty food tins to make water in; had to dash to nearest empty trench for other, trousers unbuttoned in advance. Eventually relieved and went to another field. Three days rest, cleaned up a bit, back up the line. Senior N.C.O. shot himself in foot, decided he'd had enough."

" On the 10th of July then, began the hot and desperate fight for this hill, which was to give it the name of ' Kalvarienberg '," wrote Heinz Trautmann. " Not one square metre of earth remained which had not been ploughed repeatedly by the shells. Only a week ago, in Holland, we had asked ourselves: ' The war in Western Europe—what will it be like?' Now, the only time we raised our heads in surprise was when the noise of battle ceased. The howling of the shells and the whistle of the bullets had become for us familiar music; wherever we turned up with our tanks, there we would leave behind nothing but ruins and rubble. And then again the order: '*Panzer—advance!*' The call that carried us along, surrounded by death, urged on by one single, elemental force: the determination to stand firm, to hold our ground, to halt the victory march on Berlin, to hit back against the overwhelming power of the enemy, to make him hold his breath with the shout: 'German tanks are coming'! Every day our reserves grow less. Boys of 17 are in the line, and grey old men, grandfathers; the homeland is sucked dry, there is nothing more to give. Men who desert to the enemy are not exceptional any more. But we will not desert. Often, we cannot get out of our tanks because of the shellfire, not for anything; an empty shellcase comes in handy for necessary purposes. But here on this plateau, without cover, every morning without fail, the Battalion Commander of our support infantry turns up. We can see him coming from St. Martin, in his gaiters, with his binoculars round his neck, his walking stick in his hand. Heedless of the fire he walks on, slightly stooped. From underneath his field cap shows his white hair. He goes from trench to trench, has an encouraging word for every one of his soldiers, asks about their welfare, distributes cigarettes. Then, one morning, he did not come anymore. Down by the burnt-out S.P. gun, his soldier's fate was fulfilled.

"Not one single day passes but the Wehrmacht News Bulletin does not mention this hill, until it is finally abandoned at the end of July according to orders, and the Tigers retreat from it undefeated. But it changes hands many times, its slopes saturated with the blood of our comrades and that of the English and Canadian soldiers. During the night of 12 July, the Tommies took it once again. Our Tiger 134 has to go back to workshops for repairs; petrol tanks leak, the air-conditioning is out of order; the red light glows on the driver's dashboard—damage to the radiators. For all its powerful engine and huge 60-ton weight, the Tiger needs very careful handling. Like a raw egg. Even a giant has his Achilles heel. Back at workshops in St. Martin, we are shelled, the gunner is badly wounded, the driver is wounded too, but he can be patched up, and stays on duty. Next day, 13

July, we retake that wood on the top with a dash; the burnt-out wrecks of the guns and vehicles of 11 July are still there. But the defensive fire goes on day and night. Loss after loss. The grenadiers cannot hang on there anymore, and on 15 July only the Tigers are left on the top. There is no more infantry protection, we are up there alone: the day and the night seem endless. ' Hold at all costs ' is the order. Then on the morning of 16 July, the grenadiers of the 'Frundsberg' Division re-occupy the old position. After five such days, it has changed its aspect completely. Bare, naked tree-stumps point accusingly at the sky and the countless craters make one think of the surface of the moon.

" But what we remember are the sandwiches, made from iron-hard bread with a rusty knife. And the pudding garnished with grass and sand (the ration vehicle had driven into a bomb-crater, the rations had fallen onto the raw earth, and the driver had scooped them up with a ladle—he just dug a bit too deep, that was all). ' Mess-tins ready! ' Cider in a field-flask and the ultimate ecstasy, as we all leaned back and screwed a 'sulima', a cigarette, into our faces, and read the mail: Leni is in child-birth—little Herbert has eaten soft soap—Walter next door has been killed in action, somebody got a coupon for a new pair of shoes—Frau Mikkerig on the second floor has a new . . ."

The British paid with 2,000 men for the first thirty-six hours' fighting; and the drain of blood went on, until everyone was jumpy, nerves tight-screwed. "Although we were dug in behind the actual front line now, we were still close enough for enemy patrols, and were constantly expecting them to attempt to get at the mortars," said Corporal Jones, who could not know that the German infantry had suffered a blood-letting at least as severe and had trouble enough barely to hold their ground, if at all. " During the night, while Serjeant Brewster and myself were sharing a slit trench, we heard footsteps. We knew it wasn't a member of our unit; they had all taken up positions for the night and would not move about. It was dark inside our trench, because we wanted a smoke, and had covered over the top with a gascape.

' What the devil's that, Ginger?' said Brewster.

' I don't know; have a look,' I replied.

' No, you have a look,' he said, humorously.

" Full of misgivings, I lifted my corner of the gascape, poked my head out, and came face to face with the head of a cow. I started laughing.

' What is it?' asked Brewster.

' Bloody cow,' I replied.

' Get rid of the thing,' he said.

" The potential danger had occurred to him instantly; if the cow was hit and fell into our trench, we not only could not get out, we might suffocate. With no more ado, I belted the poor old cow across the muzzle, much against my nature, hoping that, if it fell, it would fall in some other trench. At about this time, I decided to have something done about a painful boil on the back of my neck, which had burst, so I went to the First Aid Post, but when I saw the Doc surrounded by bodies, I decided he'd got far more important work for the knife, and returned to my slit." Very many men had these boils, in England and in Normandy; so it was probably something to do with the diet, which was only theoretically and for propaganda purposes adequate in vitamins.

" Often at night we heard the noises of tank tracks in the valley below, where Maltot lay," wrote Heinz Trautmann, " and one day we were told that the Canadians had occupied it, and we were to clean it up." This must have been on 22 July, when 4th and 5th Wilts attacked, supported by a squadron of Churchills from 7 R.T.R. 4 Somersets and 8 Middlesex were in reserve. Because Canadian officers were seconded to British units, and were particularly aggressive patrol leaders, the Germans often assumed, from the men they met, that a unit was Canadian, when in fact it was British. ' Panzer—marsch!' crackled the voice in Trautmann's earphones. The Tigers advanced through defensive shellfire put down by the artillery of 43 Div and the two AGRAs, independent artillery groups, for the moment under their command. The roofs and walls of Maltot were visibly dissolving under the fire, and from the top window of the church steeple, the usual point for an artillery observer, a battered Red Cross flag was flying. ' Half left—500—' crackled the voice of the tank commander, and looking left, as the turret swung, Trautmann could see four olive-green tanks rolling towards them along the road. ' Long body, small, short turret—Churchill ', thought

Trautmann. The final fire order came: *'Targets—the leading tank, and the rear tank, "Fire!"'* The first Churchill slewed right across the road, blocking it, the crew bailing out. The rear tank began to burn. The two in the middle were trapped, driving about wildly to find a way of escape. " Number 3 gets two hits in succession in the hull—nobody gets out of that one," wrote Trautmann. " The last one is hit in the stern, thin white smoke comes out of the hatches, then the heavy sternplates fly high into the air, a sheet of flame leaps up from the engine, and then the ammunition explodes." No sooner had they destroyed the Churchills than black bursts of smoke blossomed violently all around the Tigers. Anti-tank fire from a wood. They moved on quickly, and began to engage infantry, whom they could see moving amongst the trees. Then they were attacked by Typhoons, and the advance came to a halt. They were ordered back to the nearest slopes of Hill 112, overlooking Maltot.

Moving through the woods towards the Orne that morning was William Biles, with one of the two assault battalions, 4 Wiltshires. " We were told to take a small 'ouse in a wood, only five Germans inside, easy. We were attacking in Company strength, with tanks in support. As I walked up along the road, all I could see through the foliage was the top windows and part of the front door. No. 3 Section got the job of actually assaulting, and as they tore up the path, a machine-gun fired a short burst, and wounded two of them. One managed to crawl away but the other chap was 'it in the stomach. So our Red Cross bloke put a big red cross on the end of a bayonet and held it out where the Germans could see it. There was no firing so 'e crawled out; then they fired and 'it 'im in the leg. So it was decided to call up the tank from the rear. But I 'ad the bright idea, as I was No. 1 of the 2-inch mortar, to fire HE on the 'ouse. My mate opened up the cases, and I lay down behind the mortar and poked it in the general direction of the front door; I'd never fired the thing before, I was only hoping for the best.

'Well, Bill, I'll bung 'em in, you fire 'em ', said the Serjeant.

" I turned the handle, but when the first one hit, it didn't explode, it just poured smoke.

'They're not the bloody HE, they're the smoke ones ', I yelled to the Serjeant.

'Never mind,' said the Serjeant, ' we'll use those while your mate's opening the bloody HE '.

" So he was putting 'em down the barrel, and I was letting 'em off, when I hears a rat-tat-tat right behind me 'ead. It was our tank, firing into the 'ouse, which was covered in thick white smoke. 'Ell of a din. Then I was told they'd raided the 'ouse, and instead of 5 coming out, there was 45 coming out. I seen 'em coming out. We lined 'em up alongside bloody road, told 'em to put their 'ands on their 'eads; but our chaps weren't too gentle with 'em, some of 'em accidentally got their toes trod on, or got pushed on the 'ead, one or two got accidentally pushed under the chin with their elbows. Then, while I got a fag out, the chaps were going through their pockets and that, but I never once saw one of our chaps taking anything off a German except what was necessary. No time, really. No, we didn't hate 'em, not generally. Just 'ad a job to do."

Following behind and clearing up was the reserve battalion, 4 Somersets. " It was snipers we were after," said Corporal Jones. " Some were up trees, and some in trenches covered by thickets. If you saw marks on the bark of a tree-trunk, you knew a man had climbed up. So you sprayed. I remember we had an ' O ' Group by an L-shaped wood. The Major was sitting with a map on his knees. His orders were incoherent, he was picking alternately at his binoculars and compass, and yet doing nothing with them. I looked at the Captain, and by the expression on his face, I knew we were thinking the same thing; the Major was a brilliant staff man, but he'd had enough. So the Captain sent him back for a rest, and gave out the orders himself in a quiet voice, for he was a very religious man and never swore; some of the men thought him too soft-spoken. I went to do my job, to find Bren positions at the corner of the wood. I came out onto a track which led into enemy country and saw a man standing there, 30 yards away, in a sniper's jacket, his back to me. He turned round to look at me. And we both hit the deck at the same time; he rolled into the ditch by the hedge, I rolled over and over and over until I was out of sight of the track. He must have had a damned good sense of direction, for his first bullet went dead over my tin-hat and smacked into a tree-trunk behind me. I turned to Private Graham Todd, my Bren gunner, and yelled: 'Thirty yards—up the hedge—fire!' The sniper came out of the hedge and onto the field, to one side of the track, with his hands up, no rifle, after shouting 'kamerad'. I indicated to him to walk across the field and surrender to our people on the other side. Then Todd came up, looked at my tin-bonze, which I wore on the back of my head, and grinned: 'Ginger, look at yer 'at.' Bullets had hit the rim of my tin-bonze. Then I had a close look at the track, where I'd rolled over it out of the line of fire—there was a little cap, like the cap of a petrol can, sticking up. It was a mine; there were five of 'em, and I'd rolled over the lot. But my weight was well-distributed, as I was horizontal. Next morning, I went out and got that sniper's gun. It was a Schmeisser machine-pistol, and it was my personal weapon from then on."

On all sides, the infantry were flooding round Hill 112. The last battle of Caen had been fought, on 18 July, the Americans were poised finally to break through far to the west; but the Tigers were still holding, still operating like mobile pill-boxes to plug the holes, to bolster the unfortunate infantry drenched by the British shellfire. Through their positions infiltrated strong patrols. "On the night of 23 July, we were again on Hill 112", wrote Trautmann. "From somewhere very close indeed some damned mortar was killing off our grenadiers one by one. Soon after midnight, three of their NCOs came to report that something strange was going on at the corner of the next hedge. We can't see a thing, but it's no hallucination. Tensely, we waited for about an hour, judging by the mortar bombs that the Tommy had dug himself in right under our noses. Some of our MG 42s[5] fired at where they thought it was; but as soon as they had stopped, over came the next mortar bomb. Eventually, 'Staff' Baumann lost his temper. He started his Tiger, swung right, rolled forward, and sprayed the corner of the hedge to such effect that when he stopped, we saw a few hesitant hands come up. Those damned dish-washers had put their wretched thing only thirty yards away from us! Three tall Canadians, the only unwounded members of the patrol, came creeping out of their

[5] A Light Machine-Gun with a very high rate of fire, faster than the MG 34 which, in turn, was faster than the Bren. All German LMGs were called 'Spandaus' by the British.

holes. 'Hands up!' They pulled out four more men, all badly wounded, and left the six dead men who remained. With rubber boots on their feet, blackened faces, camouflage nets over their uniforms, well-sharpened hatchets like bushknives at their belts, they had tried to put Tigers out of action. They stared at us in disbelief: so that was what those devils look like who bothered us so. They had another thought coming."

On 24 July, the Tigers got eight Churchills near Maltot in a few minutes; on 25 July, they got the 'bomb carpet' treatment —"We heard the Trumpet of Jericho and the angels sing in heaven, what a choir that was!" wrote Trautmann. "And the English infantry came forward through a smokescreen with panzerfausts that looked like stove pipes, trying to hit us up the pan. We were relieved that night, and moving back, heard the cattle bellowing for food or relief from distended udders, a few ducks quacking in a pond, a stray dog howling, and saw in long, silent files the panzer grenadiers moving up along the sides of the road, carrying their MGs and heavy boxes of ammunition. *What unit?* we call. '*Hitler Jugend*' they reply. How many will return?"

Looking back at it long afterwards, it is possible to see that it was here that the desperate German defence of Normandy, with everything in the shop-window and nothing behind, began to fray at the edges. The bitter defence gave a momentarily false picture; to those up the sharp end, it seemed that the Germans would never crack, despite everything the Allies could hurl against them. The H.L.I. had come back from yet another botched attack on Evrecy, where the line bulged around behind the Germans on Hill 112: the Brigadier had been killed in the same field where Serjeant Green was dug-in, so at the crucial moment there had to be a re-shuffle, adding to the chaos which, in Green's opinion, was due to out-moded organisation and tactics. They were withdrawn somewhere around 21 July, and went to rest and re-organise in the gun area behind Hill 112, so that Serjeant Green found himself next to 6th Field Regiment, R.A., his brother's unit. He went over to see him, and was told he was up on Hill 112 with the O.P. party. "Next day", wrote Serjeant Green, "a smoke-begrimed figure came to my truck and asked for me. I turned and asked the man what he wanted. It was my brother, but I did not recognise him. He was the sole survivor of the O.P. party. They had all been sheltering under the O.P. tank, when a shell burst in front of the tracks, killing and wounding everybody except my brother Stan—how he escaped he never knew. In the course of the next day or so, we drank a bottle of whisky between us."

And on 23 July, Maltot was largely in British hands again. "An appalling spectacle, the streets and fields still strewn with the dead of the Dorsets and Hampshires who had fallen on 10 July, and lay in heaps around slit trenches," wrote the divisional historian. On 26 July, the Tigers fought their last battle around Hill 112, between Maltot and Feuguerolles-sur-Orne. " The first hours in the morning, the change from night to grey hint of day, these are the only peaceful hours we have," wrote Trautmann. " The light striking into the depths of the valleys and ravines, until the branches glitter and gleam, and the birds begin to sing. And so, too, began this 26th of July, another blue midsummer's day. The R.A.F. will have a good time. In spite of that, from ambush, we destroyed three tanks, four anti-tank guns, and ten vehicles. Then, at 1130, we moved to our old defensive hide-out, relieving Oberhuber's tank. He was unusually excited and pointing towards Maltot, where he thought anti-tank guns had come into position in the woods. Then he opened fire, the shell-bursts flickering like lightning among the trees. But there was no reply, until suddenly we came under fire from an unexpected direction, showers of dirt billowing up *behind* us. The radio crackled: 'Achtung! —anti-tank fire—start engines—load HE.' There was a brilliant flash on the right side of Oberhuber's tank. A circular black hole drilled in the armoured side, level with the radio operator's seat, showed that we were being attacked from the flank. The blast and shock tumbled Oberhuber backwards, out of his turret onto the stern, and smoke began to pour out of the hatches through which were tumbling the survivors, mortal terror on their faces, eyes wide and staring. The wireless operator was dead, but the driver had got out, in terrible pain, wildly waving the stump of a severed arm, the hand dangling down, still attached by shreds of flesh."

The Tigers reversed out of it, then counter-attacked. They spent the afternoon picking off at long range the ' soft-skinned ' vehicles which were flooding forward, the columns of smoke rising high in the still air from the burning trucks. Late that afternoon they were concentrated at Feuguerolles to meet an attack coming in on the right, probably part of the abortive Canadian Operation ' Spring ', and were caught by the R.A.F. " We had hardly started when they were overhead," wrote Trautmann. " Looking back, the diving formations resembled a star exploding into separate particles. Dirt, stones, and disintegrated trees, wrapped in clouds of black smoke, went flying past our vision slits; waves of hot air blew past us. As if chased by the devil we raced across trenches and over craters, 60 tons of tank bobbing about like a rowing boat in a storm. Behind us the diving planes, then screaming low overhead, then climbing steeply for the next attack. We went dashing into the cover of a wood, feeling as if we had disturbed a swarm of bees. We can see that the whole valley of the Orne is under shellfire, puffs of black, yellow and white smoke bursting amid thundering walls of dirt. One battery got our range, salvo after salvo screaming down and tearing up the ground around us. Sheer fright rooted us to our seats, where we cowered behind the telescopes and weapons, listening to the hot fragments strike the armour plating, the ground shaking beneath us."

But still the German lines held, until on the night of 1 August, the Tigers were switched away to meet a threatened breakthrough by the Americans at Vire. The British had held them long enough, for many more weeks than had been planned; and now, at last, the long-delayed major effort to roll up the Normandy front was being made. As a memento of the men they had fought so long and so bitterly, Heinz Trautmann took with him some captured maps and a British soldier's letter home, lying unposted on Hill 112, and dated 12 July.

" Dear Ted and Brenda,

I received your welcome letter and am very pleased to know that you are back O.K. and that the baby is keeping well and gained weight. Regarding myself, I am in the pink and have so far escaped a blighty one. I have no idea when I shall be home as I guess we will have to keep going after the retreating Germans. I suppose Paris will be our next objective, now that Caen has fallen, and I hope it is not in ruins like all the villages we have captured. There is no wine, women and song out here, as it is very seldom we see any civilians. After our last attack I don't want to go into another like it, as it was a real bloody battle and we had to fight hard to get what we wanted. We had bread today for the first time since we came over here and I certainly did enjoy it; we only got one slice for breakfast, but we really cannot expect too much yet. Well I guess there's not much more I can say at present so I send my best wishes to you all and hope that the baby comes along O.K. and I hope to be able to see you all very soon."

Only half of Caen had fallen when that letter was written, but by the time the Tigers left Hill 112, Montgomery was at last where he had intended to be on D-Day, give or take a few thousand yards, the ones that mattered.

CHAPTER SIXTEEN

THE GREATEST AIR RAID
OF ALL TIME

*'Goodwood'—the Plan—Preparations—Rommel
wounded on the Eve—4,000-Plus
16 to 18 July*

While Collins was hoisting his VII Corps flag over Cherbourg,
Montgomery was spending his reputation in a bitter siege against
the old university town of Caen. But had we attempted to exonerate
Montgomery by explaining how successfully he had hoodwinked the
German by diverting him toward Caen from the Cotentin, we would
have given our strategy away. We desperately wanted the German
to believe this attack on Caen was the main Allied effort. But he
nevertheless left himself open to criticism by overemphasising the
importance of his thrust toward Caen. When Monty failed to take it,
the correspondents blamed him for the delay.

General Omar N. Bradley

General Montgomery had planned to get, not merely Caen,
but the dominating heights behind the city, by the evening of
D-Day—and 3rd British Division had failed by a good three miles
even to enter the northern outskirts. He had then planned a
double-encirclement, through Villers Bocage and the Airborne
bridgehead: but 51st Highland had failed on the left and 7th
Armoured on the right had been driven back in their first defeat
since Alamein. With greatly increased forces, he had then planned
a tremendous ' right hook ', starting at Fontenay, which was to
sweep round behind the city, via the Odon, Hill 112, and the
Orne to the heights of Bourguebus Ridge, directly in rear of Caen
and dominating the rising plain and the dead straight road which
led to Falaise: and 30 Corps, 8 Corps, and 1 Corps combined had
faltered and then come to a standstill under the impact of the
German armoured strategic reserve, so that even Hill 112 had had
to be given up. Dispensing at last with subtlety, he had then
attacked Caen head on from the north under an overwhelming
tonnage of ' air ' which had torn the city apart: and three divisions
had come grinding to a halt in the rubble along the line of the
water barriers which divided the city in half. He was in Caen, but

he had not taken Caen. The real prize, the dominating heights in rear, the plain behind them, and the road to Paris, which tactically were one, remained in German hands.

Two minor failures, two major failures; redeemed so far by the success of the primary mission allotted to the British and Canadian Armies—to act as the honey to attract the German wasps. But by the second week in July, yet another failure imperilled everything they had so far done, and turned a serious situation into a critical one. The British and Canadian blood-letting went for nothing if the Americans failed in their part of the plan—to break-out of the bridgehead while the bulk of the German Army was elsewhere engaged, and to swing the whole Allied line through an angle of ninety degrees, with Caen as the pivot, and so push the German Army up against the Seine, where it might be destroyed in a great mobile tank battle. This was the over-riding idea, as originally conceived, but the Americans had failed again and again to break-out. Their last attempt had been timed to coincide with the British and Canadian head-on assault on Caen of 7 July, but by 10 July the Americans too had failed, and General Bradley reported that he would be unable to try again until 20 July at the very earliest; and in fact was not able to do so until five days after.

The Allies were therefore pinned in a narrow bridgehead, ten to twenty miles deep, which was barely one-fifth of the area they had planned to occupy, and in fact needed to get, by mid-July. Every field was an arms dump; there was simply no room for many of the follow-up formations and specialised units. Hitler's strategy of not yielding one yard of ground, if it could possibly be avoided, had so far succeeded; and seemed to be on the verge of stabilising the whole Normandy front altogether. If the bridgehead could be corralled off for another six weeks or so, the onset of autumn, and then winter weather, might well turn stalemate into disaster. Cherbourg was likely to be useless as a port for many months to come; the artificial harbours would probably not stand a winter storm, of twice the force which had smashed the American Mulberry and damaged the British one; and beach unloading would be a desperate and chancy business. In any event, tonnage unloaded would not anything like match tonnage required—for the Allied forces ashore had now grown almost to the strength of two Army Groups, one British and one American, controlling four Armies.

But the German forces also had increased. At long last, Hitler and many of his senior commanders had realised that Normandy was the main Allied effort; that the V.1 bombardment of London had failed to produce a surrender or provoke an attack on the Pas de Calais. German infantry divisions, so far held in reserve, were being moved to the Normandy front; in the period of a few days just before and just after the attack on Caen of 7 July, no less than four German infantry divisions reached the front, three of them going into the line opposite the British and Canadians. Now, at last, much of the strategic armoured reserve —General Baron Geyr von Schweppenburg's Panzer Group West —could be pulled out of the line, to rest, re-fit, and prepare for its proper task; not limited local counter-attacks, but a massive counter-offensive to split the narrow bridgehead in two and destroy the British and Americans separately. The Americans being reckoned much the easier proposition, the German armour began to move away from the cemetery city of Caen and the blood-soaked Odon stream, towards the American front, where Bradley's drive to take St. Lo had collapsed, and where for at least ten days, and in fact fifteen, no major American offensive action was likely to succeed. If those panzer divisions were allowed to re-group in front of the delayed American break-out, there would be at very least no break-out; there might instead be a break-in. It was imperative to hold them, or at least the bulk of them, on the British-Canadian anvil of Caen; and to crack them there. A critical situation required emergency measures, improvised and unorthodox, and therefore open to criticism if it failed in any way. And this is the reason that Montgomery's last battle for Caen, Operation 'Goodwood', has provoked more criticism, much of it biased, and most of it ill-tempered, than all the rest of the Normandy battles put together.

But one other known factor there also was. The blood-letting between British and German had been mutual and not, as newspaper readers at home then thought, one-sided. There are no easy victories to be obtained over German armies. Indeed, because most of the British divisions were 'green' when they went into their first full-scale battle, and also because the attacker, having to expose himself, is always likely to lose more than the skilful defender, the ratio of loss was running at approximately 3:1. That is, three dead British infantrymen for every dead German. Even more serious was the fact that this had not been sufficiently allowed for in the planning; in the offices where the future dead, mutilated and missing are calculated and prepared for in advance, as they must be. For D-Day itself and for approximately ten days afterwards, losses had been pleasantly lower than estimated; from then on, as the panzer divisions of the German reserve were drawn in, they had jumped to the alarming ratio of 2:1. That is, for every man who became a casualty, and for whom a replacement had been provided, and was standing by in the reinforcement holding units, two men were becoming casualties; and there was only one man to replace them both. The time was rapidly arriving—it was less than two weeks away, in fact—when there would be no more infantry reinforcements. They had all been fed to the units and had themselves become casualties in their turn. The turn-over of a British or Canadian infantry battalion at this time would make a bomber aircrew's tour of operations look like a good life insurance proposition. There simply was no way out except feet first or two feet under; and the infantry themselves knew it better than anybody else. That fact was becoming very obvious. And the only way, now, to keep divisions up to strength, was to break-up an existing division, already bled and shaken, and distribute the survivors piecemeal throughout the armies. Among other things, this would mean that the very large ' tail ', or non-combatant element of the division broken-up, would find themselves swiftly up the sharp end, learning virtually a new trade.

But this crisis affected infantry only, apart from a few specialised trades such as driver. The armoured divisions had lost many tanks—mere mass-produced machines which, like aircraft, were now expendable—but they had not lost many men; because, again, as with aircraft, many of the crews were able to bale out. This consideration was a vital factor in shaping the plan for Goodwood '. Use the armour, not the exhausted infantry, was an obviously sensible proposition. But how and where?

There were three armoured divisions available. The 11th, which had seen action at the Odon; the Guards, which was newly landed and inexperienced; and the 7th, which was very experienced but equipped with light, fast 'blitzkrieg' tanks. There were 500 reserve tanks parked in Normandy, so that colossal losses of machines could be calmly accepted; there were plenty of tank crew reinforcements in the 'pipeline'; and there were, standing by in England, two more complete armoured divisions, the 4th Canadian and the 1st Polish. There was the major error in British planning. Thinking in terms of North Africa, and even of 1940, they had over the years produced a 'blitzkrieg' army; but the place in which it was finally committed demanded a much higher ratio of infantry to armour and a great number of 'infantry' tanks capable of tackling the Panther and Tiger. Of course, once a breakout had been achieved, the British Army would be almost perfectly tailored for the task of rapid pursuit. But as long as it remained bogged down in Normandy, it was struggling not merely against the enemy and the close, constricting countryside he was defending so skilfully, but against its own technical composition; as if a jeep was trying to do the job of a bulldozer. Additionally, from the beginning to the end of the Normandy campaign, the necessity to use inexperienced formations immediately in a major battle meant delay, fumbling, and unnecessary casualties; which is a comment on the facts, not a reflection on the commanders and men concerned.

The question of how this force was to be used was also the question of where? The Odon/Orne front, as 'Epsom' had proved, was totally unsuitable for mass tank movement, because the main roads ran the wrong way; tanks can take to the fields, if they absolutely have to, but petrol, ammunition, and workshops lorries are roadbound. Moving a single division is like moving a small town, a difficult feat in itself, even without opposition. Additionally, the Orne barrier meant an assault river crossing at the outset, one certain recipe for delay and possible disaster; the other certain recipe being a large, uncleared minefield. There was only one area where the British already had a bridgehead over the water barriers which ran into Caen from the south-west and continued northwards to the sea at Ouistreham: the cramped, constricted Airborne bridgehead east of the Orne and the Caen Canal, overlooked by the Germans on the high ground of the Bois de Bavent and the Caen factory suburb of Colombelles. This finally was the area decided on, not because it was satisfactory, but because it was not quite so unsatisfactory as the alternatives. And the shape of the ground shaped the plan of attack. So narrow was the front, that there was no room to use the three armoured divisions in line abreast; they would have to advance in line ahead on a front only a few tanks wide, one behind the other; fanning out only when elbow room had been gained behind Caen to the south. 11 Armoured Division was to lead, commanded by Major-General 'Pip' Roberts, probably the best armoured commander the British had, followed by the inexperienced Guards, followed by the lighter weight of 7th Armoured, equipped with tanks suitable for a rapid exploitation of any breakthrough achieved by the two leading divisions.

There were obvious objections to this plan. In effect, it was a strong 'left hook' round Caen from the north-east, which would travel in an arc, exactly like a wild 'swinging' punch, starting due south, ending up facing south-west and west. The entire flank of the narrow thrust would be exposed to German fire at short range, and possible counter-attacks, for something like six miles. All along the left flank of the advance, or in its path, were heavily fortified villages, which the Germans had turned into a careful system of linked strong-points covering each other by mutual defensive fire. On the right flank of the advance were the equally heavily fortified outskirts and factory areas of Caen: Colombelles, Mondeville, Cormelles. The villages were set down with a neat, regular spacing, like a chessboard—Cuverville, Giberville, Sannerville, Toufreville, Demouville, Banneville, Manneville, Emieville, Grentheville, Frenouville, Bellengreville, jarring slightly at the name of Cagny, as the attack itself was to jar. Then, a mile or so beyond the railway embankment, the name forms varied widely—Soliers, Ifs, Bras, Hubert-Folie, and Bourguebus, the ultimate objective, in a commanding position between the two national highways—N 13, the Paris road, and N 158, the Falaise road. British infantry were supposed to clear the left flank and Canadian infantry the right, but clearly they would not be able to pace the planned tank advance, which was to go in at speed in order to 'saturate' the defences.

The motorised infantry component of 11 Armoured Division

was to be dropped off on the way through, to clear two of the strongpoint villages, Cuverville and Demouville. Major-General Roberts represented to 8 Corps that this was unsound and unnecessary. He needed his infantry with him, to deal with anti-tank positions, and there seemed to be no reason why the infantry divisions could not at least mop up the villages near the start line. The Corp Commander's reply was an offer to let some other division lead the advance, which Roberts did not accept, because he felt that the operation as a whole had a good chance of success with the tanks of three armoured divisions saturating the defences. But it would have to be achieved almost alone. Because the Airborne bridgehead was cramped there was little space to deploy the artillery and, as such a preliminary move forward of the gun lines would give the game away, it was decided not to do so. Therefore, halfway through the attack, the tanks, already vulnerable on their left flank, and lacking also in infantry, would pass beyond the barrage put down by the massed field guns. They would have to make the final bound for the Ridge supported only by their own mobile artillery and a 'cab rank' of circling rocket-firing Typhoons. As the Army Commander was subsequently to refuse offered R.A.F. bomber support, and as the direct radio-link between the tanks and the Typhoons was to be knocked out early by an unlucky hit, and as 7 Armoured Division were slow coming into the battle, perhaps due to traffic congestion, in the event 11 Armoured Division advanced alone with Guards Armoured Division on the left flank.

These risks were accepted because the Intelligence estimates were optimistic. They reported that the German defences were only some three or four miles deep, coming to an end more or less on the line of the Caen-Vimont railway; if the tanks could burst through the initial three or four miles, there would be nothing between them and Bourguebus Ridge. The Germans had negligible armoured reserves and would be unable to mount any formidable counter-attack. As the British had command of the air and a network of agents working among a basically friendly population, this appreciation should have been correct. But it was not. Intelligence had wrongly placed one panzer division, mislaid another, and did not know of the existence of a third. They believed that the line was held by infantry, that 21 Panzer Div was locked up in the Caen suburb of Vaucelles, and that the only German armoured reserve was the remnants of 12th S.S.

Consequently, there was tremendous optimism at Corps and Army. The German village strongpoints would be torn apart by the greatest concentrated air armada in history—more than 2,000 bombers, more than 2,000 fighter-bombers and fighters. 720 guns, which had 250,000 rounds to fire, would open a secondary bombardment. And then three armoured divisions, a complete armoured corps, would crash through the pulverised defences and race for the high ground beyond. If it cost 200 tanks, it did not matter; even 300 would not be too high a price to pay for Bourguebus Ridge. From there, the whole Caen plain could be dominated, and the broad national highway ran in a dead straight line to Falaise, distant only sixteen miles. Easy tank country and a main road for the supply convoys. Bourguebus Ridge was the minimum, with a broken German front ahead and armoured cars probing to Falaise, to see if the maximum was attainable—a breakthrough as decisive as El Alamein.

Of course, the American attack—now definitely known to be delayed until 25 July, a week after ' Goodwood '—must not be risked. The infantry must mop up and consolidate the gains of the tanks, so that the Caen sector was firm and unbreakable, the hinge upon which the Americans would pivot. But if that could be done quickly, the American break-out might be matched by a swift British tank drive to Falaise. For the ' record,' the minimum objectives were firmly and cautiously stressed; but even there, the hope of a major success is apparent. Among the staff, there was absolutely no doubt about it, and the optimism spread downwards to units and across the Channel to England. Nothing could withstand this enormous concentration of air power. The villages on the left flank would receive 2,500 tons of heavy bombs in a few minutes, the Caen-Mondeville industrial area on the right flank would simultaneously receive 2,500 tons; and the single village of Cagny, almost in the path of the advance, would have 650 tons of R.A.F. bombs directed at it. Just one village! The strong-points in the centre would be swamped with small-calibre bombs by the concentrated might of the U.S. Air Force. In comparison, the bombing of Caen itself on 7 July had been just a small-scale experiment in technique; this was the culmination, the greatest air raid of all time. And this time, there would be no delay in follow-up; that mistake had been noted. There would be no traffic jams either; the lesson of the Odon had also been learned. Subconsciously, the staffs relaxed. The bombers would win the battle for them; brisk staff work would keep the advance going and firmly under control. As for fighting—what would the Germans have left to fight with, after their positions had been pounded into the dust for a depth of many miles? 'Goodwood' was an aptly chosen name: line up the gee-gees by the starter's box, fire the guns and drop the bombs, then race for the finishing tape, hell-bent. No one was prepared for a bloody battle, and no plans had been made for that impossible eventuality. And at 0530 on 18 July, the starter's guns—all 720 of them—began to fire, and over 1,000 'heavies' of Bomber Command came in with a throbbing roar, wave after wave after wave, soon to be followed by the Fortresses and Liberators of the U.S. 8th Air Force. "The whole area in front of us seemed to erupt in one enormous column of smoke and dust," wrote Major W. H. Close, M.C., then commanding 'A' Squadron, 3rd Royal Tank Regiment, which, with 'B' Squadron, was to lead the advance of the three armoured divisions. "Nothing could have survived such an onslaught, we thought. How wrong we were!"

*   *   *

"We were told, and fully believed it," wrote the Household Cavalry historian, "that we were on the threshold of great events. 'We are ready to break-out of the bridgehead . . . we still firmly retain the initiative . . . we have punished the enemy severely.' Nothing could now stop us . . ." The task of the armoured cars of the Household Cavalry, the reconnaissance regiment of 8 Corps, was to prevent a recurrence of the Cheux traffic jam which had strangled the Odon offensive at birth. The special nature of the fighting in Normandy had altered a great many tactical conceptions, and one of them was the use of armoured cars for reconnaissance. Armies were supposed to advance and retreat behind a mobile screen of fast, W/T equipped vehicles, but the Germans in Normandy proved surly and unobliging; the first thing an armoured car met was either a tank or an anti-tank gun; result—no armoured car. For ' Goodwood ', 2 H.C.R. were being used for traffic control, and consequently Lieutenant D. B. Powle found himself posted at the Bénouville/Ranville bridges with two tasks. His orders were: to see that traffic passed across in one direction only: UP. Nothing was to come back, not even ambulances. Anything that went over, stayed over. To enforce his orders as regards personnel, he had a squad of Military Police; to cope with broken-down or damaged traffic, he had two recovery vehicles, one at each end of the bridge. His second task, equally vital, was to report by radio direct to Corps, by-passing the cumbersome ' normal channels ', exactly what unit was in fact passing over the bridge. Theoretically, the ' wonders of modern science ' had made control of widespread forces ridiculously easy; but, in fact, they were merely ridiculous. Very often, senior commanders had absolutely no idea where their forces were; all they knew was where they had been, yesterday or the day before. These new arrangements had been most carefully thought out and should have proved adequate. That they did not was due to two factors, one of which was discovered late, and the other too late.

To preserve secrecy, the armoured divisions were moved, one by one, by night, to their concentration areas. First to arrive, on 16 July, was 11th Armoured. They were informed that, that day, an unknown minefield had been discovered, laid by a since-departed British division, right across the axis of the ' Goodwood ' advance.[1] If secrecy was still to be preserved, it could not be cleared in the time now available—less than 48 hours. Only a few narrow lanes were in fact cleared. Through them would have to flow the armour of three armoured divisions, the half-tracks of the infantry brigades of those divisions, the S.P. guns of the divisional artillery, and the clutter of tankers, ammunition wagons, REME, Engineers, and so on, which formed the long but necessary ' tail '. " Many experienced officers had grave misgivings about the traffic jam which was bound to be formed," wrote the historian of 23 Hussars, the unit which was to follow

[1] So they were told; but in fact it was the precise position of the mines which was unknown—they had been hurriedly laid and corn had since grown over them.

3 R.T.R. and 2 Fife & Forfar Yeomanry through the gaps. The fighting vehicles of this Brigade alone, as concentrated, covered a complete square mile of ground. The three gaps through which they would have to funnel were one tank wide; so that the square mile of vehicles would have to squeeze themselves forward into narrow lanes; straggle through the minefield, and then reform into mass formation on the far side, in full view of the enemy, or what was left of him. And this was merely the leading brigade of the leading division.

The desire to achieve surprise, which prevented the mass lifting of the minefield, was also responsible for the decision not to move forward as many as possible of the 420 25-pounder field guns, which were short-ranged and could cover only the opening phase of 'Goodwood'. Hindsight shows that this was a faulty appreciation; by 17 July, the day before the attack, the Germans knew all they needed to know. This day, their air reconnaissance reported the mass transfer of armour from west to east; their agents reported that the date of the offensive was 18 July and that it would fall on the front of 16 Luftwaffe Field Division; the barrages fired at night to conceal the noise of the moving tanks, which could be heard miles away, thus did not screen, but in fact confirmed, these reports. 'Sepp' Dietrich, commanding I S.S. Panzer Corps, still defending Caen, told his interrogators after the war that a trick he had learned on the Russian front, of pressing his ear to the ground, enabled him to hear the tank movement in spite of the artillery fire; but this would have told him nothing he did not already know. That day he was in fact in conference at the H.Q. of II S.S. Panzer Corps with the corps commander, General Wilhelm Bittrich, and Field Marshal Erwin Rommel. The latter left early, at 4 in the afternoon, because he was in a hurry to get back to H.Q. Army Group B at La Roche-Guyon. As usual, he passed through Livarot; Monsieur R. Nicolas, who kept the main baker's shop in the town at that time, recalled that "he used to pass through every day in a kind of Mercedes, on his way to the front, and then come back in the evening, in front of our house, on his way to his headquarters." This day, the Mercedes passed many German vehicles burning by the side of the road, where they had been shot up by British aircraft attracted by the great flags of dust they towed behind them; for the Germans, as well as for the British, ' Dust meant Death '. They took evasive action, turning down several side roads, before emerging on to the main road again, the other side of Livarot, over which eight fighter-bombers were circling. Believing that they had not been spotted, the driver of the staff car drove on. Then Serjeant Holke, whose duty was to watch for aircraft, reported two fighter-bombers chasing them, at well over 300 m.p.h. The driver was told to step on it and swerve the car round into a side turning a few hundred yards ahead.

The leading fighter-bomber leapt up on them like death, its wings only a few feet above the road surface, so that the burst of cannon and machine-gun fire ripped into the staff car without any need for deflection or a hurried pull-out from a dive. Rommel was wounded, Major Neuhaus was wounded, and the driver, Daniel, was dying. The staff car slewed out of control across the road, hit a tree stump, struck a ditch, and turned over—the doors flying open. Twenty yards behind it, lying unconscious in the road, was Field Marshal Rommel. The second fighter-bomber continued the attack, trying to finish off Hauptmann Lang and Serjeant Holke, who had jumped out as the car went over. It was 45 minutes before Lang could find a car to get the Field Marshal to hospital, and his injuries were so severe that at first it was thought there was no hope for him. In a sense, this was true. A few days before, he had sent a report, drafted by his chief of staff, General Speidel, for onward transmission to the Führer, in which the Normandy situation was summed up in the words: " Our troops are fighting heroically but even so the end of this unequal battle is in sight." In his own handwriting, he had then added the postscript: " I must beg you to recognise at once the political significance of this situation. I feel it my duty, as Commander-in-Chief of the Army Group, to say this plainly." This was to say to the Führer, as von Rundstedt had already said to the Führer's staff: " Make peace, you fools! " Field Marshal von Kluge, who had succeeded von Rundstedt, did forward the letter to the Führer's headquarters in East Prussia with a covering letter of his own in the same strain: " The moment is fast approaching when this overtaxed front is bound to break up . . . . I consider it my duty as the responsible commander to bring these developments to your notice in good time, my

Leader." Thus von Kluge had signed his own death warrant also, though he anticipated it. These were not isolated grumbles, springing from the immediate situation; there was, literally, a time-bomb of long standing under the Führer; and it was ready to blow. Rommel, Speidel, and von Kluge had long been connected with it. But it was the events in Normandy and now also in the East, where the Red Army had broken through, which produced the necessary critical situation in which a minority might act with some hope of majority support. But Rommel was the keystone of it all, for he alone had the mass popularity, the figure-head quality which was required of a new German leader in war-time; and, unlike many other generals, he was bold enough to act decisively in a situation where failure meant torture, execution, and disgrace, not merely for the plotters, but for their families as well. The keystone of the plot had been eliminated, not by the Gestapo, who had begun already to round up minor figures, but almost by accident, and three days before the balloon was due to go up.

The day before ' Goodwood ', Britain and Germany lost the war; the U.S.A. and the U.S.S.R. were on their way to rival domination of the world.

* * *

" Possibly the only time in the history of the 2nd Battalion Grenadier Guards when all ranks were up before reveille was on 18 July, 1944, for at 0500 a distant thunder in the air brought all the sleepy-eyed tank crews out of their blankets. 1,000 Lancasters were flying in from the sea in groups of three or four at 3,000 feet. Ahead of them the pathfinders were scattering their flares and before long the first bombs were dropping. After a few minutes the area was a turmoil of smoke and dust with the Ack Ack tracer soaring above. Occasionally an aircraft would fall like a swaying leaf, flaming to the ground." So wrote a member of the Guards Armoured Division. The heavy 500 and 1,000 lb bombs were falling into two long, narrow rectangles, one to the right of the armour's axis of advance, one to the left. The right flank target area covered the Colombelles and Mondeville industrial suburbs of Caen, due to be mopped up by 3 Canadian Inf Div with 2 CIB in support; it was held by part of 21 Panzer

Division, including Leutnant Hans Höller's detachment of self-propelled anti-tank guns and half-tracked light flak, well dug in. One half-track, a very heavy armoured vehicle, complete with its 2 cm flak guns, was dug out by a direct bomb hit and flew twenty yards through the air. "This was another special day," wrote Höller. "While the bombing went on there was no fighting at all, everyone hid in the deepest hole; the area became completely ploughed up and impassable. There were thousands of bombers. Each wave dropped smoke signals after they had unloaded, to indicate to the next wave to start dropping more bombs." In fact, the target indicators were being dropped by the Pathfinder Force, so that there would be no tendency for the bomb-aimers to take the rapidly drifting clouds of smoke and dust as their target, or to bomb short.

Doing this job of marking on the left-flank target was Flight Lieutenant G. D. Linacre. The area contained the farming villages of Toufreville, Sannerville, Banneville, Manneville, Guillerville, and Emieville, and was due to be mopped up by 3 British Inf Div; it was not held by 16 Luftwaffe Field Division, as British intelligence had reported, but by part of the von Luck Battle Group, strengthened by the Tiger tanks of Heavy Tank Battalion 503 and part of 200 Assault Gun Battalion. The Luftwaffe division had been almost wiped out in the 7th to 9th July battle of Caen and its remnants were near Colombelles, where British intelligence had placed all of 21 Panzer Div, instead of only part of it. At the south end of the left-flank target was part of Panzer Regiment 22, including Werner Kortenhaus' 4 Company, and also part of the Tiger Battalion. Bomber Command was attacking tanks and armoured anti-tank guns largely, and not the more vulnerable infantry. "When the droning of the approaching bomber squadrons was heard", wrote Kortenhaus, "the men got into the tanks and closed the flaps, or crawled underneath for protection. We saw little dots detach themselves from the planes, so many of them that the crazy thought occurred to us: are those leaflets? We could hardly believe that they could all be bombs. Then began the most terrifying hours of our lives. It was a bomb carpet, regularly ploughing up the ground. Among the thunder of the explosions, we could hear the wounded scream and the insane howling of men who had been driven mad." Men were knocked unconscious by blast, while the bomb storm raged around them; amid the continuous whistle rising to a scream of the approaching bombs, and the thunder-crack of the explosions, men heard death coming—were reprieved—heard death coming—were reprieved—heard death coming—could do nothing—and some nerves cracked; there were cases of suicide; there were cases of permanent or temporary insanity; the stunning effect temporarily incapacitated everyone. Nerves, emotions were drained; it was impossible to think. The scenery had vanished. The farms and the fields had gone, wiped out. In their place was a wild moon landscape of brown craters, wreathed in the acrid smell of high-exposives. Tanks caught fire; tanks were buried; men were buried; a 60-ton Tiger was blown upside down. And still the R.A.F. poured overhead, the great black-painted night-bombers roaring low to make certain of their aim. Among them the Pathfinders, relentlessly marking up the targets for continuous attack, intent on getting an aiming point picture, ' or else '.

Linacre's sub-target in the left-flank farming area was the village of Sannerville, two miles north of where Kortenhaus was. " We set off in the dark at 0400 to do Visual Backer-Up," he said. " In the half-light, we could see masses of aircraft. It grew into a beautiful morning, hardly a cloud. It was the first time I had seen so many aircraft in daylight; and I remember the beachhead was amazingly quiet, not many ships there now." Now the target was coming up, and Linacre was feeding information into the bomb-sight, subconsciously expecting another flak barrage similar to that which had damaged them over Caen on 7 July. Down below, Sannerville was boiling, the fumes streaming away downwind on a wide front as if the earth was on fire. There were vivid, flickering flashes among the smoke and dust storms, as fresh bombs burst, and sticking out of the leading edge of chaos was the distinctive cross-roads which made a double triangle—the aiming point. Linacre took his photograph, and the Government's business was done. " It was very smooth, none of the opposition we'd had earlier; a cakewalk," he recalled, with surprise. " We came out down by Cherbourg, sight-seeing. All very peaceful. And we wondered: ' Where the hell *is* everybody ! ' "

They were waiting for the bombing to stop; nothing could move while that went on. And the flak did not fire, for it was no longer defending Caen against air attack; after 7 July, it had been moved out of the city and was now emplaced in an anti-tank role all along the line of the 'Goodwood' advance, and dead in the path of it, on Bourguebus Ridge. 78 Luftwaffe dual-purpose 88s survived intact, waiting for the tanks. The old anti-tank gun screen which Rommel had used so frequently in the desert against Montgomery's predecessors, which had ruined so many British near-victories, which had sent so many generals home in their bowler hats, and had at length brought out Monty himself to turn the tide of continual defeat. Bourguebus was not on the R.A.F. bombing programme, and was outside the range of the artillery programme. It was on the U.S. 8th Air Force bombing programme, which started as Bomber Command finished, having lost only nine night-bombers in what could have been a dangerous and costly operation.

The American heavy bombers were quite distinctive. " We saw the R.A.F. go in, in the normal way, spread out and low," recalled Lieutenant-Colonel Powle, M.C., who was then a lieutenant in the Household Cavalry, " but the Yanks came over in tight formations and higher." Unlike Bomber Command, which had been designed as a mass-destruction, city-pulverising force, from which no great accuracy was expected, the Flying Fortresses had been designed for deadly accuracy on pin-point key targets in daylight; and they had a bomb-sight which the more 'gung-ho' types claimed would put a 'bomb in a barrel' from 20,000 feet. Their targets were mainly in the Grentheville, Bras, Soliers, Hubert Folie, and Bourguebus area; that is, clustered beyond the Caen-Vimont railway, on the approaches to the vital heights. There was also an extreme left-flank target rectangle near Troarn, a few miles east of the Bomber Command left-flank target area in the farmlands. Nevertheless, the effort by the American heavies (carrying a much lighter load than the R.A.F.) proved to be scattered and ineffective in the most vital area of all—Bourguebus. And the medium bombers, which were to spray the corridor through which the armour was to advance, with small bombs, to avoid heavy cratering, were hindered by the drifting dust storms created by the accurate R.A.F. bombing which had preceded them. A strong force of dive-bombers would have come in very useful at this point, but the Americans had abandoned them, and the R.A.F. had always opposed them, apparently on religious grounds, to judge by the fervour of their arguments, which were in fact a legacy of the inter-service quarrelling about air power in the 1930s.

Nevertheless, the plight of the Germans appeared to be appalling. If the British came at them now, without pause, there was nothing they could do. Some units had been totally destroyed. The bombing of the American mediums on Demouville, on the line of the armoured advance, had been particularly effective. 1 Battery, 200 Assault Gun Battalion had been eliminated and 1 Battalion, Panzer Grenadier Regiment 125 had vanished. The infantry of 716 Luftwaffe Field Division were either dead, wounded or so stunned and shocked as to be incapable of resistance. Tank crews were literally digging themselves out with their hands; the tanks were plastered in earth, their engines fouled up, their air-cooling systems full of sand, their optics knocked out of alignment. The men were shaking with nervous reaction, and hardly knew what to do first, attend to the moaning wounded or see to their immobilised and useless tanks. "We cursed this insane war," said Höller. "Always the tanks had to be in the frontline, instead of being held behind as a reserve, at the point of gravity. We were just playing at 'fire brigade', being helplessly smashed up from the air. Desperately, we begged for the chance to hit at an enemy we could see, instead of one who knocked everything down from a distance. But that reminded me of when the boot was on the other foot. At Tobruk, in 1941, we had knocked out a British tank with an 88, and when the British officer got out of his little Mark II, he complained that it was not fair of us to shoot at his tank with such a large calibre gun! At this time, I had an appreciative audience for *that* story. . . ." For many of the Germans, it was their worst day in five years of war.

In these circumstances, behind the gun barrage, the British began to advance.

CHAPTER SEVENTEEN

DEATH RIDE OF THE ARMOURED DIVISIONS

'Goodwood'—18 and 19 July

Theirs not to reason why,
Theirs but to do and die:
Into the valley of Death
Rode the six hundred.

The leading tanks of the armoured corps began to move up to the minefield at about 0230 on 18th July. Far in rear was 7 Armoured Division, ahead of them was Guards Armoured Division, and in front of them was 11 Armoured Division. At the head of 11 Armoured Division was Lieutenant-Colonel D. Silvertop's 3rd Royal Tank Regiment, which was to advance with A and B Squadrons abreast, leading the whole procession. "At about 0430 hours, in the grey light before dawn, we moved through the minefield, nose to tail," recollected Major W. H. Close, M.C., then commanding A Squadron. "One of the carriers of the Motor Company wandered out of the taped lane and was blown up, then we debouched from the minefield as quickly as possible in the darkness, and at first light were forming up in very close formation on the start-line. Owing to the narrowness of the gap, tanks could only be a few yards apart at first, and we were horrified at the mass of tanks and vehicles crammed into such a small area." A and B Squadrons were the first wave of the advance—32 tanks in line. The second wave consisted of R.H.Q., the light tanks of the Recce Troop, the Carrier Platoon, a troop of Flail tanks, and half a troop of Engineers' tanks, AVREs. In the third wave was the reserve Squadron, the infantry of the Motor Company, and the SP guns of the R.H.A. Battery. Between 0545 and 0745, some 8,000 tons of bombs turned the ground ahead into a spurting dust storm, obliterating the positions believed to be held only by the infantry of 16

Luftwaffe Field Division. At 0745, the Artillery barrage began, behind which the tanks were to advance. 250,000 rounds were available, up to 750 shells and cartridges were stacked beside each field gun; and many guns fired 400 rounds or more that day. Some of them fell short directly onto 3 R.T.R. on the start-line, killing several troop commanders and wounding some of the crews who had been standing outside their tanks, enjoying a last cigarette. "This happening a few seconds before we were to start, added considerably to the confusion, and we set off after the barrage in some disorder," said Major Close.

The disorder increased at the head of the procession, as the tanks advanced in swirling clouds of dust and, hardly able to see, found the ground pitted with bomb craters which could not be crossed. Swerving blindly round them, and tending to lose direction, time was lost, and the barrage was lost; the guns steadily increased the range, as the time-table indicated, and the tanks got further and further behind. 2 Fife & Forfar Yeomanry followed 3 R.T.R., and after them came the reserve regiment of the leading brigade, 23 Hussars. By the time the Hussars had bottle-necked through the gaps in the minefield, then fanned out into the required mass formation on the other side, they were not, as had been planned, 100 yards behind the leading regiments, but a mile behind them—with the ground in front covered by a medley of straggling vehicles. Not only had the leading tanks lost the barrage, but the reserve regiment had lost the leading tanks. All might still be well if the enemy was unable to offer much opposition, but the infantry of 3 British Div, covering the left flank of the armoured advance, although they took battered Sannerville easily enough, met trouble at Touffreville and tried to get their ambulances back. Lieutenant Powle, controlling traffic at the bridge, let them through whenever there was a gap in the 'UP' traffic flow—and was blasted for it by a staff Brigadier. Then he stopped them—and got a rocket from Medical instead. Traffic began to pile up, because there was no room forward.

On the right flank, too, 3 Canadian Div was meeting trouble. Leutnant Höller's guns were well dug-in; all three 75 mms were still in action, and he had only lost one of the 2 cm flak vehicles. To take one large building in Colombelles cost the Régiment

264

de la Chaudière fifty men, even with covering artillery fire. C Squadron of the 1st Hussars supported them, while Serjeant Leo Gariepy, with B Squadron, was to take a factory and then Giberville. But the Germans had the high ground, the dust and the huge R.A.F. bomb craters hindered the tanks, and both they and the infantry were new to each other and to street fighting in a densely built-up industrial area. The German guns and mortars were still in action, and the attack went only pain-fully forward. Everything now depended on the swift advance of the armoured corps over the open ground in the centre, and at first, in spite of delays caused by the dust and cratering, this went well.

As 3 R.T.R. passed between the first groups of defended villages, there was little opposition from Cuverville and Demou-ville on the right, where the troops and guns had largely been destroyed. "Very dazed and shaken infantrymen came out of the cornfields and attempted to give themselves up," said Major Close. "Tank commanders waved them to the rear, where it was hoped the carriers of the Motor Company would soon round them up. Others remained in their slit trenches and fox-holes, offering no resistance." By the time even the 23 Hussars had come up, there was a slight change; some were beginning to recover. "They all looked white and stunned by the bombing," wrote the Hussars' historian. "For every prisoner who surren-dered, there were at least six more who merely sat dazedly in their dug-outs, occasionally popping up to snipe at tank com-manders' heads." One Mark IV tank appeared, as 3 R.T.R. passed Demouville, heading for the first railway embankment, the Caen-Troarn line; Major J. F. C. Langdon, M.C., then OC of 1 Troop, A Squadron, knocked it out. Once over the embank-ment, they were approaching the Manneville/Emieville area, where the Mark IVs of Kortenhaus' unit and the Tigers of 503 were; and among all the village strongpoints on the left flank, they noted increasing enemy movement. "We would have liked to stop and put down a concentration of fire," said Major Close, but our orders were to press on. The only thing we could do was to fire ' on the move' and hope to keep the enemy's heads down; but this policy of leaving villages uncleared was to have dire consequences later."

The two leading units of 29 Armoured Brigade—3 R.T.R. on the right and 2 Fife & Forfar on the left—were now line-abreast, with 23 Hussars trailing along a mile behind. The final railway embankment ahead, marking the Caen-Vimont track, marked also the point where the barrage would end and the slope up to Bourguebus Ridge began. Just before this embankment was the fortified village of Cagny, which marked the parting of the ways for the three divisions of the armoured corps. 11th Armoured was to drive straight on for Bourguebus, but Guards Armoured, coming up behind, was to wheel left between Cagny and Emieville in a drive direct on Vimont, while 7th Armoured was to pass Cagny on the other side, also wheeling left, and fan out in between the other two divisions with the German gun area of Secqueville as the target and readily able to help either the 11th or the Guards at will. Cagny was the hub from which the three spokes of the armoured corps drive would radiate, and was therefore vital; but there were no infantry available to take it—they had all been dropped off, on the Corps Commander's direct order, to clear Cuverville and Demouville, miles behind. But as the entire area along the left flank of the advance was thought to be held only by infantry, and as Cagny itself had had 650 tons of heavy bombs delivered in the last ten minutes of the R.A.F. attack, it was thought that the matter was taken care of. But it very soon became obvious that (a) the defenders of Cagny had not been eliminated, and (b) that they were equipped with something more formidable than rifles. And also, they were under bold and effective leadership.

In contradiction of the intelligence reports, this area was held by the Battle Group Luck—that is, Panzer Grenadier Regiment 125, plus part of Panzer Regiment 22, plus the Tigers of Heavy Tank Battalion 503, plus the very special equipment of 200 Assault Gun Battalion. Oberst Freiherr Hans von Luck was the last member of his Battle Group to become aware that ' Goodwood ' had started. At 0900, long after the bombing had stopped, he drove up to his HQ in Frenouville, wearing his best uniform—long trousers with the red stripe of the staff down the sides—fresh from what he described, with a grin, as " three days' attachment " in Paris: " Honi soit qui mal y pense ", which roughly translated, means " Nice work, if you can get it." In command of the Battle Group, meanwhile, had been the CO of I Battalion, Panzer Grenadier Regiment 125. He reported to von Luck that all contact had been lost with both battalions of this regiment and with the battalion of 16 Luftwaffe Field Division which had been incorporated in their front, after the destruction of that division during the last battle for Caen. In point of fact, his Regiment's I battalion had been so thoroughly eliminated that he never saw any of them again until after the war. The bombing had paralysed the unit, and then the British advance had rolled right over them. By 0930, von Luck was in Cagny, seeing the situation for himself. At that moment a solid mass of British armour, some 30 or 40 Shermans, he thought, were crossing the Caen-Vimont road and the railway line just beyond, heading for Bourguebus. They were in fact the leading squadrons of 2 Fife & Forfar Yeomanry, with 3 R.T.R. beyond. Having been in Paris, and consequently out of touch, he was in the same unfortunate position as British intelligence: he thought there was nothing at Bourguebus to stop them, and that it was entirely up to him. In fact, 1 S.S. Panzer Division, 'Leibstandarte S.S. Adolf Hitler', the senior formation of the Waffen S.S., had just been relieved by an infantry division and was being held in reserve, 'at the point of balance', on the Falaise road behind Bourguebus. Now, in the next few hours, all the half-cooked chickens of Generals Dempsey and O'Connor were due to come home to roost.

The area had been chosen because it was 'good tank country'; and so it was, wide and open; much better in fact for the German tanks and anti-tank guns, with their tremendous range and high velocity, than for the British. And now, the irresistible torrent of armour roaring through the German lines on the heels of the bombers rapidly turned into a 'death ride'. Tiny though the German forces were, they were well-designed, coherently handled in accordance with the thoroughly-understood Guderian doctrine for 'mobile defence by armoured groups' ('beweglichen Abwehr mit Pz. Verbänden'), and resolutely led.

When von Luck saw that the mass of tanks, the vanguard of the 700, were not making for Cagny, but were passing all along the line of his strong-points, exposing their vulnerable, lightly armoured flanks to long-range fire; and that they had no infantry with them, he decided that there was a chance to disrupt the whole charge. The first orders he gave were, naturally, for Cagny itself. All he had there, which consisted of HQ Company, one Mark IV tank, one 88 mm anti-tank gun, and a battery of Luftwaffe 88 mm flak guns, was hurriedly deployed on the western edge of the bomb-shattered village, facing the flank of the moving corridor of British armour. They must have been very quick about it, for Major Close saw a squadron of the Fife & Forfar on his left wiped out " in a matter of seconds ". Twelve Shermans of C Squadron were in fact knocked out, and 23 Hussars in rear came to a stop behind a suddenly halted mass of vehicles. Ahead, they could see smoke spiralling up from blazing tanks and then " sad little parties " began to come back on foot, smoke-grimed or black from severe burns.

Next, von Luck thought of counter-attack; with the Germans, it was automatic. Panzer Regiment 22 and the Tigers of 503 were well-placed, had they survived the bombing, to hit the left flank of the British armoured corps. There had been about 40 Mark IVs in the Emieville area, but they had been badly hit by the bombing; not many had been actually destroyed, but most were temporarily immobilised in the ' moon landscape', half-buried, their engines fouled with dirt. Kortenhaus, who was with them, recalled: " When the enemy tanks came rolling towards us, wave after wave, we knew there was no more hope here. A short struggle, and four of our tanks were destroyed, five simply over-run, the crews taken prisoner. Only one tank of our Company rolled back from that encounter, gouged and scarred, an object of admiration and wonder. It was our own 431 which, however, was not to survive the cauldron of Falaise later." Here, the British advance had been fast enough to take full advantage of the bomber effort.

But the Tigers of 503, in the same area, had fared better. Typical of them was 3 Company, commanded by Hauptmann Freiherr R. von Rosen. Of his ten operational tanks, only two had been destroyed; the other eight were temporarily unserviceable. Sixty minutes after the bombing, six out of the eight could at least put up a fight; and, whereas the British would charge Mark IVs without hesitation, they were likely to be very cautious with Tigers. None of the tanks were really on the top line—they all needed workshop attention—but at least they could move slowly, and the guns would fire. Hindered by the bomb craters, they picked their way forward to Manneville, and began to engage 23 Hussars, charging along a mile in rear of the leaders. The guns proved unaccountably inaccurate (the sights having been thrown out of alignment by the bombing), and they lost two Tigers.

The British leaders, meanwhile, had run into more trouble. 3 R.T.R. were fired on by anti-tank guns from Le Mesnil Frementel, as they passed to the west of the village, lost one tank, then silenced the opposition. From then on, things became grim. This central area, the main axis of the advance, was not held by infantry; but instead was packed with anti-tank guns of 200 Assault Gun Battalion. There were five batteries, each equipped with six 105 mm and four 75 mm guns; also a mortar platoon with multi-barrelled weapons of 80 mm calibre, a flak platoon, and an armoured engineer platoon. They were commanded by Major Becker, who was also the designer of all their special equipment, which in the main consisted of powerful German guns married to a French Hotchkiss tank chassis. The guns had only a limited traverse and light armour, but they were very heavy for the size of the vehicle. Of the five batteries, only one, that at Demouville, had been knocked out by the bombing. 2 Battery survived intact at Giberville; 4 and 5 Batteries stayed in the Le Mesnil Frementel area long enough to engage 3 R.T.R., then withdrew because they had no infantry protection for the guns; but 3 Battery, at Grentheville, just beyond the last railway embankment, held on until 3 p.m., by-passed on both sides by British tanks, firing both East and West, and doing great damage.

3 R.T.R. hit them first, under direct orders to by-pass all villages and go head-on for Bourguebus Ridge. "As we approached the village", said Major Close, "we could observe considerable enemy movement along its north-west edge and among the orchards; there were several anti-tank gun positions among the trees, and we could see the gunners frantically swinging their guns round towards us. In the cornfields around us were many nebelwerfer (multi-barrel mortar) positions, which were already firing over our heads. They were quickly dealt with, in some cases

simply by running them over with the tank. But the anti-tank guns were a different matter. Opening fire at almost point-blank range, they hit three of my tanks, which burst into flames; and I could see that the squadron on my left also had several tanks blazing furiously. My orders were still to press on and by-pass the village." By using the normal tactics of bound-by-bound advance, one group of tanks moving while another group gave them covering fire, they all got through to the shelter of the railway embankment. "AP shot was whistling about all over the place, but fortunately none of my squadron were hit. At the west side of the embankment, we were reasonably sheltered, and were joined by the rest of the Battalion. Our objectives, the villages of Bras and Hubert Folie lay ahead, over some 3,000 yards of very open ground, on a prominent ridge. It looked comparatively quiet and we could see no signs of enemy activity. As there was practically no cover, it was impossible to move as we would have wished, bound by bound."

3,000 yards to go to the ridge, which was marked by the three villages of Bras, Hubert Folie, and Bourguebus; with Soliers a little in front. Montgomery's minimum objective was not only in sight, but it appeared to be, as intelligence had said it would be, beyond the area of the fixed defences; and with no German reserves at hand to restore the situation. In mass formation, 3 R.T.R. and 2 Fife & Forfar roared up the slope to the attack, not as strong as they had been in the morning, but still strong enough. The distance between them and the ridge steadily decreased, without a shot being fired, until the compact mass of armoured vehicles was within a few hundred yards of Bras, aiming to pass between that village and Hubert Folie. Slightly ahead of A Squadron of 3 R.T.R. was the tank of Major Langdon, then O.C. of 1 Troop, rolling across the road which connected the two villages. There was the shattering impact of solid armour-piercing shot striking metal, and the tank was in flames. Out of the roaring inferno the crew, two of them slightly wounded, dragged the badly wounded gunner; and they all flopped in the ditch, breathless at their escape.

Major Close had time to see two tanks of his left-hand Troop hit and knocked out; then his tank also rocked to the thud-crack of solid shot. His crew started to yell, "Bale out, sir!" And out they went. But the tank did not burn, the shell having merely removed the rear sprocket and severed the track. Major Close then ran over to the next tank, told the commander to get out, took his place, and resumed command of A Squadron. " On the left, the remainder of the Battalion were heavily engaged, at least seven tanks were blazing, and baled out crews were making their way back to the embankment," he said. From their position in the ditch, Langdon's crew could see " a mass of tanks brewing up " to the left, where B Squadron was, and beyond them the Fife & Forfar, and to the right " other tanks of our squadron had also been knocked out, and the remainder were withdrawing off the Ridge," said Langdon. " The ammunition began exploding in my blazing tank, and we had to move away without delay. At least 200 yards to the nearest cover, uncut corn, the ground between completely open and covered by enemy fire from Bras and Hubert Folie. We picked up the wounded gunner and carried him across this open ground; we must certainly have been seen, but nothing was fired at us. The gunner died at the Dressing Station and I returned to the Squadron and took command of my Troop Corporal's tank."

The first the Brigadier knew of it was when the Fife & Forfar went off the air. Guessing trouble, he sent forward 23 Hussars, who crossed the railway line and advanced to support them. Their tanks were still massed in the open near Soliers, many sending up clouds of smoke. B Squadron of the Hussars drove forward into the centre of the ring of blazing tanks before they realised that it was a ghost unit they were supporting; almost all the Fife & Forfar's tanks appeared to be 'dead'. A Squadron commander ran out to say that only four were left in action; much later, it was discovered that eighteen out of 52 had survived. But he had hardly finished speaking, when fire struck the Hussars. 1 Troop of B Squadron "were hit and blazing in a matter of seconds", and the remaining tanks began to reverse. The fire was coming from the leading Panthers of the 'Leibstandarte Adolf Hitler', which had just followed their SP guns onto the ridge in front. The position of B Squadron was hopeless, caught in the open, out-ranged by the Panthers, with most of the 17-pounders knocked out and only the 75 mms left. On the left, C Squadron came up to help, but was suddenly hit by point-blank fire from the village of Four, back by the railway embankment and, like all the other villages, uncleared. " With no time for retaliation, no time to do anything but to take one quick glance at the situation, almost in one minute, all of the tanks of the three troops and of Squadron H.Q. were hit, blazing and exploding," wrote the historian of the Hussars. " Everywhere wounded and burning figures ran or struggled painfully for cover, while a remorseless rain of armour-piercing shot riddled the already helpless Shermans. All too clearly, we were not going to ' break through' today. It was going to be a matter not how much we should advance, but whether we should be able to hold on to what we had gained. Out of the great array of armour that had moved forward to battle that morning, 106 tanks now lay crippled and out of action in the cornfields."

" Our C.O. was not quite happy about his position down by the embankment," said Major Close, " so he instructed one of his officers to peep over the top. The young officer did so, rather gingerly, and there, only a few feet below him, were two Panther tanks advancing towards the gap under the embankment. In his own words, he could have tossed a peanut down their cupolas. Every tank in H.Q. frantically traversed its gun on the opening, fully expecting two Panthers at any moment. However, nothing happened; they must have been forced to withdraw by fire from our tanks from the other side. We were now in a somewhat precarious position, some 2,000 yards ahead of the rest of the Division. The by-passed villages behind us had not been cleared by infantry, and stretching back to the start-line, for a distance of some 6,000 yards, was a mass of tanks and vehicles. The Guards were held up there, west of Cagny, having lost 60 tanks, and 7th Armoured had not yet cleared the minefield. Even they were having casualties from enemy guns which had now come to life."

* * *

The battle of Cagny began at about 10 in the morning and lasted until about 4 in the afternoon, because infantry were not immediately available. When they did arrive, the village fell almost at once—because the Germans had no infantry, either, only the guns and a single tank. One of the infantrymen who took it was G. H. Marsden, a wireless operator of the 1st Motor

Battalion Grenadier Guards. "After we had moved through a huge minefield," he said, "I heard a call on my wireless: '*Watch for snipers and Germans in the cornfields.*' I could see Caen just to my right, the whole area was on fire, the earth shuddering from the bombing and shelling. I saw at least 40 Sherman tanks blazing; even after this hideous bombardment the Germans were still trying to hold us back. I know for a fact that one German 88 mm S.P. gun knocked out 11 Shermans. We kept on moving around the outskirts of Caen towards a place called Cagny. Our captives were mere boys, running towards our lines with hands on head, and leaving many of their comrades dead and wounded. But they still retaliated with shellfire and most of all the dreaded 'Moaning Minnies', the electrically propelled mortar; to be caught in their fire was certain disaster. The whole area was ablaze, tanks on fire and abandoned, carriers, half-tracks, motor vehicles, all knocked out. I saw the enemy dug-outs, their dead, and out-of-action artillery. When we reached Cagny, then, more or less, Caen was engulfed. We took our positions and started to dig in, rather desperately, I thought. I could hardly believe the impact of three armoured divisions could be slowed down; but the job had been done, and I must pay tribute to the skill and cunning of the German Army. The area we had to hold was typical of any English village. I had to dig my trench in a potato field; the ground was hard and stony. By now it was growing dark. Just on my left I saw my dead comrades being buried already, about seven graves; now I knew why the white crosses had been issued before the battle."

Throughout the afternoon, the few remaining semi-serviceable Tigers of 503 had been probing into the open flank of the armoured corps. Little more than half-a-dozen were at first available, but only one, a Tiger II, was lost—and that in a most unusual manner. It was put out of action by a Lieutenant of the Irish Guards, who recalled: "This was my first time in action and I was excited. I had got across the little stream running into Cagny from the north-east, but the rest of my troop got stuck. However, I pushed on alone for a bit and found plenty of targets and was beginning to think this war business was not too bad after all; in fact, I was beginning to enjoy myself. But this didn't last long for, on glancing to my left, I saw to my horror the unmistakable shape of a Royal Tiger coming through a hedge under 200 yards away. I ordered my gunner: '*Traverse left—on—fire!*' He fired and I saw with dismay the 75 mm shot hit the front of the Tiger, bounce off and go sizzling up into the air. I ordered the gunner to fire again, but a hollow voice came up from the bowels of the tank, saying, '*Gun jammed, sir.*' This was a situation for which I had not been trained and I did not know what to do. Glancing anxiously again at the Tiger, I saw with horror that his long gun was slowly swinging round in my direction. Someone had once told me that when in doubt the thing to do was advance, so I ordered my driver to advance at full speed and ram the Tiger. We lurched forward, gathered speed, and hit him amidships with a terrific crash, just before he got his sights on to me. Both crews baled out on impact and, since there was quite heavy shelling, both crews dived for cover. My wireless operator saw a convenient slit trench and, jumping into it, found it already occupied by the Tiger's crew. However, they both stayed there together, keeping their heads down. I crawled back, brought up my 17-pounder Sherman and managed to brew the Tiger. I then collected my crew and the Tiger's crew, and we went back and got another tank."

The delay at Cagny enabled the Germans to bring up the only reserve the British knew about—the remnants of 12th S.S. from Potigny; by late afternoon groups of young grenadiers, experienced anti-tank fighters, were working their way towards Frenouville along the Caen-Vimont railway. They were poised to do this, because the operations around Hill 112 and Maltot, which had immediately preceded 'Goodwood', had been recognised as a feint, and General Eberbach had alerted them on the evening of 17 July with an order to expect a major offensive in the next few hours. But not all were available, because one Battle Group had been sent to Lisieux, in case the British offensive from the Airborne bridgehead should be directed east, to link up with possible seaborne landings between the Orne and Pas de Calais, another face of that chimera which haunted the German High Command and helped bring their Normandy front to ruin. Because of the British lack of infantry, 12th S.S. were able to infiltrate, both with tanks and anti-tank weapons, while 29 Armoured Brigade was actually attempting to rush the Ridge.

Equally because of the lack of infantry, the batteries of 200 Assault Gun Battalion were able to withdraw through the battle area, sometimes after having been by-passed, without losing a gun—apart from those destroyed by the bombing. Even where there were infantry, on the flanks, some of the decimated German units escaped, those holding the Caen factory area retiring directly across the path of the armoured corps' advance.

The factory area, from Colombelles to Vaucelles, was the responsibility of II Canadian Corps. 8th and 9th Brigades of 3 Div were to sweep south, on the east bank of the Orne, parallel to the axis of the armoured corps drive, while 7 Brigade attacked directly over the river into Vaucelles, from the heart of Caen. Their gains were to be exploited, later in the day, by the newly-landed 2 Div, which had not fought since Dieppe. Leutnant Höller, having lost only one flak half-track from the bombing, brought his guns back to the Caen-Mondeville steelworks, now a total ruin, from which his 75 mm anti-tank guns could cover the exits from the factory area; in front of them were the remnants of a Luftwaffe infantry unit, 1 Panzerjäger Company. This steelworks was an early objective of the Régiment de la Chaudière, which had lost so many men at the first objective, Colombelles chateau, that they had to be reinforced by the North Shore Regiment. They found the roads so badly cratered that their vehicles could not get forward, and were separated from the rifle companies. Höller noticed this at once, when he went forward with his company commander, Oberleutnant Braatz, that afternoon. One of his guns had been knocked out by Canadian artillery, probably directed by an observer in Colombelles, they thought; but as no enemy had actually been seen, they carried out a recce forward from the Mondeville steelworks. " We went across the bomb craters parallel to the factories of Colombelles ", he said. " Near the edge of the factory buildings, we worked our way into a ruined house from which we would have a good view forward. But the enemy cut short our recce, and we were splattered with plaster from the walls. Then we saw Tommies in a cratered field about 200 yards away, and retired at once, jumping or crawling through the torn-up ground. The enemy, too, could only move with difficulty under these conditions."

At dusk, the Canadians who had got across the river by direct assault were in Vaucelles, in rear of Höller's position at Mondeville, while the other two brigades were in front. " We could hear the machine-pistols rattling even behind Battalion H.Q.," said Höller, " but the Battalion Commander had decided to stay and resist to the end. He sent a message to Div H.Q.: ' *Second Battalion surrounded in Mondeville—fighting to the last—long live the Führer—Sieg Heil*' (or something like that). However, we managed to make him change his mind. Within minutes we were ready to break out with our self-propelled guns. We saw two enemy tanks in front of the railway viaduct (Caen-Vimont), but discovered that they were ' dead '; on we went, and due to our numbers and the fact that the Tommies were rather scattered, we got out of this ticklish situation with hardly any difficulty. In view of our ' fighting to the last ' message, Div were rather surprised to see us; but glad also to receive this reinforcement."

Even those Tigers of 503 which were still immobilised by the bombing, or had broken down later because of it, were got away from Manneville on the other flank, before the British could over-run them for an easy victory. " The German counter-attack with Tigers at Manneville must have been in front of our attack ", recalled Marsden, " because I could see so many tanks already knocked out, or being knocked out, and I did see some dug-in Tigers—and believe me, if the Germans tried to move immobile Tigers they certainly needed some moving (it was generally known that even the best British REME Recovery units could not shift them)." However, moved they were, the last of them a bare five minutes before the first British tanks arrived. The German officer who did it was the last to leave, at about 7 p.m., and he waited a moment to watch the entry of the Guards. In spite of three years on the Russian front, this for him, because of the terrible bombardment, had been the worst day of the war. The secret of moving an immobile 60-ton Tiger was three other Tigers—or, at least, that was how Heinz Trautmann's Tiger 134 was shortly to be towed out of action, after it had been knocked out.

On the Ridge, one last effort was made to get forward by a fresh unit, 2 Northants Yeomanry; it failed, with the inevitable heavy casualties, in face of the line of dug-in Luftwaffe 88s. Then, just as it was getting dark, the Leibstandarte counter-attacked with Panthers. The moment they came into the open and exposed themselves, they had casualties, but the remnants of 29 Armoured Brigade were forced to withdraw for the night from the embankment, thus allowing Höller's unit room to slip past them in the darkness. Two of the German tanks used in this attack were captured Shermans; one knocked out several British tanks before being destroyed.

Meanwhile, incredible confusion reigned, not only in the armoured corridor, but in the various headquarters, all seemingly out of touch. A complete infantry formation—32 Guards Brigade —spent most of the day sitting in their vehicles, stuck in a traffic jam, being shelled by the artillery of 21 Panzer and 16 Luftwaffe Divisions. The British divisional organisation at the time was muscle-bound; infantry and armour in big, separate packages, physically unable to help each other. Then the armoured corps commander, Lieutenant-General Sir Richard N. O'Connor, personally intervened. "A last picture of 'Goodwood' is worth recalling", wrote the Household Cavalry historian. "General O'Connor, coming forward to see for himself what was holding things up, jumped onto a tank containing one of the tank battalion's commanders in process of ordering forward his Squadrons. On the back of this tank was also the Brigade Commander and behind him the Divisional Commander, Major-General Adair, all urgently ordering one another on in descending order of seniority, the final version doubtless reaching (in wireless form) some harassed subaltern as he struggled through Cagny. A Household Cavalry trooper, witness of this unusual party, turned aside to his companion: 'Well, I thought that when I had the Colonel and two other bastards giving advice on the back of my Daimler at Linney Head it was bad enough, but three Generals is bloody murder!'"

While the Corps Commander was making this praiseworthy but hopeless attempt to sort out the confusion, the Army Commander, Lieutenant-General Sir Miles C. Dempsey, was turning down an offer by Tactical Air Force to come back in the afternoon and blast Bourguebus Ridge, which had been left out of the morning's bombing programme because of shortage of aircraft. The R.A.F. were particularly keen to see a big advance south of Caen, because it would give them much-needed airfield sites for their short-ranged fighters, but General Dempsey thought the bombing of Bourguebus was unnecessary. Similarly misinformed was General Montgomery himself, who, at 4.20 p.m., as the first Panthers of 1 S.S. Panzer Division roared onto the ridge behind their S.P. guns, sent a jubilant message to the Chief of the Imperial General Staff. " Complete success . . . bombing decisive . . . spectacle terrific . . . ordered recce regiments to crossings between Mezidon and Falaise . . . difficult to see what the enemy can do . . . few enemy tanks met so far . . . ." The list of fallen towns and villages (with timings) attached included one strongly held by the Hitler Jugend and another in possession of the Leibstandarte Adolf Hitler, neither of them British formations. Based on this report, a Monty 'special announcement' was issued in time for the B.B.C.'s 9 o'clock news that night. The fatal words " Second Army attacked and broke through ", combined with " General Montgomery is well satisfied ", gave the newsmen what they thought was their cue. They concluded that here was another Alamein in the making instead of, as it really was, another Balaclava. In fact, some 200 tanks had been lost on this first day, and a night raid by the Luftwaffe did more vital damage to the armoured echelons back in the glider fields at Ranville; Fife & Forfar alone lost 40 tank crews, including both reinforcements and men who had baled out. The minimum objective, as stated by Montgomery, had been to " write down " the German armour; instead, it was the British armour which was being " written off." And next day, the attack went in again.

*   *   *

" The Regiment had received 11 tanks during the night from the Forward Delivery Squadron," said Major Langdon of 3 R.T.R. " This brought our tank strength to approximately 25, and of these A Squadron had 11." At approximately half-strength, even including the reinforcements, 3 R.T.R. moved forward at first light, about 0430. " Our orders were the same," said Major Close, " to get up on the ridge and occupy Bras and Hubert Folie. As we reached the line of our tanks burned out the day before, we again encountered heavy fire, intensified by the presence of more enemy tanks on the ridge."

"My troop was given the task of going to the left of Bras," said Major Langdon. "As we moved up to the ridge I could see my original tank still smouldering; it was an extremely unpleasant feeling, as we edged past it up the ridge. Moving through the corn, we met German infantry; and at the edge of the corn, again near Bras, we were again knocked out. This time, no one was wounded, as the shot hit the rear of the tank; and as we were still in the corn, we had immediate cover. I collected the crew and we made our way back on hands and knees until we met our own infantry. They had collected about 20 prisoners from the Hermann Göring Regiment, and asked us to escort them back."

"Several of my tanks were knocked out in the first few moments," said Major Close, "the two squadrons on my left also lost tanks, and we very quickly found ourselves in the same predicament as the previous day—unable to get forward. Again, I personally was extremely lucky. I had just hopped out of my tank in order to help some of my wounded crews to get clear of their blazing tanks, when my own tank was hit slap through the turret, gunner and operator being killed instantly. Once again, I had to turn out a tank commander and take command from his tank. A Serjeant who had done good work the day before, this day was able to brew up a Panther and two anti-tank guns in Bras; but we were completely unable to advance. The enemy positions had been noticeably strengthened, but at about 3 in the afternoon I was called to an 'O' group by my C.O., and told that 3rd Tanks were to make a direct attack on Hubert Folie at 4 o'clock. Northants Yeomanry were to attack Bras and give us covering fire."

The situation now, on the afternoon of 19 July, was altered by the bringing forward of the field guns, so that both attacks would go in under a barrage, with far greater chance of success. The Northants Yeomanry went in first, lost direction unaccountably to the right, and exposed their flanks to the strongly defended village of Ifs. "In as many moments about half their tanks were brewed up or knocked out, and they withdrew in some disorder towards the Cormelles factory area in our rear," said Major Close. "My C.O. had seen the plight of the Northants, and he suggested to our Brigadier that 3rd Tanks should switch their attack from Hubert Folie to Bras. With little or no delay, and merely by wireless orders, this was done, and shortly before 4 o'clock we advanced on Bras. The promised artillery barrage came down on both villages, and an excellent smokescreen enabled us to move rapidly, in a proper manner, Troop by Troop, giving supporting fire." Close behind the tanks, this time, came the infantry of 8 K.R.R.C., the British panzer grenadiers. By 7 p.m., the Leibstandarte had been driven out of Bras, leaving many dead and a dozen S.P. guns behind. But 3 R.T.R. were through. They had started with 52 tanks, been given 11 replacements, making 63 tanks in all. With Bras now in their hands, they had nine tanks left. Major Close's A Squadron had lost 17 tanks in two days, seven being completely destroyed, the others recoverable; all Troop officers had been killed or wounded, and only one Troop Serjeant was left. The Fife & Forfar had fared rather worse. Every Regiment which had gone up that ridge had been knocked to pieces, and 11th Armoured Division was spent.

The impetus of the armoured drive was spent also, irretrievably. In the British view, it was their own traffic chaos and the delay imposed by the Battle Group Luck which were paramount; that is, bad organisation and faulty intelligence. In the view of von Luck himself, delay was also the paramount factor: failure to advance fast enough on the heels of the initially paralysing bombardment; failure to mop up the fortified strong-points fast enough, because insufficient infantry accompanied the tanks; and above all, failure to take the Cagny strong-point instantly. But these are the views of the men who were there. The views of those who were not there, but were concerned elsewhere with the planning, are different.

Motives were mixed, because the collapse of 'Goodwood' became the bone in an inter-Service as well as inter-Allied dog-fight, with theories of long-standing at stake, and the irritant personality of Montgomery thrown like pepper into the eyes of the snarling animals. Chester Wilmot has chronicled this at length; the official history by Major Ellis follows roughly the same line; and Omar Bradley who, like Dempsey, was Monty's immediate subordinate, gives a not dissimilar picture from the American side. They are all basically favourable to Montgomery, technically, as a general. The anti-Montgomery faction was only partly American; mainly, it was R.A.F. In the fury of the controversy, many interesting facts and illusions concerning the two main battles for Caen have recently come to light; notably those expressed in a review of the official historian's work by Air Marshal Sir Philip Wigglesworth, who was the Senior Air Staff Officer for ' Overlord '.[1] He states that the plan to attack enemy strongpoints north of Caen with heavy bombers, which in fact resulted in the destruction of the city on 7 July, was prepared by Professor ' Solly ' Zuckermann, scientific adviser to Leigh-Mallory, and his planning officer, Air Vice-Marshal Kingston-McCloughry. Leigh-Mallory, who had commanded the controversial 12 Group during the Battle of Britain, had now gone on to bigger things with ' Overlord ', but was not universally regarded with admiration inside the R.A.F. However, this plan was opposed by Tedder, ' Bomber ' Harris, and the American air general Spaatz. It was only sparked into life when Churchill forcibly put on the pressure concerning the delay in taking Caen, and was told by Montgomery that the city could be taken if the ' heavies ' were used.

Sir Philip Wigglesworth reveals that when Omar Bradley admitted the failure of his first major break-out operation, General Dempsey made a " specific, bold and imaginative recommendation " early in July, that the plan should be reversed; his Second Army should make the main effort, without waiting for Bradley to try again. Montgomery would not at first agree (and no wonder, for it meant seeking a decision where the bulk of the German Army, and particularly its armour, was gathered), but later approved a plan which was essentially ' Goodwood '. Dempsey issued the detailed orders on 13 July, and these included establishing an armoured division in the Falaise area. Two days later came what the Air Marshal calls Montgomery's famous ' write down ' directive, which made clear that the Caen hinge must be made impregnable before any risks were taken far away at Falaise. Then, he goes on to say, " Dempsey revised his own orders to conform, but there is evidence that he anticipated a collapse of the enemy permitting an advance well beyond Falaise." It is very likely that he did; it would explain the tremendous optimism which undoubtedly existed in Second Army before the attack, and is itself explained by the faulty intelligence

[1] " Royal United Service Institution Journal ", May, 1963.

reports. But, after this, the Air Marshal becomes airborne on lighter-than-air principles, stating: "Thus Dempsey's far-reaching intentions were frustrated by Montgomery's inflexibility and defensive caution. There seems little doubt that had Dempsey not been restrained, this combined land and air operation would have achieved decisive results leading to the much earlier conquest of Normandy: our Intelligence had revealed earlier that the enemy was becoming incapable of offering adequate resistance." So they had, of course. And they continued to do so for a month more, until finally illusion became reality, largely through the intervention of Adolf Hitler.

In fact, on 20 July, 'Goodwood' was more or less corralled off by 21 Panzer, 1st S.S. Panzer, 12th S.S., and 272 Infantry Division, with further armoured reinforcements on the way—for 116 Panzer Division, up to strength and fully equipped, came up from reserve at Amiens and went into the line behind 12th S.S. the next day. But certainly Montgomery had risked criticism by his complacent communique on the evening of 18 July; and for him, the storm burst on 21 July, when, according to Wigglesworth, Eisenhower "insisted on Dempsey maintaining the force of his attack towards Falaise, prematurely halted by Montgomery." For Canada, this was to have dire results. And on the battlefield, as elsewhere in Europe, the storm had already burst.

CHAPTER EIGHTEEN

O CANADA!

The Last Day of ' Goodwood '—the Plot of 20 July—the
Canadians attack Verrières Ridge—the Front stabilised
again—the Landing of the Last Divisions
20 July 1 August

The 20th of July, 1944, was heavy and sullen with heat, oppressive with a mounting charge of electricity rising to the point of ultimate, explosive release. The sort of day during which the dulled mind tends to make mistakes, longing for the cool rain. By nightfall, the rains had come, but before then, men stumbled through the day: it was hot behind the glass windows of offices, in London, Paris, Berlin; hotter still for the burdened infantry of 2 Canadian Div, waiting at Bras and Hubert Folie to climb yet another deadly slope, to the summit of Verrières Ridge, on the last day of ' Goodwood'; and hotter even than that inside the oven of an armoured car, as the Household Cavalry probed through Emieville towards Troarn. Perhaps that was why, blinded by the dust of the leading cars, Corporal-of-Horse Booth missed the way. Turning a bend in the road, he saw a Tiger tank abandoned by the ditch, an old German tunic incongruously hanging over its side. Advancing cautiously, Booth stopped his armoured car alongside, got out, and went through the pockets of the coat. Among the possibly useful documents he removed was a soldier's paybook. Then a burst of machine-gun fire whip-cracked overhead, Booth jumped back into his armoured car, and as the driver hurriedly reversed, a second Tiger opened up at them from a wood. He had located the very Tiger which was holding up the advance of the Welsh Guards in that sector, and pinched the owner's documents while he was having a brew-up!

* * *

General Heusinger was speaking. " Strong Russian forces are turning to the north and west of the River Düna. Their leading columns are already west of Dünaburg. My Führer, if we do not at once—now—withdraw these Army Groups, there will be a catastrophe . . ." And then it happened.

One witness, Oberst Count Claus Schenk von Stauffenberg, had kissed his four children goodbye for the last time the previous night, and said farewell to his Countess. Cardinal Preysing of Berlin had told him that what he was about to do was not necessarily a sin, but rather a matter for his own conscience. At approximately 1237 he had placed his heavy briefcase against the thick oak support of the conference table, and as the Führer would not be ready to take his report for some minutes, excused himself to make a telephone call. Oberst Brandt, chief of staff to Heusinger, found the briefcase in his way; he moved it to the far side of the heavy oak support, the side furthest from Adolf Hitler. So stifling was the heat, that all the windows of the Nissen-type hut were open. At 1242 the acid reached the fuse of the explosive charge inside the briefcase.

It was as though a shell had exploded inside the wooden building; the windows burst, part of the roof collapsed, thin, high-pitched screaming came from the ruins. Stauffenberg nodded with satisfaction, ground out his cigarette under his heel, got into the staff car, and was driven to the first barrier manned by the S.S. They let him through.

*   *   *

There had been a delay in attacking Verrières, which was on the ridge west of Bourguebus; 7th Armoured were late in moving out and letting the Canadians in; there was time for the Germans to bring up reinforcements. 272 Infantry Division were up there, and some 70 tanks of 1st S.S., and a battle group from 2 (Vienna) Panzer Division which had been hurriedly transferred to help block 'Goodwood'. It was not until early afternoon that 2 Canadian Div went forward to the attack. The South Saskatchewan Regiment were going into their first real action, and with them went Private Rubin Bider from Winnipeg. On the right, the attack made progress, slowly, but the German armoured counter-attack from Verrières hit the S.S.R. and hurled them back down the slope. The last step was to evacuate the wounded in the carriers, before the rifle companies caved in, and Bider helped with this. There was no one left to give him orders any more. His company commander was dead, his platoon officer was wounded, his section leader was dead. It was rough, for a first battle. "I just stayed around and found some fellows who had been wounded. Among the last was Pte. V. A. Aston, he was hit in the leg and had lost a lot of blood. I gave him a smoke. I was told to stay there by a Major, and I did, till another Eastern outfit came to re-take our position, four hours late. I was all alone till then, cut off from our own lines. I got myself a Bren, two Stens and two rifles. Some Germans were advancing. I shot at them with the Bren and saw some fall. I then saw a German tank move up, and their soldiers pull back. I crawled to another position near where I could see our tanks advancing. Some troops from Ontario came along, and I joined up with them and stayed there that night. I didn't get back to my unit till two days later. I got a clipping in the *Winnipeg Free Press*, and I got put in for the D.C.M., but I didn't get it. I guess if my name had been James M. Smith I would have got a ribbon." Bider was small, dark, 23, and Jewish.

There had been a delay in Berlin in ordering a 'Valkyrie' Exercise. No orders were given until the late afternoon, when Stauffenberg flew in from East Prussia. Twice in the last few weeks he had set off for the Führer's headquarters with a bomb in his briefcase, and twice come back to report failure. "A horse which refuses a jump twice, won't go over the third time," they thought, and waited. Then the 'revolution by telephone' began. By telephone, by teleprinter, and by bluff. The code word 'Valkyrie' was flashed to units of the Home Army and to the conquered capitals—Vienna, Paris, Prague. A plan within a plan. Outwardly, it was a scheme to meet a possible revolt by the millions of foreign slave workers by taking over all key points in all key cities; and the army units began to move, obeying orders passed down normal channels by the properly constituted authority. Only a few of the officers knew that the occupation of those key points was to coincide with the elimination of Hitler, and, if possible, of Himmler and Goebbels, too so that, in the resulting confusion, the Army would be firmly in control and able to suppress the Party. Possibly it meant civil war, but that was a risk they had considered and weighed; also the consequences of failure. Then the Nazis began to fight back, by telephone and teleprinter. Führer Headquarters to all commands: "*The Führer is alive.*" H.Q. Home Army to all commands: "*The Führer is dead, the Army has taken over. Disarm all Party members, by force if necessary.*" In the confidential directive they had added: "There are to be no acts of private revenge". The French Resistance, who had sickened their Allies by an orgy of indignity wreaked on 'collaborators', might have learned from that. By evening the Führer, who had been damaged, but not eliminated, was screaming for blood with a violence that surprised even his intimates and shook his Italian visitors, including Mussolini, to the core. And victory, this day, was riding with the ruthless, professional revolutionaries—Hitler and the National Socialist Party; not the amateurs, who baulked at a bloodbath.

On Verrières Ridge, the battle swayed to and fro, with blood and blazing tanks in the corn. "We were reserve with the Essex Scottish in the 4th Brigade," recalled Gordon Amos, of Gun B2, 18 Battery, 2nd Anti-Tank Regiment, supporting the Highland Brigade of Canada. "The weather was hot and the roads were dusty. We were green, but we soon ripened up. It was here that Serjeant Boyd, of Irish and French mixture, said: 'The Irish never had a fireworks display on the Glorious Twelfth, like we got.' A piece of shrapnel took his rifle butt off, three inches from the belt, and he blessed the mortar crew that did it in his best Irish. It was here that B2 and B3 had their gun tyres flattened. It was here that our coffee pot got hit and went to glory. Geo. Edgington was cooking, and he used his best language. It was here also that the Essex Scottish mortars were bombed by the German air force. It was here that two nice black horses, and a white one, wandered about; how they didn't get hit was a miracle. When the shelling started, they would turn their rears to it and lower their heads. We all felt sorry for them. The late Bill Antoniuk said: 'They sure humped their backs and took it.' Wilf Carter grinned back: 'Well, Bill, they aren't the only ones'. Bill Antoniuk, he was happy-go-lucky, nothing bothered him, and he always had a wisecrack; about 5 feet 10 inches and 180 lbs, and we called him Bacon Butt Slim. C Troop were badly beaten and there wasn't much left of the

5th Brigade, but our gun crew only had one wounded up to now, but in the next few days it was different."

By 6.30 p.m., the telephone and teleprinter battle had risen to a climax. In Berlin, Goebbels had been placed under arrest by an officer obeying orders, who was not in the conspiracy; Goebbels had telephoned Hitler, and Hitler had spoken to the officer who had arrested Goebbels, appointed him Colonel on the spot and ordered him to use his troops, which were to have supported the revolt, to suppress it. The officer spoke to attention on the telephone, when he realised that it really was the Führer on the other end of the line. At 6.30 p.m. Goebbels got out a brief announcement from Berlin radio, which the plotters had failed to hold. An attempt had been made on the Führer's life, but the Führer was miraculously alive. At Rommel's former headquarters in Normandy, now controlled by the wavering conspirator, Field Marshal Hans von Kluge (' Clever Hans '), von Kluge was speaking to the chief of the conspiracy, ex-General Beck, in Berlin, and simultaneously, a transcript of Goebbels' broadcast announcement was placed before him. He had agreed to act, if Hitler was eliminated, but if the Führer was still alive . . . " Does it matter?" crackled the voice of Beck from Berlin, " if in the long run we are prepared to go ahead?" And von Kluge replied, finally, " I'll ring you back in half an hour."

" For Verrières, my squadron was held in reserve," said Serjeant Leo Gariepy, of 6 Armoured Regiment, 2 Canadian Armoured Brigade. " But A and C Squadrons were ordered to support the Fusiliers Mont Royal into Beauvoir and Toteval Farm. Since the 27th C.A.R. was already into St. André-sur-Orne with our ' little friends ', this was thought to be a real easy one. So our crew commanders were told not to engage if they could avoid it. But apparently the enemy did not know of our plans, because the fight became so fierce that, not only were they engaged, but they suffered high casualties. After severe fighting, the objective was reached and our little friends solidly entrenched."

At about 8 p.m., Winston Churchill was teaching the words of *Rule Britannia* to the officers of the cruiser *Enterprise,* lying off the beachhead. And Field Marshal von Kluge, at La Roche Guyon, was wondering how, if he decided to support Beck, he should make the first peace overtures to the Allies. Stop the V.1 offensive against London, was his first decision. Then another message came in, signed Keitel, to all commands: *The Führer is still alive.* Kluge hesitated, and began another long round of telephone calls, to find out the truth. He was very much alone, for the Allies, having accepted Roosevelt's 'Unconditional Surrender' declaration, would offer no terms to the conspirators. From ex-Colonel Eisenhower, imbued with the spirit of a 'Crusade in Europe', there could have been little encouragement; but Churchill, thinking ahead to the peace and British interests (which were not the same as those of the U.S.A. and the U.S.S.R.), might possibly have taken advantage of the situation, had he known. But, apparently, there were no channels of communication and the conspiracy, which had been in existence since 1938, was being ignored. The U.S.A. and U.S.S.R. were determined, not on the capitulation of Germany, but her destruction; however, if the British had accepted the surrender on terms of the German Armies in Normandy, there would have been nothing the two great powers could have done about it, except froth at the mouth. They were not powerful enough, without the British Empire, to bring matters to a conclusion. It was only a slim chance in any case, requiring a bold man to carry it out. There were even now, war correspondents weeping with rage because they thought the Allied stalemate in Normandy was a deliberate move to ruin the progressive Russians; and this faction had grown very strong, from the moment Hitler had attacked the U.S.S.R.[1] But it also required a bold man on the German side, such a man as Rommel, put out of action three days before; a man acceptable to the British at least. Von Kluge was not that man.

"We were in a gravel pit on top of Hill 70, off a sunken road; I was on lookout with a Black Watch private. He told me he was on leave three weeks before, staying with his girl friend at her house. He asked when I was home last. I said: 'Four years ago'. He groaned. 'My God, that's a long time.' I told him that's the way the ball rolled, so why worry. Geo. Edgington

[1] See Omar Bradley's *A Soldier's Story*, p. 336. Both British and American war correspondents were involved; and, of course, some of President Roosevelt's assistants, such as Harry Dexter White and Algar Hiss, did not fare so well when the climate of opinion changed, much too late.

learned to swear here but not from me. It was hot, about 90 degrees, and no wind to take the dust away. George said: 'You know, Amos, this shouldn't happen to a dog.' I said: 'I know, but a damn dog would know better than stay in a place like this.' I don't know if it was the place or the stew we had that Geo. was talking about. It happened to be P.V., and I never saw a dog that would eat it, or could either."

A sweltering evening succeeded the unbearably hot day. By dark, von Kluge knew that, not only was Hitler not dead, but that counter-action was in full swing; he backed down. After he had done so, he learned from General Stülpnagel, Military Governor of Paris, that he had ordered the Paris part of the plot to get under way. By now, some 1,200 members of the Sicherheitsdienst, the Nazi Security organisation, should be under arrest. Some of them, ironically, were destined for Fresnes Prison, where as part of their duties they tortured Allied agents and members of the French Resistance. Stülpnagel, unlike most of the Berlin conspirators, believed in utter ruthlessness at the critical moment. Sandbagged execution stands were already being set up for the most notorious of the Gestapo men. There would, of course, be a trial—a drumhead court martial for each man, lasting a minute at the most. One Gestapo man who had escaped the round-up telephoned the HQ of 12th S.S. Division, but there was no reaction from there or from 'Sepp' Dietrich at HQ I S.S. Panzer Korps. Some of the Waffen S.S. leaders had been cautiously sounded out beforehand by the plotters. But elsewhere in Europe, the revolt was collapsing before it had hardly begun, the vital counter-blow being delivered by Goebbels, who got Hitler to make a broadcast late that night. After exploding at Stülpnagel in a wild paroxism of rage, von Kluge as abruptly calmed down, and said, "If only the swine were dead." And into every news bulletin on the radio was inserted the death-knell of the rebellion: "*The Führer will speak tonight*".

Soon after 10.30 p.m., as the Paris operation got under way, the counter-attack closed in on the headquarters of the Berlin revolt in the War Ministry building. Men ran along the corridors, cradling machine-pistols, and shouting: "For or against the Führer?" Stauffenberg made a run for it, was shot and hit in his left arm; he had left the other arm behind in Tunisia, so could not use a gun. Beck attempted to commit suicide, but only wounded himself. He was finished off by an N.C.O., an officer having refused to do it. Stauffenberg and three others were led out into the warm night and placed up against a wall. A car was run into position, so that the headlights illuminated them. The rifle-bolts snickered, the commands rang out, the rifles fired and the butts kicked against the soldiers' shoulders. Four bodies lay in front of the wall. The brickwork was pitted. An officer's cap was in the dust. The staff colonel with the artificial right hand and the black eye patch had kissed his four children and his countess good night, last night, for the last time; nevermore. Then the storm broke. Lightning ripped apart the clouds over Berlin, over all Europe, and the rain came pouring down, tension released, on the bodies lying still in front of the wall, on the soldiers still fighting in Normandy. The war would go on.

"About 0200 next morning we two gun crews were in mud and water up to the knees," said Amos, "and trying to man-handle the guns into position. Bill Buton looked up and said: 'If bull strength and ignorance goes a long way, we should go on forever.'" 'Goodwood' was ended.

*   *   *

Tank losses for the three days of 'Goodwood', for the armoured corps only, have been put by quite well-informed people as high as 413. This does not include losses suffered by the supporting tanks of the two flank Corps. The official historian, however, puts 8 Corps losses at 271. Other historians, by referring to 11th Armoured only, and the first day only, manage to get it down to a little over the 100 mark, which makes it more respectable; indeed, for many years, this was the standard way in which the 'Balaclava' aspect of the operation was treated. For the record, it is unfortunately true that the true figures were not known at the time, and never will be known. Casualty returns were made during a fluctuating situation: strength at any one time would include, on the one hand, fresh tanks just brought forward by delivery units, but would not include tanks which were merely missing and would rejoin. And there is the distinction, after the battle, for the side which holds the battle-field, between tanks completely written off and tanks recoverable and repairable—a 'brew up' on the one hand, a broken track on the other. 300 tanks written off, and a lot of work for REME, is probably as fair an approximation as any. The losses of crews, although heavy, was not in proportion, because of the 'bale out' factor.

The fiasco was naturally not publicised at the time, nor the terrible drain on the infantry which had reduced battalions to about half-strength. The British and Canadians had been prepared to take punishment for two or three weeks, while the Americans massed for the major break-out around 1 July; they had held the Germans for twice that time, and still the Americans could not get going. For his part, Bradley needed to be sure that his new break-out attempt, Operation 'Cobra', would really go; there was little time left for another failure. It was supposed to have been launched on the heels of 'Goodwood', to take full advantage of the flow of further German reinforcements to the Caen sector which would be the obvious result, win or lose; but the bad weather which set in after 20 July put back the date to 24 July, and then, finally 25 July. Weather was vital to 'Cobra', because the plan was similar to 'Goodwood'—attack on a very narrow front preceded by an enormous air bombardment. The Americans now had 19 divisions in Normandy, facing a hotch-potch of German forces amounting to 9 divisions (with 110 tanks, none of them Tigers). The British and Canadians had 14 divisions facing 14 German divisions (with 600 tanks, many of them Tigers). The only way to prevent some transfers to the American front was to make yet another threat to Falaise and the Paris road; this time, a hopeless one, head-on at the strongly-held heights. It was to be launched regardless of weather on 25 July and was called Operation 'Spring'. The infantry and armour of II Canadian Corps attacked at 0330, with the surviving British armoured divisions, 7th and Guards, ready to exploit a breakthrough.

But the German defenders were unshaken by what their own newspaper, *Front und Heimat*, called "a small treason-group of insane generals" who had now been "eliminated". The banner headline: "The Miracle of the Führer" was followed by the ominous sub-title: "Now, the way is clear for Total War!" Hitler's escape from death, said the leading article, was: "a fiery sign that this man has been singled out by Providence to fulfil a task so great that no power on earth can halt his progress on his pre-destined path to victory." It was real, honest-to-goodness 'schmaltz', but the message was clearly stated: "There must be no capitulation."[2] The one thing of which the Führer was afraid was peace. But he need not have worried: the Allied leaders thought the same way. After 20 July, they declared that their policy was still 'Unconditional Surrender', regardless of what government was in power in Germany.[3] There was therefore no more point in trying to overthrow Hitler, particularly when the fate of the men who had tried to do so was noted. Following Soviet precedent, not merely the plotters, but their wives, their children, their relatives, were to be "eliminated". At one time, there were ten von Stauffenbergs in Buchenwald, waiting for the gas chambers.[4] The plotters themselves were tortured to the point where they "ceased any more to be human", another Soviet precedent which Hitler had been instrumental in re-introducing into Europe. For the Germans, there was no way out but fight to the bitter end for the dregs of a cause. It is difficult to see, now, how the position of the Allies differed in any material way; certainly their effective leaders cannot evade the charge of wanton destruction, the murder of millions.

The first to die in this manner were the Canadians on Verrières Ridge. 2 Div advanced west of Route National 158, the road to Falaise and Paris, 3 Div went forward on the east. From their strong positions in fortified mine galleries and shafts, and from the little villages which lie east and west of the road, "the enemy cut our battalions to pieces", admitted Colonel Stacey in *Les Canadiens dans la Bataille de Normandie*, one of two official histories he wrote. The village of Verrières and the ridge on which it stood was the highest point in the area and the main effort centred on it. The Black Watch of Canada, 5th Brigade of 2 Div, their Colonel dead, assaulted up the slope,

---

[2] Copy in possession of the present author; picked up in Normandy.
[3] *The Struggle For Europe*, p. 831. Chester Wilmot.
[4] *Victory in the West*, Vol. I, p. 374. Major L. F. Ellis.

through the corn, under fire from three sides. Probably 60 men reached the summit. About 15 came back, to report that there was a German stronghold on the crest. 342 men of the Black Watch lay dead or moaning in the corn.

The Royal Hamilton Light Infantry, under Lieutenant-Colonel J. M. Rockingham, 4th Brigade of 2 Div, assaulted the village of Verrières, "the most solid success of the whole operation", according to Stacey. He says they got it, but they didn't; not the first day. Gordon Amos went up there with them, on gun B2, a 17-pounder anti-tank of 18 Battery, 2nd A/T Regiment. "On the morning of 25 July we moved up to Trottville Farm, just back of Verrières; it was just daylight and some Engineers were there and sixteen of the 1st Hussars tanks. It was here that B1 got four tanks. The R.H.L.I. came up and these four German tanks were sitting around. B1 was man-handled in, pushed, the crew staying behind the gun-shield. Rockingham wanted them knocked out, so they went to work. As a tank was hit, there was a bright red flash of fire, and some smoke. They took one round each, and then they got three more each. The crews never baled out, but you couldn't trust them; then they started to burn and we knew they were O.K. The boys moved back from their gun and then it got a hit on the layer's side; that was it, it started burning. They stayed, and dug in, and could have fought as infantry if needed.

"B4 was man-handled up, and the boys left, and it got a hit in the same place; it burnt also. They dug in, and took up positions, and would have fought as infantry. B2 and B3 were left. Lieutenant Kennedy said to have the guns just back of the ridge and have them ready. The four crews were dug in and ready for an anti-tank role or infantry, whichever was required. The 25-pounders were putting up a barrage and the R.H.L.I. went in. They took one hell of a beating, and the 1st Hussars took one with them, 16 tanks knocked out. They were all burning, except one had a blown track and the other had its 17-pounder gun barrel shot off; Murray Hurter from Glen Ewen, Sask., drove that tank; he said it was a wonder they got out, they were sure casing them. Three of the crews that were left went with the infantry. The R.H.L.I. didn't get to their objective but close to it, and dug in and held. The field artillery and mortars and Typhoons of the Air Force saved them. They couldn't get reinforcements up, and they couldn't get out. They got about a dozen prisoners out of it and we looked after them for a while.

"On 26 July, about 0400, we went with B2 and B3 to the left outskirts of Verrières; B3 200 yards to our right. We had a crew of seven and we lost four. Duguid was wounded and Avery was killed. Lieutenant Kennedy and Serjeant Davies, two of the best you could ask for, they made it back. Kennedy was wounded twice more after this, and Davies once. At about 0530, Rockingham crawled into my slit trench, and asked how many men we had. Then, it was 11, on the two guns. 'Good,' he said, 'that gives me 87.' He looked at our gun, B2, two flat tyres, pieces of shrapnel in the telescope sight, and a few holes in the shield. 'The old girl's a sad and sorry looking sack, this morning,' he said, 'but she can still talk real estate.' He went on to his men. From what I saw of Rockingham, he feared neither man nor devil but I believe he put a lot of trust in God, because the rest of us did.

"After the guns B1 and B4 were knocked out, it was impossible to get over the Ridge, except fast. The 88s were right on. The jeeps made it O.K., but a man on foot didn't stand a chance. The dead layed out for a week, as we couldn't get out to bury them. Four stretcher bearers went out on 27 July, and they were killed by mortar fire. The 6-pounder troop of the 23rd Battery were knocked out, then C Troop of the 18th Battery were brought up, and they were trimmed down also. By this time our B Troop had lost three of their four guns. B2 was left, and odd but strange, she finished with us at Oldenburg, Germany. Life was very cheap on Verrières Ridge and it was well scoured with 88s and mortars. We heard a lot of noise, the air was blue, the time Bob Cruse had a 1,000-cigarette carton hit. Serjeant Boyd done the cooking there for our gun crew. He would toss a can of stew about 25 feet to me, and I've seen it hit in the air; but we tried it again and made it. We lived through it but didn't go hungry. They got tired of shooting at the food cans and about the time they figured it was opened and dished out, a shower of mortars would come over. They filled it with dirt once, then we waited till the dust cleared.

"The Germans used the Beetle here against the R.H.L.I., a

miniature tank filled with about 150 lbs. of explosive, and radio controlled. The crew of a 6-pounder and half a dozen R.H.L.I. boys would take a gun to the top of the ridge, knock out the Beetle, and pull the gun back. It looked funny at the time, but Judas it wasn't for them. It was from Verrières that the Essex Scottish went in a house on the ridge about 700 yards from us. Captain Maidens was our Battery Captain; he went in with a section of the Essex to see what an attack was like. He found out. His comment was: 'You get it or you don't'. The boys felt a bit rough about a fellow being hit or killed. After all, when you have lived with them from five years to a year, you get to know them. It was never too much trouble, and I don't think it bothered them too much, to crawl out to the wounded and get them in even if it was rough. I pulled a wounded man out of a burning truck filled with gas and ammo one night, at the time he needed help. I never thought at the time of being hit or hurt, but I got him out. After, I thought I might have been killed or wounded, but somebody else would have helped both of us. At times like that, you don't think; or if you do, it's the other fellow you think of.

"It was around the end of July that Dave Munn came down at dusk and stopped his jeep by the trench Edginton and I occupied. The mortars fell, a fair shower, about 20, and the jeep was riddled. Munn said: 'Those buggers meant them for me.' I told him not to be so damn miserable and share things. The R.H.L.I. was relieved on the night of 2 August by the S.S.R. I didn't see Serjeant-Major Outhwaite from Oxbow go by our gun, but about 20 yards from it, I heard him. I knew it was the S.S.R.

"Oxbow was a small town on the prairies, about 500 people. There was a creamery, 2 garages, dry goods, drug store, hospital, 2 blacksmith shops, Doctor, picture show, barber shop and pool room, and a good school, 12 grades. It was in the drought area and there wasn't much work. Some of the boys went away to work; I was away two years working on a farm. When we were 14 or 15, we shot rabbits, skinned, stretched and dried the hides, and sold them for ten cents apiece, when a dance was coming up. I shot my share, as it was the only way we could get money. There was also a rush of cream at the creamery; there was a sign on the wall: *'All I have, I owe to udders.'* There were two boys from

Oxbow, Bill Davidson and Mac Rutledge, in the S.S.R.'s support company, and I met them when I was out repairing telephone wire. I asked them down for coffee that night; they both started out. Mac made 200 yards, took 2 hours to make it, then the coffee was cold. Bill made it later, but didn't take so long. There were trenches all along, so they had cover.

" Some tanks from the English 7th Armoured Div came down. After they had been there three days, I was on lookout and watching a house about 700 yards away. I was watching with field glasses and noticed a curtain move, and a shadow behind it. There was an English tank Major with me, he got in on account of mortar fire, and I told him about it and asked him to use the 17-pounder on one of their tanks. Our gun had two flat tyres and we figured the Germans thought it was dead. He said he couldn't, as he had to contact our Brigadier for permission to fire. I told him we didn't have radio or phone to get in touch with our Brig. He finally asked for permission and was given the go ahead. The building soon burnt, and after that we got less sniper fire and their mortars weren't so accurate. I know the English soldier is a brute for punishment, but I can't figure out why they don't take the bull by the horns and do something to make life more pleasant. The English crew had lived for three days in that tank, not daring to peek out of the turret night or day. And if the Brig. would have said ' No ', I don't think he would have fired a damn round. I know Rockingham would have told him to fire and to hell with the Brig.

" Later, I met Geo. Clark of the 23rd Battery on the way to Falaise. There were three gunners and a 17-pounder, three ton of gun. Geo. and the boys were going up and into action; there were only three left, but they were in there and still loggin. A gun was needed, and knowing Geo. and his driver, they wouldn't have backed down from Satan himself. I didn't know the third gunner, but guess he was in the same class. I guess the Canadian Army was like that."

*   *   *

" Talk about the B.L.A.—it's the B.D.A.—the Bloody Destruction Army ", wrote a Gunner Officer of 59 Div to his parents on 27 July. " This stabilised front area is just like

Flanders must have been—every building a pile of rubble, every field a showpiece of a soldier's desire to get underground, if he's stopping 5 minutes. My own O.P. is just in front of a village which must have been very old and quaint not to mention beautiful. Now, all that stands above ground level are two burnt out Panthers and a Tiger balanced on its nose, one of the Panthers still housing the charred remains of two of Europe's chosen race. The stink is appalling. I am sure I smell just as bad as those two Gerries lying downstairs—and they, I should imagine, have been there some time. I am very sorry for the Norman peasant who will have to reclaim his ravished fields and homes. I am at the moment in the attic of my shattered farm house: how on earth the stairs haven't been hit I don't know: they are the only thing that hasn't. My Ac. is observing. He is an Irishman from Sligo—a deserter from the Eireann Army. I have just finished reading the O.P. log of the chap I took over from. Last entry reads as follows:—'*Waiting for 481 to relieve me so that I can hand over 1 shattered Normandy farm + normal accoutrements and the dead, which include 2 Germans, 1 Grave, British, unknown, 1 Cow, 1 Horse, 2 Pigs, and a Chick.*'

"Prisoners, more often they're deserters, are very funny the way they behave. Two came in the other day, saying they were Poles—but one turned out to be Bavarian, the other Austrian. They thought they would get preferential treatment that way. A couple of real Poles came in and volunteered the information that the Germans always put one Pole and one German to share a dug-out. The spokesman said: 'I saw my mate running across the field, and I looked down and saw my German asleep, so I just bashed him one and ran across too.' For every round Gerry fires, we give him a hundred, so it's no wonder these Poles, Belgians, Russians, Austrians, etc., whose hearts were never in the war, desert in large numbers. However, the German mobile field units near us are all S.S. and certainly know how to fight. We've had some hard battles with them, but know now just how good they are and their weak spots. Another point is that a lot of us (including yrs. truly) have got dysentery—some badly. It is the swarm of flies we have; but there is nothing you can do about it. Sanitation has been pretty good throughout the Regt., yet everybody I have met has got it fairly prevalent in their unit. It is largely due I think to some very bad sanitation by Jerry, more particularly by foreigners or units with foreigners in, than by German S.S. units, for example."

" Jerry's mosquito-ridden mortar and 88 mm range ", was what the British called their share of the ' stabilised front'; there was a constant drain of casualties. But as Joe Illingworth, the *Yorkshire Post* war correspondent, wrote of the British soldier: " He belongs to a race which has coloured the map red, and all he wants are the green fields of England. . . . If you picture him in any other way you will forget who he is. Here is no massive figure flashing through some legendary scene. This soldier is your neighbour and mine." And first of all, he liked his sleep. He could never get enough of it, for in action he never got any. Battles are not fought by keen-eyed, bright-faced young heroes, but by drugged men, walking in a daze, jumpy from noise and strain and lack of rest. " In the first case," said a Major, " the destiny of them all is determined by the Battalion Commander, who gives out his orders, having had two hours sleep in the last 24; then the Company Commanders, trying to awaken the young Platoon leaders from their death-like slumber. All of them heavy and drained of energy. Thirty minutes to make plans, then they lead the dog-weary men against the Spandaus, the everlasting mortar—to the first, the second, and the third objective."

When the advance stops and the front is stabilised, they get their heads down, if they can. A soldier of the K.O.Y.L.I., 49 Div, after 60 hours of combined waiting and action, wrapped himself up in a gascape at the bottom of his slit, and had barely dropped off when he was woken by a German at two in the morning. The German shook him awake, saying urgently: " Kamerad, Tommy, Kamerad." The soldier stirred, and grunted: " Wot, after 60 hours! Bugger orf and find some other feller and let this one sleep!" After sleep, food. Good farming country, Normandy— and the rations, designed with a shipping shortage in mind, were deficient in a good deal; so much so, that bread and potatoes were luxuries. Consequently, men would go out foraging; and the best spots were those occupied by nobody. Hence, on a misty July morning, just before first light on Tessel Wood, another K.O.Y.L.I. private crept forward cautiously, rifle at the ready. But you can't pick spuds with your rifle in your hand. So he laid it down, and as he moved along the rows of ' pomme de terre '. saw another early riser similarly engaged. As they slowly moved together along the row, they realised that they represented opposing forces. The British soldier's rifle was 30 yards behind him, and he made for it like a deer. the German panting frantically after, waving a ' Schmeisser ' (the M.P. 40 machine-pistol). But the German caught up, breathing hard, and handed over the Schmeisser. The Englishman proudly paraded his prisoner back, hands on head, to where his section were dug in. " Never mind about him," they said. " Where the devil are the spuds?"

And after food. . . . Well, there wasn't any beer. Indeed, B-Day, the day of the First Beer Issue in the Beachhead. was a memorable occasion, remembered for long weeks afterward. But there was one soldier of one unit, both nameless, but he came from Sussex, who was in the not too unusual position of holding a forward position with a house in front still occupied by the inhabitants, but not apparently by the Germans. Some French families were, inevitably, cut off like this between the opposing forces, sometimes for weeks. The Sussex man noted women coming out of the house and going in again, but keeping close to it. One of the women was young, they clearly had no cigarettes, and he had. So he took a very long detour, it being suicide to crawl directly across, got to the house, introduced himself, had the young woman, and looking out of the window afterwards, found himself looking down onto a Spandau on a tripod mounting, its three-man crew lounging beside it, smoking. He could have plopped a grenade into the middle of them, if he'd had one. But, as he said, he wouldn't have been so silly, anyway; obviously, the Germans were using the house for the same purpose as he had. But he was most annoyed with the young woman, for not mentioning the Germans. " I could have got shot in a most unmilitary position," he complained.

* * *

But the stabilised front was not to last much longer. After having been bombed twice by their own airforce, with over 1,000 casualties, the Americans had got going with ' Cobra ', and were surprising themselves with the speed of their advance. The additional space gained by ' Goodwood ' now enabled Montgomery

to bring more troops ashore. General H. D. G. Crerar, the
Canadian commander, was able to cross and set up his headquarters so that, by the end of July, First Canadian Army was
operational, in addition to Second British Army, the pair forming 21 Army Group. And by 1 August, the two remaining
armoured divisions, 4th Canadian and 1st Polish, had been
landed, ready for the final breakout, under Canadian command.

The 1st Hussars, returning from Verrières, less the men and
the tanks they had left for good on top of the ridge, came
across a brand-new Canadian Armoured Division. "We could
hardly believe our eyes," said Serjeant Gariepy. "Resplandissant,
in their clean new battledress, black belts, black gaiters, shiny
new tanks with some sort of gleaming polish over them, squadron
signals and pennants all new and crisp. These boys were all ready
for a triumphant march-past through Paris with Hitler in a cage
for all the world to see. They were an exact replica of the British
Guards Armoured we had seen in England. They looked at us
with as much surprise as we at them. Dirty, battle-scarred, tanks
patched up, unshaven men, berets in all sorts of colours instead
of steel helmets (which were too uncomfortable on the earphones),
dirty old coveralls which had seen filth and fighting grime ever
since the landing, no insignias of rank on our shoulders. . . .
These fellows were shocked. As we passed them, the ribald
questions began. 'Whose side are you guys fighting for?'—
'Were you fellows prisoners with your tanks?' They could not
understand our bedraggled appearance, and most of us felt very
sorry for them. We remembered the day we landed and how we
felt so vastly superior to the enemy, until after the first day, and
then we realised that we knew nothing at all."

This was the division which, when at last the game in Normandy went the British way, had the ball placed at their feet;
and this is why they fumbled it. There is no blame attached.
Everyone has to learn, and there were no experienced divisions
left. Their partners with the ball were to be 1st Polish Armoured
Division, as a division inexperienced, but some of the Poles knew
only too well what they were in for, and the atmosphere of that
division was different. To start with, they all had their heads
shaven (to prevent hair getting into a wound and infecting it).
One of them had actually fought with the German Armies in

Russia, then against the Americans in Italy, where he was captured, and was now going to fight the Germans in France. For
the record, they did sing. As the 8,000 ton Liberty ships slid
downstream from Tilbury on the night of 29 July, *South of the
Border* and a Hawaiin War Chant, beautifully sung, echoed
across the water over the soft beat of the engines and the put-
putter of the incoming flying bombs, and the thunder of the
barrage, and the earth-tremor explosions where the roofs dissolved
in reddened dust under a red moon. For the record, the ship's
company's radio played dance tunes as the great convoy sighted
the beachhead at sunset on 31 July, and the British soldiers
aboard were springing violently to attention whenever Joe
(Stalin) and the Royal Navy were mentioned, as these, they maintained, would see them safe home again. The Poles were grim and
silent. Ack Ack hammered and thumped above the thin drone
of the high-flying Ju 188s of Generalmajor Peltz, commanding
IX Flieger Korps, and the ranging British night-fighters. " Every
raid we made, four attacks by night-fighters," said Siegfried
Radkte, " and Peltz led nearly all these raids himself!" It was
a nightly performance, as the newly-landed troops were to find
out. That night, for the record, the sea was black and the moon
was red, and the low line of Normandy lay under a high, fantastic
castled world of clouds.

Next morning, for the record, the bridge radio of the Liberty
ship *Ocean Vigour* was playing the march " Le Pere de la
Victoire" (The Father of Victory), as the troops transferred to
LCTs, scrambling in full kit down the swaying rope ladders,
praying not to fall, as the steel hulls of the landing craft ground
against the steel sides of the big transport. After the men, the
vehicles were lowered over, with men underneath them, to guide
the many tons of steel into the right place on the rolling, swaying
decks. In one LCT, a British soldier was sitting on the turret of
a Polish tank, earphones on, listening to the B.B.C. six o'clock
news from London. At the bows of another, two more British
soldiers, about to go for a swim, stopped a moment to watch a
man on a parachute slowly drifting downwards into a field
behind the beach defences; then they dived overboard, went
straight to the bottom to find the depth, and finding it shallow,
breast-stroked around the red flags flying from the warm sea to

mark the hulls of sunken vessels. One went straight in for the beach, dodging the patches of oil fuel, to be the first man of his unit to land in Normandy, but was called back by loud-hailer.

The Poles looked unsmiling on, lost inside themselves. "Of course, the Polish Armoured Division played, in a way, a unique role," commented Major Kamil B. Czarnecki, G2 of the division. "They were fighting, liberating step by step the territory of France, whilst their own country was being 'liberated' step by step, at the same time, by the Russian Army. Everybody knew what that meant. Nevertheless, it was this division which closed the famous 'Falaise Gap'." The British sensed the tragedy of the Poles, but could not share it; the Polish tankmen did not seem personally to expect to survive, and as Poland was then being over-run by the Red Army, there seemed little point in their sacrifice, except revenge. Nor did the British then, with their toasts to 'Joe' and the R.N., realise what to be over-run by the Russians really meant; they found out later. Only for one moment did British and Pole come close together. As the anchors roared inboard, and the LCT went in to beach, and at a soft-spoken Navy order, the flat bows went down onto the sand. "How many rounds have you got in those pouches," asked an A.B., almost wistfully. But the soldiers hardly heard him. They were staring ahead, the hair on the back of their heads bristling. Going to an unknown fate, they were trying to read the future. "Fifty," said someone, mechanically.

*　　*　　*

The German air effort over the beaches nightly varied from 80 to 120 bombers, many of them mine-laying sorties. "West of the Seine and in the Paris area, I think there were more British night-fighters than German bombers!" said Radtke, who flew 21 missions in five weeks. "The flak varied from moderate to the strongest we had ever seen: the beachhead was like a boiling kettle of water, comparable to Malta in 1942. But our most difficult raid was on the night of 26/27 July, against a troop and tank concentration in the Giberville area south-east of Caen. The distance between our troops and the British was only 1,800 feet. We took off from Soesterberg near Utrecht at 2300, flying at low-level until we reached the Seine, when we climbed from 300 feet to 13,000 feet for a 45 degree dive-bombing attack (but without air-brakes). During the climb, our gunner dropped 'window' against search and night-fighter radar, but we were attacked three times by English night-fighters and lost a lot of time in dodging them. From high in the black sky we saw the front-line like a glowing snake writhing across the landscape. Our troops had been ordered to light green pocket lamps on the ground to mark their positions, and our Pathfinder Group 66 was to lay both ground and sky markers for us. And there they were! A great green glow on the ground (730 coloured incendiaries) and four yellow parachute flares hanging above. We dived from 13,000 to 1,000, towards the fires and explosions on the ground, our aircraft rocking from the flak detonations. At the note from the 'Boschhorn' which meant we were at 1,000 feet and must drop our bombs, we pulled out—fast!—and at that moment were hit by light flak. We steep-turned towards our own lines, port wing and engine on fire, then struggled for bale-out height. We were much too low at that moment. But the engines were still running and we got vectors back to an emergency field in Belgium. They had the searchlights turned on for us. At 0325, wheels up, port wing blazing, we crash-landed on this field."[5]

Next day, 28 July, Lancaster 'J for Johnny' of 635 Pathfinder Squadron was airborne from Downham Market, south of King's Lynn, bound for Hamburg. For once, not an invasion target. Bomber Command by now had lost 2,000 aircrew in two months, mostly in support of 'Overlord'. This was a murder mission pure and simple. Incendiaries only. Target: people. They were refugees from the holocaust of Hamburg the previous year, living in temporary hutted camps. Some probably were war-workers, a legitimate target, but their wives and their babies were there too. The Pathfinders had been briefed: "You're going for the people!" For once, Flight Lieutenant Linacre felt sick at what he was going to do. "Hamburg was out of context. The rest had been Normandy battle area, railways, V1 sites, Duisburg, etc.

---

[5] An undue proportion of bombs and torpedoes off the beachhead was harmlessly absorbed by two old battleships sunk in the shallows as part of the 'Gooseberry' breakwater; Radtke remembered attacking one of them. They were the French *Courbet*, which had served during the Battle of Britain as a floating flak battery in Portsmouth Harbour, and the British *Centurion*, which had spent her time between the wars steaming without a crew—a radio-controlled target ship.

All military targets. I don't go for this stuff about our being 'Terror Bombers'. We were just doing what we were told, and an industrial town *is* a military target. However, when we bombed factories, we'd been told, they'd been working again three days later. So the policy now was bomb the houses where the workers lived, upset their lives. When factories were bombed, normally the workers were not there, so they escaped. The Hamburg huts were part of this policy. But, this time, Hamburg was wide open. If you have opposition, then self-preservation is the paramount factor in your mind. Nuremberg, for instance, when we saw aircraft going down left, right, and centre—94 in all, I think, that night. We used to save one bomb for Beachy Head, even; they shot at us, so we kept one to hurl back at them— self-preservation. And the night we were routed out over London, to hearten the populace; we got mixed up with a German raid and there were more British bombs dropped on London that time than German. But the first time I ever had feelings for the people down below was Hamburg: it was wide open. I was on radar on approach, picked up the coast, made sure the landmarks were right, then ten minutes before the target, ducked down to the bomb-sights, to finish on visual. I thought we got better bombing by radar than visual, but this was a visual."

The name of the man who originated this policy was Lindemann, later Lord Cherwell, scientific adviser to Winston Churchill, and now dead. The name of the man who originated the scheme which destroyed Caen was Zuckermann, scientific adviser to Leigh-Mallory, and now Sir Solly Zuckermann. He is still alive.

CHAPTER NINETEEN

DICKIE'S BRIDGE

*'Bluecoat'—The Break-Out from Caumont Begins
30 July to 4 August*

By the end of July, an American commentator could truthfully say: "Up those beaches came a million men, and Dinah Shore." When the Germans are added, there were more than two million soldiers locked up in part of Normandy. The area held by the British and Canadian Armies at that date equalled roughly half the size of an average English county; including the Cherbourg peninsula, the American Armies held an area the same size as an English county, although their front was no longer than the line held by the British. As the new units—the last of the many—landed on 1 August, the thing which impressed them in the most vivid way was the narrowness of the beachhead, the lack of depth. Their backs were to the sea and the continuous drumfire of the artillery was around them in a great semi-circle. The 'sharp end' seemed to be just down the road, although in fact it was fifteen miles away; and just to rub it home, their vehicles were not allowed to move from the area just behind the beaches until nightfall, when they first heard the jingle: "We believe in luck, in God we trust; but the Hun still shoots at a cloud of dust."

To quote from the diary of a soldier who arrived on 1 August—D plus 56—nearly two months after the Allies had first landed: "Soon after 10 p.m. we rolled off to the east, and were immediately blinded by dust. The moon shone down on a countryside like England; now and then there were gun flashes from the beach or a riot of red tracers from the front lines; we saw our first French girl, talking to soldiers; someone from the rear truck cried, 'Vive la France!' and was rewarded by a shout of 'Muck off!' delivered in Yankee accents; someone else asked, 'Where are we, cock?' and found himself addressing a Brigadier; and in a little while we were well and truly lost. The moon moved all round the horizon about four times; every now and then the truck hit a young shell hole; we passed the same place several times; the rear truck hit a stone bridge and bounced off again; and it was anticipated by many that it was the German Army we would be reinforcing. A Verey light rose up from behind a wood, seeming to us very close; startled, we went back the way we had come, with more flares going up and bursts of machine-gun fire coming from the other side of the nearest trees; and we arrived at our destination at 0230 on 2 August, having apparently made an exhaustive and unofficial tour of the Normandy beachhead. Stiff and sore, we moved too slowly to please the reception committee (of one), who snarled: ' You'd have been dug in by now, if you'd been here on D-Day!' " This was not quite so bitter an experience as that of Corporal Jones of 4th Somersets, who landed on D plus 12, to be greeted by a group of elderly pick-and-shovellers of the Pioneer Corps with the taunt, " What kept you, eh?"

But between D plus 12 and D plus 56, the British front had moved forward only about half-a-dozen miles, at enormous cost; and as it was not continuously held, it was in fact possible to drive straight through. Fifteen miles at 30 m.p.h. is only half-an-hour; by stepping on it, you could make the German lines in 20 minutes. Rarely can front and rear have been so near; rarely can so many men have been gathered for battle in so cramped a space. By the end of July, the Allied beachhead was still only a tiny triangle, with the corners at Caen, Avranches, and Cherbourg. At this time there was no thought of Falaise as anything other than one of many objectives; that it very soon became very much more was manna from heaven or, more precisely, from the Führer's Headquarters on the other side of Europe. There never was a plan to encircle the German Armies in Normandy until the end of the first week of August, when an opportunity suddenly presented itself. Up to that time, the objective of the American armies was in the exactly opposite direction, both to Falaise and to Paris—it was to race westward into Britanny for the ports. With bases secure, then the Allied line could wheel eastward to Falaise. Argentan, Alencon, Le Mans, Angers, and Rennes: a wide wheeling movement to drive the Germans back to the Seine and force them to fight a great tank battle with the river at their backs. This was the point of holding Caen securely, for it was intended to be the pivot on which the armies would wheel. But the breakthrough to Britanny, which began at the end of July, was long-delayed; the Allies had expected to be on the Seine by now.

Therefore the British part of this operation, which was called 'Bluecoat', must be seen in the context of the original plan, not as it finally and unexpectedly developed. In spite of grumbles at the top, Montgomery still commanded all the Armies in Normandy, British, Canadian, and American. The Germans were holding firm at Caen, where most of their armour still was; but the German front at Avranches, the opposite end of the line, was visibly disintegrating. So Montgomery decided to strike in the centre, at Caumont, at the junction of the American and British forces, and start the left-wheel from there, in time with the right-wheel of one American Army into Britanny. The move positively invited a counter-offensive at the point where the twin thrusts began to part company; any amateur strategist could grasp it instantly, and Hitler did not fail to do so. But Montgomery was no amateur, and he judged that, with the forces available, it could not be done; and the German generals agreed. Montgomery cannot be blamed for failing to foresee that Hitler would complete the ruin of the German Armies in Normandy. He switched the bulk of the British striking force from the Caen area to Caumont, where there was little German armour, and on 30 July, the Americans and British began to seep forward, slowly, painfully, but inexorably, like the incoming tide. And again, as at the Odon, the front was to be set ablaze from right to left, in succession, so that the Germans would have no respite, but be compelled to switch their reserves here, there, and everywhere. As at the Odon, the main attack was to be made with the armoured corps, 8 Corps, with 15 Scottish Division in their Odon role—to break open a gap through which the armour could pour, for a quick exploitation. A vital role would be played by the armoured cars of the Household Cavalry, which would go through the infantry gap first, to find a ' soft ' spot for the armour to follow up.

The 30th was a confusing day for the advance. The ' teeth ' of 8 Corps were attacking at Caumont while the ' tail ' was still at Caen, 50 miles away. The roads of Normandy were never really designed for the movement by night of immense streams of traffic, including the heaviest and most cumbersome vehicles. And some of the teeth were knocked off on a stubborn German defence laced with a new and formidable weapon called 'Ferdinand'. The British 'infantry' tanks had a horrible time. The Argylls of 15 Scottish, less their anti-tank guns, but supported by the Churchills of the Scots Guards, took and held a height known as Quarry Hill, when there were three shots, and three Churchills 'brewed'. Then two enormous S.P. guns, covered by a third, lumbered into the open, up the hill, through the British position, and down the other side, leaving in all eleven shattered Churchills behind them. One of the SPs passed within a few feet of an artillery officer who had a close view of the German commander, who was standing up, wearing only a vest, presumably because of the heat, and laughing. These enormous vehicles were Jagd Panthers, which mounted a 128 mm gun some 23 feet long on a Panther chassis.

In spite of them, 15th Scottish and 11th Armoured had bitten six miles into the German front, as at the Odon; and, as at the Odon, a lagging flank division, this time 43 Wessex, was contributing to the creation of a second 'Scottish Corridor'. They were lagging, because in front of them was the main 'mountain' chain of Normandy, which the Germans had to hold, if their forces on the American front were not to be cut off and surrounded. The ominous *massif* of Mont Pincon, which they had first seen as strongly marked contour lines on a map back in England, now loomed before them in fact; its nickname was 'Little Switzerland'. They, too, met Jagd Panthers, supported this time by very determined infantry.

* * *

South of Caumont lay the real bocage, an intricate pattern of earth-banked fields and high hedges; twisting leafy lanes; and rivers, at this time of the year, little more than streams, crossed by bridges many of which were not stressed for tanks. Ideal ambush country for small groups of armoured vehicles or S.P. guns, protected by infantry; and the ambush, as ever, formed the basis of German tactics. Not only let them get into the open, let them come right up to you before you fire—that was the method. In both British and German narratives, the figures ten or eleven tanks (Churchills or Shermans) instantly knocked out, occur with sickening regularity. It was almost impossible to work round a Panther or Tiger, and shoot it up from the rear or in the flank; almost always, the encounter was head-on, where the armour was impenetrable. Not infrequently, two Tigers could hold up an entire Armoured Brigade for hours. 23 Hussars had already tried their guns on dead Panthers (knocked out from a flank): unless the shell hit the turret ring, a 75 mm was useless; a 17-pounder at 300 yards would penetrate the turret, but frequently not the sloping front plate of the hull. In full knowledge of the facts, 11 Armoured Division went forward, and in front of them the probing reconnaissance cars of 2 Household Cavalry.

Throughout the morning of 31 July, messages were coming back from the leading cars, often from behind the enemy front; and, sometimes, no messages at all, just silence, from a particular car. Mixed up with these vital radio transmissions were lengthy and self-important warblings from Corps HQ, broken into now and then by a continual "*I can hear you now fine and dandy*" from some long-winded American at Cherbourg, or completely drowned by a high-powered transmitter worked by an operator calling himself 'Blackboid'. In all this mush, at about 10.30 a.m., a half-understood message was received from C Squadron. What it implied was so unbelievable that the CO, Colonel Abel Smith, demanded an instant re-check. And back it came again, quite definite:

"*I say again, at 1035 hours, the bridge at 637436 is clear of enemy and still intact.*"

637436 was a bridge which carried the main road to Le Beny Bocage and Vire over the River Souleuvre. It was six miles behind the German lines. It was being used by the Germans for two-way traffic. It was being observed by one armoured car and one scout car. There was a chance to get it. The entire Corps plan was altered, and the advance of 29 Armoured Brigade was switched to back up the lonely reconnaissance unit, hiding in the woods. At the moment, only a Frenchman knew they were there. He was Monsieur Desiré Papillon, owner of a farm some 200 yards from the bridge, which he had abandoned that morning because there was obviously going to be trouble. There were rumours of English tanks close at hand, and the Germans were tense and bad-tempered; he had hidden in the woods and observed all movement. Very accurately indeed, for when the 2 H.C.R. historian revisited the spot three years after, instead of the usual 'What I did to the Boche' line-shoot, he was able to describe exactly how he had seen the two cars cautiously approach the bridge, cross over, and disappear among the trees. "Yes," he chuckled, "I knew that the English were there, but the Boches didn't."

What had happened was this. Most of the cars had been blocked, one way or another. Corporal-of-Horse Munn had gone swanning at high speed, passed the line of sight of a Panther, and been hit three times—one shot passing between the driver's legs, one removing the front suspension, one travelling through the car from front to rear, starting at the engine and coming out at the back. The following car, seeing this, tried another route and, nosing up to a corner, found themselves spectators of a German unit, fifty strong, on parade. Corporal Bugby, the commander, opened fire with a Bren until he heard his Troop Leader calling: "*Retire at once. Enemy tank advancing on you. Have laid down smoke.*" In Bugby's words, "We retired like scalded cats. But why were the enemy not capable of returning one round to the hundreds we had fired? This gave us confidence that they were not the super soldiers we had been led to believe."

However, Lieutenant-Colonel D. B. Powle, M.C., then a lieutenant commanding 1 Troop of C Squadron, had what he afterwards considered the good fortune to part company with his two rear cars, half-way through. Otherwise, he thought, he would have been too conspicuously British. The first few miles were difficult, with four cars belting along. The first German lookout was despatched by a grenade hurled from the leading scout car by Corporal G. B. Bland: the explosion would not give the game away, as a burst of machine-gun fire would have done. The two rear cars became immobilised in a narrow lane just as they approached a main road, which was covered by an 88. Consequently, only Bland's scout car and Powle's armoured car roared across, the 88 was late in identifying them as enemy, and could not swing round quickly enough to knock them out. However, it was now ready for whoever tried it next. Powle pressed on, shouting to Bland: "*We may as well try what's in front—it can't be worse than trying to neck it back through that lot!*"

They now went flat out down a track leading through the Forêt l'Eveque, unknown to them the boundary between two German divisions—2nd Parachute and 326 Infantry. As is usual in such cases, each thought the other was holding it, and transport of both divisions was using it as well, of course, as the Household Cavalry. And most of this traffic was going back—that is, it was travelling in the same direction as Powle and Bland, who found themselves roaring along in fast convoy for two miles with a German four-wheeled armoured car. All most Germans saw was an unmistakable German armoured car blinding along, followed by two other armoured vehicles in a cloud of dust. Even had they recognised the two fellow-travellers as British vehicles, it meant nothing; the German Army in Normandy was using some British equipment, including Bren carriers, captured four years before at Dunkirk. Then the genuine German vehicle turned up a side road, and the British cars arrived at the bridge, at which a sentry was posted. Both cars halted, and while Powle covered them, Brand and his driver, Trooper H. P. G. Read, dealt with the unsuspecting sentry. "We quietly finished him off," said Brand, "as otherwise we were sunk." They then crossed over, hid the cars in the wood, and leaving Corporal Stables to transmit the famous message, went back to observe the bridge, spotted only by Monsieur Papillon. So far, they were only five men on their own, with a wireless set, six miles behind the German lines.

Lieutenant R. A. Bethell, commanding 5 Troop of D Squadron, was despatched at once to support them; and very shortly went off the air. Next day, two of his four cars were found, burnt out on the road to St. Lo, with no survivor to tell the story. A complete Troop had disappeared. It was only pieced together long afterwards. They had run into a simple infantry ambush with bazookas. Corporal-of-Horse C. K. Soper found himself trapped behind the two leading cars, both blazingly furiously;

and dismounted to help them. Lieutnant Bethell had had his right leg severed, but did not realise it until he tried to stand up; how he got out will never be known. " His leg had been shot away from the knee and his foot was hanging on by two strings of flesh," said Soper. " I cut away the foot with a jack-knife and treated the wound as best I could. Then the Germans moved in on us from all sides. They treated us quite well." Soper was put in a large house with some fifty Americans, mostly aircrew, then next day they were all marched off, the French in the villages giving them food and wine. " I shall never forget a Frenchwoman who brought us food," said Soper. " When the Germans were not looking she lifted up the apron she was wearing and underneath she had a British and an American flag." Meanwhile, for the wounded men, wrote the H.C.R. historian, " it was to be a story of a disorganised enemy lacking anaesthetics, pain-deadening drugs and even the most elementary surgical necessities. Their bandages were made of paper. A German doctor spoke to Lieutenant Bethell in English and did his best for him, but said he would have to clean up the wound with nothing more than a local anaesthetic—explaining it was the same for his own men."

By sunset on 31 July, 29 Armoured Brigade were moving on what was now to be known as ' Dickie's Bridge', and soon their tanks were rumbling across. " The capture of the bridge and the advance southward which it made possible was un-questionably a turning-point in the campaign," stated the author of the *History of 11th Armoured Division*. It might even have been more. On the following day, for a space of perhaps two hours, there was the possibility of a complete breakthrough, but if this had been attempted 11 Armoured Division would certainly have been cut off as there were no troops immediately available to hold open the jaws of the gap. The chance was fleeting, but Major-General Roberts was not prepared to take such a risk with all the implications of air supply when no time was available for any planning. By 1 August, however, both 11th Armoured and the 19th American Division, the latter without permission, were using the main road which led south-east from the bridge. Lieutenant Ainsworth of D Squadron, 2 H.C.R., was the first to contact the Americans. Moving off before dawn, he drove through St. Martin de Besaces southwards, parallel to the thin thrust to Dickie's Bridge. St. Martin was abandoned. No civilians, no British, no Germans; just houses quietly burning and a dead dog in the road; the reek of death, and another odour. "I can smell Germans, sir," said a Trooper. The keen scent-faculties which neolithic man must have had, had returned; to save lives. The Germans *did* smell different; and the Germans maintained, for their part, that you could always smell an Englishman. This may have been from the remnants of the anti-gas chemical with which their battledress was impregnated. The German odour may have been weapon oil or synthetic petrol, or even food; certainly, it was unmistakable. The cars moved quickly forward until they heard wild bursts of shooting, which turned out to be not the Germans after all, but a dogface Colonel and his men.

" The strangest of cavalcades appeared out of the darkness, and we watched them pass with curiosity. It was our first meeting with our Allies under active service conditions. They were infantry moving in single file and, being also dog tired, they did not take the slightest notice of us. If British faces have a reputation for stolidity, then surely those of the Americans are graven. Quite expressionless, sallow with fatigue, one and all masticating gum and silent in their rubber-studded top boots, they padded by in their tight-bottomed trousers. In the middle of their column and sitting like a Buddha on a mound of kit in the back of a jeep was an officer chewing a large cigar and studying by its glowing ash a crumpled map. He nodded to me and, casually glancing from his map to the shadowy outline of a tree, sprayed its topmost branches with a Tommy gun. 'Snipers,' he grunted. Long after they had scraped by our cars we could still hear them firing at the tree tops."

Anything less like the Hollywood 'G.I.' than the genuine American 'dogface' could hardly be imagined. Quiet and modest, they admitted that their policy was to blast the objective with airplanes and artillery, and if even so much as a single Spandau replied, to blast it again, before going in. The Germans then, felt much as the British had in 1940, firing at dive-bombers with rifles from the sands of Dunkirk. 5 Parachute Division, to which Karl Max Wietzorek belonged, was now retiring before

the Americans towards Vire and Falaise, the meeting ground
of all the Armies. "This place sure has been liberated," said
an American M.P. to an H.C.R. crew, when eventually they
reached the waste of brick and stone which had been Vire.
"There was no real front any more," said Wietzorek, "friend
and foe were all mixed up. I wonder how many Americans
and British were actually butchered by their own bomber-leaders.
We saw the bombs come down, glinting in the sun, mostly right
among the American positions. Lucky for us. But their twin-
tailed Lightnings mowed us down, and the thick hedges didn't
help us much then. Our communications were paralysed, we got
no rations. We nibbled on a bit of bread-crust and drank any
cider we could 'organise'. We went down with enteritis,
although we had a blunter word for it. Ashen-pale in the face,
dirty, filthy, over-exhausted, dead beat; so much so that I personally would have been grateful for the 'coup de grace'. I am not
ashamed to admit that when an American soldier, hit in one
arm by a mortar, came staggering towards us, throwing his good
arm round my neck and crying out, 'Comrade, help me!'—I was
so shaken that I started to vomit. What could we do with our
first-aid kit? A little packet no bigger than a pack of 20 American
cigarettes. The American soldier had so many splinters in him,
he was like a sieve. He bled to death with a rattle in his throat;
it is quite true, but so horrible that I cannot put it on paper
properly. I saw my best friend, Parachutist Lötte, who was a
machine-gunner. Suddenly his head was not on his body; I could
only identify him by the barrel of his gun, which was still
strapped round his neck. It was a wild flight, no organised
retreat any more, although the Wehrmacht communiques spoke
of 'shortening the front'. We called ourselves Retreat Candi-
dates, and I believe the Allies called us War-prolongers, but in
fact the Military Police had to work hard on us, but now even
the hanging of soldiers from wayside trees, and horrors like
that, were not successful any more. On the ground, man for
man, I would say we Germans were one hundred per cent better
soldiers, but what chance did we stand against the mass of
material and superior equipment, our rifles against the American
automatics? We never experienced an attack by the Allies
without the heaviest preparation by bombers and artillery. It

was indiscriminate, and even our Red Cross men were cut down, white flags and all. They told us about the V1, V2, and V3, which were so effective that the Island Kingdom would drown in the Channel and disappear from the map. But we did not believe these fairy-tales any more; with blistered feet, we 'old comrades' of 18 and 19 streamed back, accompanied by the American Air Force."

But on the British front, once again, resistance stiffened. Rightly or wrongly, the Germans consistently regarded the Americans as inferior fighting troops. This was the really basic reason for their fierce defence of Caen and the surrounding heights. Now, they were planning a great counter-offensive against what they thought to be the 'weak sister' of the three nations against them. At Mortain, as in the Ardennes, it was the American they intended to hit; but in order to cut the line of communications of the American Britanny breakout, they had to hold the 'shoulder' of their road network, stretching along the heights from Mont Pincon westwards. And this was why, on the night of 1 August, as a swift reaction to the British coup at 'Dickie's Bridge', Willi Fey and Heinz Trautmann and the rest of S.S. Heavy Tank Battalion 502 found themselves withdrawn from the 'Hill of Calvary' and, with most of II S.S. Panzer Corps, rushed towards Vire, to halt the British and American forces now pouring southwards from Caumont, along the newly-captured road. And it was a Tiger which finally got 'Dickie' himself.

On 2 August, an Auster artillery spotter dropped a message to 2 H.C.R., reporting the ridge in front, Chenedolle-Sourdevalle, strongly held by armour, and some of the cars were reporting Tigers. In the first village, the French were reporting mines. The Mayor came rushing up to the leading cars, shouting his head off in an attempt to stop them. When they looked more closely at the road, they saw it resembled the aftermath of a paper chase—the villagers had lain in hiding, watched the Germans laying them, noted each spot and then, at considerable risks, gone out and marked each one with a piece of paper.

'Dickie' Powle halted his troop on the road from Presles to Estry and while his crew decoded an enormous backlog of messages received, Powle decided to take a stroll and reconnoitre the enemy on foot. He quickly came back, to report a Tiger with a track off, borrowed a captured German rifle from one of the cars, and set off for a slice of lone sniping. When he did not return, Corporals Bradbury and Bland moved cautiously down the lane on foot. "Then," says the H.C.R. historian, "they halted, for in front of them, standing in solitary splendour, was a pair of British Army boots! Of their Troop Leader—not a sign." Lieutenant Powle had met his match. The Household Cavalry was the most glittering Regiment of the 'Establishment'; and on his first (quite unofficial) reconnaissance back in July, their Colonel had been hopelessly distracted by a covey of partridges, which he had attempted to 'walk up', in spite of the fact that the birds were in a minefield. Old habits die hard. But now Powle met the appropriate sort of German, lying back at his ease while he watched his crew repair the broken track. Frankly, he thought it was presumptious of Powle to try to interfere with a 60-ton tank, armed with no more than a rifle, and while Powle stalked the Tiger, he stalked Powle. A British revolver would have been no use to him, but his Luger, like all German automatic pistols, had a high accuracy even in inexperienced hands. He hit Powle in the arm, spinning him over.

The German then stalked forward and introduced himself, in perfect public school English. "I was at Winchester. Where were you?" After fifteen minutes of security-conscious conversation on both sides, the Tiger was repaired, and the German said casually, "As a matter of fact, we're rather pushed. Your chaps, as far as I can make out, should be advancing towards this spot, and we have been ordered to retire. I trust you not to look where we are going. When we are out of earshot you can make your way back to your lines, I hope? However, as a formality, I shall have to ask you to leave your boots behind."

On 3 August, the reconnaissance regiment of 9 S.S. Panzer Division, newly arrived from the area of Hill 112, drove the British out of Presles, but the division could not retake the vital, commanding ridge of Perrier, held by 11 Armoured Division, although a game of hide and seek developed in the bocage, with no firm front at all, and twenty-two Tigers and Panthers were seen by a single armoured car. Now the Germans were seeping

back, the most ominous and indicative sign being the groups of
French refugees, who could not be admitted to the British
positions, because it would have been too easy for the Germans
to infiltrate an agent or two among them. In the evening,
Lieutenant M. A. J. Smallwood probed forward three miles,
ran into a Tiger, and went off the air. As Smallwood baled out
and ran for it, he was bowled over by a burst of machine-gun
fire in the legs, the high rate of fire of the M.G.34 making this a
most serious business. The Germans fixed him up with rough
crutches, and helped him to their aid post, where he got an
anti-tetanus injection and a paper bandage. The orderly left
the boots on, because, with his primitive equipment, he said,
any cleaning up of the wounds might result in a flow of blood
which he could not stop. " They seemed a pretty casual crowd,"
said Smallwood, " and I thought I might get away during the
night. Their Major was very chatty—he spoke perfect English,
and I gather he had worked on the Manchester Cotton Exchange.
They had recently come from Russia and their morale was very
high. I must say I was very well treated. After a long harangue
about Bolshevism and the true ' Democracy ' to be found in the
German Army, he told me that another British scout car had
been knocked out down the road and the crew killed. Would I
like to superintend their burial and see if I could make a note
of their names for next of kin? I agreed; but when I got to
my feet again, I had a sharpish twinge, and passed clean out."

Lieutenant Smallwood was taken prisoner near Le Brien and
was evacuated towards Paris as the Falaise Gap was actually
being closed. " We were in an open and antiquated lorry. I
was lying next to a poor devil of a Canadian in a bad way—the
remainder were German wounded. They screamed and moaned
without any restraint, but the Canadian kept dead quiet through
it all. The French leaned out of their upper windows and I
don't want to be looked at again in that way. There was no
exaggerated expression on their faces, but one didn't have to be
very imaginative to see the hatred and triumph there. The
knowledge that it was not directed against oneself did little to
soften it. Sometimes they spat almost impersonally. It was a
sort of vicious circle. The more the wounded screamed, the
more intense was the French reaction; the windier the driver

became, the faster he drove; the more the trunk jolted, the more the wounded screamed. There was absolutely no doubt that, as far as France was concerned, the Germans were completely beaten."

CHAPTER TWENTY

'LITTLE SWITZERLAND'

The Battle for Mont Pincon—Battle of the Orne Bridgehead
5 to 12 August

" I remember walking down the road with all me mates, there was no tanks with us; we came to a stop, didn't dig in, told to get ready for battle. Lay down in field, hearing scores of our own shells coming over the top of our heads. This went on for quite some time. Then we got back on the road; walked along about half a mile, and suddenly saw in front of us this bloody great hill. Another half hour, I think early in the afternoon, and we actually started to go up Mont Pincon." So recollected ' Bill ' Biles of 4 Wilts. " It was really hot, really hard going; it took all your time to walk up the side of that hill without thinking so much about why you was walking up there. And suddenly there was some m.g. fire, didn't know where it came from, or whose it was, but I remember we all fell flat on our faces, and got ready to open back if it wasn't ours. Like most every other battle, you don't see the Germans until you're practically on top of 'em. Maybe not you they're firing at. Your own little area might seem dead as a door nail, then you get the order to get up and move on, and then you suddenly bloody well spot 'em. You might start firing, or it might be your mates start firing, you don't know, it's all done instinctively, and then it seems everyone is firing all round you and it lasts perhaps only ten minutes, and then suddenly up goes their hands, once again, they want to pack it in. I remember we eventually came to what I presume to be the top of Mont Pincon, because we got the order to dig. It was pitch-dark, and my own particular mate of that time, poor chap, had been plagued with boils. In bloody agony with 'em, he was absolutely wore out. I knew we had to dig, I tried to get him to do his share, for it takes two of you, but he was absolutely beat. Somehow I dug this bloody trench, don't know how deep it was. Must 'ave been 2 or 3 o'clock in the morning then, very quiet, occasional shell, and you could distinctly 'ear Germans talking. Wasn't until next day that we were told, as we were digging in on one side, they were digging in on the other. But they found we were so close on top of 'em that they decided to get off home. We couldn't get no tanks up there."

Mostly, there was no tank support for the infantry; those that did attempt the hill, which was 1,200 feet high, were from 13/18 Hussars. "We went at night into the German lines," said Raymond Arthur Frank Hill, a Sherman gunner of the Hussars. "We took off into the blue, driving into the dark, told to prepare for anything. It was close wooded country and we saw and heard little. Normally, we felt comparatively safe, compared to infantry, but not in this position. In general, we couldn't hear much, all speech done on intercom and a 400 h.p. engine belting away. A bloke would get out of a slit trench to yell at you there was an m.g. over there. But you couldn't hear. We were frightened of the ditches along the roads, and bazooka teams in them. If attacking along a road, the infantry would stay parallel with the tank, and protect us from bazookas, while we fired with both m.gs. at the trees and everything else in sight, to protect the infantry who were protecting us. We felt reasonably safe, if we had infantry beside us; if not, then just naked. Now, we were south of Mont Pincon, virtually surrounded, but getting around the back of it. The tank I was in got bogged down, nearly to the top of its tracks. Two other tanks had gone on ahead, we heard firing and one came back. The one that didn't, two of the crew, you could have scooped 'em up and put 'em in a blanket. In a tank, you were not so vulnerable as infantry, as long as you weren't in the tank that was leading. Our serjeant-major was killed that night; he was in charge of the lorries and so on carrying the petrol, ammo and diesel supplies; they were vulnerable to shellfire."

As well as 5 Wilts, part of 4 Wilts also reached the top that night. J. Jones, a Battalion H.Q. signaller, was attached to a rifle company on this occasion, with an H.Q. wireless set. The company commander was new, a reinforcement. First he had them set up a machine-gun where it was promptly knocked out by the tanks of 13/18 Hussars, then when the H.Q. set went dud, he said it was the battery, and very bravely went back in a carrier to get a spare. Unfortunately, the battery he brought back was for the ' 38 ' set used by the rifle platoons, and would not fit the larger H.Q. set. So they were out of touch with Battalion. The officer set off for H.Q. again, and returned with an order to withdraw, as they were surrounded. " While we were preparing to make for the road," said Jones, " we saw two shadows leap over the skyline, behind us and to our right, then dive into a slit trench and begin to fire tracer bursts across the field. We moved carefully for the road, spread out. Suddenly, an enemy machine-gun opened up, the company commander and several others fell, and blue sparks flew from the bullets hitting the road as we threw ourselves into a hedge and then jumped into a stream. As we crawled on, we could hear German voices in the woods, and the sound of digging, and how we managed to find our way back is something of a mystery to me. Due to the casualties in this action the rifle companies were amalgamated, and I lost my job, returning to H.Q." In the morning, when 5 Wilts re-organised, they had two rifle companies left.

The third battalion of 129 Infantry Brigade, 4 Somerset Light Infantry, had been in reserve to 4th and 5th Wilts on the first day, 5 August. 30 Corps, to which 43 Wessex Division belonged, had just changed hands—Lieutenant-General B. G. Horrocks, still convalescent from a serious wound received in Africa the previous year, had taken over on 4 August. Presumably, he is the target of various barbed remarks in the divisional history, concerning ' timetables ' which might have been possible in the desert, but were not applicable in present circumstances. In any event, 4 Somersets went forward to the attack on the morning of 6 August, together with the survivors of 5 Wilts. In front of the mountain at this point ran a stream which had to be crossed before the battalion could start up the slope. From the point of view of Corporal D. B. Jones, of Bristol, there was a field in front, sloping down to the stream, and a bridge over it half left. His platoon was to assault right of the bridge. Another platoon, with Captain Scammel, was to assault left of the bridge. And that, as far as they were concerned, was it: a two platoon attack. What everyone else was doing, they knew not.

"As we went forward, quick, L/Corporal Hooley was hit in the shoulder," said Jones. " He tumbled over like a rag-doll, spinning backwards and to the right. I stopped running and had a look. There was a hole in the muscle at the top of his right shoulder. 'You've got a good one there, Jim. Grab your rifle and get back.' He did, and was off like a jack rabbit. Then I started running to catch up with the rest of my platoon, and heard an explosion as a British SP gun hit a mine on the bridge, blocking it, just as Jerry wanted. Previously, we had reccied that bridge and found it clear of mines; what Jerry had done must have been to deliberately let us have a look first, then get really ready for us. We went on over the stream, and up the hill to a hedgerow which was in line with a farm over on our left—and that was the objective of the other platoon. I brought my section into line on the right of our platoon, where there was a bank some 3 or 4 feet high at the hedge. Good cover for us; nasty for our tanks to go over, because they'd expose their bellies for a second or two. That was all the time the German panzer grenadiers would want; they were good soldiers, very good at that sort of thing. Now L/Corporal Moore on my left was signalling that he'd spotted something suspicious, and I had to do something. So I cradled my captured Schmeisser, and rose up to my knees, blasting, determined to be firing at the moment I put my head up. As I rose to my feet, blazing away, I found myself looking down a Spandau barrel, poking me in the eye, as if for inspection. But there was no Jerry there; they deserted this gun and another we also found on the left. I had a look through the sights and found it was on fixed lines, aimed at the hedge we'd started from, but a dip in the group hid our further advance. They'd just had time to hit Hooley before we disappeared; then they'd run for it.

"I opened up with our Spandau on another Spandau in the farm on our left. That made them keep their heads down. We couldn't actually see them, just the smoke haze from the weapon pit; but it stopped firing, so I supposed I'd got him. However, the firing of our Spandau brought fire on us from our own side, probably from our own Company. These new-fangled methods like radio don't do the trick. By the time the message has got to the troops it's meant for, it's out-of-date. Antiquated signalling methods—like flags—would have saved time. So what I did was to stick a bayoneted rifle into the ground and put a British tin hat on top of it—and that did the trick. After that, we settled down to a long-drawn-out cig-smoking campaign, I got rid of 60 fag ends; the butts are probably still there. Queer position; just couldn't do anything, couldn't go on with just 16 men. Jerry policy was to inflict casualties, then run away to fight another day. I'd thought they'd crack before we did. Seemed they'd a guilty conscience, made excuses. When we searched POWs, pretty forcibly, saying: 'What do you think of Hitler now, eh?' they'd reply: 'Hitler kaput.'

" We were there for about six hours, and during this time the Germans counter-attacked twice to get those two m.gs. They crawled across the potato field in front, and from our flank near a gate, until they were close enough to hurl grenades—one blew my tin hat off. They used grenades, because we were behind a bank and anyone with a sub-machine-gun would have to come through that hedge and expose himself; they didn't want to do that. Also during this time, our own people on the left tried twice to get that farmhouse, and so help us. The first attack was led by Captain Stewart: he was found afterwards inside it, with his batman and nine Germans, the lot being dead. We presumed he'd attacked more or less alone. Captain Scammel led the second attempt, and tried very hard, but as they went through the orchard of the farm, he was so badly hit in the leg that the bone showed through. By now, we were down to about half strength: five able-bodied, four badly wounded, ten slightly wounded. Eventually, the point was reached where German resistance was breaking, but our platoon was out of ammunition and the seriously wounded men urgently needed medical attention. I gave the order to withdraw, and chancing a shot in the back, we put the badly hurt men over our shoulders and began to crawl. We'd reached the point when we couldn't care less whether we were bloody blown up, or shot, or not. Back on the start line, I reported to the battalion commander, and complained about the lack of tanks, which are the answer to m.g. positions. He said it was difficult to use them here. However, the tank commanders eventually found the correct terrain to advance up the hill. This then put the enemy in full retreat."

A platoon at full strength is about three dozen men; this one had been cut down to five effectives. 5 Wilts, who had been cut down to two full-strength rifle companies, had also gone up that hill in the morning with 4 Somersets. But, shattered by their experiences of the previous day, they had at first refused to go beyond the stream, the men lying down in the water for cover. Their C.O., Lieutenant-Colonel J. H. C. Pearson, had got out of his armoured carrier and walked defiantly across the bridge over the stream, swinging a walking stick, and with a red rose in his hat. Of course, he fell; but the men got up out of the stream and went forward. Then they came under more intense fire, and stuck again. By now, there were 60 left out of 800.[1]

If 'Dickie's Bridge' had been the start of the break-out from Caumont, the turning point was the capture of the summit of Mont Pincon on the evening of 6 August; and again, it was a handful of men and vehicles who acted in the right place at the right time. Most of 13/18 Hussars were pinned down with the Wiltshires, by fire directed from the top, but two Troops from A Squadron found a way, and seven Shermans reached the summit, occupying it in conjunction with the Germans. Trooper S. F. Hitchcox wrote home about this epic action: he stated that his troop was the first to reach the summit, and that they had a wonderful view of France from there. That, of course, was precisely why the place was so important. Normandy was the story of an advance from one set of commanding heights to the next; but Mont Pincon was the highest of all. By 7 August, most of it was firmly held, a German counter-attack being rumoured to have lost direction in a fog which came down suddenly. And on 8 August, an officer of 7 S.L.I. was watching 7 Armoured Division's tanks crawling round the base of the massif, to initiate the next phase of the advance, when he heard a voice asking for the Corps Commander. "Good God, you don't expect to find him this far forward, do you?" he replied, and found himself talking to a major-general. Lieutenant-General Horrocks was in fact on Mont Pincon, having just 'bowler-hatted' three of the most senior officers of the armoured division now at his feet, and was personally putting units 'in the picture'. It paid handsome dividends in morale, even if they didn't believe a word of it. None of the

[1] The best description of 5 Wilts at Mont Pincon is in Alexander Baron's *From the City, From the Plough*, a novel, written as fiction, but factually by far the best thing ever done on the Normandy campaign: few of the factual books are really satisfying, because they record merely the facts that don't matter, the chess-game side of war.

13/18 Hussars did, when Horrocks got around to them. "He told us", said Hill, "that the next time we moved, we'd be doing 60 miles a day. We laughed, but he was right. In a few weeks more, we were in Belgium."

* * *

Mont Pincon taken, new battles had broken open in succession, from right to left: one, the Orne Bridgehead; two, the Falaise road. While these were opening, the Wessex and their supporting tanks of 8th Armoured Brigade were moving forward to the Orne also, which on their front was much further away. During this advance, Hill's tank was knocked out for the first time, with a snapped track. It did not brew, and the remaining tanks instantly put paid to the argumentative anti-tank gun. There had been a great change in the Hussars, since they had landed on D-Day, two months ago. "We had become experienced," said Hill. "We wouldn't dream of doing things we'd done earlier; we were definitely more efficient; now, I think, we had pride in the Regiment and in what it had actually done. Of course, we still felt that the only way to get out of the Army was to beat the Germans; our stomachs still turned over before action; and if we were told to go back for a rest, then there was a reprieved, 'I'm in the clear for a few days' feeling. I remember an infantryman, a bullet from my m.g. hit him in the arm; he was happy, he came over and thanked me."

"The next battle I remember going to was the River Orne," said Bill Biles. "We went up to this on a beautiful day, riding on tanks. Then, in a large cornfield, we got off the tanks as there was firing all round us and we couldn't see where it was coming from. I was walking behind the tank wondering what the hell we were firing at and who was firing at us, when suddenly we stumbled across the Germans in their trenches: young, unshaven, well-built, badly shocked, glad to get out of it. I think I told 'em, 'Get off out of it, back where the others are going', and pointed, for by this time there was scores of German soldiers with their hands up, trooping back the way we had come. I still didn't know really what was going on. Most of the others were just going forward like a lot of sheep, jumping over any dead or wounded. Then I noticed a bloody big gun poking through the top of a hedge. It wasn't firing, but I knew it wasn't one of ours. I didn't know what to do, but knew I should do something. Then I remembered: at back of our tanks was a buzzer; press it, and you could speak by phone to the occupants. I ran up to the tank and I couldn't for love or money see where this bloody buzzer was. Quite by chance, I stumbled on it, the turret opened, and out poked a young serjeant.

'What's up, me ole mate?'

'Look, f-----g great gun over there, don't know what you want to do about it'.

'Thanks, pal, I'll get 'im.'

"He put his head down, closed the turret, the tank made straight for the gun, went right through the hedge, over the gun, all the time firing m.g. bullets. Next thing, I saw half-a-dozen Germans running for dear life. I was wondering when we'd reach this River Orne. I was told we'd already crossed it, but I couldn't remember seeing it." By this time, as Biles remembered it, his company had lost fifteen men through self-inflicted wounds. One of them was a battle-experienced man from the Desert Army to whom, at first, everyone looked up. Then he developed a peculiar habit of diving in on top of someone else in a slit trench, as the shells arrived, and then jumping up excitedly: "Christ, that one was only over there, Bill!" After some weeks, he came over to Biles and said: "I'm going over to see Tom. Take your Sten gun, mate, that all right?" Then there was a shout: "Hey, Bill, your mate went and shot himself with your gun." Half-an-hour later, he came up to Biles, hand bandaged and blood seeping through. "There was I, sitting with me hand on the end of the Sten gun; I banged it, and this is what I got. Well, cheerio, I don't know if I'll see you again."

"No," said Biles bitterly, "I don't suppose you bloody well will, you're out of it."

*　　*　　*

Eastward of 43rd Wessex were 7th Armoured and 50 Div; eastward again, with orders to establish a bridgehead across the Orne at the nearest point, was 59 Staffordshire Division. By the evening of 6 August, the day Mont Pincon fell, 59 Div were about to make an assault crossing of the River Orne. By that day, the infantry brigade of 7th Armoured had been virtually used up; the worst hit battalion being 1/6th Queens. As the four rifle companies trudged forward that day, one only was respectable, numbering 55 men, approximately half-strength. There were 40 men in the next company, 15 in the next, and a pathetic little group of 8 men (not even a section) represented the last company. 59 Div was now advancing to the same fate. When the roll call was made, there were to be six, seven, or even perhaps fifteen men left out of each one hundred.

6 North Staffs, the regiment with which Lieutenant John F. Brown was serving as an anti-tank gun officer of the support company, had fought at Caen on 7 July, and after that battle been transferred to the front opposite Villers Bocage. On 16 July, they had put in a very successful attack on Haut des Forges, capturing 290 Germans for the loss of 32 men. From then on, the front was static, but they lost heavily in patrol actions, capturing only one prisoner, who trod on a mine on the way back; that cost, not only the prisoner, but eleven men from the patrol, killed and wounded. But by 4 August, the static front was no more; opposed only by mines, boobytraps, and demolitions, they swept forward to Villers Bocage, scene of the defeat of 7 Armoured Div in mid-June. At 7.30 p.m. on 6 August, the rifle companies made an assault crossing of the Orne, during the night the sappers built a bridge, and on the morning of 7 August, Lieutenant Brown went forward to get his anti-tank guns across.

"As I crossed the bridge, shells began falling in the river alongside, sending up high spouts of water," he said. "One of my guns was knocked out and the towing vehicle set on fire. The rest of us pressed on across the bridge to the far bank. A carrier in front was burning furiously, sending up a high pillar of black smoke, and slewed right across the narrow track, effectively blocking it. I managed to get my guns across one by one, without further loss, but the next problem was to deploy them. I had given each gun commander a pre-arranged position based on the assumed locations of the rifle companies, but when I reached the far bank I discovered that the two forward companies no longer existed as such. The remnants had been pushed back to join the remains of a company holding the immediate area of the bridge. I positioned one gun to cover the bridge approaches, then led the others up the track past the burning carrier and dispersed them in a field on the right. A counter-attack by an S.S. Division, with Tiger tanks, came in at this moment. I was anxious to get the guns properly deployed against the tanks, so set off for Battalion H.Q. on the left, taking an N.C.O. from each crew. On the way, we came up against a Spandau post in a copse; it had been hit by our own mortars, and we found only one machine-gunner alive. He was severely injured about the legs, unable to move. His number two was face-downwards with a wound in the middle of his back the size of a tea-plate, and covered by a seething mass of black flies. We disarmed the badly wounded survivor, and despite his urgent cries of 'Kamerad! Kamerad!' one of the N.C.Os. was anxious to finish him off. He was a typical blonde German youngster, not much more than eighteen, and in no fit state to do us any more harm, so we made him as comfortable as possible and continued towards Battalion H.Q.

"I came across the R.S.M. in a slit trench and asked him where I could find the C.O. He started to get up to direct me, then I saw him clutch both hands to his head. At the same instant, I found myself on my back staring up at the clear blue sky. I was shivering with shock, and my right leg hurt badly. The others who had been with me were scattered around, and all appeared to be dead; but one in fact was only unconscious. I turned on my side and dragged myself to the nearest bit of cover. I remember very little after that, just occasional bits of consciousness: shells falling, then someone giving me a cigarette, then an agonising journey back over the bridge in a jeep. I had a broken leg and thigh, from a shell or mortar burst, no idea which; and there was no splinting, the broken leg just flapped about; there was a German underneath me, also with leg wounds, in the same state. The R.A.P. was in a house on the far side of the bridge, an M.O. diving out of it between shellbursts to give injections, then diving back again. Actually, all this was in the middle of the German counter-attack, as I learnt later. Any shift of my foot hurt, but there seemed to be no blood. I was in a tented hospital at Bayeux the same day, and within minutes was on the table, being operated on. The last thing I remember for a long time was the mask coming down on my face." Against continuous counter-attacks, so numerous that no one could remember how many, the Battalion held its position, "but matters could easily have gone the other way." By 9 August, 6 North Staffs was reduced more or less to Battalion H.Q. and D Company; A, B, and C Companies were "in skeleton only", according to the War Diary. 202 men were dead, wounded, or missing. There were no replacements. On 12 August, news came of the impending break-up of the Division, to provide other, equally decimated divisions with reinforcements. Both armies were being burned away in the fires of Normandy, and now the question was: would there be enough men left to make sure and decisive the impending victory?

The holding of the precarious Orne Bridgehead, however, was primarily due to "the magnificent shooting of the artillery", according to 6 North Staffs war diary. A Gunner Officer wrote of "the physical effort of firing 1,000 rounds a gun a day during the battle. This was done for two days running, but has not often occurred, I believe, in the history of war. It was necessary to pour water over the guns the whole time to keep them from melting. I remember being so tired that I slept through the unloading of surplus bombs by a returning wounded Fortress on the next-door Troop. Definitely, it is superiority of fire power, not accuracy, that counts. Troop and Battery targets were unheard of. Regiment was the smallest effective unit and in static positions we used such a concentration on such a small area that it is incredible to think of. I have seen Battleships, Cruisers, Destroyers, Superheavies, Mediums, Heavy A.A., Light A.A., and Field guns all pour shells as hard as they can into one field for five minutes. The particular party I am thinking of had over 500 Field guns in that square of 600 yards, so you can imagine what it was like with all the others in, too. When synchronisation is perfect, first you have an ordinary field, maybe full of Jerry dug-outs and lined with Tigers; you look at your watch and for Time on Target; a roar and the area boils for half a minute; after that, you can see nothing, and you proceed on your way knowing that that field at least will not molest you. You don't, of course, go across it, as all it consists of is several feet of loose earth."

CHAPTER TWENTY-ONE

'THE MAD CHARGE'

The Battle for the Falaise Road: 'Totalise' ('Down the Corridor') and 'Tractable' ('The Mad Charge') 7 to 15 August

On 4 August, Flight Lieutenant Linacre went to Troissy-St. Maximim, 20 miles north-east of Paris. The Squadron's previous show had been an army support effort on 30 July, rendered abortive by 10/10ths cloud. This one was a fringe target for Normandy, to hit storage caves for V-weapons. Not much opposition to be expected, they were told. The three Pathfinder aircraft came roaring in first, leading the gaggle. They were not quite in the right order—the Deputy Master Bomber was up in front, followed by the Visual Backer-up aircraft flown by Squadron Leader 'Basil' Bazalgette, followed by Linacre in the Master Bomber's aircraft. There were not many guns opposing them, but they were heavy pieces and dead accurate. The Deputy Master Bomber went first. There was a bang, and he was hit; the tail came off, and the aircraft went down, drifting like a leaf, turning over and upside down. Obviously, no one was going to get out of that one. Then 'Basil' caught fire. "He was really burning," said Linacre, " but we saw him fly on and drop his bombs on the target; then he veered off, lost height, and we saw two parachutes open." Four men out of the seven actually got out, with the aircraft breaking up in the air. One of those who jumped saw an engine cowling fall off and flutter down after him, actually hitting him as it went past. The three still in the Lancaster were ' Basil,' one dead man, and a chap who had lost an arm and was refusing to jump. 'Basil' stayed with the aircraft until it blew up, killing them all, and was awarded a posthumous Victoria Cross on the grounds that his motive must have been to avoid letting the bomber crash into the village of Senantes. Linacre doubted this. It was far more likely he had thought 'I can't leave poor old Charlie', and tried to put it down in order to save his friend's life. "Taking risks for a friend is conceivable, in fact you can't

leave him," said Linacre, " but not for any bod you don't know."
In three weeks, the four men who had got out were back with
the Squadron; they had gone into hiding with the French and
been liberated by the armies advancing helter-skelter out of
Normandy.

Three days later, on 7 August, they were airborne at 2140 in
support of 21 Army Group, marking up for over 1,000 aircraft
over the Falaise road just south of Caen. Their previous support
sorties had been massed daylights; this was a massed night raid.
The onus of marking was on the Army. The Germans, in similar
case, had got their front-line troops to mark their own positions
with coloured flash-lights; this was an advance on that. As they
roared over, Linacre could see the British and Canadian guns
firing coloured tracers in a distinct lane and putting down target
indicators both sides of the unbombed corridor through which
the troops were to race forward. The objective was Falaise, but
unexpectedly bitter resistance by the Germans made it in fact a
two-part operation: 'Totalise' and 'Tractable' to the planners,
'Down the Corridor' and the 'Mad Charge' to the troops. The
general plan of 'Totalise' was for two columns of armour and
armoured infantry to roar straight through the enemy front by
night, on both sides of the Falaise road, covered on the flanks by
a 1,000 bomber raid. Through the gap they made, next day
would pour two armoured divisions—4th Canadian and 1st
Polish. The use of tanks by night was not entirely unorthodox:
Horrocks, commanding 30 Corps, and Bittrich, commanding II
S.S. Panzer Corps, both favoured it; but it shook most tank men,
including those in Gariepy's unit, who had actually to carry it
out. Tanks at night are very vulnerable to infantry and the
searchlights which were to reflect their beams off the clouds and
so provide a kind of moonlight, turned the night landscape,
blind with bomb dust, into a pattern of nightmare shapes; made
the supporting infantry hard to see in the shadows and other
times lit them up starkly. The use of armoured and tracked personnel carriers for infantry was not entirely unorthodox either—
General Bittrich's II S.S. Panzer Corps had numbers of them,
for instance. But the British and Canadians had had none up to
now, in spite of the fact that Major-General Fuller had been
advocating their use for some twenty years. Therefore, some were

borrowed from the Americans, but the majority were improvised from the S.P. gun known as the 'Priest'. The gun was taken out, and room made for infantrymen, the resulting vehicles being dubbed 'Unfrocked Priests' or 'Holy Rollers'. With the leading armour were to go 'flail' tanks for minefield clearance.

The basic concept was to eliminate the slow, bloody advance of infantry and tanks to a position from which the defenders would, with equal lack of speed, withdraw. Instead, the armour and armoured infantry, cloaked by night, were to rush through the defences, without stopping to fight them, and go hell-bent for the rear. This, it was thought, would cause the front behind them to offer little resistance to the next onrush, in daylight, of two complete armoured divisions, advancing under yet another bomb carpet. Additionally, this attack was timed to start immediately on the heels of the Orne Bridgehead offensive, which in turn followed Mont Pincon; and a battle group of 12th S.S. had in fact been sent to the Orne.

"After the bombing our column pushed ahead in this greatly feared action," said Gariepy. "It was such an easy one that we suffered absolutely no loss of tanks at all. After getting all keened up to fight hard, there was very little resistance and the objective taken in one of the easiest actions of the war." But this was only the first phase, carried out by experienced units. The second phase, the onrush of two brand-new armoured divisions in daylight, went less well. To start with, they were bombed on the start-line, the 51st Highland Division sharing in the rain of misplaced explosives. 60 men were killed, 300 were wounded, a number of guns were destroyed, and a great quantity of ammunition went up, as 638 bombers of the U.S. 8th Air Force roared over, having taken on the job at short notice. "I watched like all the others for the bomb sticks to drop on Jerry," said Gariepy, "when we suddenly realised that they were coming straight at us. Our Verey light recognition signals made no difference; the ground was dry and dusty, and after the first bomb hit the whole area was just a shambles—fires, dust, and smoke made the Verey lights ineffective. To add to the confusion, I saw Jerry firing various coloured lights also. To make things worse, we carried out our attack just the same, immediately the last bomb had dropped on us, so the enemy was fresh from a very spectacular show and must have wondered at the methods used by our commanders to induce us to fight."

Various stories circulated to explain it: one was that a Fortress had jettisoned owing to fire in the bomb-bay and the rest had thought he knew best what the target was. Something like this had in fact happened on the first, abortive day of Cobra, 24 July, when the 8th Air Force killed 25 and wounded 131 men of the American 30th Division; but it had happened again the next day, 25 July, when 8th Air Force killed 111 American soldiers and wounded 490, plus a number of war correspondents and official observers. And now they had done it again, to the Canadians, the Poles, and the Highlanders. Some Germans were killed, too, because in fact the bombs showered down over a wide area, hardly any of them on target. On their heels, a lone Messerschmitt sneaked in and sprayed an ammunition dump, with good results. From this day's work sprang the German gibe: "When the Luftwaffe comes over, the Allies duck; when the R.A.F. comes over, the Germans duck; but when the Americans come over—everyone ducks!" The sarcasm would not have been so marked had it not been for that boast about being able to put a bomb in a barrel from 20,000 feet.

More important than the misplaced bombs were other, interlocking factors: the inexperience of the two attacking armoured divisions and the determined, efficient defence by 12th S.S., fighting to the end. The cynical summary at H.Q. First Canadian Army next day was noted in a private diary: "The Yanks have taken Le Mans, the Canadians are driving down to meet them. The Canadian Armoured Div has lost 1 tank; the Polish Armoured Div went bald-headed for the 12 S.S. Panzers dug-in in wooded country, and lost 30 tanks. One of the German inf divs is proceeding in large numbers in a northerly direction (i.e., to the POW cages). The current plan is for the Canadians and Yanks to meet at Falaise, enclosing the German 7th Army in a pocket and destroying it. Should this be a one hundred per cent. success, the war is over. The rest will be a motor tour into Germany. It has not been laid on who is to take Falaise; it depends on the progress the two pincer arms can achieve. The Canadians are driving down from the North, the Yanks are coming up to Argentan from the South. In Brittany, the Yanks are fanning out for the ports, but these have not fallen yet. The German 15th Army, not a very good one, is moving down from the Pas de Calais."

As this was being written, on 9 August, 4 Canadian Armoured was trying to make up for its initial laggard progress by making the opposite mistake. Having failed to take risks at the outset, when it was vital to do so, and before 12th S.S. could possibly have re-grouped in time to stop them, they made a daring, lightning night march, lost the way, captured the wrong hill, were counter-attacked by 12th S.S., who, assisted by Allied fighter-bombers, drove them off it, and retired with the loss, to the British Columbia Regiment, of 47 tanks in one day. The Canadian Army had advanced eight miles towards Falaise, precisely half the distance; there was still another eight miles to go. A series of orthodox attacks broke down, with heavy casualties; therefore another unorthodox operation was planned—' Tractable ', which might be called Totalise by daylight.

However, the admirable summary of the situation, as seen at the time at General Crerar's headquarters, describes and dates precisely the gathering together of factors at the decisive moment of the Normandy battle. Two factors only are omitted. The first, the German armoured counter-attack against Mortain which, having been launched on 6 August, was stale news by the 9th. Hitler had, in effect, thrust the head of his armies into a noose; and the Canadians had seen the chance to tighten it, with possibly fatal results. It was true: if the German Army could be, not merely decimated but destroyed at Falaise, the war was over. And this was the intention at Canadian Army. But General Bradley did not see it this way, and this was not then known. The Americans were aiming for a much wider encirclement on the Seine, and their main forces (apart from those in Brittany) were directed east in the Paris direction, and only minor forces were sent to sweep left and up to the north towards Argentan; Bradley was in fact adhering to the original plan of a wide left-wheel and a tank battle in front of the Seine. This was fatal because, although the salient driven into the Allied lines by the westward drive for Mortain looked vulnerable on the map, it contained the bulk of the German armour which had made the drive—two Panzer Groups. It would take more than a nut-cracker to encircle, let alone destroy, that formidable force. It is perfectly possible for half-a-dozen men to encircle an enraged rhinoceros, but the encirclement by itself does not dispose of the beast.

On 10 August the U.S.A.A.F. put on a comic turn over the beachhead which must have had the largest audience of any air display in history—over a million. A four-engined Liberator, prematurely abandoned and out of control, performed stunt aerobatics for quarter of an hour before being shot down by R.A.F. Spitfires. While the parachutes drifted slowly earthward, the giant bomber dived, pulled up in a climbing turn, and fell off the top into a roaring dive, repeating this performance in full view of the Canadian, British and German armies until finally the fighters tore in with cannon and m.gs. blazing. The Liberator flicked up on its tail, then fell away in a slow spin to port, white smoke streaming from the starboard inner, and vanished from Canadian sight behind trees to the north. Particularly during an advance, control of the air could be a mixed blessing, in spite of the careful bomb lines drawn and redrawn on the great headquarters' maps. Not exceptional, but typical, was the bomb-reception record of the Régiment de la Chaudière, attacked on 17 July by the Luftwaffe, on 8 August by the U.S.A.A.F., on 14 August by the R.A.F., and on 15 August by the U.S.A.A.F. again. Of these four attacks, incomparably the most effective was that of the Royal Air Force. It was delivered in support of ' Tractable ' on 14 August.

Aptly, the troops called it ' The Mad Charge '. It was another ' Goodwood ', but coldly deliberate. Whereas the British had stumbled by accident on a front held in depth by anti-tank guns and 88s, the Canadians knew they were there. They planned to go through, nevertheless, blinding the guns with smoke and ordering the armour not to engage them except on the move. There were 160 tanks in the first wave, 90 tanks in the second; plus the armoured infantry carriers, the ' Holy Rollers ', now dubbed ' Kangaroos ', because each had ten men in its pouch. Their flanks would be protected by a rain of smoke and high explosive and the bombing attack would be simultaneous with the advance, giving the Germans little time in which to recover. " This is perhaps the only time in the war on the western front where eight squadrons of tanks, followed by four more squadrons, were to go roaring across country to overwhelm a reported impregnable anti-tank gun screen by sheer weight of numbers," said Serjeant Gariepy, who, by accident, was soon to find himself ' point ' tank of the whole damned advance.

"We, the crew commanders, knew then that many of us would not make it; it was inconceivable, in view of these tremendous defences. Each of us looked at the other, wondering: How many? Who? At the start of a big push, everyone is afraid, because we know some of us will get it, but once the move is begun we are then too busy to be afraid. There seemed to be tanks as far as the eye could see, and behind them were our 'little friends' in their Kangaroos. At precisely 1200 hours, the ' Mad Charge' began. Those who were there and lived through it will always remember the sight. It was a beautiful sunny day, and this great column of armour moving through fields of waving grain like eerie avenging centaurs straight from hell. The artillery began to fire marker shells for the bombers, and a few minutes after, began laying a tremendous smoke screen; and at 1142 hours, wireless silence was broken by the command ' Move now.' As the armoured brigades began rolling to the start line, the bombers, sweeping low over the charging tanks, attacked the valley for a quarter of an hour. The smokescreen supposed to blind the enemy turned out to be a thick dense mist in the path of our advance, soon supplemented by the dust clouds created by the terrific bombing; the area was ' vision zero'. Very little could be done to keep direction, except by aiming the tank ' at the sun '. The German gunners had been alerted beforehand because an officer had been captured (on the evening of 13 August) with the plans of the attack on him; they knew the main axis of our advance exactly and kept playing merry old hell with us. The only reason why our casualties were not very much higher, is that the smog obscured us to them as much as it obscured them to us. Speed, nothing but speed, and on we went, crashing through obstacles at 20 to 25 m.p.h., very rough inside a tank going cross country, and each hedge hid from four to six anti-tank guns, pointed right at us, waiting.

"Only, by then there was no line of frontage, owing to the dust and smoke. We just barged ahead, some of the tanks appeared to be going on at crazy angles, and in the confusion I did not know who was right and who was wrong; I just kept charging 'at the sun', blasting everything large enough to hide a field gun, and taking a terrible whipping in the turret of the bucking 32-ton monster. Enemy infantry was scarce, most of those we saw were running, in all probability they were really gun crews seeking refuge. Our guns, co-axial and co-driver's Browning, were firing constantly; the pace was hot, the ground rugged; I had to brace myself, look out for direction, look out for 'priority' targets, mostly 88s (I was credited with four). This went on for what seemed hours, till we finally reached a creek. This was the 'river' we had been told about, the Laison; in Europe many Canadians got fooled by this, for in Canada some of these so-called rivers would not have been given the title of 'ditch'. However, this was the Laison, which we had to cross, and which intelligence had told us was not an obstacle. But it was a serious tank trap, not because of width and depth, but because of its muddy bed. Some of the tanks had already been bogged, others were looking for a better crossing point, and the tremendous clouds of dust and burning smoke all round made us realise that either we had lost our way or some of our flank tanks had lost theirs. I kept insisting I was aiming at the sun until I reached the high ground which was our eventual goal, and when we finally forded the river I was told that, owing to a swing we had become the 'point' squadron instead of the 'support' we were supposed to be. This came through on the air from my 'sun-ray', the squadron commander, urging us to press on at all cost, and this was the last signal I received, for my set was hit by a piece of shrapnel. A puff of smoke, and that was that, no more contact by radio. I asked my crew how they fared (the shaking of the tank was breaking everything loose inside), they reported 'O.K.' so I told them, we are 'point' tank now, our 'little friends' depend on us to bring them home safe and sound, let's get rolling."

Back at HQ First Canadian Army, a staff officer was explaining that the attack for the high ground commanding Falaise had gone in an hour ago, as planned, and that he was having great competition with the B.B.C., who had already taken Chartres, Rennes, and Falaise. "If that's so, then I guess this morning's big effort will be an awful waste of time." (Two days later, 16 August, 3 British Div's Intelligence Summary solemnly recorded: "A rare honour has this day fallen to the Division. It has captured a town ahead of the B.B.C.")

As Gariepy drove on from the Laison, the engineer tanks, the AVREs, were already arriving with 'fascines' to lay across the river bed; and the infantry, protected by their armour, were driving straight through the German infantry (of two divisions newly brought from Norway), who were staying to fight it out, although the tanks were far in their rear. The Régiment de la Chaudière was on its way to Rouvres, on the Laison, the support company, with its heavy weapons, and all the transport, staying behind at St. Agan de Crasmesnil. At 1400, disaster struck them there. As Lancaster 'J for Johnny' came thundering over the top, with Linacre as bomb-aimer, on the last trip of his tour, he identified aiming point 21B, which was a wood with a lot of roads leading into it. "Wizard show", he wrote in his logbook, for his squadron had got one hundred per cent aiming-point pictures; but someone was badly off, for he could hear the Master Bomber 'doing his knut', shouting: "Keep off that one at the back; Keep it going forward!" And as the Lancaster came back, bombs gone, he could see a wood erupting yellow smoke, with odd reds popping out. Someone was shouting: "Look at that Auster!" Linacre himself didn't see it, but others did— a little three-seater artillery spotter going round in circles among the bomber stream at 6,000, firing red Verey lights. The mass of yellow was the support company of the Régiment de la Chaudière, and other Canadian units, showing the standard recognition colour which denoted friendly troops. The reds were being fired by Lieutenant E. M. G. Belfield, R.A., of 661 A.O.P. Squadron, who had taken off in his light aircraft to try to stop the bombing. But yellow and red were among the different target indicator colours being used by Bomber Command that day (unknown to the troops), and the more yellows and reds they let off, the more bombers they attracted. Lancaster after Lancaster came roaring in, 77 of them in all, killing and wounding nearly 400 men. "Not one vehicle, not one gun, not one tank was left undamaged," wrote the Chaudière historian. "The bombardment lasted from 1400 to 1530 hours, killing Captain J. L. A. Giguére and many soldiers; of two of them, not a shred remained for identification. It was an inferno; many men became insane. Two sections of the carrier platoon were wiped out, the truck containing the records was destroyed by fire." Twenty-five minutes after the bombardment ceased, the rifle companies of the Régiment, unstoppable behind their armour by the German infantry, were in Rouvres.

"In all it took less than half an hour for the tanks which survived the charge to reach the Laison," recorded the historian of 6 Armoured Regiment, "but the B Squadron charge, led by Major Gordon, originally in reserve, actually became the leading squadron when the other two deviated from their course." Serjeant Gariepy, with B Squadron, his radio out of action, soon found himself in a sticky situation. "I knew that shortly after the river crossing we were to make a right sweep (to Falaise), but I knew not exactly when. I did not want to begin rolling at a 90 degree angle in front of our own tanks, for in this dust and smoke we were sure to be clipped by our own ' bears ', so I only slightly veered to the right. This was a mistake, for, after a while, I found myself going away from the battle; some resistance still, but not the deadly accuracy we had met before. I had two choices: bear to the left again, or stop dead in my tracks. An immobile tank in action is a sure gonner, so to move on was preferable, although I was becoming more and more sceptical that we were going in the proper line of advance. The time was after 6 p.m., we had been going since noon, and then my gunner reported that our co-axial trigger was burnt out and that the Browning barrel was red hot from constant firing. I told them to carry on with the mechanically-operated trigger for the time being, we should find some friendly ' bears ' and do some maintenance. I moved cross-country to a small group of farms which looked a good place for this. Arriving there, I saw a German officer carrying a white flag. I warned my crew to hold fire and could see behind the officer several German soldiers, not showing any hostility.

"I jumped out of the tank, told my gunner to come on top with a Tommy gun, not to hesitate to shoot at the first signs of a fight, and approached the officer. He saluted me, I saluted back and asked for his firearm. He began talking, but I told him ' Nicht spraken Deutsch ', and he called an N.C.O. who spoke English. This N.C.O. told me that the Hauptmann had been waiting for us quite some time. I did not understand, but did not let on, just told the N.C.O. that all the officers and men were to come out from their cover and line-up, sitting down, in front of my tank. In the meantime, my gunner and radio operator had mounted a Browning on a tripod on top of the turret and were looking very business-like, and the Jerries were filing out in twos and threes from the rubble of the farm buildings. They would drop their rifles and sidearms in a pile and quietly come and sit in front of the tank in rows of four. I asked the Hauptmann how many men he had, and he replied 280.

" They were the remnants of a battery which had been abandoned for lack of transport. I told the Hauptmann that it was now too late to make the POW cage, we would have to remain in the open for the night and move on at first light. He was quite satisfied with this. There was no fight in these men, who were a mixture of French and Russian 'volunteers'. The six officers were Germans, and the Hauptmann, I learned, was a lawyer from Bremen. I established 'sentry' duty with my men, telling them to look as though General Crerar had sent us specially to pick them up; this was the impression they had, and I did not want them to realise that we were as lost as they were. My crew were much less nervous than I was; they were quite happy, eyeing 'souvenirs' such as Lugers, which I permitted them to take. I found the Hauptmann very calm and resigned. He asked if we were English, Polish, or something else, and was very happy when I replied we were Canadians, as he thought he would be sent to Canada as a POW. He said the afternoon attack was something he would never forget; he had never seen so many 'Yankee' tanks in all his life, as a matter of fact, he had never seen so many tanks even on parade. I would not encourage conversation with him, although he appeared eager to talk; I was afraid I might say something not quite right. In view of the 'shambles' which had preceded my getting lost, I was not too sure of the outcome of the battle and would not have been surprised if during the night the roles of jailers would be turned around. I knew that in the dark, with a tank that had no guns or radio, I would not stand a

chance. I told my radio operator, on the quiet, to simulate
contact with 'sun-ray' in the usual manner, although the wireless
was dead, so that they would think, though we were alone, our
whereabouts were known.

"During the night, small groups of enemy soldiers kept
walking in, and each group was told by the German officers they
must pile their weapons and join the others. When I asked
why some of these fellows were carrying weapons, if they wanted
to give up, the Hauptmann told me that if they were caught
roaming around without weapons by S.S. officers or N.C.O.'s, they
would be shot immediately. I asked what would happen if such
an officer or N.C.O. came upon this group. He replied that the
S.S. had decamped, leaving the remainder behind to hold as
long as they could. The night was long and fidgety, I allowed
only one of my men to sleep at a time, the others were on 'guard'
on top of the turret with the Browning pointed at the sleeping
Jerries. During the night we added 24 men to our group, which
made a total of 304 prisoners. At daylight I gave orders, loudly,
for my wireless operator to warn 'sun-ray' we were marching
the prisoners back in 20 minutes; and he made much ado about
it, bringing me the fictitious answer, '*OK, Roger, Out.*' I made
a fire of the piled weapons, pouring gasoline on them. That
brought comments from the officers. The Hauptmann, smiling,
said that such an act in their army at this time would bring
an instant field court martial. I told him that supplies were
plentiful in our ranks, and he replied that after seeing this
aggregation of tanks, he was sure we did not lack anything.

"The tank was started up with the gunner still on top with
the Browning, the driver in his seat, and the rest of the crew
with Tommy guns, walking on each side of the column. I walked
in the rear with the German officers, the tank covering us from
behind. My reasoning was, that since all was quiet we had
succeeded in our attack and every German in this sector was
still licking his wounds. I must admit I was scared; but defiantly
we moved ahead and after about four miles, I believe, we started
to see Bren carriers and a few scout cars; then a troop of a very
business-like recce outfit came charging on the column, not firing
but very ready to do so. Then we began to see a lot of our 'little
friends' and a multitude of burnt-out tanks; and a Major from

Brigade in a scout car asked where the prisoners had been collected. He laughed very loudly and said that surely I did not need any help, but gave me eight infantrymen; my crew were then able to embark back in the tank and felt better, they never did like walking (a loss of prestige for a tank man, especially when there are infantry around). Upon reaching the POW compound I was met by an interrogating officer who said he wanted to talk to me about the capture of these men, but knowing our standard orders were not to bother with prisoners, I felt a little reluctant to comply, so we quietly slipped away from the area. Then we could see the ravages of the advance—burnt-out tanks everywhere, from every squadron of the two armoured brigades; and enemy gun emplacements galore; we could not count them. At Regimental HQ I told the Intelligence Officer simply that we had laid low for the night, and did not tell him of the enemy we had captured.

"It was only much later, in Holland, that I was called to the CO's office. I marched in rather nervously, wondering where the hell I had made such a blunder as to be called before the 'old man'. Colonel White had a Brigade staff officer with him, and some documents. He asked me if this was my real rank and name. I assured him it was, and called on the Colonel to prove it, for I had known him years before the war, when I was a trooper in the Dragoons and he was a lieutenant in the Lord Strathcona Horse. The Colonel smiled and said this was true. I was preparing to defend myself as much as I could, when the Brigade officer retorted that apparently I did not like to give my name to everyone. I was puzzled but kept silent. He them asked me if, on the day of the 'Mad Charge', had I not broken away from the battle line and made for a farm? I replied: yes, this was true, but my tank being disabled and disarmed, I had to withdraw. Did you not, he continued, while there take on 342 prisoners of war and march them back to our rear lines? I replied that he was in error, the count of prisoners taken was only 280, the others, I explained, joined our happy group only later while marching back to our lines.

"Colonel White then said that it had been reported to him that a tank of the Hussars had been seen escorting some 300 prisoners, absolutely alone, from a position which at that time was beyond the boundaries of the line of advance. A troop of scout cars had then been despatched to the scene, to find one of our tanks apparently marching very quietly towards our lines with a Battalion of the enemy.

" I was told never to repeat the performance (of not reporting) or disciplinary action would be taken; and I was then handed the French Croix-de-Guerre and a citation signed by General Juin."

CHAPTER TWENTY-TWO

'THE CAULDRON'

The 15th of August was the worst day of my life.
Adolf Hitler.

Again and again I meet soldiers in the Department Eure who, as cyclists, do not keep their legs stiff when saluting. This is against orders, when the bicycle is freewheeling, and the journey is not uphill. I request that all units be informed.
Gollnitz, Oberst, District Commander, August, 1944.

The 'Mad Charge' of the Canadians to Falaise had not gained the high ground, but by 15 August, they were pressing in on the town. On a rocky height above the wreckage of the houses stood the great Norman castle, contemptuously shouldering aside the shellfire. The thunderous detonations of Canadian 25-pounder shells splintered the facings of the massive stonework, the livid yellow explosions leaping out sideways from the walls, shrouding them in rolling clouds of smoke and dust. The walls were pock-marked, that was all. Only where a screaming shell thunderclapped against a weak point, a window slit or an edge of the roof, did stonework shower down and a black hole gape. As a fortress the castle remained. The field guns of the 20th Century were impotent against it. In the rocky ravine at its foot flowed the stream where Arlette, the tanner's daughter, is said first to have caught the eye of Duke Robert the Bold, lord of Falaise. In 1027, in a room at the top of the castle, she gave birth to a male child whose name was William and whose destiny lay over the sea in England. Now, in 1944, after 900 years, the new nation he had forged had come back to the assault of his birthplace, not with a whistling storm of arrows, but under the thunderous scream of the diving Typhoons and the smoke trails of their speeding rockets. And of the field-grey defenders, at least half were kin to the Saxons he had conquered in England so long ago.

"On the night of 15 August we were marching in an unknown direction," recalled officer-cadet Kurt Misch of 12th S.S.

344

Panzer Grenadier Division. " During the night we suddenly saw Verey lights on three sides; we looked at each other meaningly —surrounded? Next day, we were sure. We tried to keep it from the men as long as possible. But they realised it as soon as the field kitchen did not turn up and the rations got smaller. Something new, unknown, takes possession of us. All the usual joking is silenced. We are all inwardly preoccupied, wondering how to meet the situation, as individuals. If it does not mean death, being taken prisoner will mean a long separation from home. We ' old ' ones stick together. Our chief leaves no doubts in our minds about the gravity of the situation, and I walk back from the conference deep in thought. The Verey lights hang like great signs in the heavens. The front lies beneath them in a breathless silence. Low-flying German planes drop rations, and a large container of chocolate lands near me. A nice surprise, and a greeting from the outside world. We have not yet been abandoned."

Caen had paid off at last. The bulk of the German forces in Normandy, consisting of 7th Army, Panzer Group West, and Panzer Group Eberbach, was concentrated in a small salient, sticking westward like a thumb; it had been driven even further west by Hitler's decision to counter-attack the Americans; and meanwhile, the Americans had torn through the thin front far to the south and were racing for the Seine and Paris. Two ' pockets ' were forming: one just south of Falaise, small and concentrated; one covering a huge area where mobile warfare, the blitzkrieg made famous by the Germans, was now in progress. The latter was the direct, planned result of the Caen battle; the former was a gift from Hitler, who would not allow his generals to fall back to the Seine in time, but on the contrary had ordered them to drive their armies still deeper into the trap. With the ' 20 July ' Trials now proceeding in Berlin, none dared disobey. Such was the tension and suspicion that, when Field Marshal von Kluge was making a personal reconnaissance of the rapidly developing encirclement and lost contact for most of the day with his own Headquarters, Hitler thought he was attempting to cross the lines to arrange the surrender of his forces.

As the Canadians fought their way down from the north

to Falaise and Trun, trying to seal the mouth of the 'pocket' with the bulk of the German forces still inside—and so end the war; then so did the pocket shrink, spewing out streams of vehicles and troops escaping eastward to the Seine. There was no question that a German disaster was impending; the question was—would it be decisive, a 'Stalingrad' in Normandy?

Already, in mid-August, the 'Resistance' was being activated, far away from Normandy, in anticipation of swift German collapse and rapid action on the lines of communication of their retreating forces. Even as distant as the Ardennes, on the Belgian border, three British agents were dropped with a radio set in order to tie-in Maquis operations with the 'blitzkrieg'. Although they were dropped in the wrong place, and lost their radio, they found that the Maquis group was an effective version of the largely mythical German 'fifth-column' of 1940. "The group we joined," said one of the agents, "were about 120 strong, armed youths in plain clothes, living in the woods, led by a regular French Colonel, a fine officer. I was with them for a fortnight and formed a high opinion of their patriotism and courage. Political considerations did not appear to be their motive, and there was no liaison with another group in the neighbourhood who were communists. Discipline and morale were remarkably high, considering the circumstances. They were operating in country favourable for guerillas, densely wooded, few roads. Armed with automatic weapons and a bazooka, they were capable of tip-and-run attacks against German columns using these roads. They operated on both sides of the Belgian frontier, and one of the regular visitors was a Belgian capuchin friar who brought us provisions. During this period the Germans made a concentrated attack on the group, which forced it to split in two. We had just started our midday meal. The first shot killed one of the outpost sentries, and before long the attacking force penetrated to within a hundred yards of our forest command post, which came under mortar fire. There was heavy firing, and casualties, on both sides, and our Colonel was wounded in the leg. Just when it seemed that we must be over-run, the German fire slackened, and then ceased. Presumably they had over-estimated our strength, for they broke off the engagement and withdrew, leaving their dead behind. We did

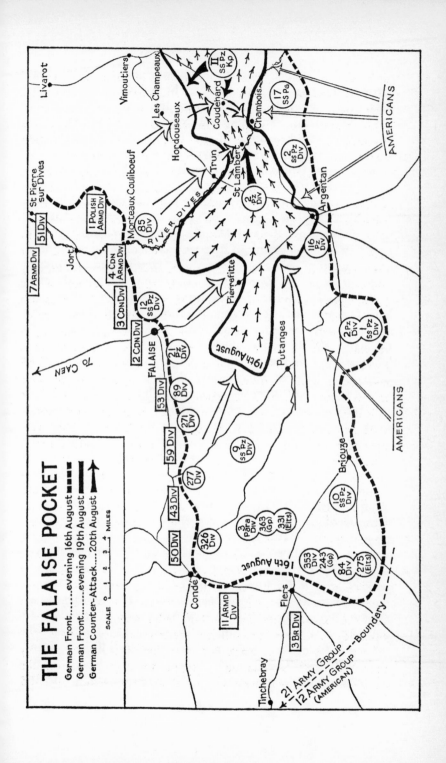

THE FALAISE POCKET

German Front......evening 16th August
German Front......evening 19th August
German Counter-Attack....20th August

SCALE 0 1 2 3 4 MILES

likewise, the Colonel limping on foot, one gravely wounded lad carried on an improvised stretcher; he was in great pain and died soon afterwards. We were now less than 50 strong, and it was not until later that we were rejoined by the other group of survivors who had been cut off. But the end was nearer than we thought and when, a few days later, we heard tanks moving along a forest lane, we were surprised to find that their crews were Americans."

In Normandy also, as the fighting began to move and become more open, and the Germans being pressed into the pocket still more disorganised, the real Maquis, waiting its chance, came to life. "In all the fighting to date we have had the most tremendous amount of co-operation from the Maquis," wrote a Gunner officer of 59 Div. "Especially in fast-moving ops, they do most of the mopping up for us, allowing us to get well ahead and not have to worry about our communications. To see them cycling about all over the place in red, white and blue armbands, with German rifles slung over their shoulders, is a wonderful sight. They are just as keen as the L.D.V. of '40, considerably more efficient, and better armed, both the efficiency and the arms gained at the expense of the Germans." The Germans noticed it, too, for even inside the pocket, packed with German troops, there were acts of sabotage. On 18 August, wrote Heinz Trautmann, of S.S. Heavy Tank Battalion 502, "the cauldron is closed. Everybody is depressed at H.Q. 'Panzer' Meyer is missing, after going out in his recce car. On the way to Trun, we are shelled and put our foot down for the next village, where we are halted by a road-block near the church—three-foot thick oaktrunks have been rolled across the road. As we get out and push them aside, two lads standing in the porch of the church watch us with interest." The Waffen S.S., Hitler's equivalent of Napoleon's Imperial Guard, which 'died but did not surrender', were still fighting, holding off the Canadians and Poles, but many units had already had enough. On 14 August, M. Guitter, a jeweller of Bois aux Veneurs, and his mother, an old lady of 68, together with two others, managed to negotiate the surrender of the 150 German troops in the village, incidentally saving the village.

"A common sight in these Normandy lanes are refugees," the

Gunner officer wrote home. "On bikes, in small carts, in big carts, on foot: all weighed down with what household goods they can carry, with the inevitable chicken poking its head out of a side pocket. They are amazingly cheerful folk, taking all their misfortunes with a stoicism worthy of the highest praise. More often than not, they have nothing to which to return, just a heap of smouldering desolation. There was a young French lad who begged us to take him with us to a town a few miles away where he had lived with his parents until the week before. They had sent him out to a farm for safety, but remained themselves. Little did he know that this particular town had been razed to the ground: hardly a wall above ground except those of the church, and not a civilian alive in the place. We thought it better not to tell him all that. He will find out soon enough." For there were French civilians trapped in the pocket, as well as the German Army. "We like the inhabitants to flee, because they block the roads and create a frightful problem for the Hun," an officer of 2 K.R.R.C. wrote home in a letter. The men in the Typhoons and Spitfires, and the men at the guns, hardly thought of it, death was so familiar now. "The pocket was terrific," wrote the Gunner. "Just a case of banging concentrated hell into an area packed with terrified Jerries."

Rolling through the chaos was a battle group led by the wounded General Freiherr von Lüttwitz, all that remained of the once-proud 2nd (Vienna) Panzer Division. "That night of 19 August, we heard our passport for escape from the cauldron," said Oberfeldwebel Hans Erich Braun. "It was, simply, 'Forward'. Forward with a mixed battle group of tanks, SP guns, flak and mounted artillery, scout cars, light tanks, and armoured troop carriers packed with Grenadiers, Paratroopers, and soldiers of all kinds of units. Forward through hell, but also towards the enemy, past the dead and the wounded. We had been tempered, like the steel plating of our tanks, and inside us now there was hardly any human feeling left. We were alive, but inside we were dead, numbed by watching the horrible scenes which rolled past on both sides, just like a film. The Grenadiers sitting on their vehicles cowered low, grasping their weapons and holding on to the wounded. Anyone dying on top of these rolling steel coffins was just pitched overboard, so that a living man could take his place. They were sitting behind their tank guns, their flak guns, behind their automatic weapons, with one thought in their minds—to destroy the enemy who would soon appear now, to be without mercy, just like him.

"The never-ending detonations—soldiers waving to us, begging for help—the dead, their faces screwed up still in agony—huddled everywhere in trenches and shelters, the officers and men who had lost their nerve—burning vehicles from which piercing screams could be heard—a soldier stumbling, holding back the intestines which were oozing from his abdomen—soldiers lying in their own blood—arms and legs torn off—others, driven crazy, crying, shouting, swearing, laughing hysterically—and the horses, some still harnessed to the shafts of their ruined wagons, appearing and disappearing in clouds of smoke and dust like ghosts—and the horses, again, screaming terribly, trying to escape the slaughter on the stumps of their hind legs. But also there were civilians lying by the roadside, loaded with personal belongings, often of no value at all, and still clinging to them in death. Close by a crossroads, caught by gunfire lay a group of men, women and children. Unforgettable, the staring gaze of their broken eyes and the grimaces of their pain-distorted faces. Destroyed prams and discarded dolls littered the terrible scene."

Night in the cauldron was almost lighter than day, lit by burning villages, blazing vehicles, and the muzzle-flashes of a thousand guns, the sheet-yellow flame of exploding shells. And by day, the fighters and fighter-bombers roamed above the pocket, hindered only by the drifting clouds of smoke. Wing Commander A. G. Page, D.S.O., D.F.C., flying a Spitfire out of D.11 airstrip, north of Bayeux, found the scene incredibly changed. Before this, he said "nothing moved on the German side of the lines, in contrast to the masses of vehicles milling about on our side; so we shot at anything, even Don Rs. on motor-cycles—I don't know how the Germans lasted as long as they did, it was a terrific demonstration of air power." The demonstration was even more conclusive over Falaise. "I went over the Falaise Gap at 200 feet," said Page, "and I saw a truck crew, sitting on the steps of a farmhouse, dejectedly looking at the burning wreckage of their vehicles in the road, so I shot them up as well." Karl Max Wietzorek, retreating with the Paratroopers from Vire towards Alencon, witnessed an attack on a packed supply column. For the Germans, the old days of blitzkrieg were over; most of the transport of the infantry divisions was horse-drawn, including the old-fashioned field kitchens. " The Jabos shot out of the clouds and fired right into the middle of the horse-drawn wagons," said Wietzorek. " Panic broke out. The horses tore loose and plunged into a ravine, the petrol tanks of the motor vehicles were blazing, soldiers were trampled to death by the stampeding horses. And into all this, the rockets screamed, hitting men and animals alike; a gigantic fireball of charred horses and charred soldiers; no room for heroics any more. We only had carbines and bayonets, against tanks and aircraft."

But, for the Allies, things were not so easy as the Germans imagined. The closing of the Falaise Gap was a battle, not an exercise; the door had not merely to be slammed, but held shut. And, in fact, it proved to be, not an iron barrier, but a steel sieve. The battle-tried units, such as Serjeant Gariepy's, were run ragged. " It seemed that higher command was trying to pulverise us into the ground," he said. " On 15 August, our Regiment could not put even one complete squadron into the field. And whenever we found a hole in the enemy lines, it was impossible to exploit, for fear of our own artillery or air force. When permission was granted to follow through, the enemy had plugged it again. The closing of a pocket is one of the most intricate manoeuvres I have ever encountered; time after time, when you feel you have succeeded, another gap is opened and more enemy are filtering through. By the time A and C squadrons combined had got down to only four operational tanks between the two of them, morale was at its lowest since our arrival on the continent."

This was an experienced unit, still meeting determined Tiger crews, and taking heavy losses; but the bulk of Canadian Army's armour consisted of the two new divisions, 4th Canadian and 1st Polish, still learning the hard way. Even had they been fully efficient, there were still not enough of them to overwhelm the German armour concentrated in, at the shoulders of, and outside the pocket, which was now south-east of Falaise itself, the ' Gap ' being between Trun and Chambois. Halfway across the gap, which was on the line of the River Dives, stood the village of St. Lambert sur Dives. To this vital point, commanding the exit through which the Germans were pouring, and breaking it up into two gaps instead of one, like an island in a fast-flowing stream, there was sent on the evening of 19 August a force from 4 Canadian Armoured Division under Major David Currie. Unbelievably, it consisted of fourteen Sherman tanks (C Squadron, South Alberta Regiment) and a single, under-strength infantry company (B Company, Argyll and Sutherland Highlanders); in all, 125 officers and men. They probed into the village that evening, to find the square commanded by a Tiger, which promptly knocked out the 'point' Sherman, and the air commanded by two Spitfires, which brewed up Currie's own command tank with rockets. Currie withdrew for the night to the northern part of the village, listening to the sound of the German troops passing through St. Lambert; with his small force, he did not want to get involved in confused night-fighting, but in the morning he sent forward a patrol under Lieutenant G. G. Armour to get the Tiger. The infantrymen crossed the bridge over the Dives, stalked the Tiger, and rushed it. Lieutenant Amour was sitting on top of it with a grenade in his hand, when the German commander appeared beside him; after a hand-to-hand scuffle, they both fell off the Tiger, an infantryman shot the German, the Tiger started up, a German poked his head out, another infantryman shot him, Armour jumped back on and popped a grenade down the turret hatch, and that was that.

And then the battle began, and the offensively-minded Canadians were driven back onto a desperate defensive. The remnants of many German divisions were heading for St. Lambert, to pass through, or flow around it; and II S.S. Panzer Corps was poised outside the pocket for a counter-attack to break it open from the east, while the forces inside tried to break out from the west. "The order to break out was a relief," said Kurt Misch of 12th S.S. "It seemed a hopeless situation to us, but as always at such critical moments, when man stands alone in the midst of chaos, God is near. The words of the Psalms came to my mind: 'Lord, you are my refuge.' And once again, prayer proved to be stronger. 20 August was a Sunday, and it started as a misty morning, for which we were glad, as the enemy could not see our movements. But by 7 o'clock the mist was gone, and the morning sun stood brilliant in the sky, and the artillery began. ' This is the Lord's Day,' said someone near to me. Hunted by the shellfire, we tried to cross a stream, I cannot remember the name (it was the Dives). One vehicle got across, then the next sank in the mud, and immediately a tangle of vehicles blocked the way to the stream. The enemy artillery observer saw it, and brought down more fire. Nearly all tree-bursts, dreadful wounds, men rolling, screaming, with torn stomachs. With gruesome irony, I recalled the words of that song which begins: ' *No better death in all the world, than by an enemy's hand.*' Traction engines rolled over bodies. The sight of squashed flesh in the caterpillar tracks was unbearable. All order was gone, panic triumphed. I jumped onto a passing half-track. A splinter flicked my cap, to remind me that there are such things as steel helmets. We drove a long way over gruesome fields of bodies, until we met a group of parachutists; and by about 4 p.m., after a short hand-to-hand fight, we had broken out of the cauldron."

Heinz Trautmann, in Tiger 134, detoured round St. Lambert to the south, towards Chambois, the southern edge of the gap. As soon as they came into view of it, so they came under fire; and the Tiger suddenly stopped. "Have you gone off your rocker, stopping here!" roared the commander. "Can't get a wheeze out of the engine anymore," explained the driver, " temperature's off the clock." A tow was impossible, so they blew up the Tiger, and went ahead on foot, until picked up by another Tiger. "We saw a serjeant waving desperately at us from a gravel pit," said Trautmann. "He waves at every vehicle, but no one seems to take any notice of him. His right arm is shot to bits and dangles about in his sleeve. We stopped and took him in, the wireless operator making room by getting out and onto the back of the Tiger. The hills around us were packed with tanks and anti-tank guns; they followed our every movement with a hail of fire. We pick up everyone we can and all ranks are now present on the tank, right up to General. But not for long, we draw enemy fire, and move on, swept clean of passengers. Generally, we feel like zero. The roads are not just for marching, they serve us now also as table, bed, and grave in one." In the afternoon, they joined a fighting group led by a paratroop colonel, heard tank engines, and saw a column of Churchills approaching. Rather than risk their last Tiger, some of the tank men went forward with panzerfausts; and as they did so, a group of French refugees blundered into the ambush. With the threat of their machine-pistols, the Germans made the refugees lie down and be quiet, just as the leading Churchill approached. " The ' boxes ' roll past so close we can almost touch them," said Traut-mann. "We can see the aerials vibrating, read the names and numerals on them. As the last one passes, two men stand up and fire their panzerfausts simultaneously. The Frenchmen scream, but it goes unheard in the crash of the explosions. ' Betty ', the last tank, goes straight into the back of the tank in front, and now they are both hopelessly entangled. Unforgettable. Not one man gets out alive. Precision work. Then our two tank-crackers run back towards us, for the Churchills in front have started to fire." Eventually, they too broke out, near Coudehard, where part of the Polish division was under attack from all sides, from out-side the cauldron as well as in, the wounded piling up with no hope of evacuation or proper attention and no rations or supplies coming in.

Meanwhile, Major Currie in St. Lambert had received a reinforcement—two army photographers, Lieutenant D. I. Grant and Serjeant Jack Stollery. They were to get the photographs of their lives (including that reproduced on the jacket of this book). No one, on either side, could really remember the sequence of events, and the inter-meshing of eye-witness accounts would have been impossible but for the negative evidence their cameras produced. There, quite clearly, are the motor bikes and sidecars of the unit which tried to get through St. Lambert a few minutes before the major attack of the day, the arrival of the furious remnants of 2 Panzer Division under the wounded General von Lüttwitz. " Then the Battle Group rolled into St. Lambert sur Dives, which was burning fiercely," said Hans Erich Braun. " Twice I saw soldiers thrown against houses by the terrific force of the explosions, seemingly nailed against the wall, reminding me of a crucifixion. Torn-off arms, and legs still clad in jack-boots, bodies covered in rags of uniform, these were lying in a doorway. And, standing in a side road, burning fiercely, dozens of motor-cycles and sidecars of an M.C. unit, the drivers still sitting in their saddles, being roasted by the flames. Shouts, unintelligible, accusing, could be heard through the din. Threateningly lifted fists were raised from foxholes, trenches, behind windows, followed by a flood of obscene curses. Religious statues, hands outstretched in a blessing, and cut off by shrapnel, down in the bloody and hard-baked dust of the road. The cemetery, ploughed up, but offering shelter to many soldiers in the burst-open crypts, pressing their bodies close to the coffins of those already dead, hoping to survive. Torn bodies, men and horses, hit a hundred times over by bullets, lying both sides of the road. And a few bars of jazz music, coming from a portable radio standing on a window sill.

"And still the armoured force rolled towards the bridge across the Dives. Loud boomed the guns of the panzers, their turrets turned to the left. Murderous German m.g. and 2 cm cannon fire raked ahead of us and half-left. Hand-grenades were hurled, and bazooka bombs went hissing, into the enemy-occupied part of the village. An almost empty square came into view, and, still firing, the Panthers and the SP guns pushed through and over a chaos of wrecked vehicles, human bodies, the carcases of animals. And then the bridge came into sight, under a hail of enemy shellfire. Full speed ahead and across, the river below almost brimming with the bodies of men and horses and the ruins of vehicles. A paratroop serjeant who had been standing beside me for a long time, fell onto the floor among the wounded, shot through the head. Someone else took his place, firing his machine-pistol at the enemy."

By now, Major Currie had received further reinforcements, C Company of the Argylls and C Company of the Lincoln and Welland Regiment; but they were pushed back, Currie's H.Q. came under rifle fire at 50 yards range, and he called for artillery fire on his own position. When it came, it was from the Mediums, firing a missile which, unlike the 25-pounder field gun shell, could demolish a Sherman.

"Flashing detonations everywhere, in houses, gardens, fields, making a maze of craters," said Braun. "At full speed our armoured troop carrier rumbled across a heap of shot-down horses and their wagons, keeping to the broad lanes in the living flesh and wreckage made by the panzers ahead of us, the piercing screams of the tortured creatures ringing in our ears. Without pause, the enemy fire whistled and banged around us; we could hear shouts for help from our own soldiers; roof tiles cascaded into the road and walls collapsed. For a moment, the four 2 cm barrels of the light flak guns on the vehicles in front of us stopped, as the panzers concentrated the fire of their heavy guns on the enemy-held houses, which he had turned into fortresses. Then it began again, the harsh, machine-like purr of quadruple barrels sending hundreds of 2 cm shells into a definite target. The Canadian defenders, driven out by direct hits, tried to escape by fleeing to a nearby farm. Every gun opened up at them, their bodies were instantly and unrecognisably torn to shreds, leaving two lone steel helmets bowling along still in the direction of escape, spinning like mad as the bullets kicked them." The ' farm ' was probably the barn in which hundreds of German and Canadian wounded were lying, tended by a German doctor and two American-born German soldiers.

"As we went blinding on, a Panther in the lead got a direct hit from an anti-tank gun, which swept the Grenadiers clinging to it into a heap in the road. A jet of flame shot out of it. At any moment, a devastating explosion would tear the giant apart. But, instinctively, our driver accelerated and twisted the steering wheel hard right. The troop carrier crashed through a low wall, throwing us about violently, then lurched back onto the road beyond the Panther, festooned with the wreckage of somebody's garden fence. Then it happened. A huge sheet of flame leapt skyward behind us. The thunder of that explosion drowned everything. As though held by a ghost, the mighty turret with its long, protruding gun barrel hovered seconds-long ten yards high above the rooftops, before crashing to the ground. Our driver was still rooted behind the wheel, accelerator pushed to the floor, when we reached open country, and our guns were firing left and front into a forest, when the inhuman tension began to ease. We stopped to take care of the wounded and the dying. Those beyond help we laid in a small field. May the enemy bury them with honour."

Major Currie's equally desperate defenders had lost one third of their number when, on 21 August, they were relieved by 3 Div; and he himself was to receive the V.C. When he awoke from his first sleep for three days and nights, he had forgotten where he was, so strange was the quiet. "All I could hear," he said, "was the chirping of birds and the incredible silence."

*　　*　　*

As there had been no general capitulation, the clearing up of the Falaise pocket went on throughout the last week of August. "We had all read the claims made by the Air Force, but with the normal cynicism of the British soldier had expected to see a few lorries and wagons knocked out," wrote Major P. Vernon of 2 K.R.R.C. "But the whole country was packed with destroyed and abandoned transport and equipment. Prisoners came in their thousands and were guarded and marched back to their cages— men who were hardly men; they had lived through ten days of indescribable terror; they had had loosed on them every horror of modern war." Major H. Wake, M.C., of the same unit, was downright contemptuous. "The retreat from Moscow can have been nothing compared to this. I lined up 60 and asked where they came from: they were mostly Germans, but included Poles, Russians, Mongols, Czechs, Yugoslavs, Frenchmen—and even an American—all in Nazi uniforms." Arthur Knight, also of 2 K.R.R.C., noted that they had driven their half-tracks, in the narrow lanes, over mangled horses and the corpses of men, because there was no other way to get forward. The Gunner Officer wrote home: "I only once had trouble with a prisoner—a great, big tough-looking chap standing in a group of unarmed Germans. Dashing past in my jeep, I splashed a puddle over this chap, heard a shout, stopped, and saw the prisoner cursing and raving, very annoyed (unlike most of them) at being caught, and shouting about what would happen to us when the Wehrmacht decided to fight. One of our chaps told him to shut up; he didn't, so the Jock hit him on the back with his rifle butt, none too gently; whereupon all his fellow prisoners started roaring with laughter, which shows just how much they care. . . ."

Serjeant Gariepy's unit, directly in the path of those Germans still trying to escape, was alerted by a report that another unit had been 'over-run' in the night; the sound of an 88 and m.g.

fire all around convinced them that Germans were near. At first
light, they saw them—a group of 200 men, sitting down barely
fifty feet from the tanks, quietly waiting to be taken prisoner.
"But whenever an airplane came over, they would dive right
under our tanks in a frenzy, pushing us out of the way. Groups
of S.S. troops would sometimes show up, and the bag of prisoners
would look fearfully at them, but all the fight had gone out of
the S.S., they would silently join their countrymen; and then
there would be skirmishing in the prisoners' compound at the
sight of the S.S.; we tried to separate them from the regular
Wehrmacht for the tense atmosphere was not safe."

C. J. Wenman, of an R.E. unit, driving through the pocket,
saw many horrible contrasts. Fields of golden corn, and a
deserted, ruined village, rabbits playing in the street. The feeling
was of a holiday held in the midst of death, especially where a
complete German unit, including its ambulances, had been
caught by Typhoons. "We saw a young French girl riding along
on a pedal cycle oblivious, as if she was in Kent; she passed us,
in a nice bright cotton dress, as gay as if she was going to the
seaside."

"I went to a service by our Padre this morning, followed by
Holy Communion," the Gunner Officer wrote home on 26
August. "It is glorious country around here, with views stretching
for miles into some distant hills, 'La Suisse de la Normandie',
it is called. It was a wonderfully exhilarating feeling, on top of
the world with civilisation at your feet, attending an outdoor
service in the cool morning air. War was quite forgotten, while
down in the village below the church bell was ringing, although
it is not Sunday, nor is it the usual Norman hour for daily
prayer. I was idly watching a farmer's boy trying to catch a couple
of horses, all the time, perhaps subconsciously, imbibing the
Padre's sermon—'Why does God, the God of Love, allow War',
and I thought 'why indeed?' when one had only to lift one's eyes
from the grass to see all the beauty there was in the world. A
shattering roar, and we were being showered with earth and
stones, bits of wood and metal. A 3-tonner had had an argument
with a Tellermine 42. We said a prayer for the two chaps who
had had it, and for the third, who will have had had it in a couple
of days' time, after they have finished fiddling about with what

is left of his kidneys." On 31 August, he was in Paris, visiting his Aunt's flat. " Paris looks infinitely better fed, better dressed and cleaner than I would have believed. They don't appear to have suffered nearly as much as we thought and have been well treated. No word of German bad behaviour. I don't think there is much to worry about on Aunt A——'s behalf, and I have written to Granny to this effect."

The Gunner Officer's division, the 59th Staffordshire, no longer existed. At that moment, those who were not infantry already were becoming so with a few muttered words and the click of a typewriter, back in Bayeux in Normandy. " Day after day, the reinforcements for the next push, marshalled and documented, line up in the morning, heavily laden, and tramp away. Poor devils. Without them, the offensive into Germany might fail, so they must go. But sometimes, as I look at their faces, and hear them call out their age . . . ' nineteen ' . . . ' twenty-two ' . . . ' twenty ' . . . I wonder why those who have not yet lived should die. In the evenings, you can hear them singing . . . dance tunes, songs, and, as always, " Jerusalem " . . . with a weird melancholy, these men who have fought in the fateful battle of the Falaise gap, sing, and then march away to another battle. For the Germans are clear of the second trap now, in spite of the valiance of the Sunday spectaculars to destroy him; and without these reinforcements, we may get stuck on the Siegfried Line—a winter campaign, for which we are not prepared."

A hundred thousand men had been trapped at Falaise, but the terrible scenes, and the demoralisation, were half an illusion, such as the British themselves had left behind them at Dunkirk, four years before. The plain unlucky, the panic-stricken, the men who did not want to fight, the weak. The strong had burst their bonds, and got out; there had been no capitulation; riding in tanks, or walking with a machine-pistol, often wounded, the German generals had led the way. The Canadian Army had hoped for a total annihilation, which would have swiftly ended the war with a ' motor tour into Germany ', but had secured only half-success. Of the 100,000, 10,000 were dead, 40,000 were prisoners—but 50,000 experienced and determined men had escaped. And the second, wider encirclement at the Seine, pressed by Montgomery and Bradley, had, too, been but a half-success.

There *would* be a winter campaign. The war would go on, until half Europe was in ruins and under foreign occupation, much of it as evil as the occupation it had replaced. Well might the voices of the infantry be melancholy as they rose in chorus in the Norman night, *" Jerusalem, Jerusalem, lift up your hearts and sing . . ."*

Through Caen, the lorries were groaning, the trucks, the tanks, the tank transporters, headed north-east on the road of the great retreat of the German armies, through the broken city of Duke William. ". . . just a waste of brick and stone, of buildings which had cost so much to build, and so very much more to destroy. The people gazed at us without emotion of any kind; we could hardly look them in the face, knowing who had done this. These were the people we came to free, and this is the price that freedom cost." The Battle of Caen was ended.

SOURCES AND ACKNOWLEDGEMENTS

The bulk of the source material consists of about 1,000 pages of English, French and German narrative supplied by some 65 witnesses specifically for the purposes of this particular work. Frequently, however, the witnesses were drawing on, or expanding, letters, notes, and narratives written either at the time or shortly afterwards, without thought of publication, purely for reasons of intrinsic historic interest. In some cases, the narrative had been written originally as source material for a unit history. I must express my gratitude to all those who so willingly gave of their time in this way, and also to my wife, who translated for me most of the French and German documents. Usually, unit or formation histories helped to fill in the background to the eye-witness stories; exceptionally, where the unit histories quoted from eye-witness narratives at length, I have gratefully borrowed. There were also a great many witnesses to whom I talked at the time, or very shortly afterwards, sometimes briefly, sometimes at length, jotting down the gist of the conversations in a diary, without always recording their names. Especially fruitful was a short stay in 9th (British) General Hospital at Antwerp, where, there being little to read, conversation flourished. Some of the general background, and one or two scenes, originate from personal knowledge; it will be sufficient to indicate that the author served in an infantry division defending the south coast of England, in the Highland Brigade of 15th Scottish Division, with the H.Q. of First Canadian Army, and with the 49th West Riding Division. The witnesses whom I contacted specially for this book, and to whom I am particularly indebted, are:—

Brigadier S. J. L. Hill, D.S.O., M.C.	3 Para. Bde.	6 A/B Div
Captain H. H. T. Hudson	9 Para. Bn.	6 A/B Div
Lieut. D. A. Breeze	3 Para. Sqdn. R.E.	6 A/B Div
H. Green	10 H.L.I.	15 (S) Div
D. B. Jones	4 S.L.I.	43 (W) Div
J. Jones	5 Wilts.	43 (W) Div
W. Biles	4 Wilts.	43 (W) Div
L. Uppington	1 Worcs.	43 (W) Div
Gordon J. Mucklow	5 D.C.L.I.	43 (W) Div
Major A. C. Packer	43 Recce Regt.	43 (W) Div
Reverend J. E. Gethyn-Jones, M.B.E.	43 Recce Regt.	43 (W) Div
W. V. Crichley	43 Recce Regt.	43 (W) Div

C. Heald	4 Y. & L. Hallams	49 (WR) Div
Lieut. J. F. Brown	6 N. Staffs.	59 (S) Div
Gunner Officer '	481/116 Fd. Regt. R.A.	59 (S) Div
Major K. B. Czarnecki, M.Sc.	H.Q.	1 Pol. Armd. Div
A. H. Markham	5 R.H.A.	7 Armd. Div
Major-General G. P. B. Roberts, C.B., D.S.O., M.C., J.P.	Cmdr.	11 Armd. Div
Major W. H. Close, M.C.	3 R.T.R.	11 Armd. Div
Major J. F. Langdon, M.C.	3 R.T.R.	11 Armd. Div
D. Blyth	7 R.T.R.	11 Armd Div
T. E. Harte	23 Hussars	11 Armd. Div
Lt.-Col. A. G. Heywood, M.V.O., M.C.	2 Gren. Gds.	Gds. Armd. Div
G. H. Marsden	1 Gren. Gds.	Gds. Armd. Div
R. A. F. Hill	13/18 Hussars	27 Armd. Bde. & 8 Armd. Bde.
A. Knight	2 K.R.R.C.	4 Ind. Armd. Bde.
Lt.-Col. D. B. Powle, M.C.	2 H.C.R.	VIII Corps
H. B. Smith	23 Bomb Disposal Coy. R.E.	
C. J. Wenman	12 Airfield Cons. Gp. R.E.	
S. Green	6 Fd. Regt. R.A.	2 AGRA
G. Amos	2 A/T Regt.	2 Cdn. Div
R. Bider	S.S.R.	2 Cdn. Div
P. Walsh	Chaudière Regt.	3 Cdn. Div
L. R. Gariepy	6 Armd. Regt.	2 Cdn. Armd. Bde.
' British Agent '		S.O.E.
C.P.O. A. V. Johnson, D.S.M., B.E.M.	' P ' Commandos	Royal Navy
C.P.O. R. H. G. McKinlay, C.G.M.	' P ' Commandos	Royal Navy
Lt.-Cdr. W. Y. McLanachan, B.E.M., M.B.E.	Bomb & Mine Disposal	Royal Navy
L. A. Bridge	HMML/BG 204	Royal Navy
W/Cdr. A. G. Page, D.S.O., D.F.C.		Royal Air Force
S/Ldr. F. R. Leatherdale	115 Squadron	Royal Air Force
F/Lt. C. D. Linacre, D.F.C.	635 Squadron	Royal Air Force
S/Ldr. A. E. L. Hill	Balloon Command	Royal Air Force
Miss Rosanne Whelan	H.Q.	21 Army Group
Sister Eilis Malone	Good Saviour Convent	
Madame Luce Tribulet	Sainte-Croix-Grand-Tonne & Caen	
Madame L. Corbasson	Caen	
Professor René Streiff	Caen	
Monsieur M. Guitter	Bois Aux Veneurs (Orne)	
Monsieur R. Nicolas	Livarot	
Hans Erich Braun	Pz. Jäg. Abtl. 38 (Sf)	2 Pz. Div
Oberst Freiherr Hans von Luck	Pz. Gr. Regt. 125	21 Pz. Div
' Officer '	Schw. Pz. Abtl. 503	21 Pz. Div
Leutnant Hans Höller	Pz. Gr. Regt. 192	21 Pz. Div

SOURCES AND ACKNOWLEDGEMENTS

Werner Kortenhaus	Pz. Regt. 22	21 Pz. Div
Karl Max Wietzorek		5 Para Div
General Wilhelm Bittrich	Kdr.	9 S.S. Pz. Div & II S.S. Pz. Korps
Oberst Walter Harzer	H.Q.	9 S.S. Pz. Div
Lothar Griel		9 S.S. Pz. Div
Oberst Hubert Meyer	H.Q.	12 S.S. Pz. Gr. Div
Cadet Kurt Misch	Artillery	12 S.S. Pz. Gr. Div
' Company Commander '	S.S. Pz. Regt. 12	12 S.S. Pz. Gr. Div
Heinz Trautmann	Schw. S.S. Pz. Abtl. 502	II S.S. Pz. Korps
Berthold Fink	Schw. S.S. Pz. Abtl. 502	II S.S. Pz. Korps
Kurt Erich Groetschel	Light Flak Unit 98	Pz. Lehr Div
	Heavy Flak Regt. I/53	12 S.S. Pz. Div
Siegfried Radtke	IX Flieger Korps	Luftwaffe

I am grateful also for permission to use quotations, mainly eye-witness narratives, from the following: —

" The 43rd Wessex Division at War: 1944-1945 " by Major-General H. Essame (Clowes, 1952), " The History of the 51st Highland Division " by J. B. Salmond (Blackwood, 1953), " The Gordon Highlanders: 1919-1945 " by Wilfrid Miles (University Press, Aberdeen) (by permission of The Gordon Highlanders Regimental History Committee), " Second Household Cavalry Regiment " by Roden Orde (Gale & Polden, 1953), " History of the 13th/18th Royal Hussars: 1922-1947 " by Major-General Charles H. Miller (Chisman, Bradshaw, 1953), " The King's Royal Rifle Corps Chronicle: 1944 ", " Le Geste du Régiment de la Chaudière " by Majors A. Ross and M. Gauvin (Holland, 1945), " Victory in the West " by Major I. F. Ellis (H.M.S.O., 1962), "A Soldier's Story " by General Omar N. Bradley (Holt, Rinehart & Winston, 1951), " Pour Retrouver Mon Fils A Caen " by Luce Tribulet (1960), ". . . ceux des Equipes d'urgence " by Prof. Rene Streiff (Caen, 1945), " The Royal United Service Institution Journal " (May, 1963). I was unable to contact the publishers of "A Short History of 7th Armoured Division " (B.A.O.R., 1945) or " The Story of the Twenty-Third Hussars: 1940-1946 " (B.A.O.R., 1946), from which quotations were also made.

INDEX

People